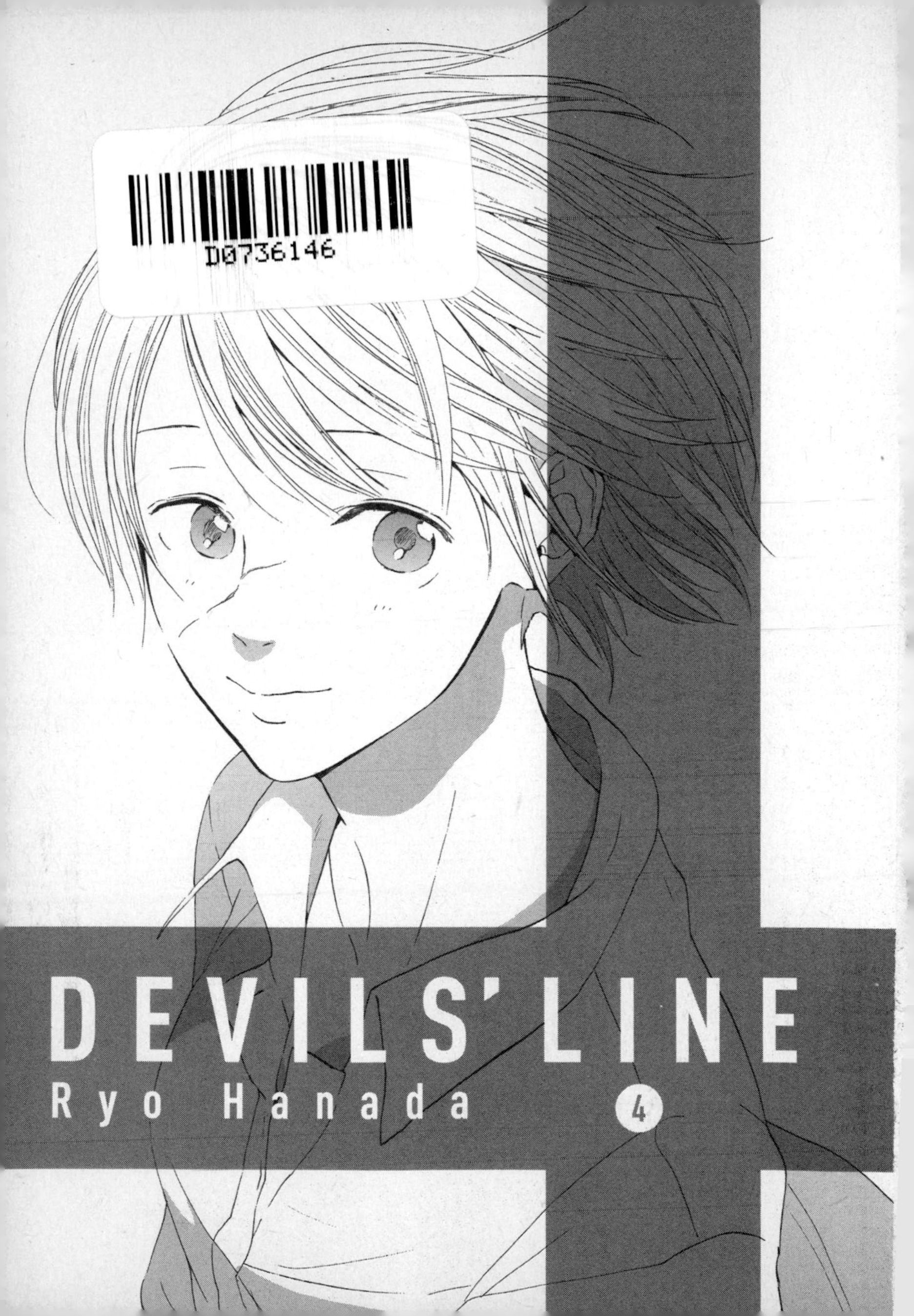
DEVILS' LINE
Ryo Hanada
4

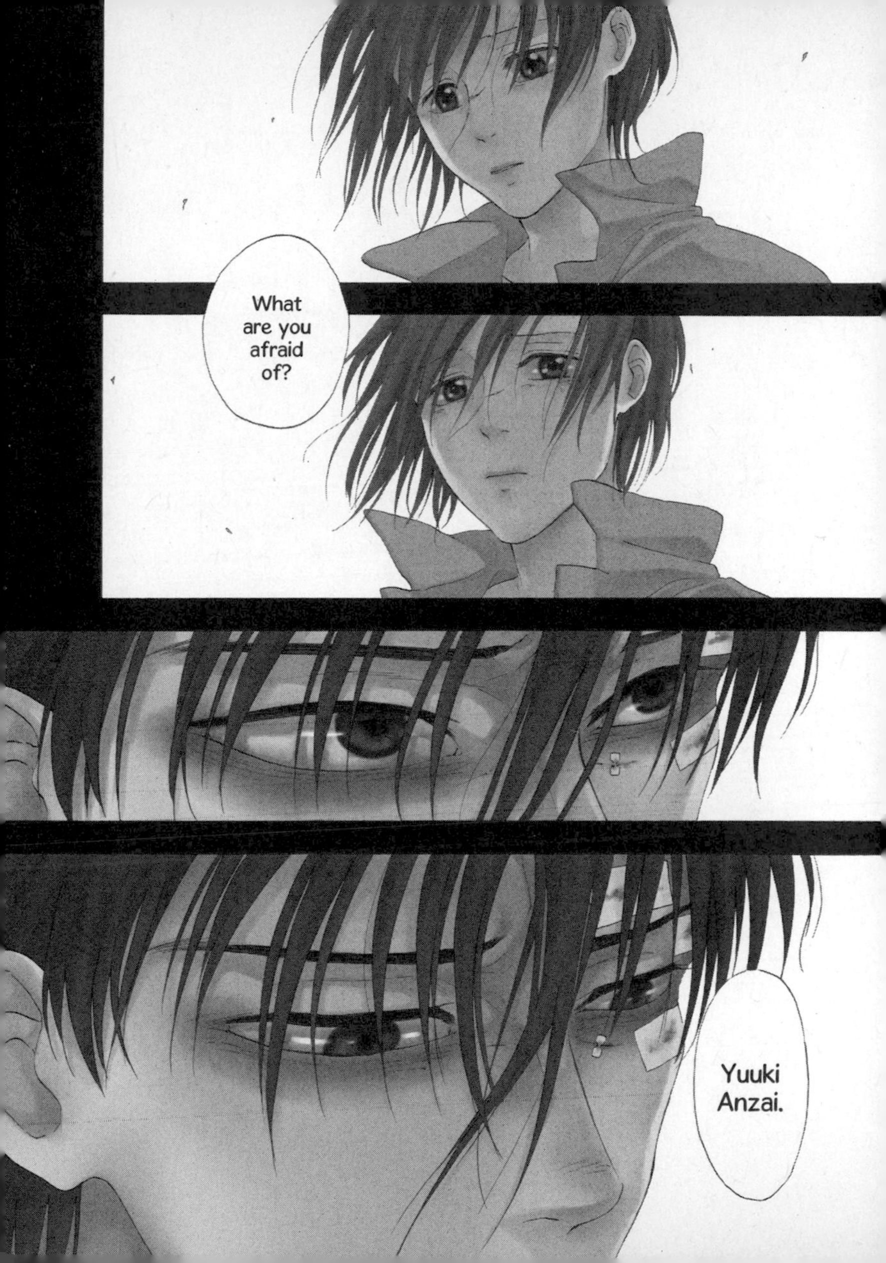
What are you afraid of?
Yuuki Anzai.

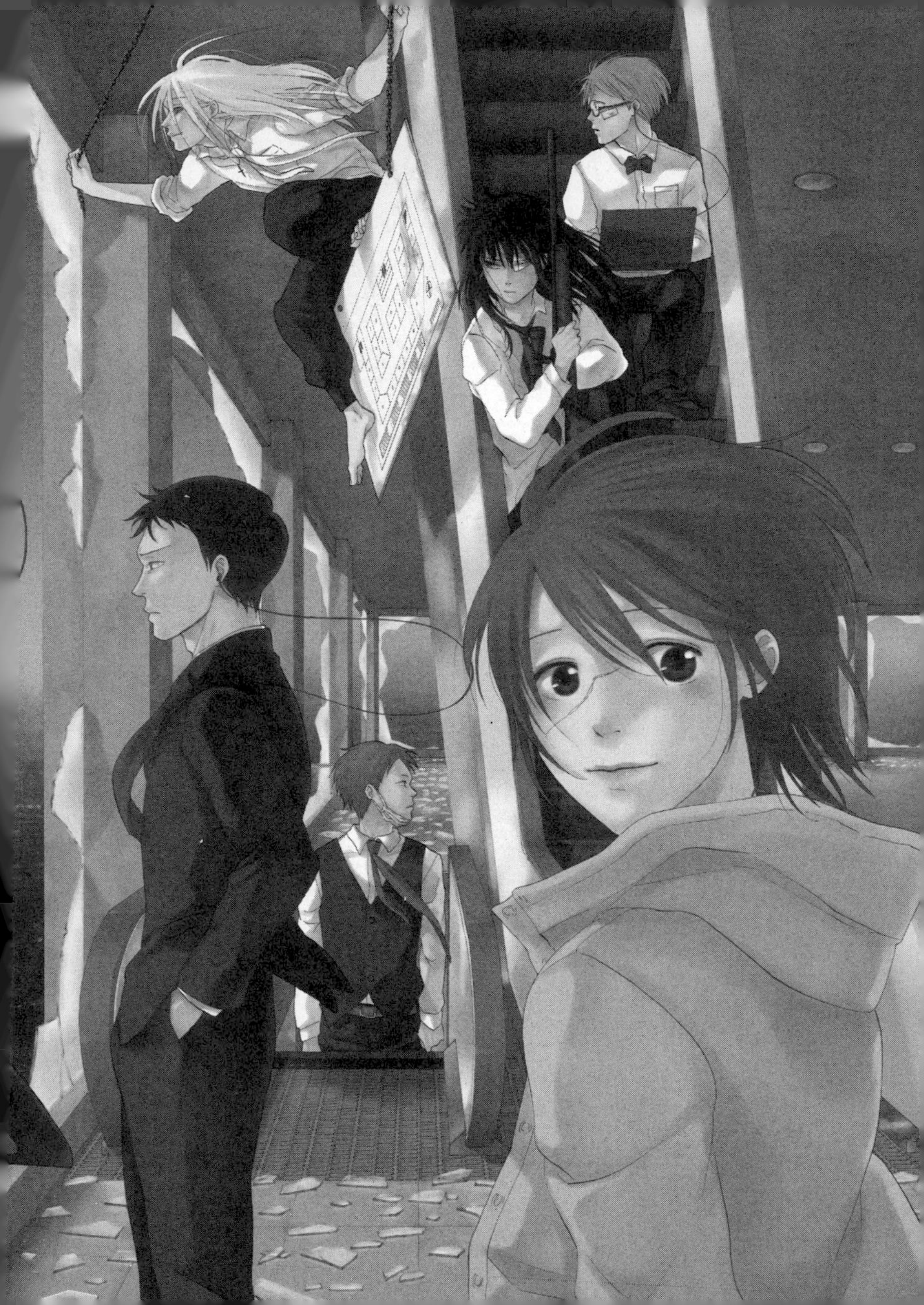

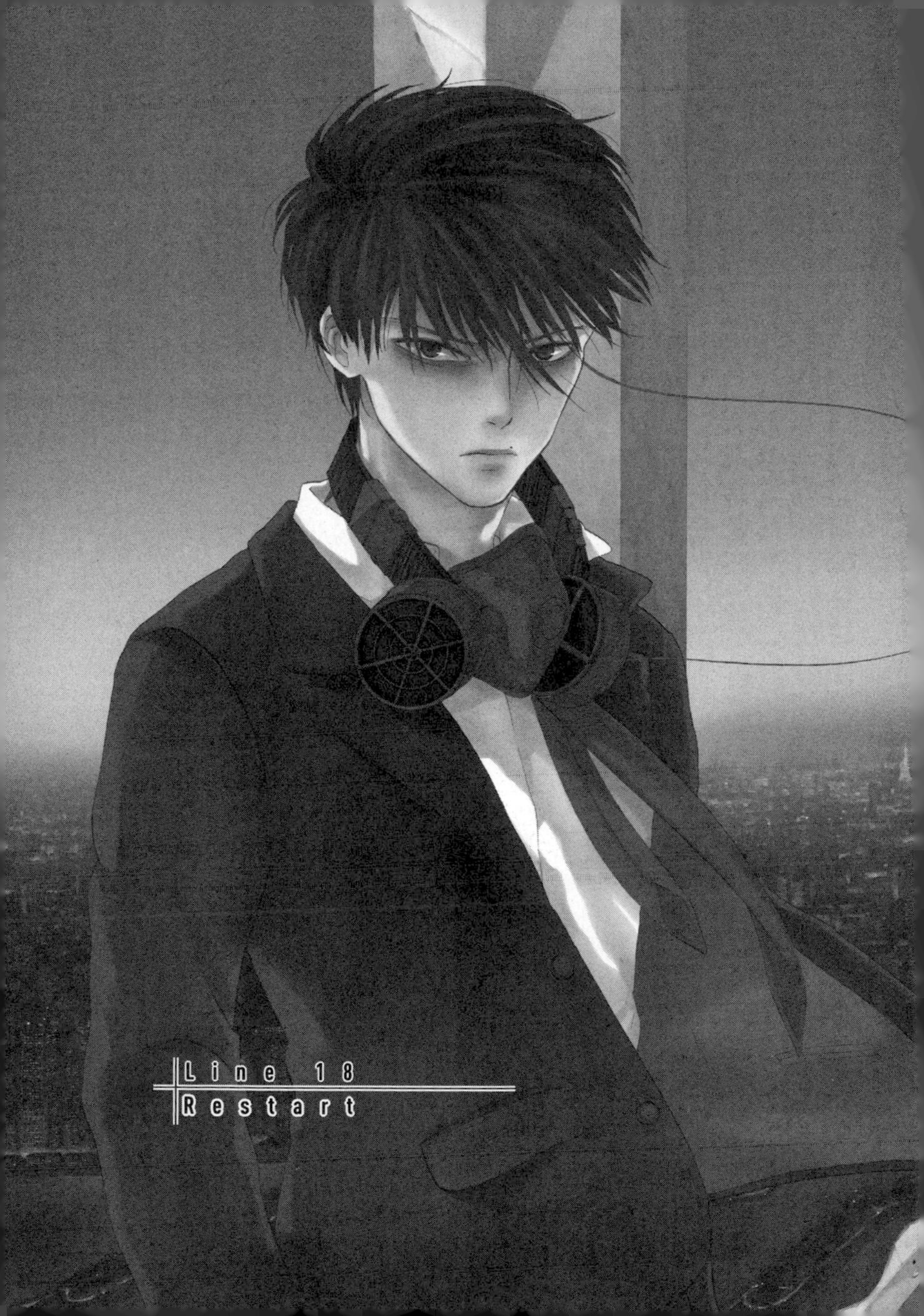
Line 18
Restart

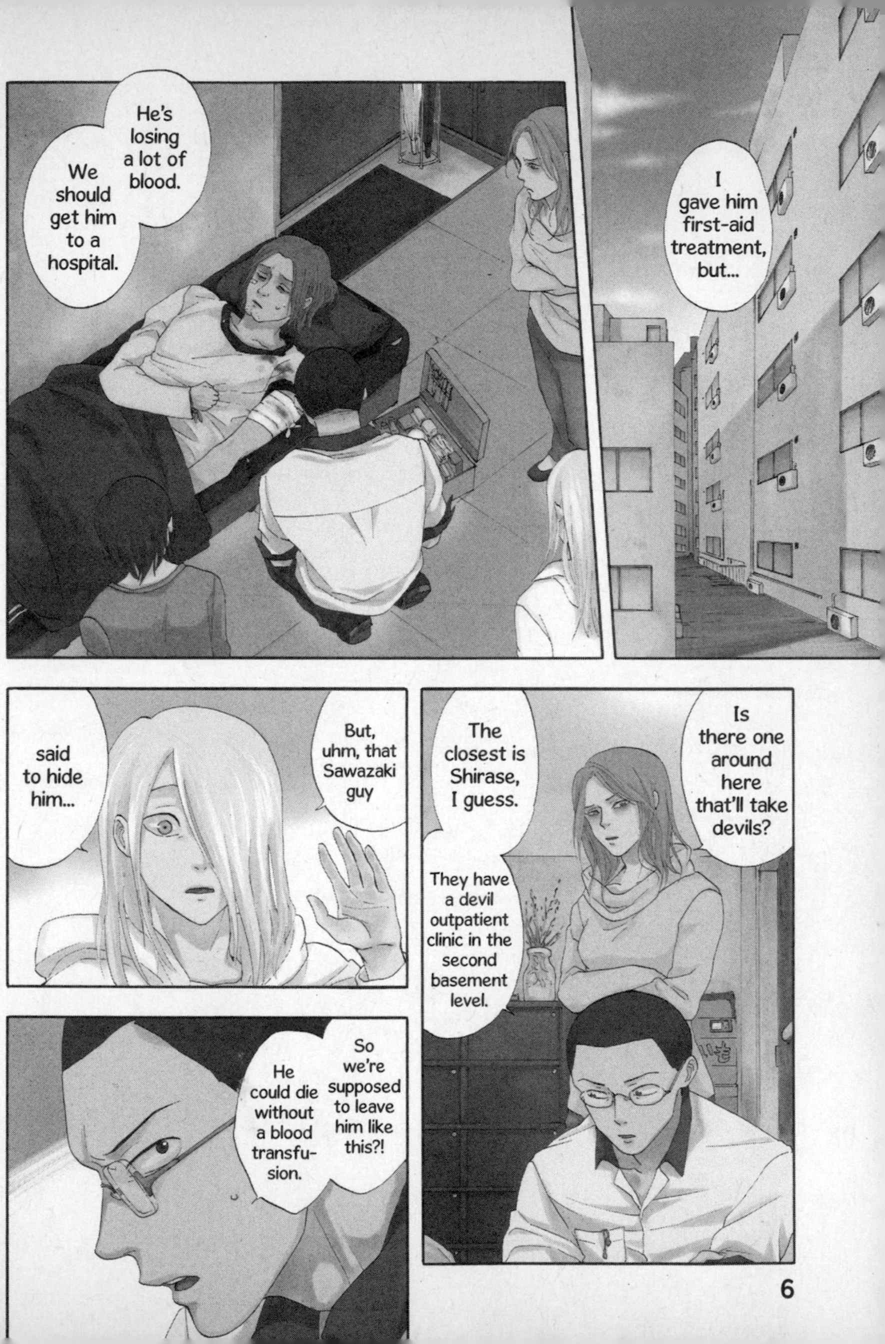
I gave him first-aid treatment, but...
He's losing a lot of blood.
We should get him to a hospital.
Is there one around here that'll take devils?
The closest is Shirase, I guess.
They have a devil outpatient clinic in the second basement level.
But, uhm, that Sawazaki guy
said to hide him...
So we're supposed to leave him like this?!
He could die without a blood transfusion.

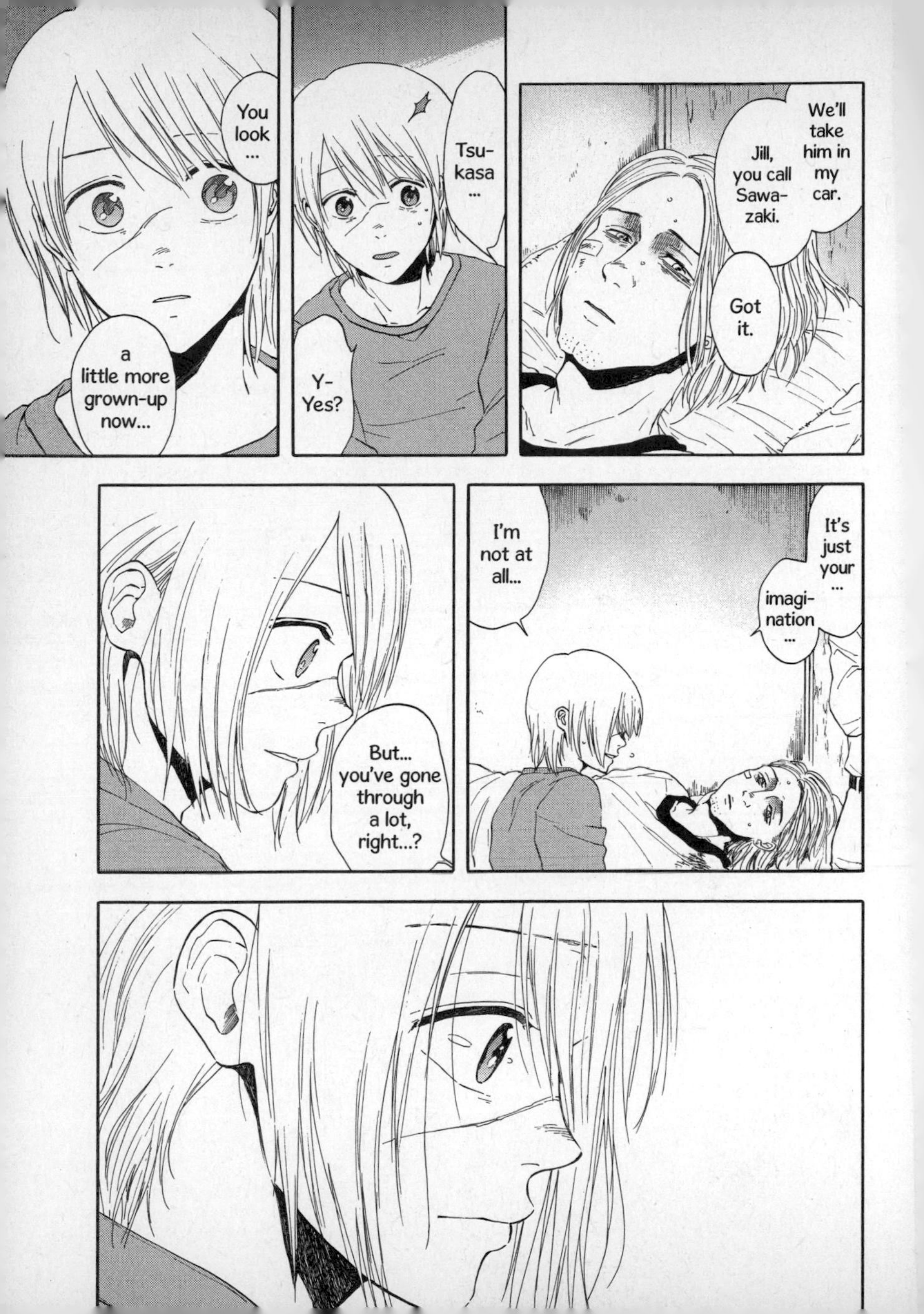
We'll take him in my car.
Jill, you call Sawazaki.
Got it.
Tsukasa...
Y-Yes?
You look...
a little more grown-up now...
It's just your... imagination...
I'm not at all...
But... you've gone through a lot, right...?

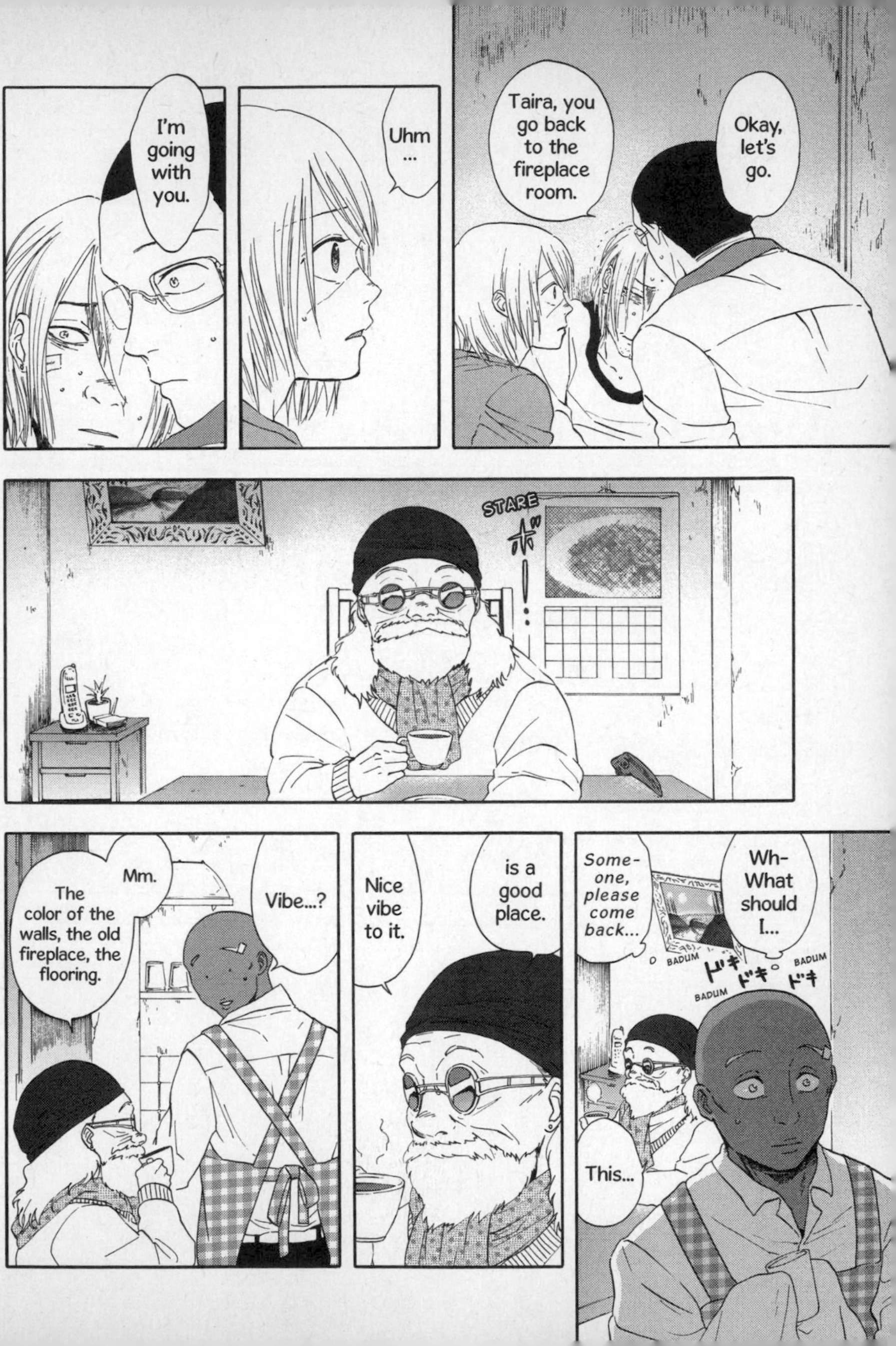

Okay, let's go.
Taira, you go back to the fireplace room.
Uhm ...
I'm going with you.
STARE
Wh- What should I...
Some-one, please come back...
BADUM
ドキ
BADUM
ドキ
BADUM
ドキ
This...
is a good place.
Nice vibe to it.
Vibe...?
Mm.
The color of the walls, the old fireplace, the flooring.

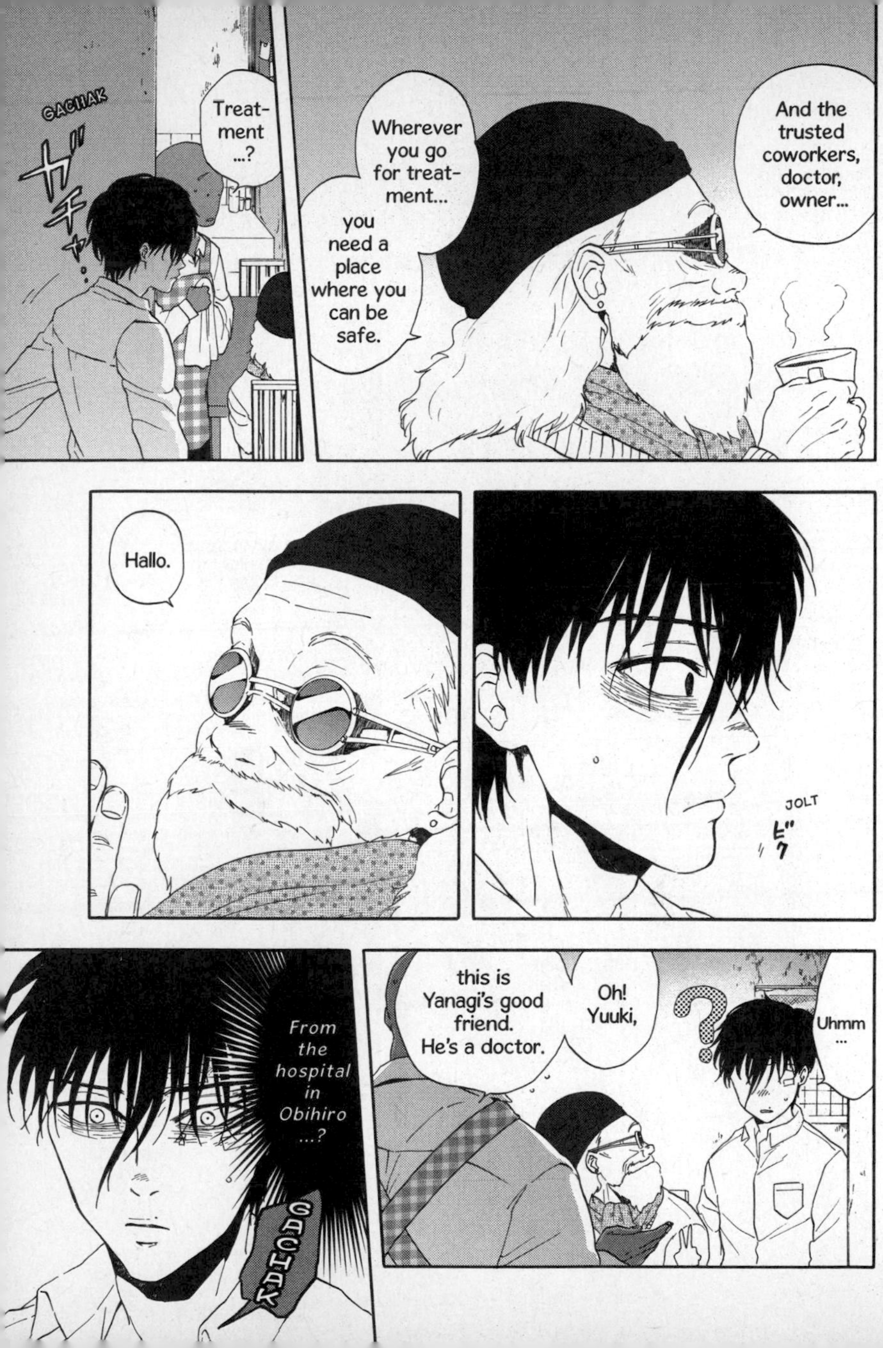
And the trusted coworkers, doctor, owner...
Wherever you go for treatment...
you need a place where you can be safe.
Treatment ...?
GACHAK
ガチャ
JOLT
ビク
Hallo.
Uhmm ...
Oh! Yuuki,
this is Yanagi's good friend. He's a doctor.
From the hospital in Obihiro ...?
GACHAK

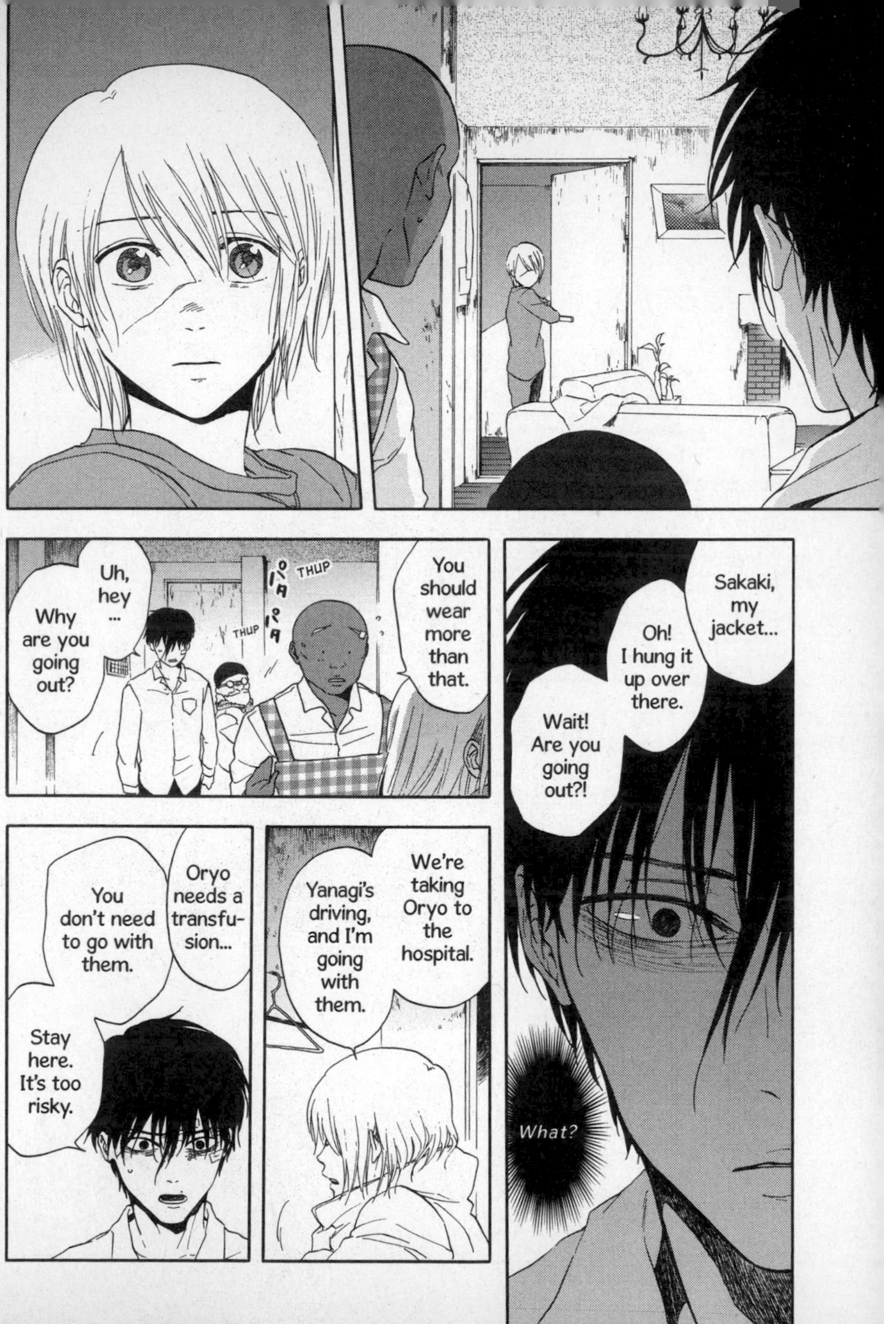
Sakaki, my jacket...
Oh! I hung it up over there.
Wait! Are you going out?!
What?
You should wear more than that.
THUP
THUP
Uh, hey ...
Why are you going out?
We're taking Oryo to the hospital.
Yanagi's driving, and I'm going with them.
Oryo needs a transfusion...
You don't need to go with them.
Stay here. It's too risky.

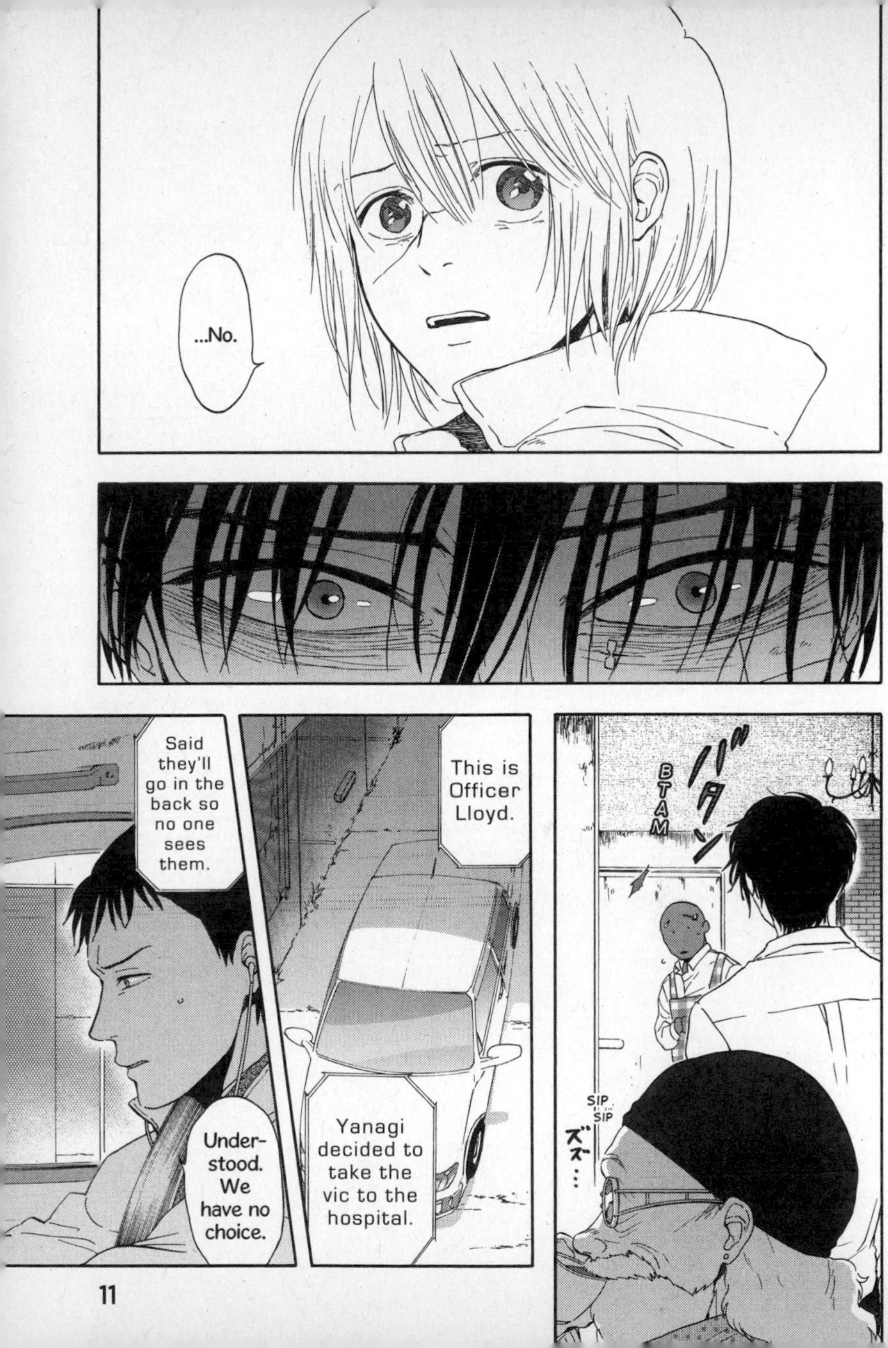

...No.
バタン
BTAM
SIP SIP
ズズ…
This is Officer Lloyd.
Yanagi decided to take the vic to the hospital.
Said they'll go in the back so no one sees them.
Understood. We have no choice.

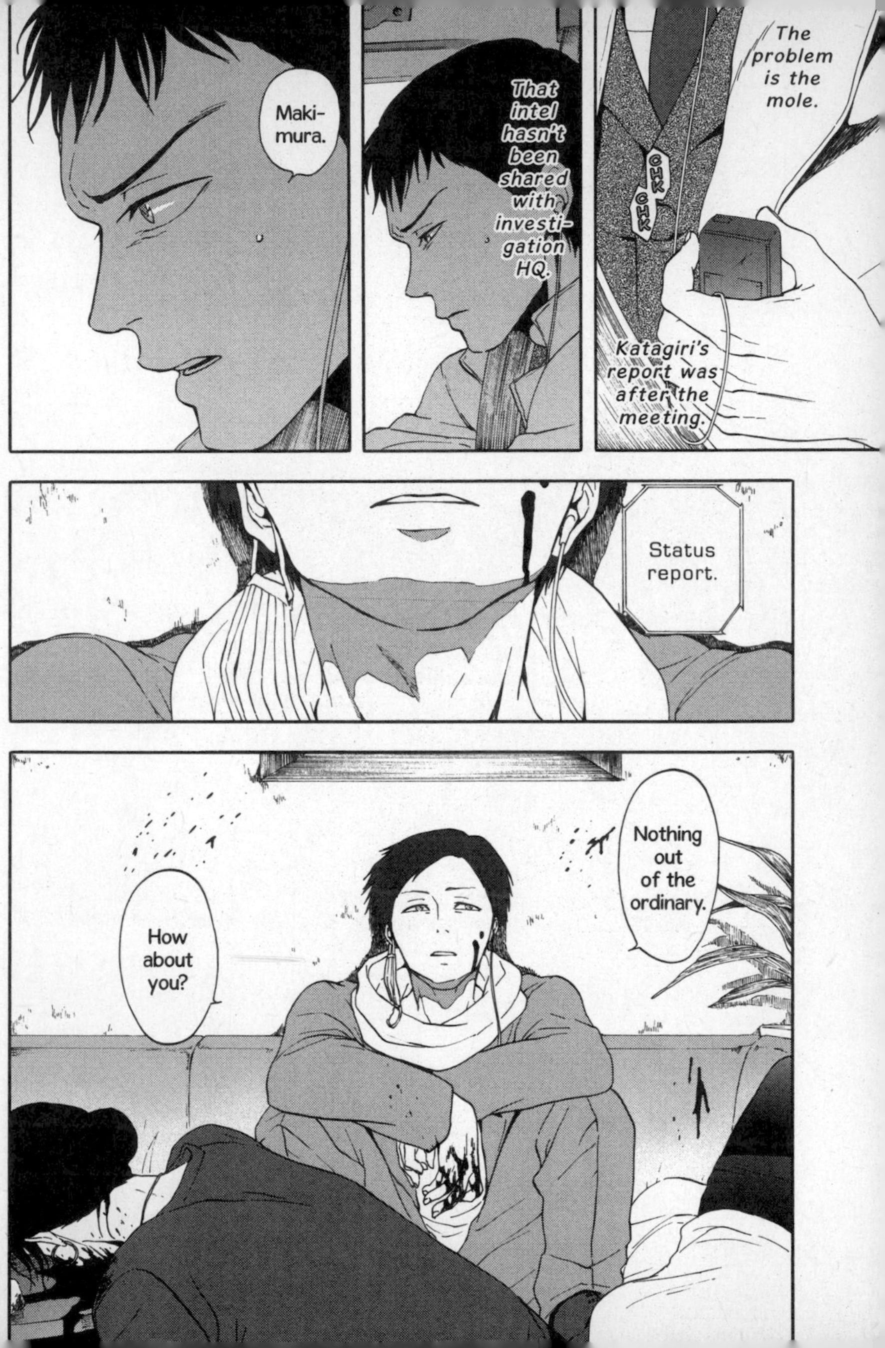
The problem is the mole.
CHK CHK
Katagiri's report was after the meeting.
That intel hasn't been shared with investigation HQ.
Maki-mura.
Status report.
Nothing out of the ordinary.
How about you?

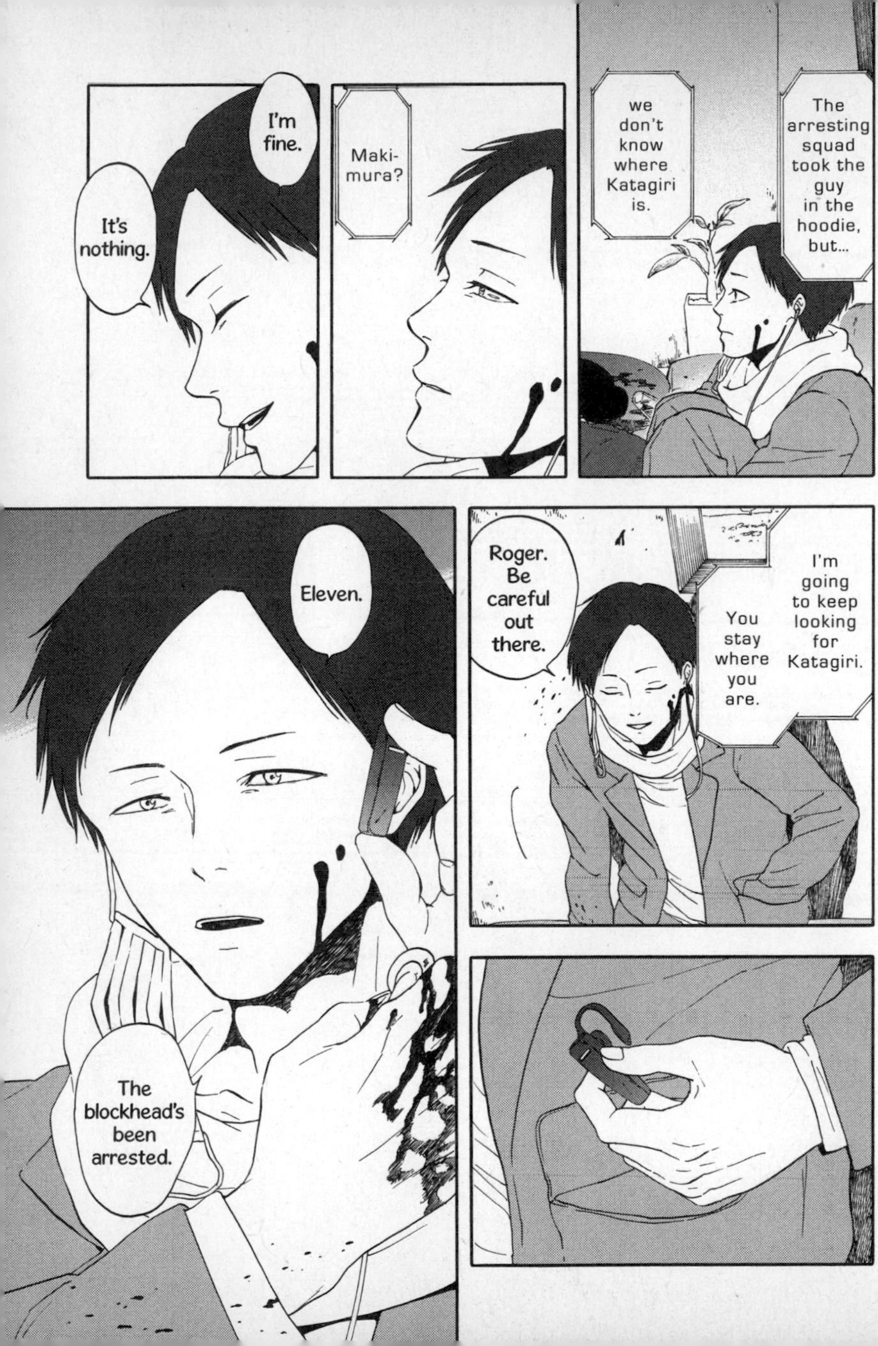
The arresting squad took the guy in the hoodie, but...
we don't know where Katagiri is.
Maki-mura?
I'm fine.
It's nothing.
I'm going to keep looking for Katagiri.
You stay where you are.
Roger. Be careful out there.
Eleven.
The blockhead's been arrested.

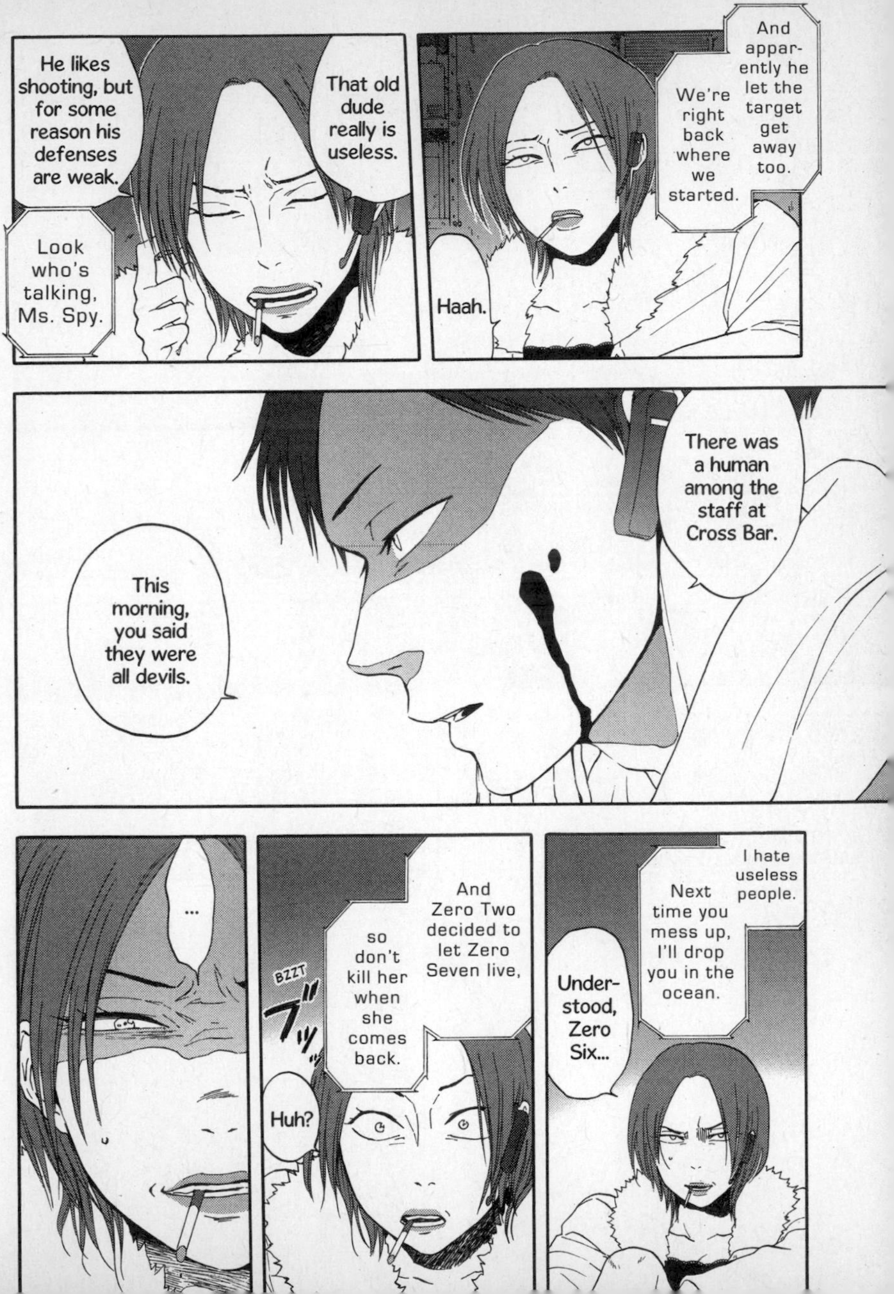
And apparently he let the target get away too.
We're right back where we started.
Haah.
That old dude really is useless.
He likes shooting, but for some reason his defenses are weak.
Look who's talking, Ms. Spy.
There was a human among the staff at Cross Bar.
This morning, you said they were all devils.
I hate useless people.
Next time you mess up, I'll drop you in the ocean.
Understood, Zero Six...
And Zero Two decided to let Zero Seven live,
so don't kill her when she comes back.
BZZT
Huh?
...

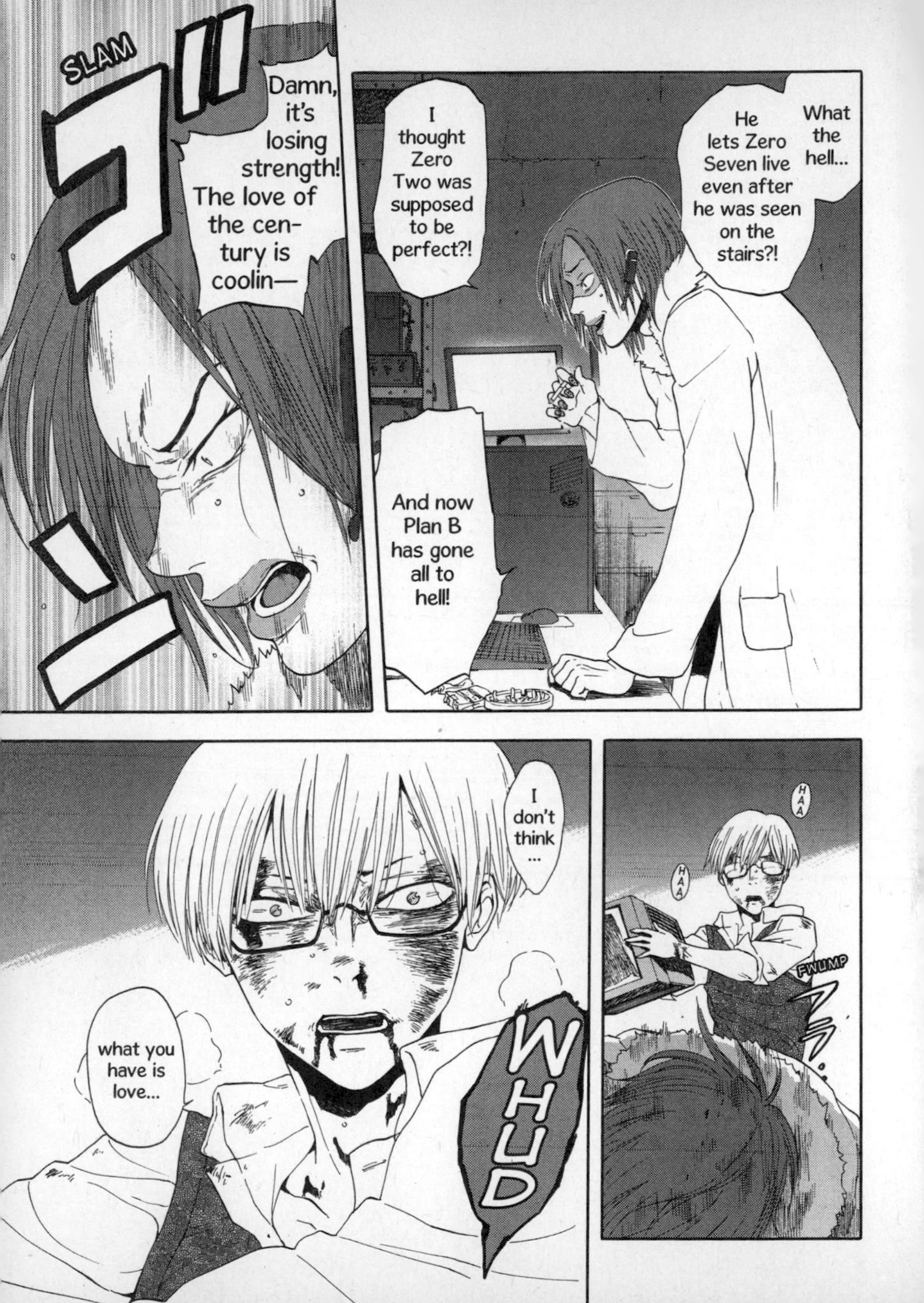
What the hell...
He lets Zero Seven live even after he was seen on the stairs?!
I thought Zero Two was supposed to be perfect?!
And now Plan B has gone all to hell!
SLAM
Damn, it's losing strength! The love of the century is coolin—
HAA
HAA
FWUMP
I don't think ...
WHUD
what you have is love...

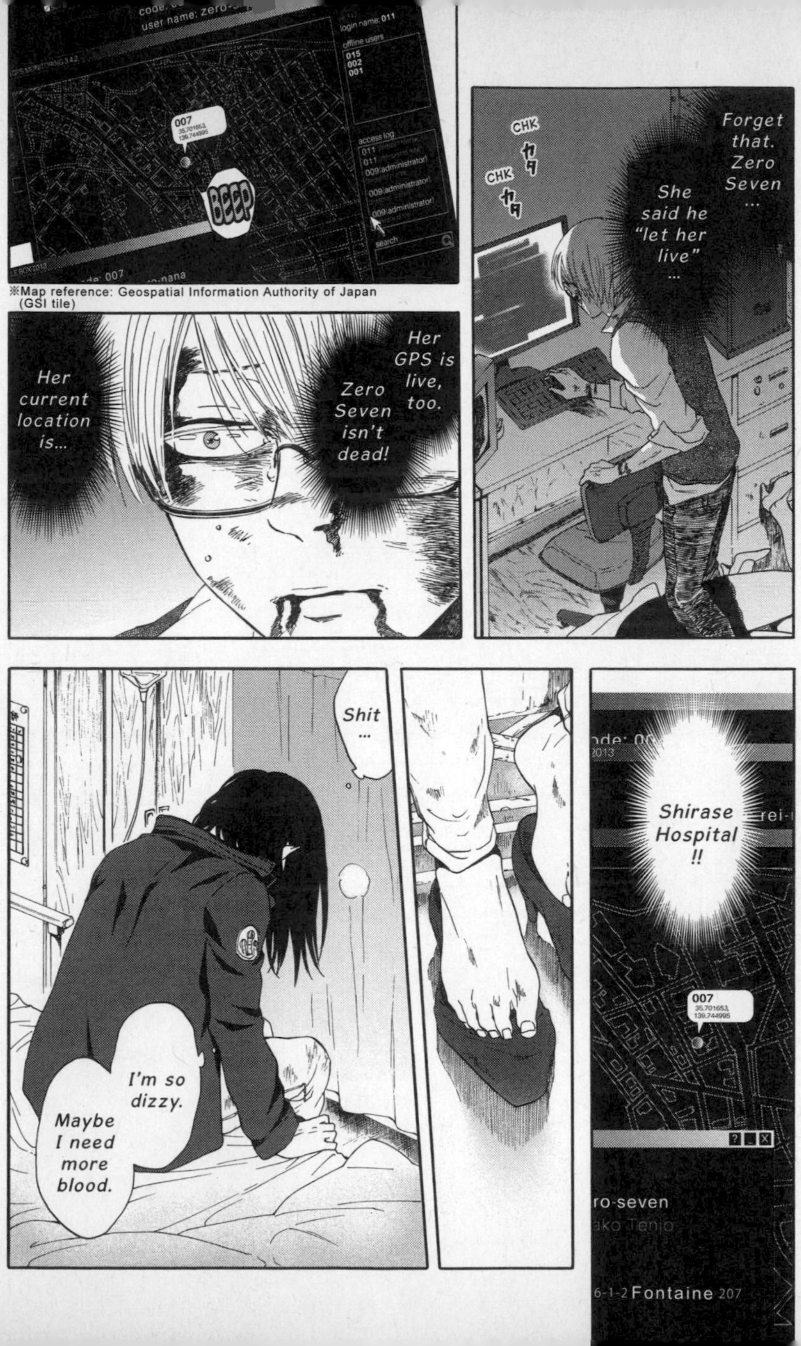
CHK
カタ
CHK
カタ
Forget that. Zero Seven ...
She said he "let her live" ...
user name: zero-
login name: 011
offline users
015
002
001
007
35.701653,
139.744995
access log
009(administrator)
009(administrator)
009(administrator)
search
BEEP
Her GPS is live, too.
Zero Seven isn't dead!
Her current location is...
Shirase Hospital !!
007
35.701653,
139.744995
ro-seven
6-1-2 Fontaine 207
Shit ...
I'm so dizzy.
Maybe I need more blood.
※Map reference: Geospatial Information Authority of Japan (GSI tile)

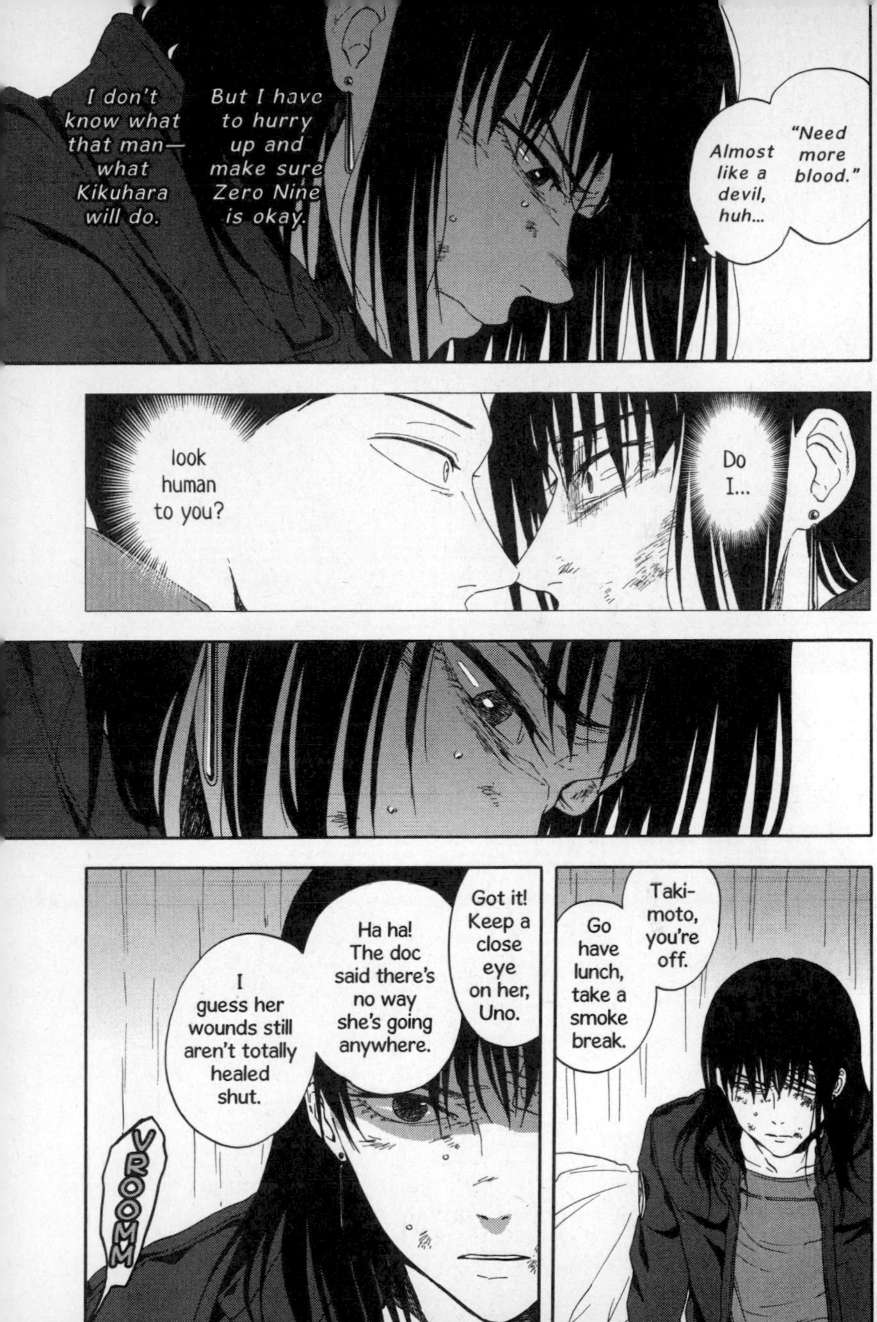
"Need more blood."
Almost like a devil, huh...
But I have to hurry up and make sure Zero Nine is okay.
I don't know what that man—what Kikuhara will do.
Do I...
look human to you?
Taki-moto, you're off.
Go have lunch, take a smoke break.
Got it! Keep a close eye on her, Uno.
Ha ha! The doc said there's no way she's going anywhere.
I guess her wounds still aren't totally healed shut.
VROOMM

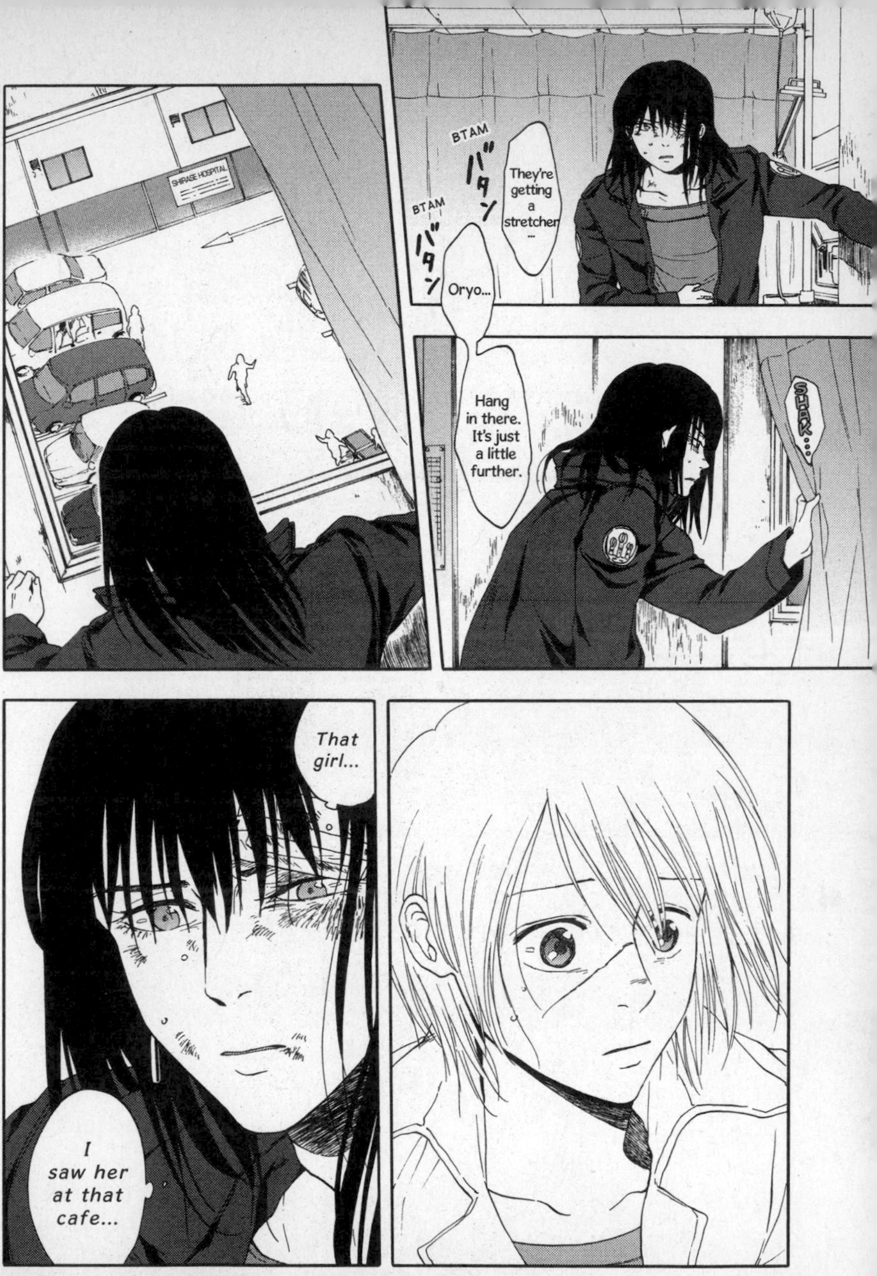
BTAM
バタン
They're getting a stretcher...
BTAM
バタン
Oryo...
Hang in there. It's just a little further.
SHAK...
SHIRASE HOSPITAL
That girl...
I saw her at that cafe...

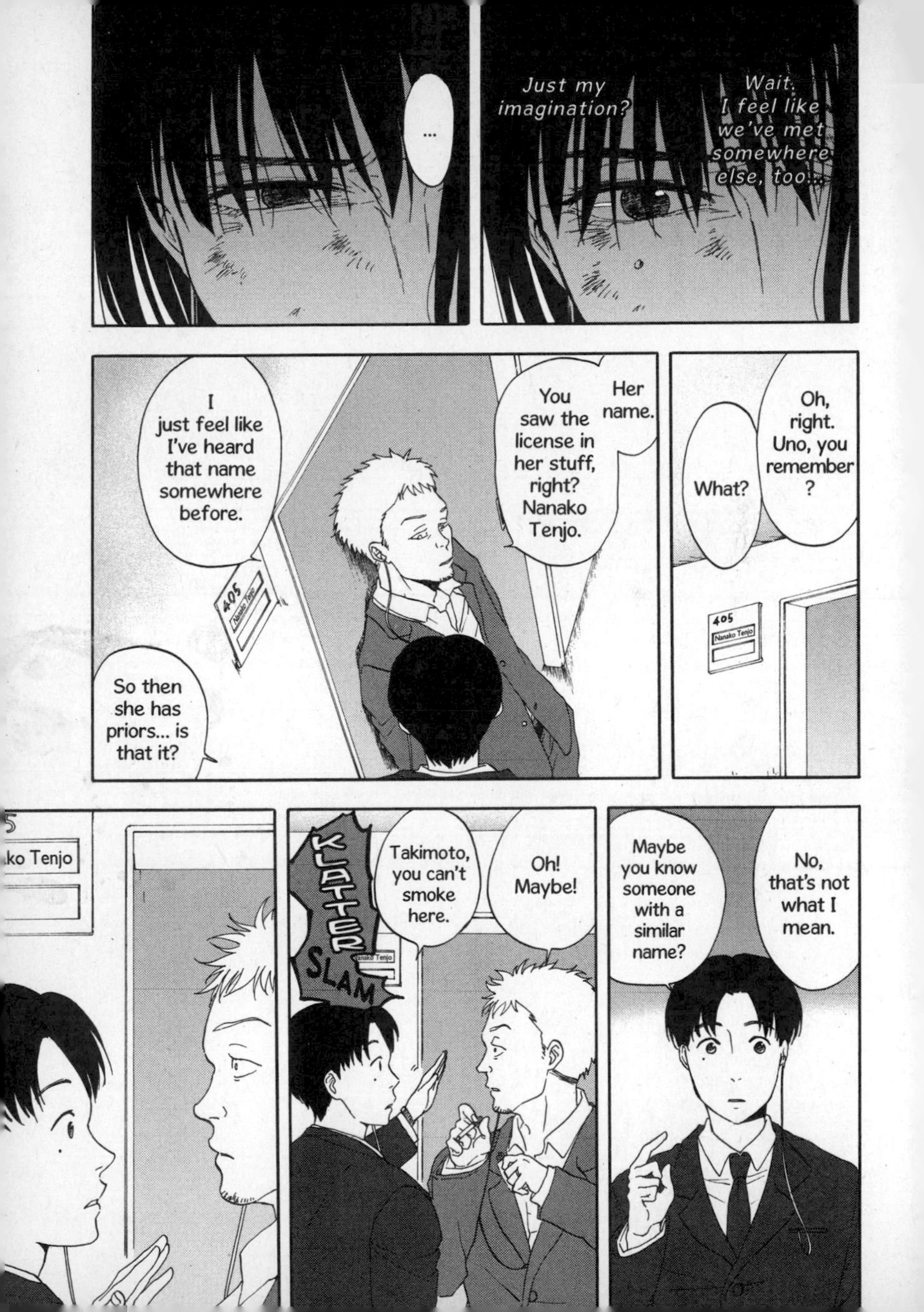
Wait. I feel like we've met somewhere else, too...
Just my imagination?
...
Oh, right. Uno, you remember?
What?
Her name.
You saw the license in her stuff, right? Nanako Tenjo.
I just feel like I've heard that name somewhere before.
405
Nanako Tenjo
So then she has priors... is that it?
No, that's not what I mean.
Maybe you know someone with a similar name?
Oh! Maybe!
Takimoto, you can't smoke here.
KLATTER
SLAM

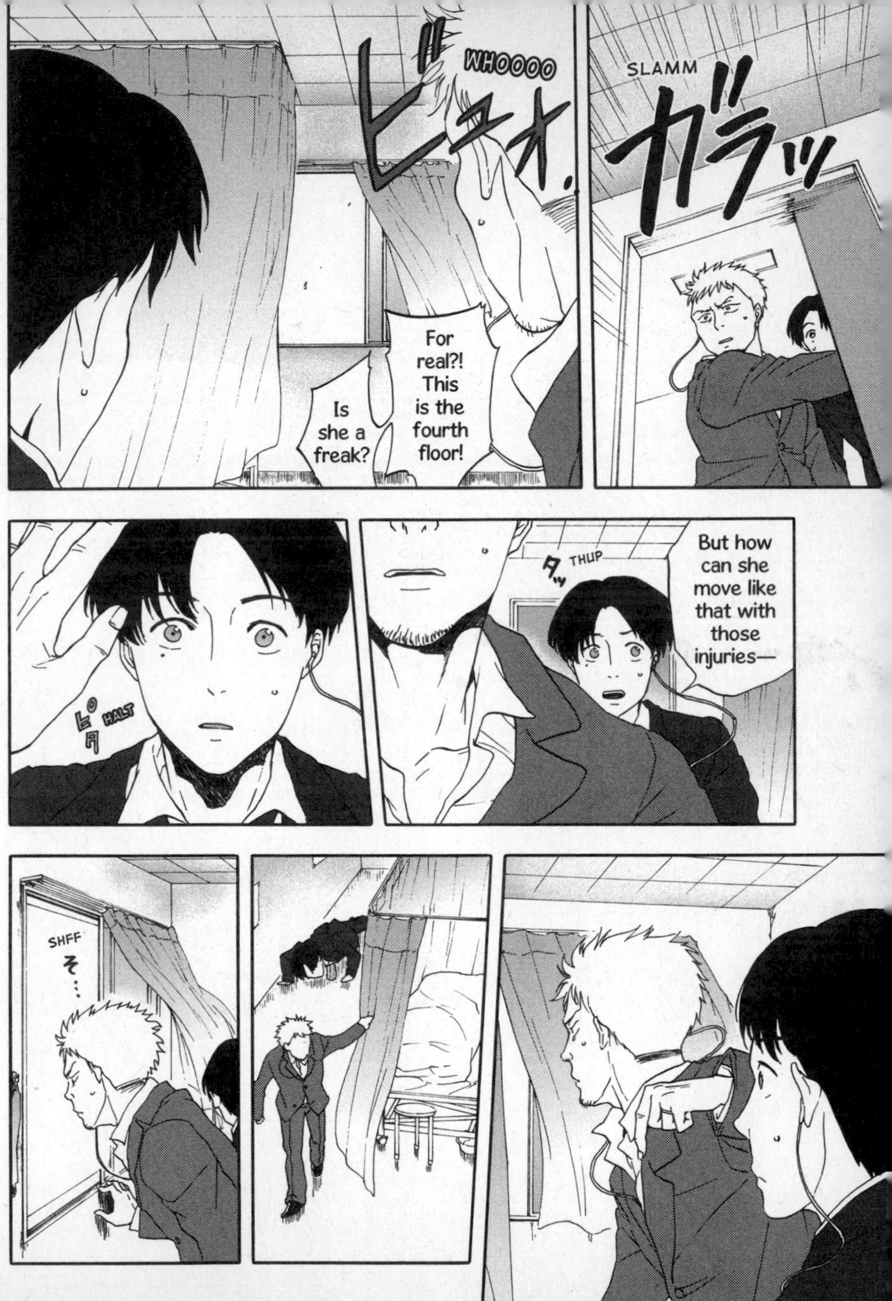
SLAMM
ガラッ
WHOOOO
ビュオ
For real?! This is the fourth floor!
Is she a freak?
THUP
タッ
But how can she move like that with those injuries—
ピタ
HALT
SHFF
そ…

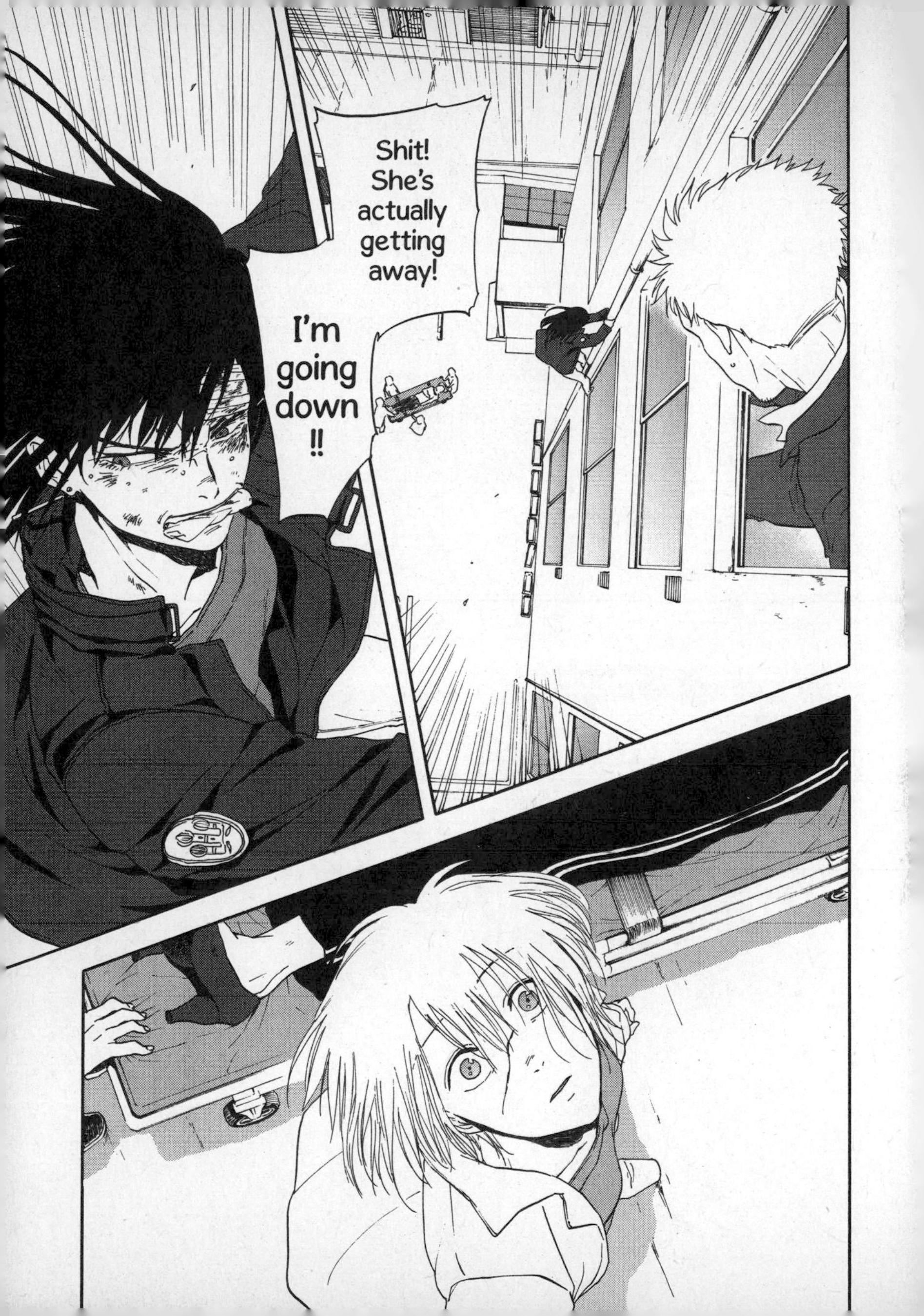
Shit! She's actually getting away!
I'm going down !!

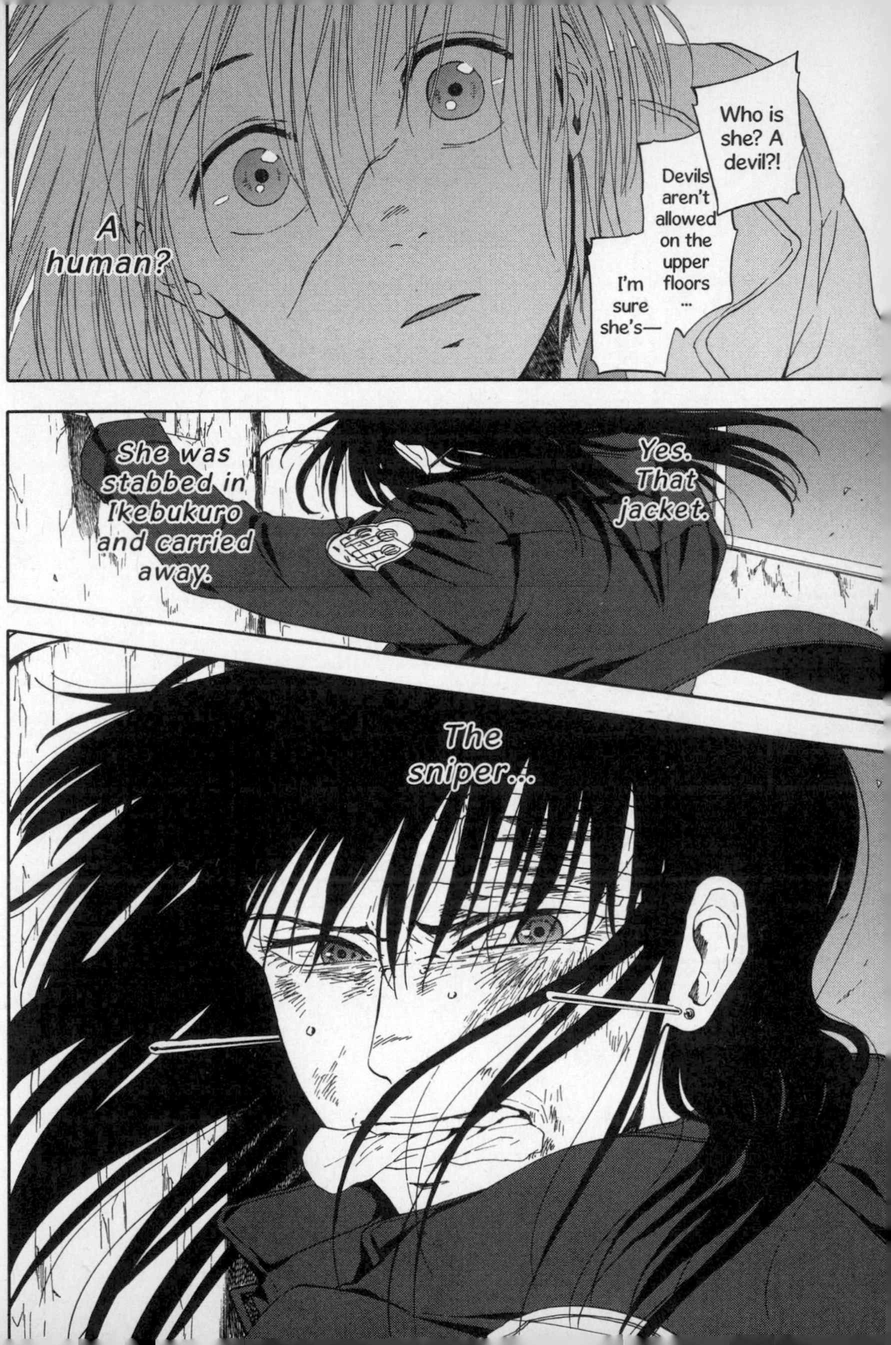
Who is she? A devil?!
Devils aren't allowed on the upper floors…
I'm sure she's—
A human?
Yes. That jacket.
She was stabbed in Ikebukuro and carried away.
The sniper…

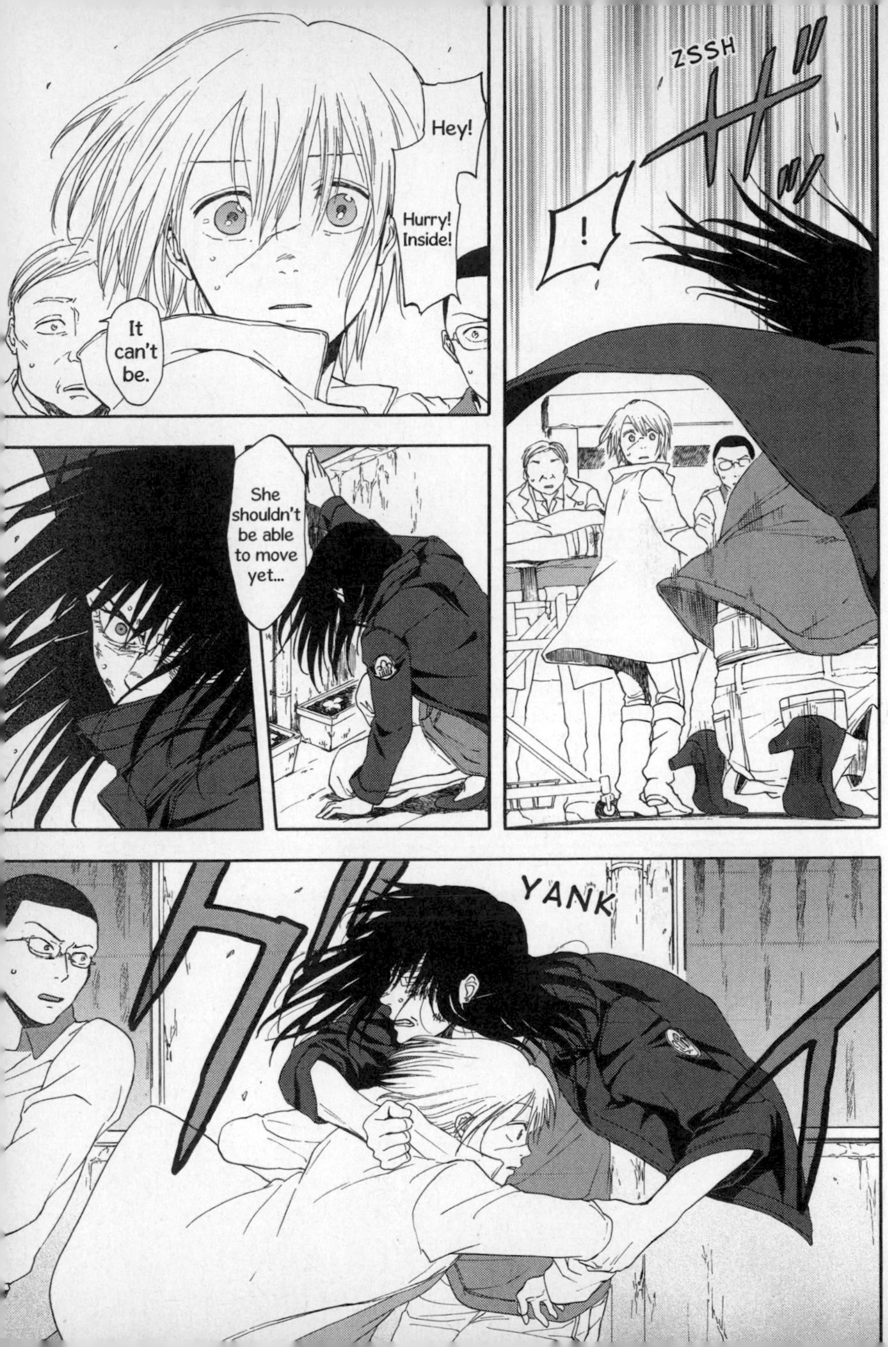
ZSSH
!
Hey!
Hurry! Inside!
It can't be.
She shouldn't be able to move yet...
YANK

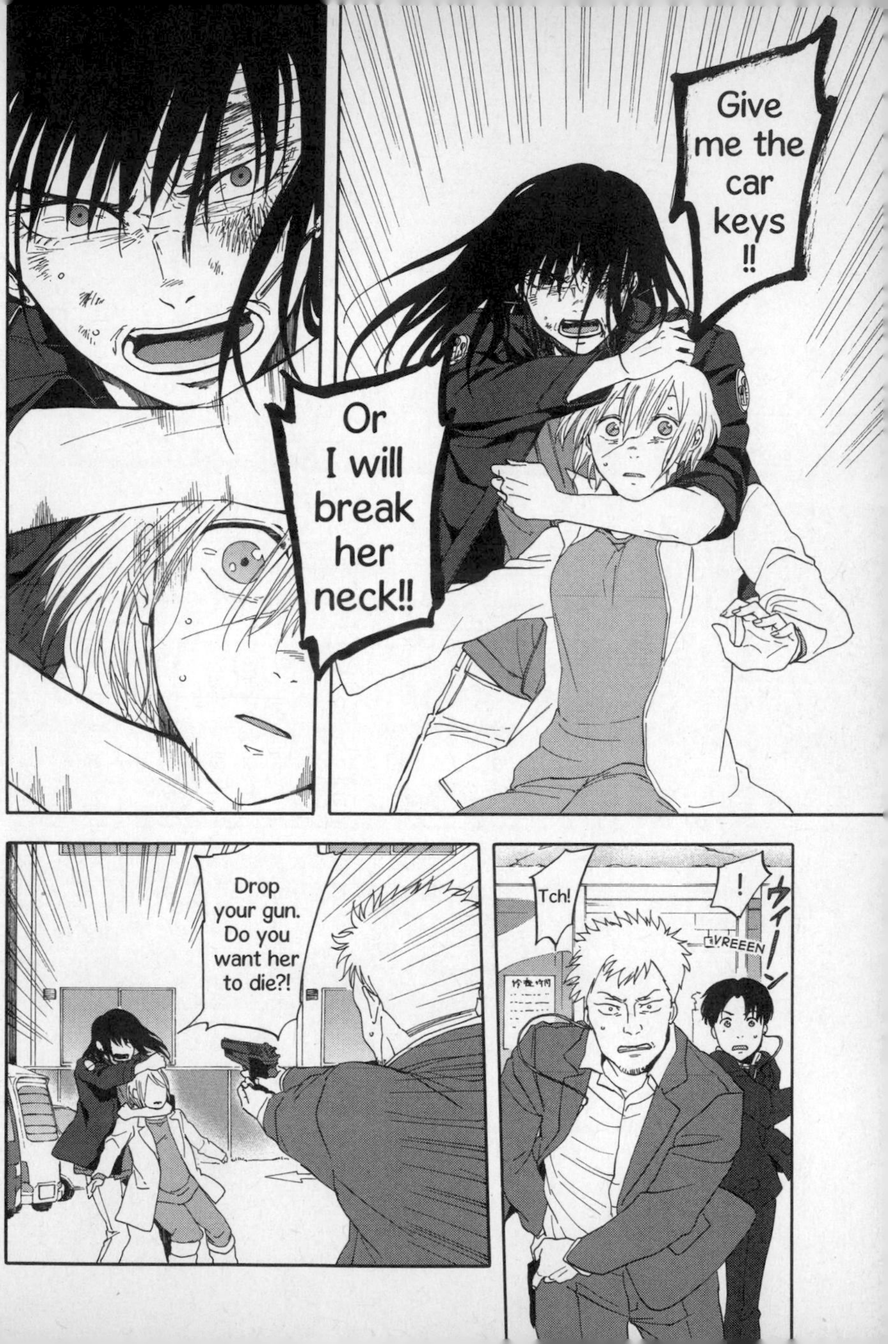

Give me the car keys!!
Or I will break her neck!!
Tch!
!
VREEEN
Drop your gun. Do you want her to die?!

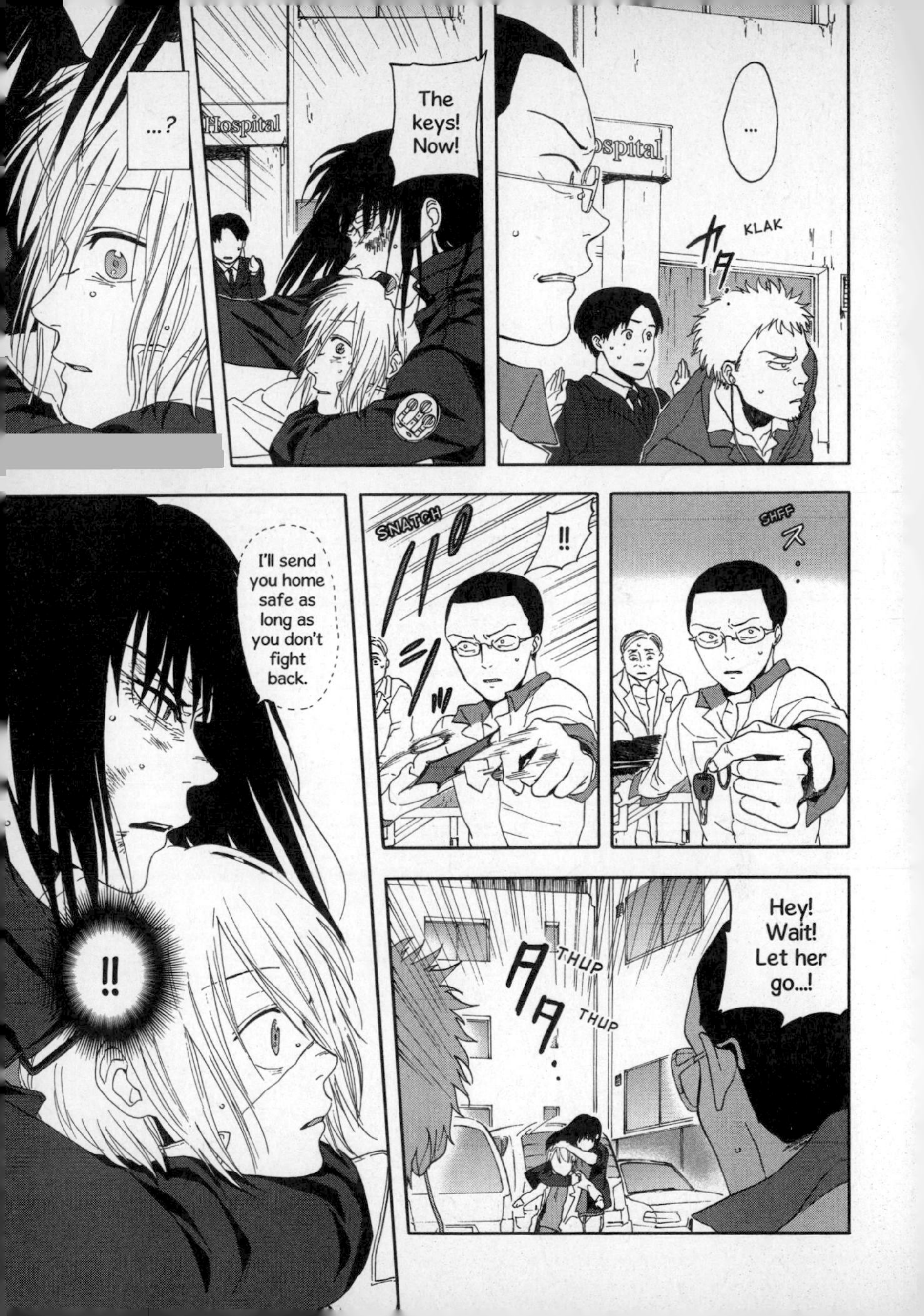
...
KLAK
The keys! Now!
...?
SHFF
SNATCH
!!
Hey! Wait! Let her go...!
THUP
THUP
I'll send you home safe as long as you don't fight back.
!!

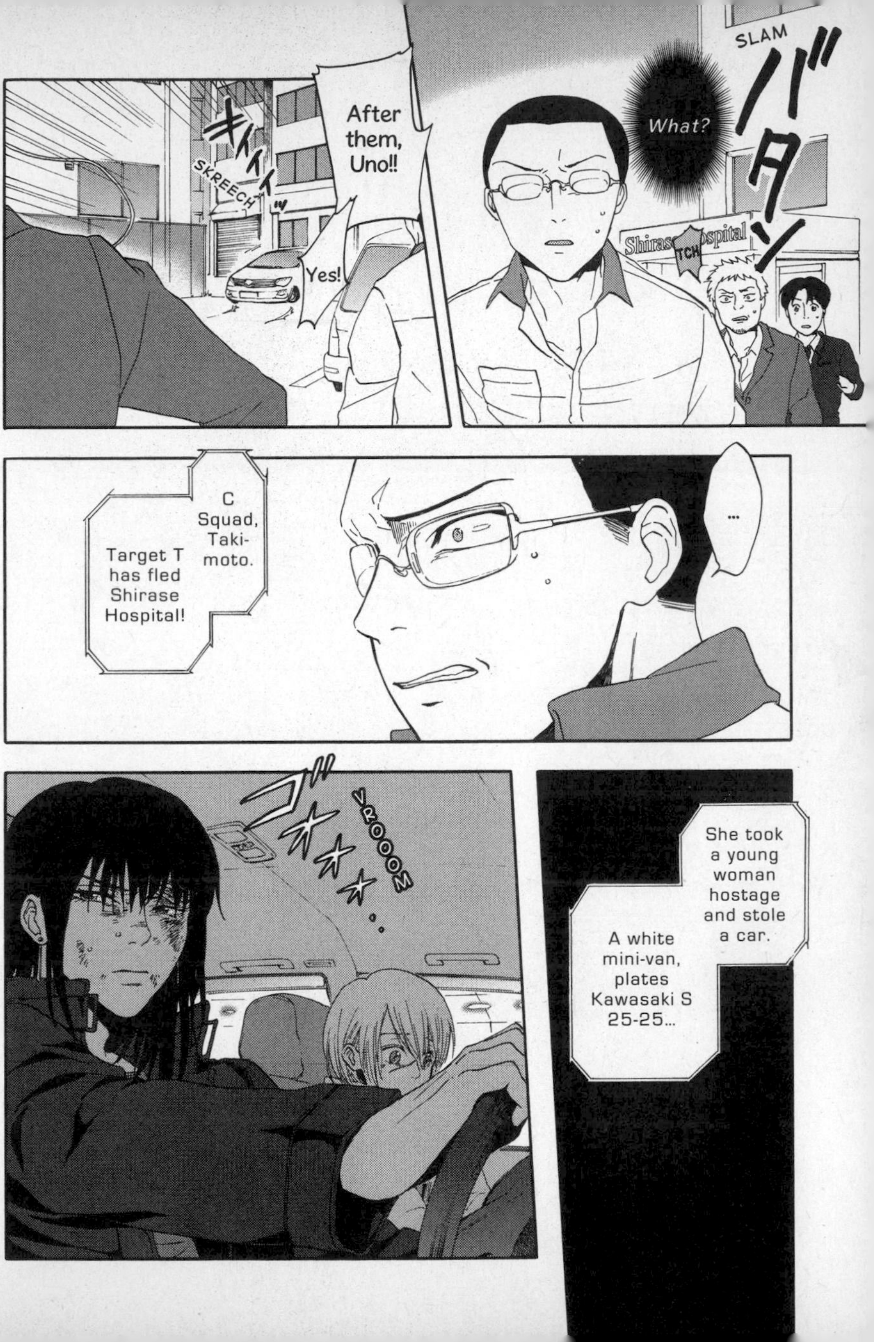
SLAM
What?
Shirase
spital
TCH
After them, Uno!!
Yes!
SKREECH
...
C Squad, Taki-moto.
Target T has fled Shirase Hospital!
She took a young woman hostage and stole a car.
A white mini-van, plates Kawasaki S 25-25...
VROOOM

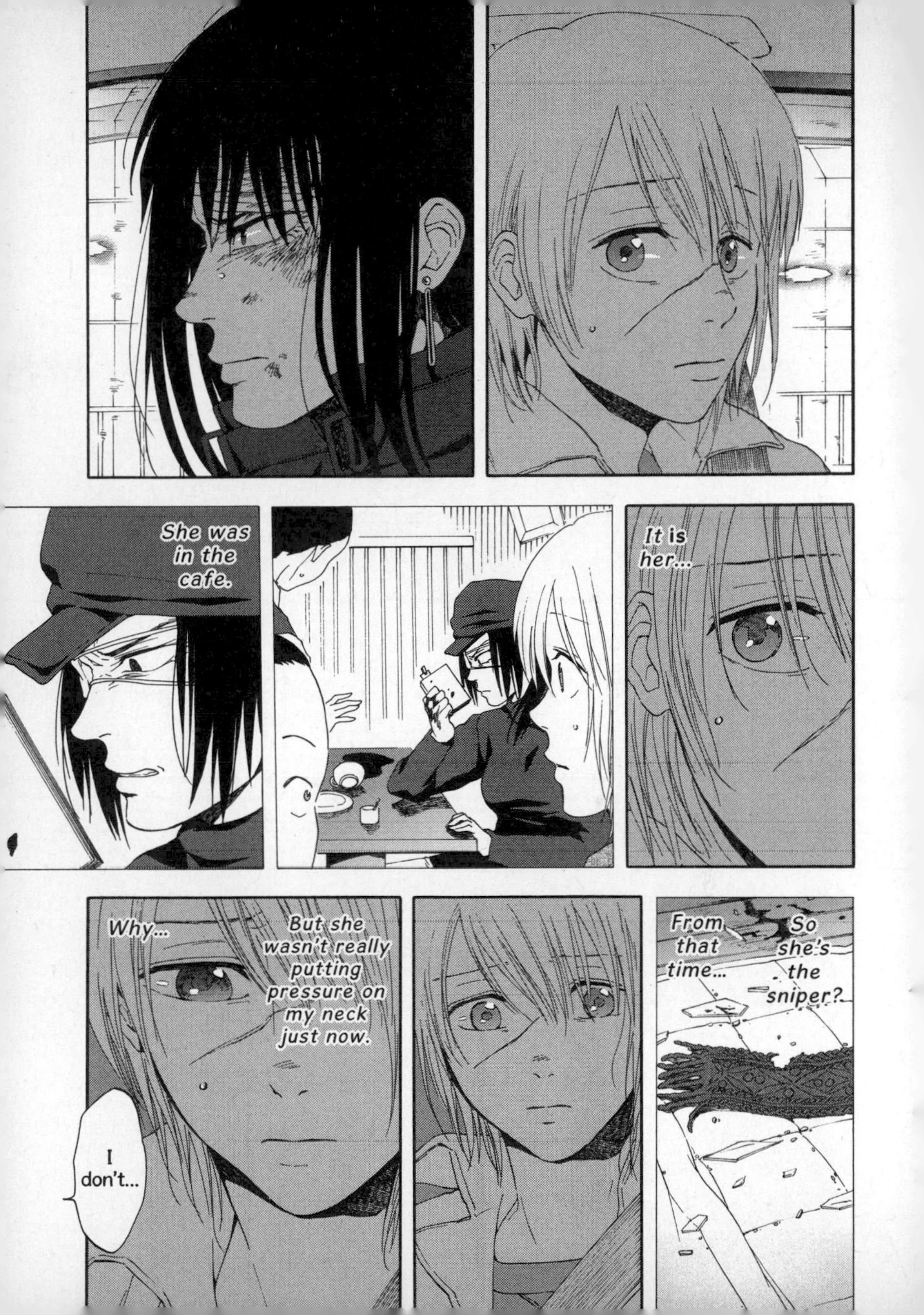
It is her...
She was in the cafe.
So she's the sniper?
From that time...
But she wasn't really putting pressure on my neck just now.
Why...
I don't...

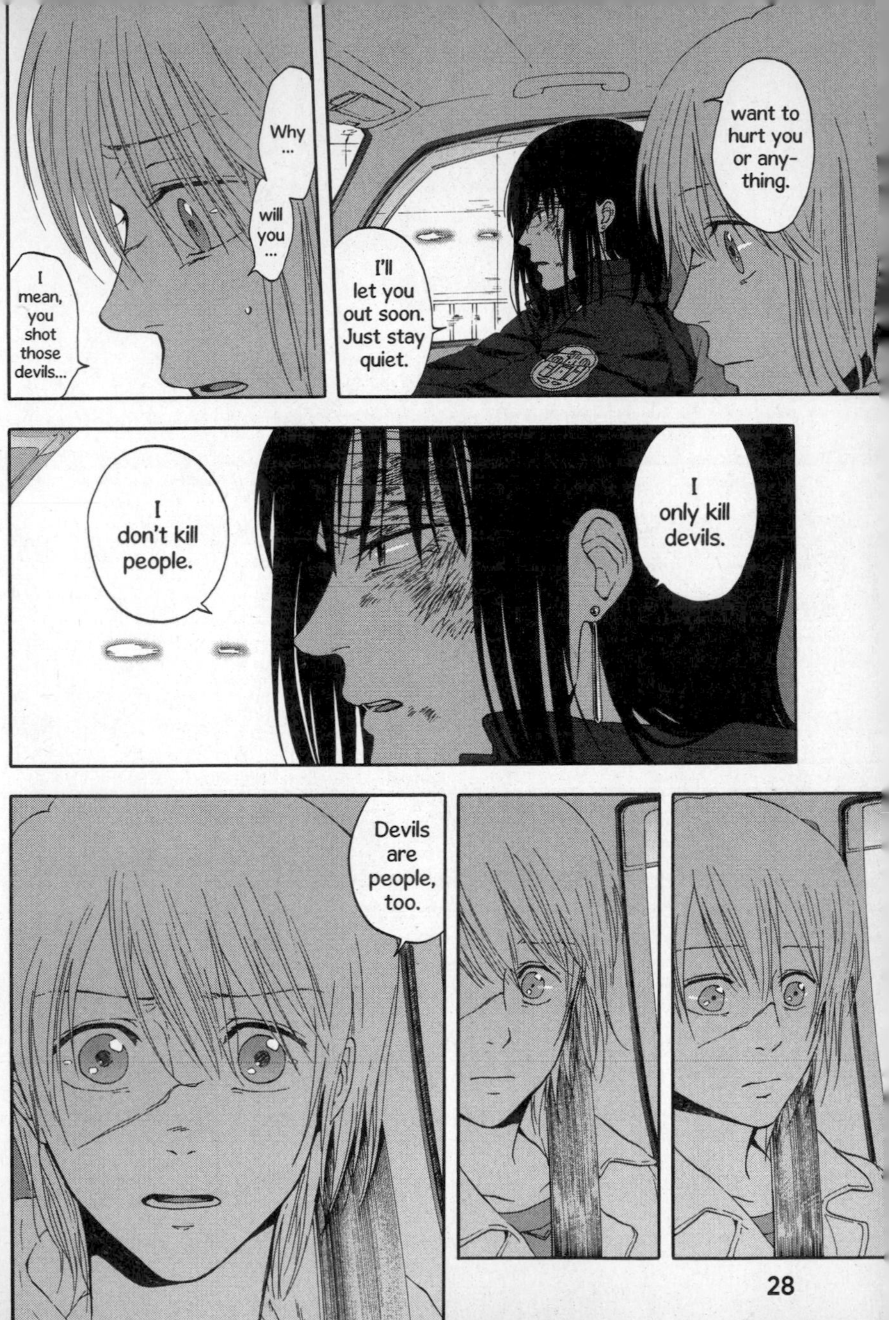
want to hurt you or any-thing.
I'll let you out soon. Just stay quiet.
Why ...
will you ...
I mean, you shot those devils...
I only kill devils.
I don't kill people.
Devils are people, too.

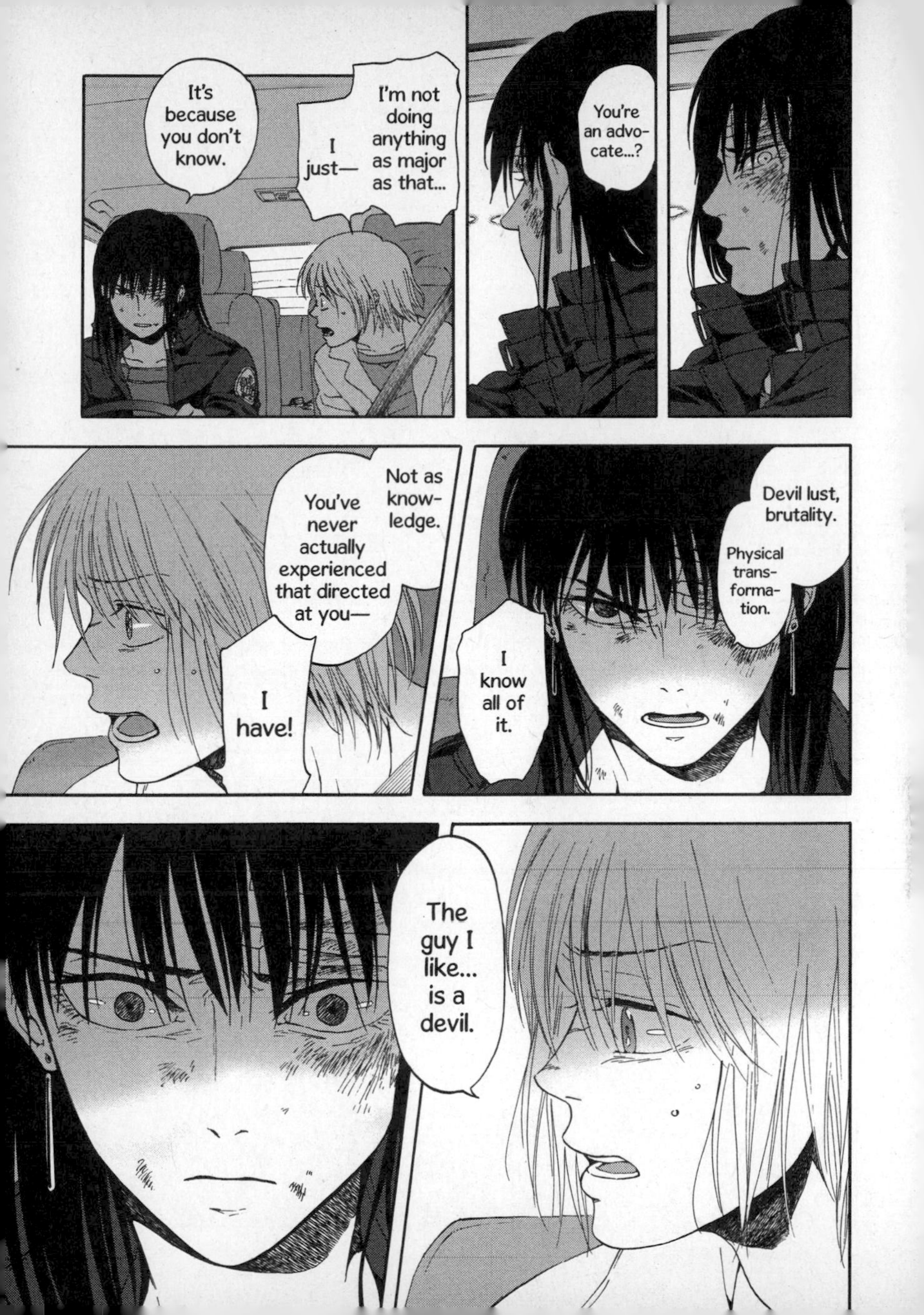
You're an advo-cate...?
I'm not doing anything as major as that...
I just—
It's because you don't know.
Devil lust, brutality.
Physical trans-forma-tion.
I know all of it.
Not as know-ledge.
You've never actually experienced that directed at you—
I have!
The guy I like... is a devil.

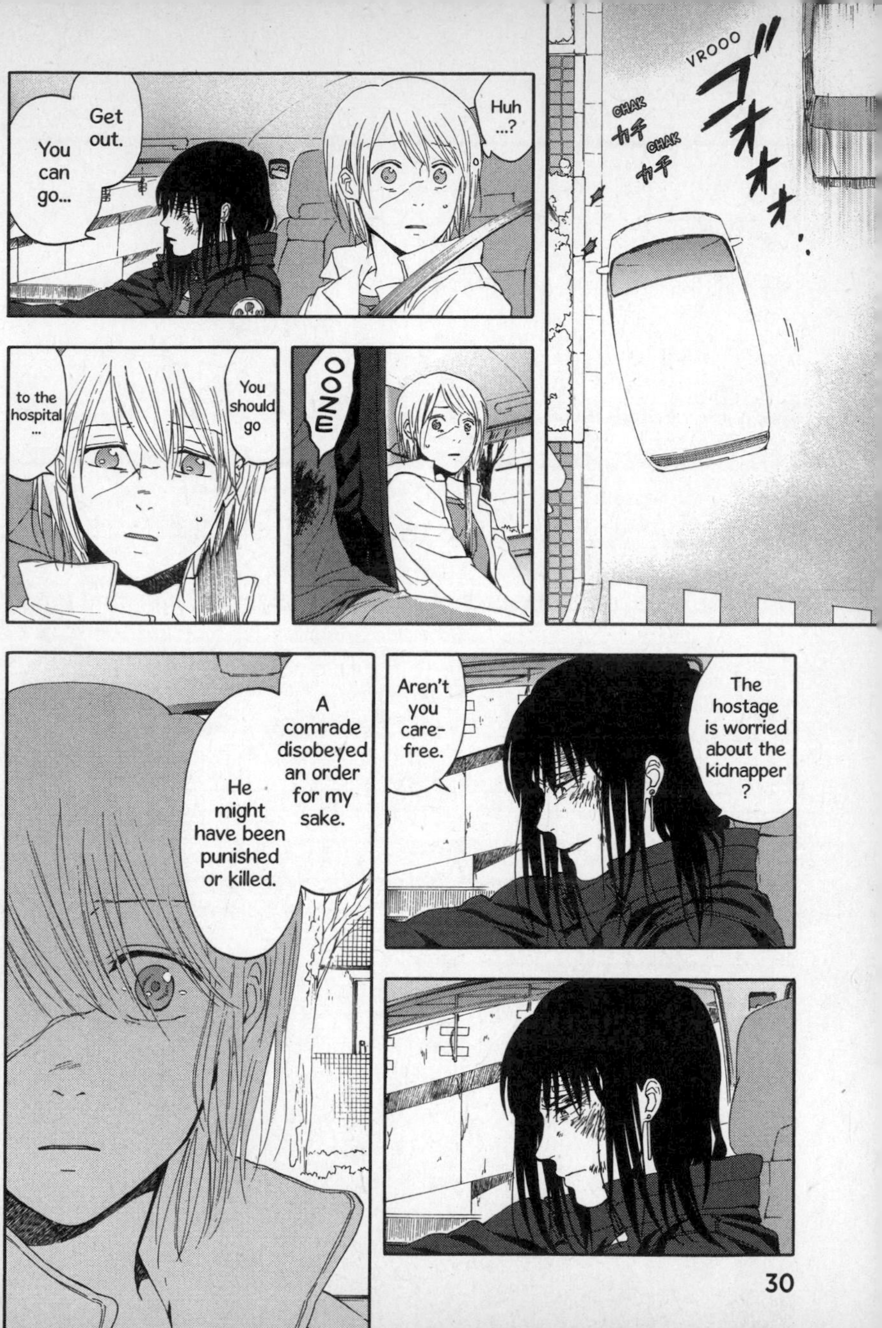
VROOO
CHAK
CHAK
Huh ...?
Get out.
You can go...
OOZE
You should go
to the hospital ...
The hostage is worried about the kidnapper ?
Aren't you care-free.
A comrade disobeyed an order for my sake.
He might have been punished or killed.

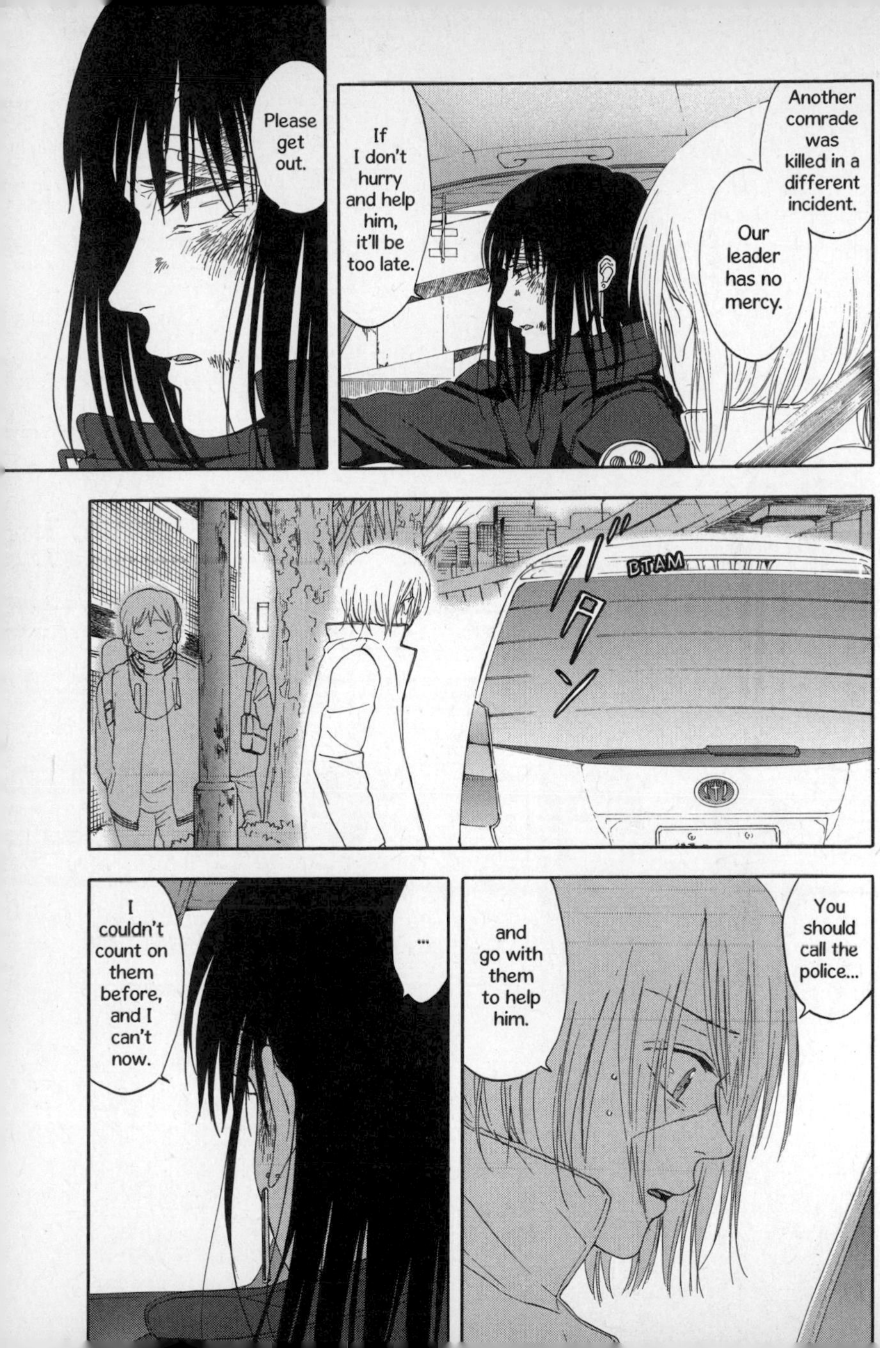
Another comrade was killed in a different incident.
Our leader has no mercy.
If I don't hurry and help him, it'll be too late.
Please get out.
BTAM
バタン
You should call the police...
and go with them to help him.
...
I couldn't count on them before, and I can't now.

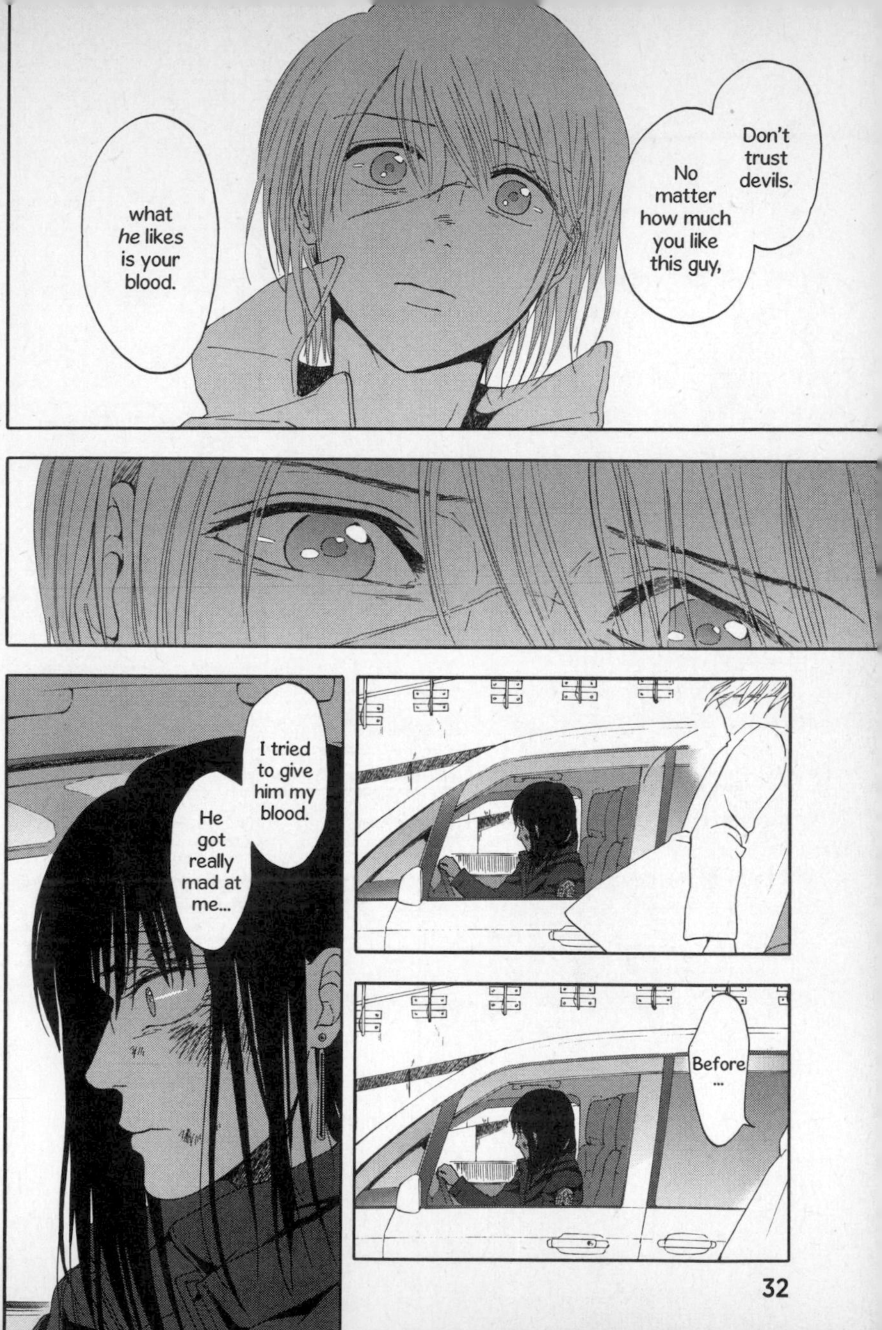
Don't trust devils.
No matter how much you like this guy,
what *he* likes is your blood.
Before...
I tried to give him my blood.
He got really mad at me...

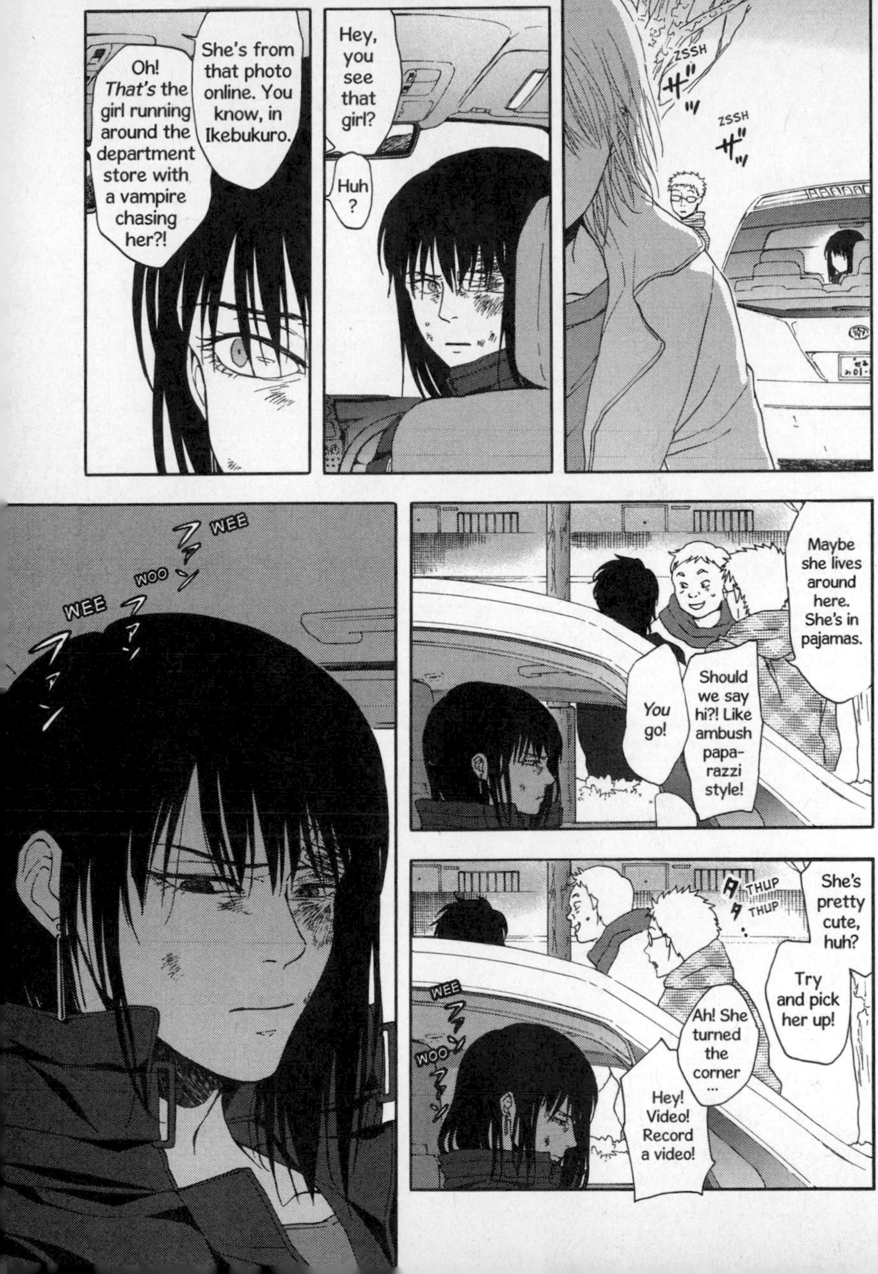
ZSSH
ZSSH
Hey, you see that girl?
Huh?
She's from that photo online. You know, in Ikebukuro.
Oh! *That's* the girl running around the department store with a vampire chasing her?!
Maybe she lives around here. She's in pajamas.
Should we say hi?! Like ambush paparazzi style!
You go!
THUP THUP
She's pretty cute, huh?
Try and pick her up!
Ah! She turned the corner ...
Hey! Video! Record a video!
WEE
WOO
WEE
WOO
WEE

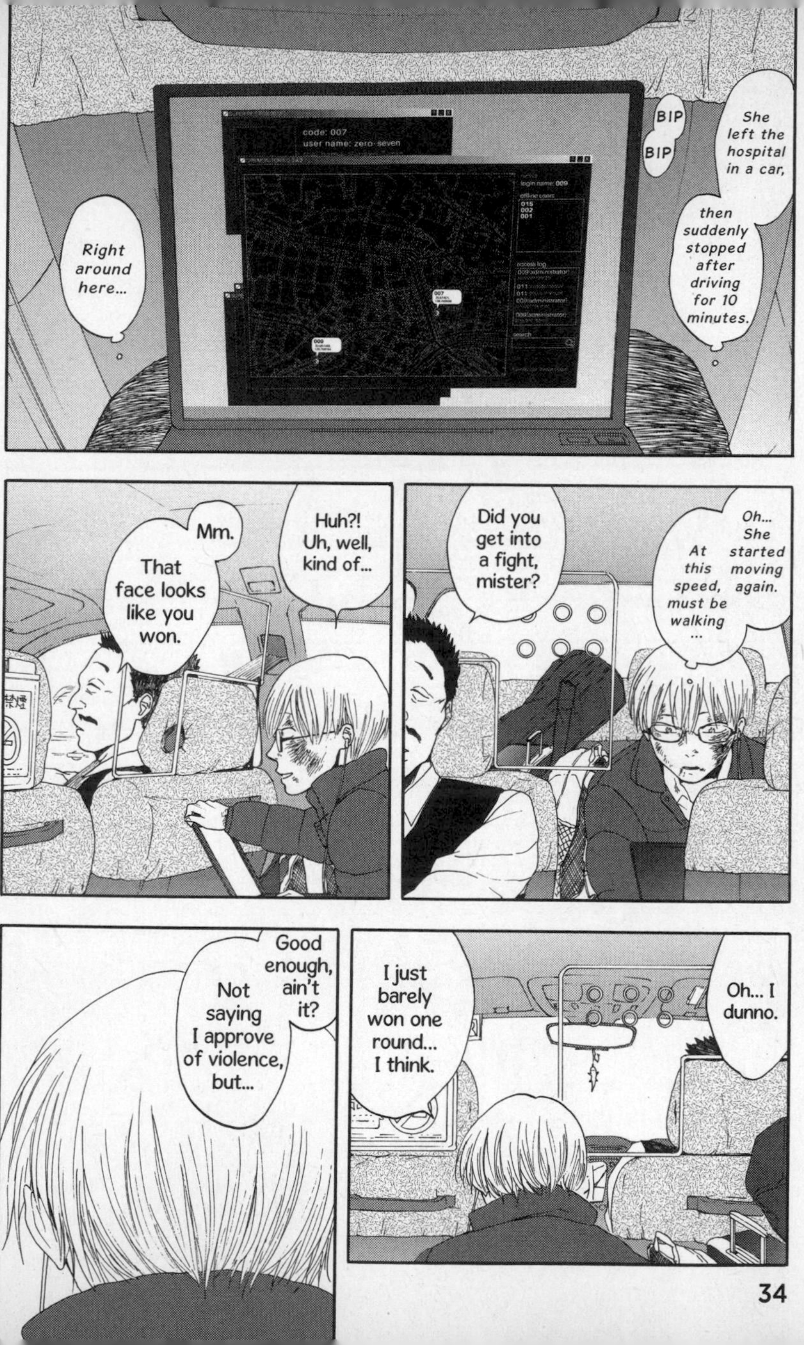
She left the hospital in a car,
then suddenly stopped after driving for 10 minutes.
BIP
BIP
code: 007
user name: zero-seven
login name: 009
015
002
001
Right around here...
Oh... She started moving again.
At this speed, must be walking...
Did you get into a fight, mister?
Huh?! Uh, well, kind of...
Mm.
That face looks like you won.
Oh... I dunno.
I just barely won one round... I think.
Good enough, ain't it?
Not saying I approve of violence, but...

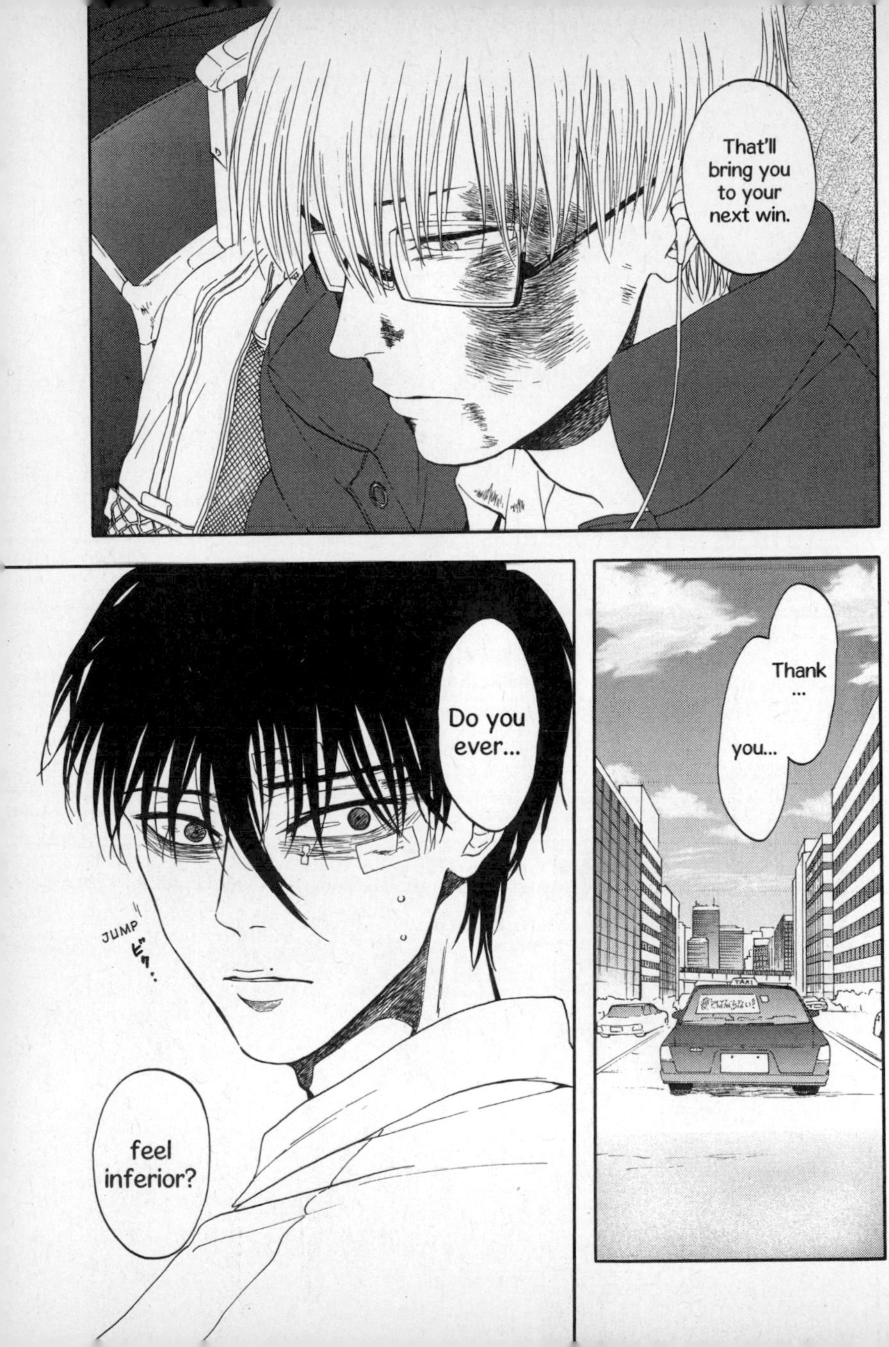
That'll bring you to your next win.
Thank... you...
Do you ever...
JUMP
ビク…
feel inferior?

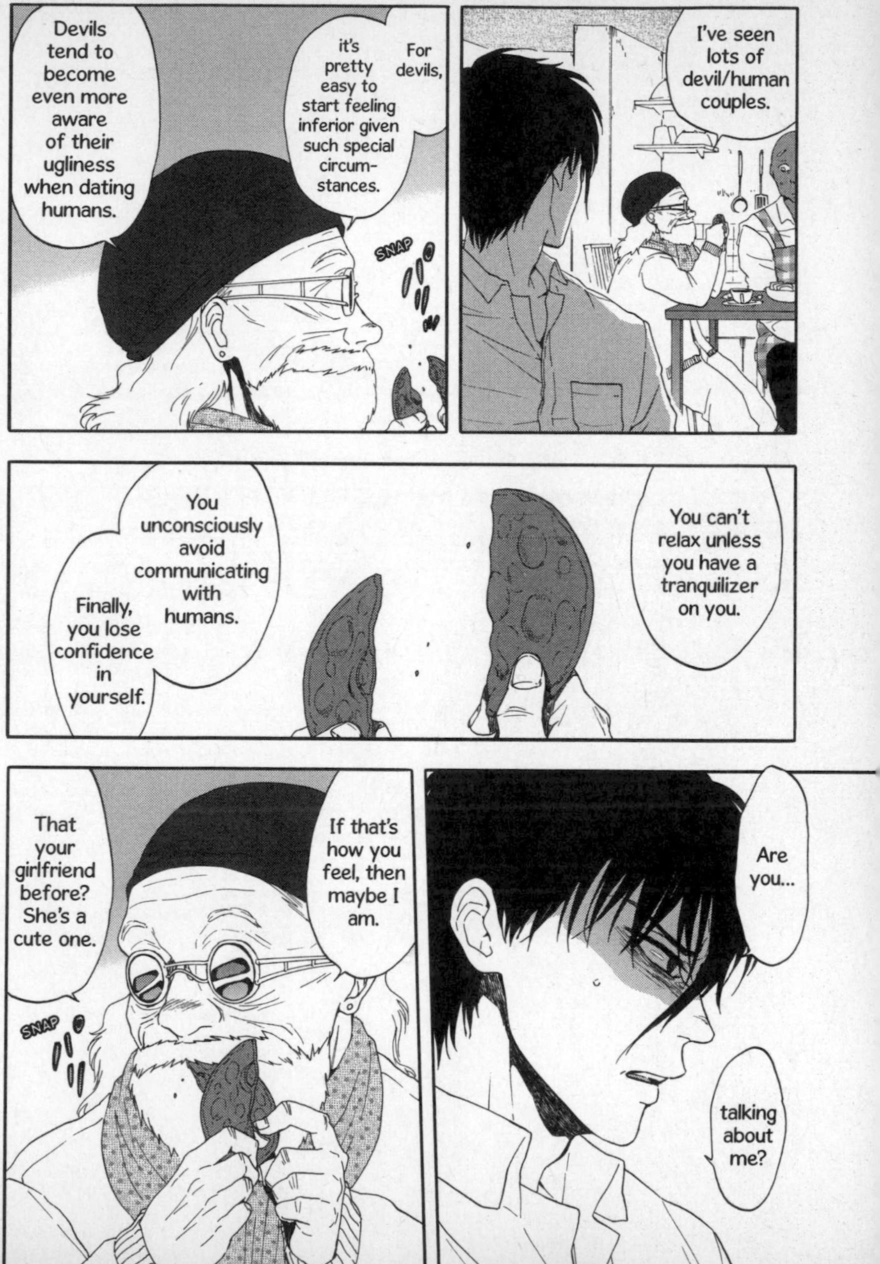
I've seen lots of devil/human couples.
For devils, it's pretty easy to start feeling inferior given such special circumstances.
Devils tend to become even more aware of their ugliness when dating humans.
SNAP
You can't relax unless you have a tranquilizer on you.
You unconsciously avoid communicating with humans.
Finally, you lose confidence in yourself.
Are you...
talking about me?
If that's how you feel, then maybe I am.
That your girlfriend before? She's a cute one.
SNAP

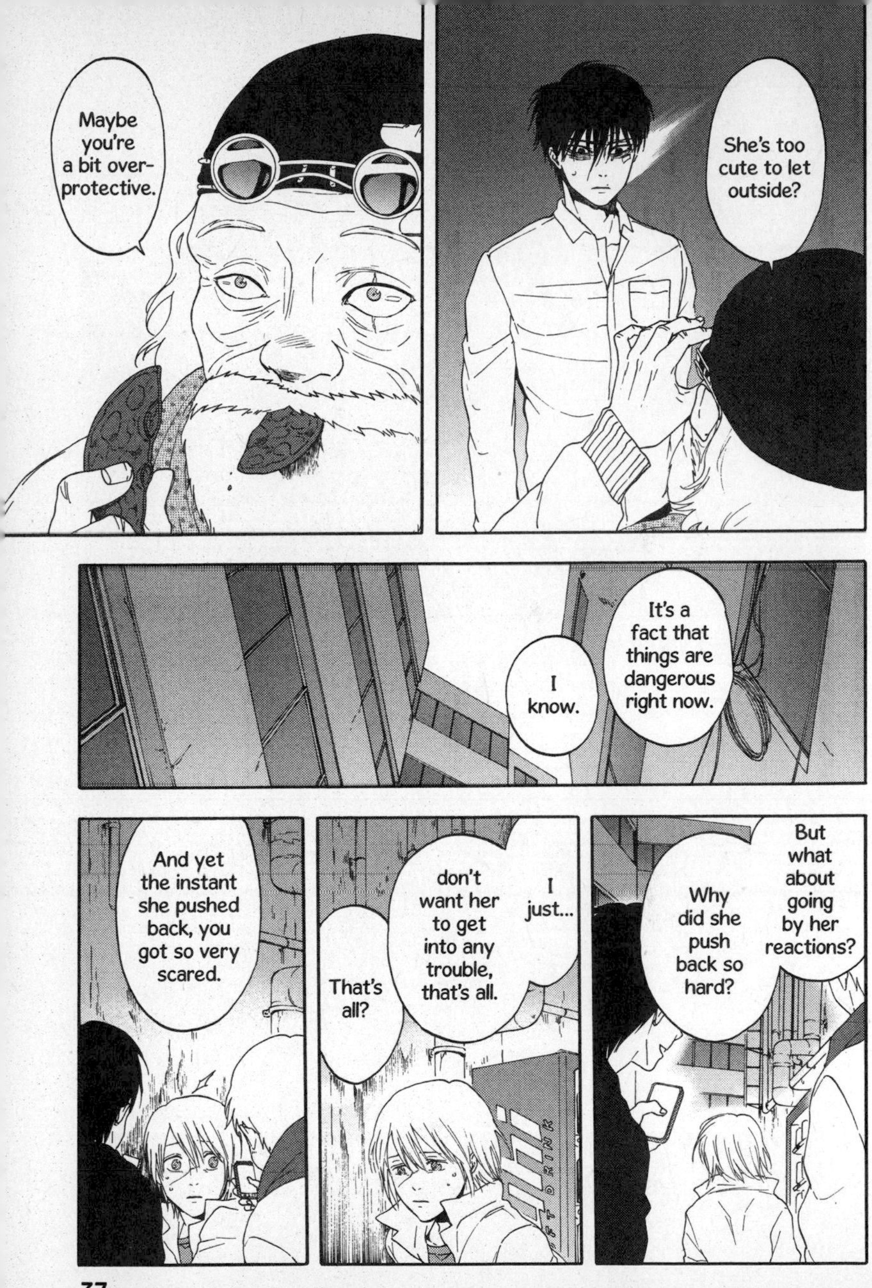
She's too cute to let outside?
Maybe you're a bit over-protective.
It's a fact that things are dangerous right now.
I know.
But what about going by her reactions?
Why did she push back so hard?
I just...
don't want her to get into any trouble, that's all.
That's all?
And yet the instant she pushed back, you got so very scared.

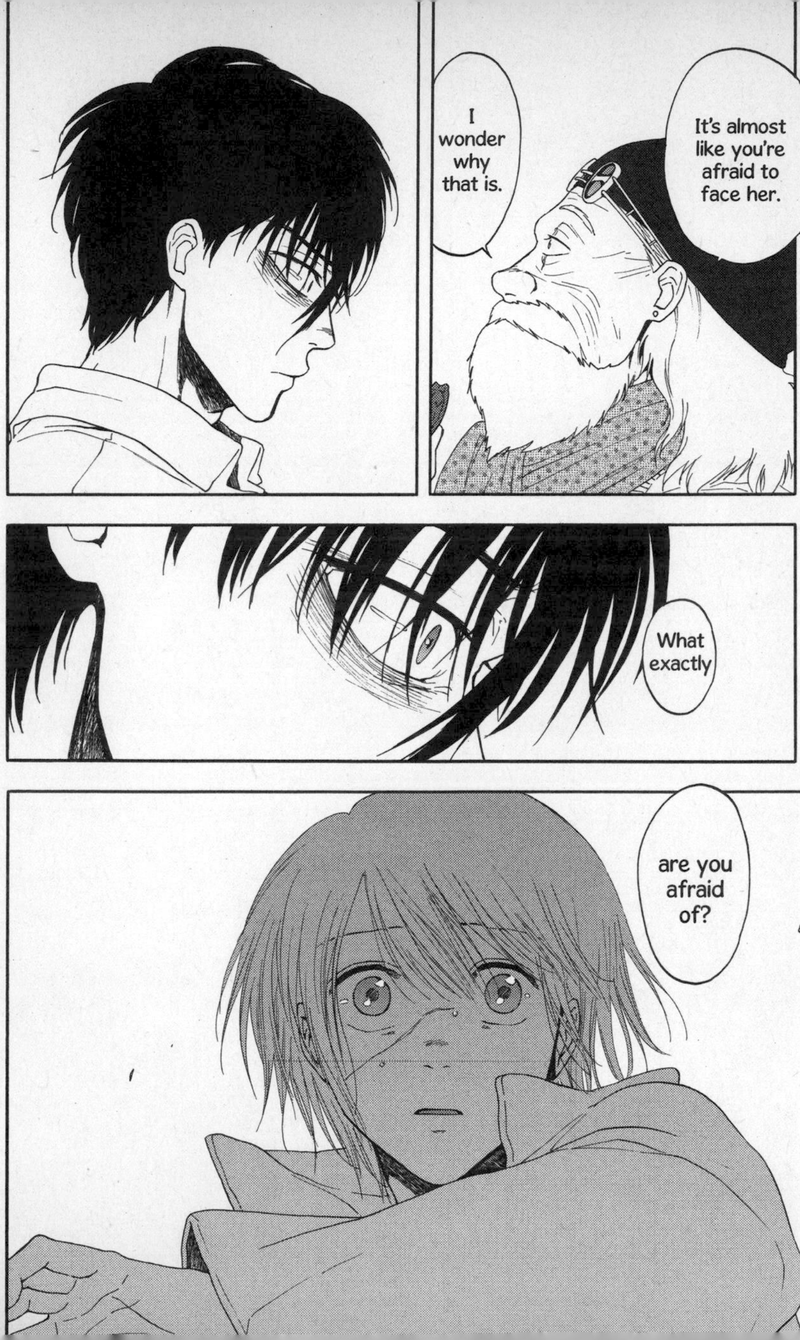
It's almost like you're afraid to face her.
I wonder why that is.
What exactly
are you afraid of?

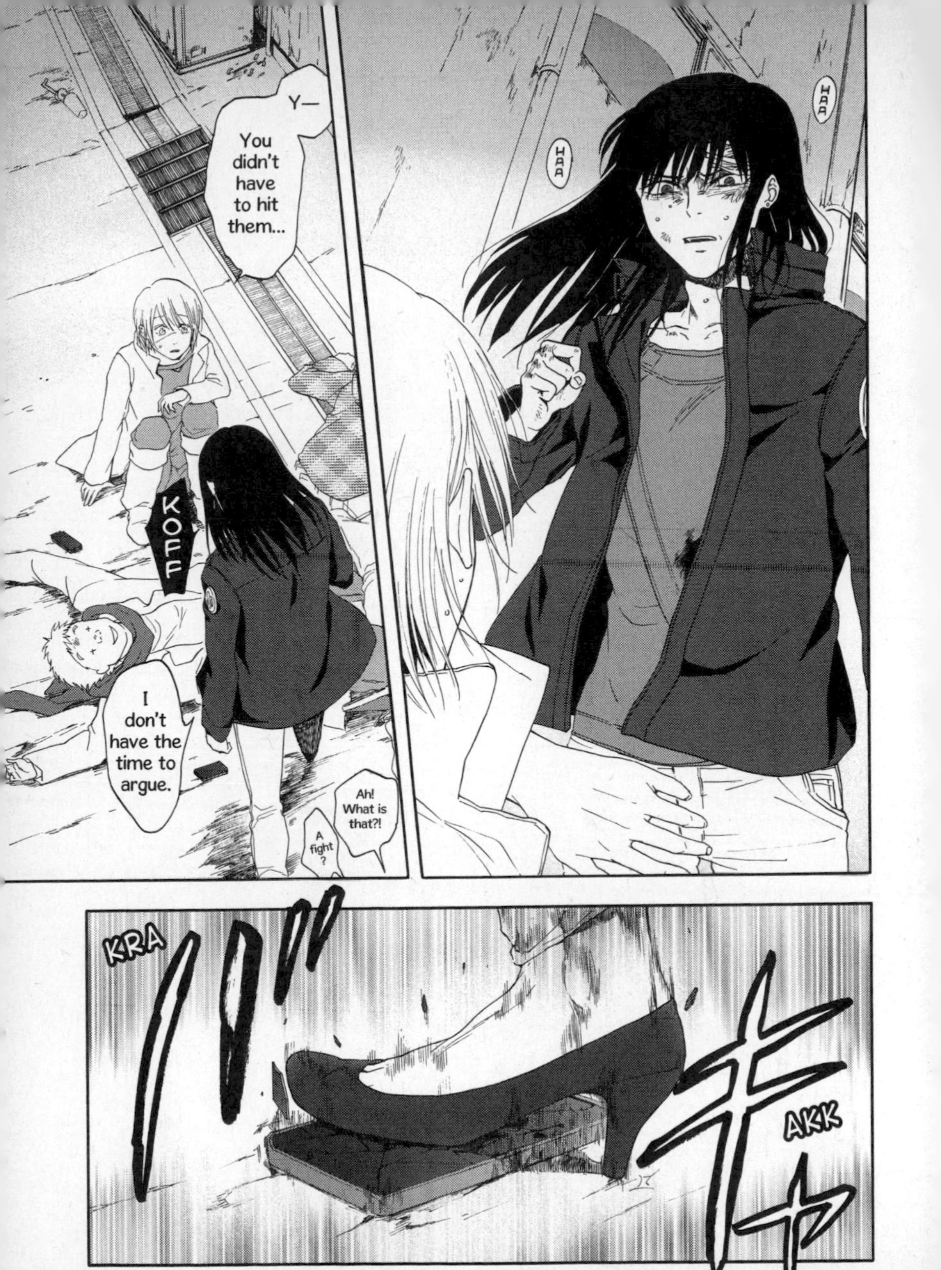
HAA
HAA
Y—
You didn't have to hit them...
KOFF
I don't have the time to argue.
Ah! What is that?!
A fight?
KRA
AKK

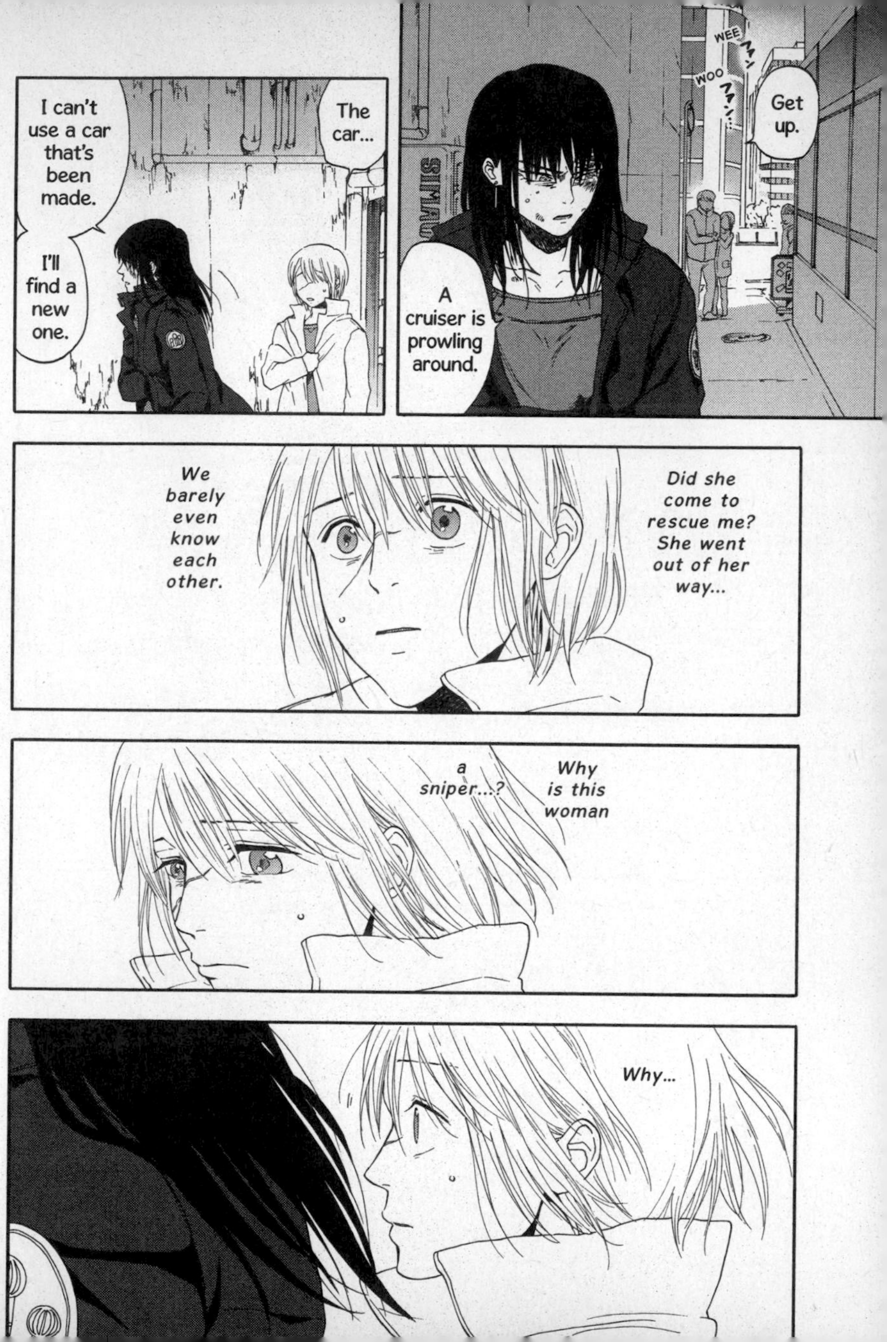
WEE
WOO
Get up.
A cruiser is prowling around.
The car...
I can't use a car that's been made.
I'll find a new one.
Did she come to rescue me? She went out of her way...
We barely even know each other.
Why is this woman
a sniper...?
Why...

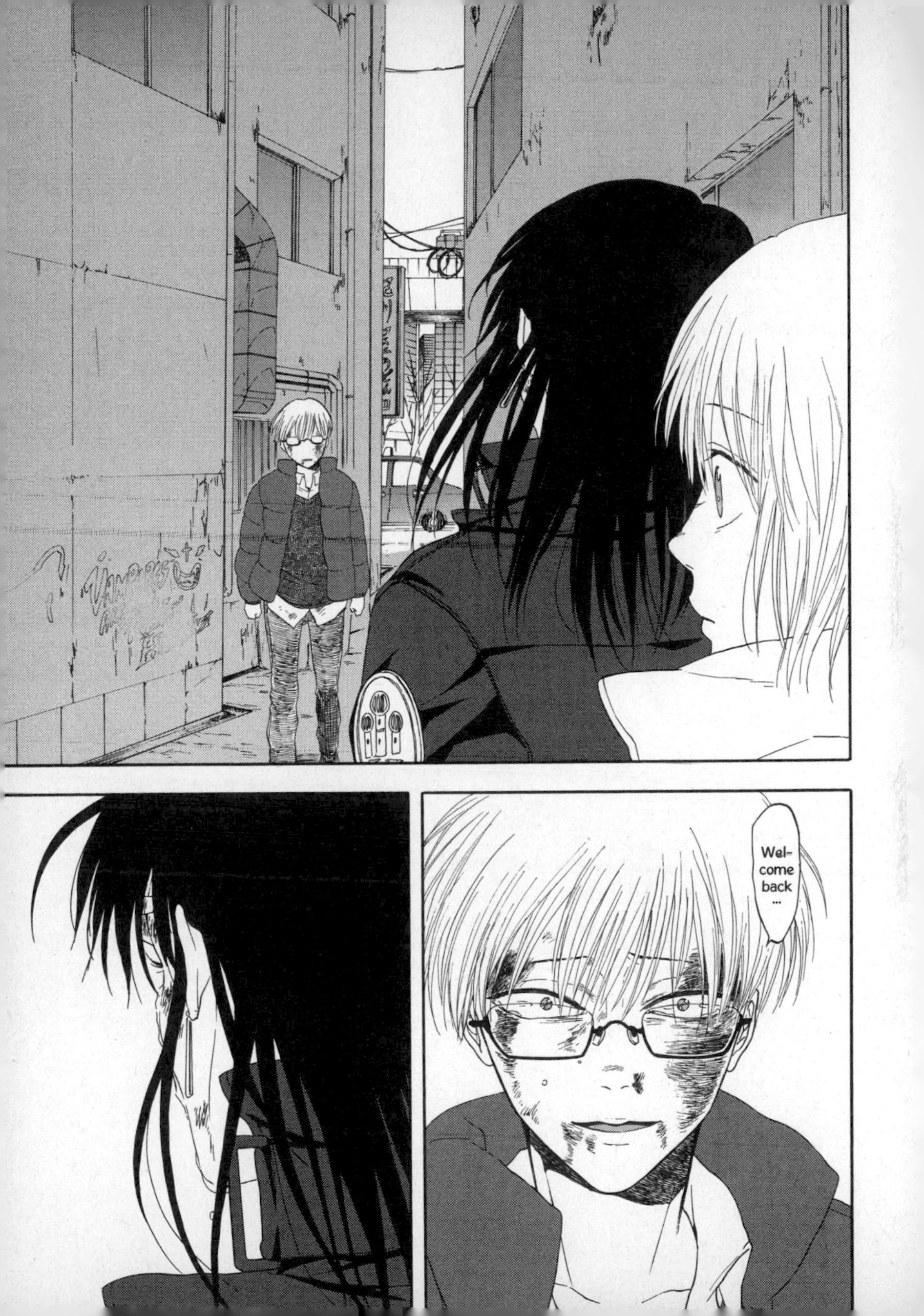
Wel-come back ...

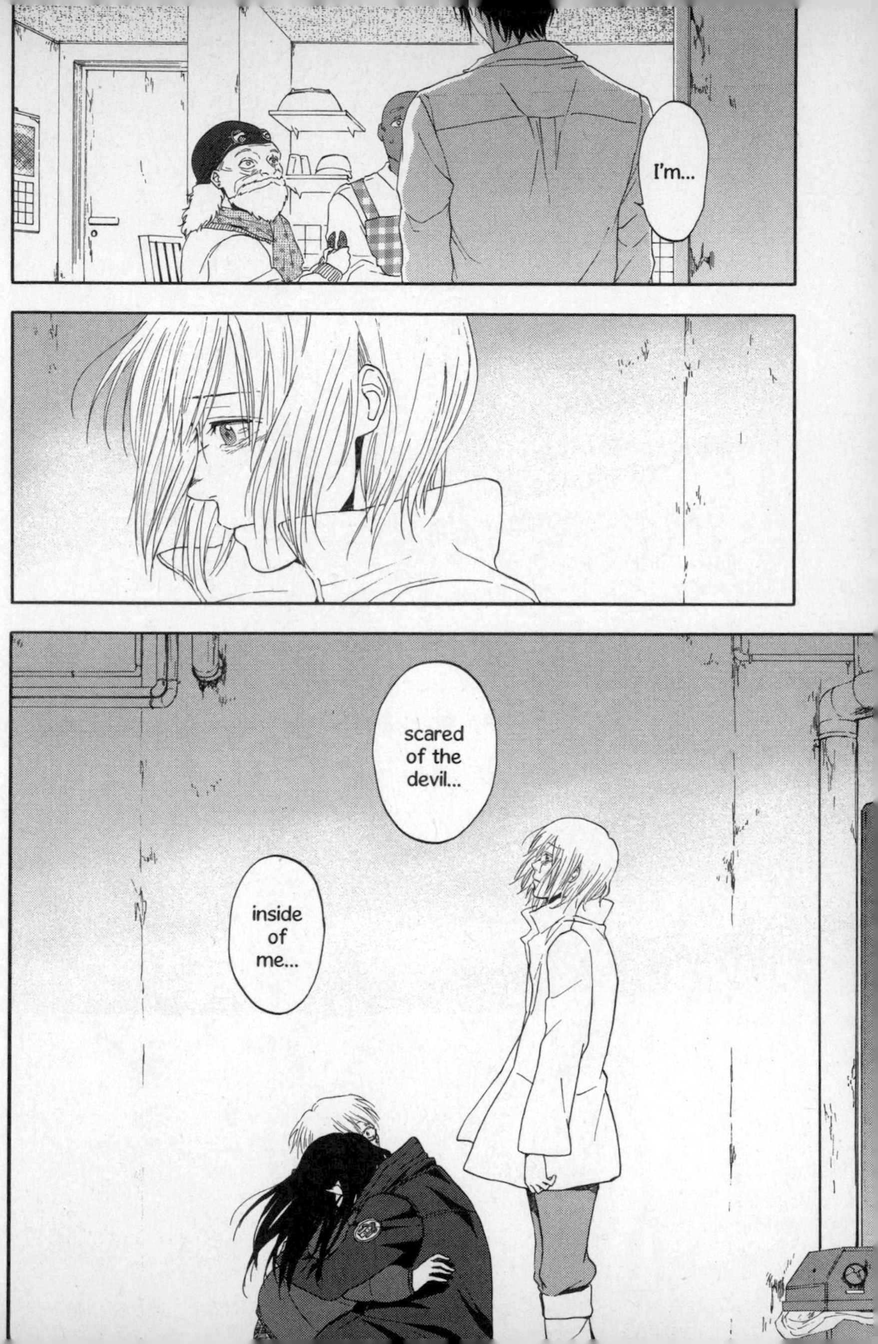
I'm...
scared of the devil...
inside of me...

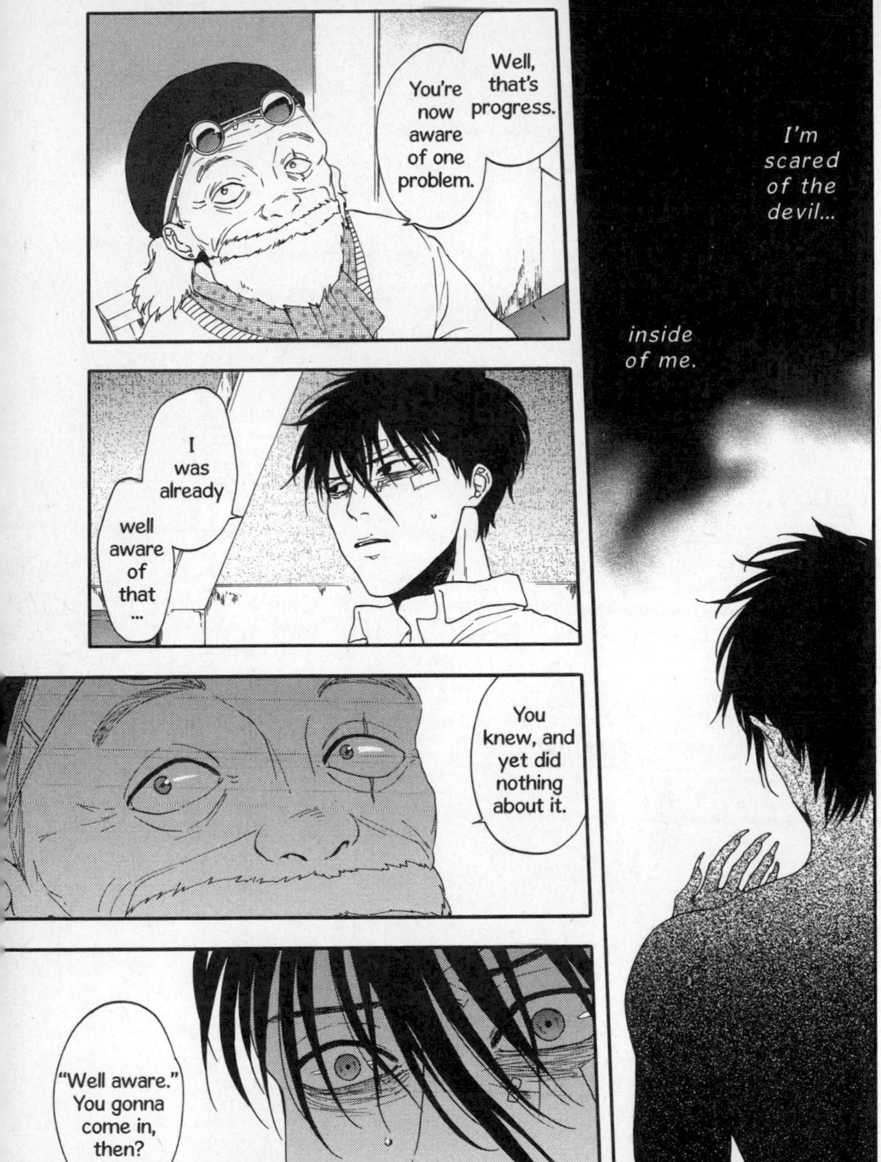
I'm scared of the devil...
inside of me.
Well, that's progress.
You're now aware of one problem.
I was already
well aware of that ...
You knew, and yet did nothing about it.
"Well aware." You gonna come in, then?

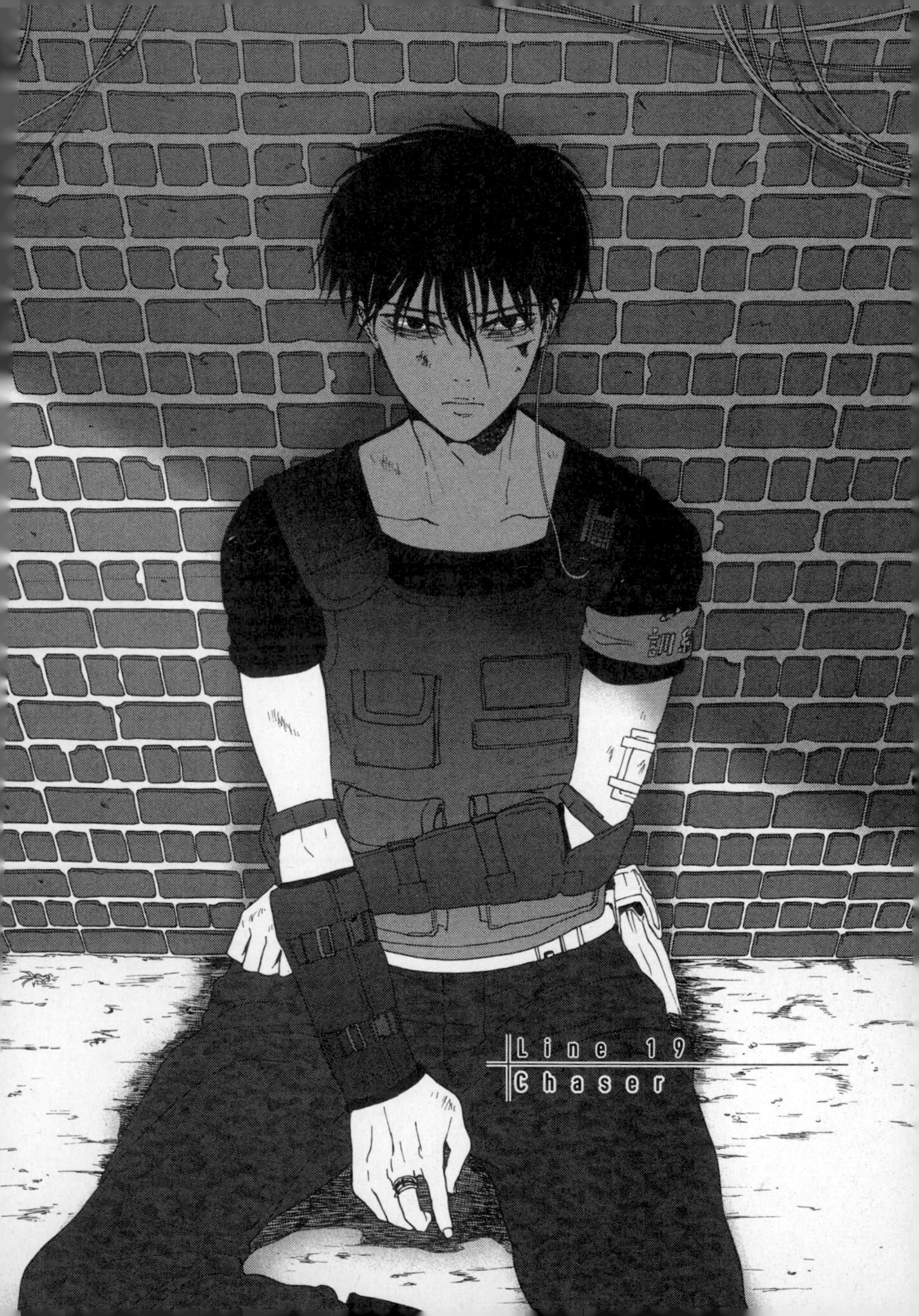
Line 19
Chaser

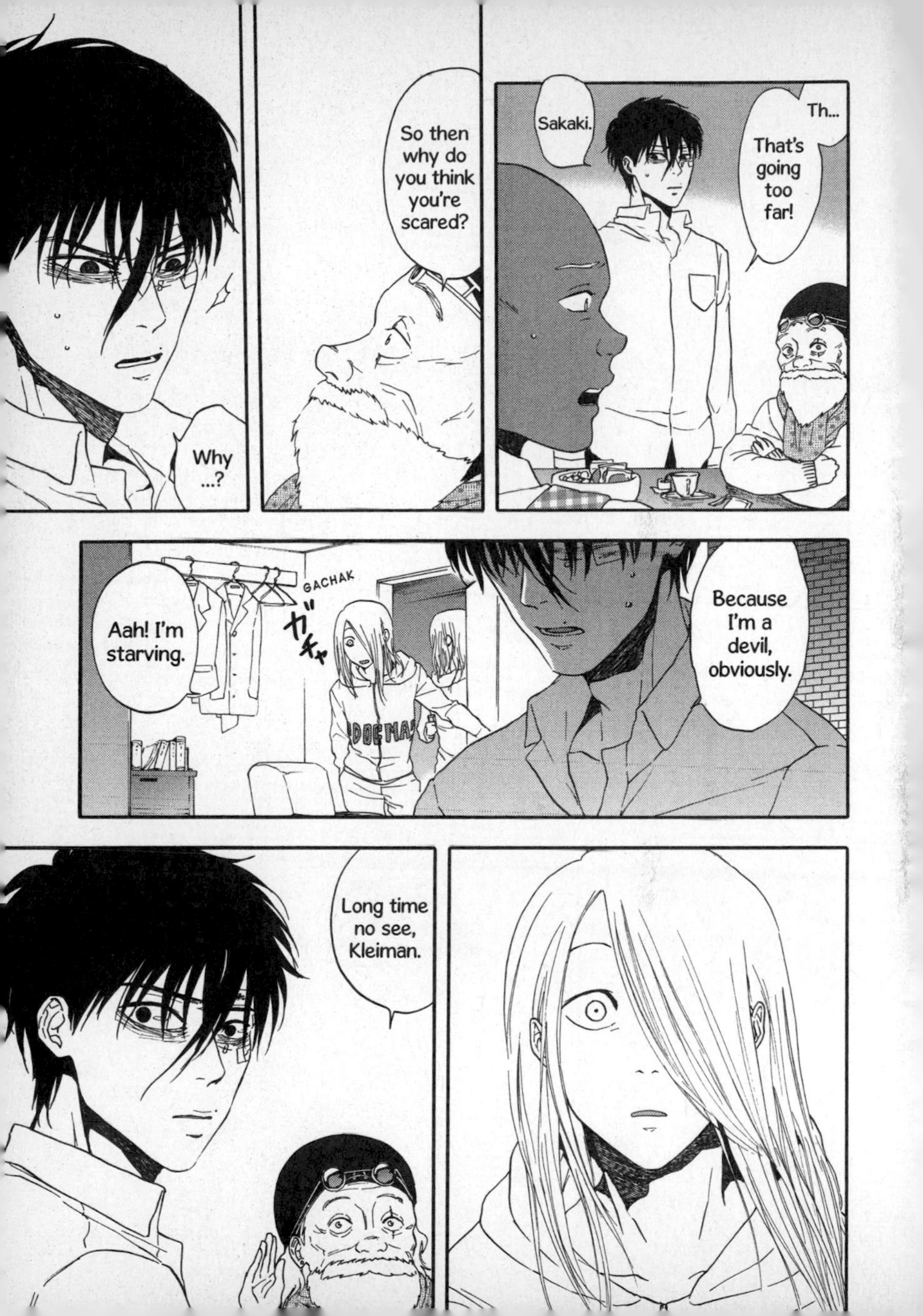
Th...
That's going too far!
Sakaki.
So then why do you think you're scared?
Why ...?
Because I'm a devil, obviously.
GACHAK
ガチャ
Aah! I'm starving.
Long time no see, Kleiman.

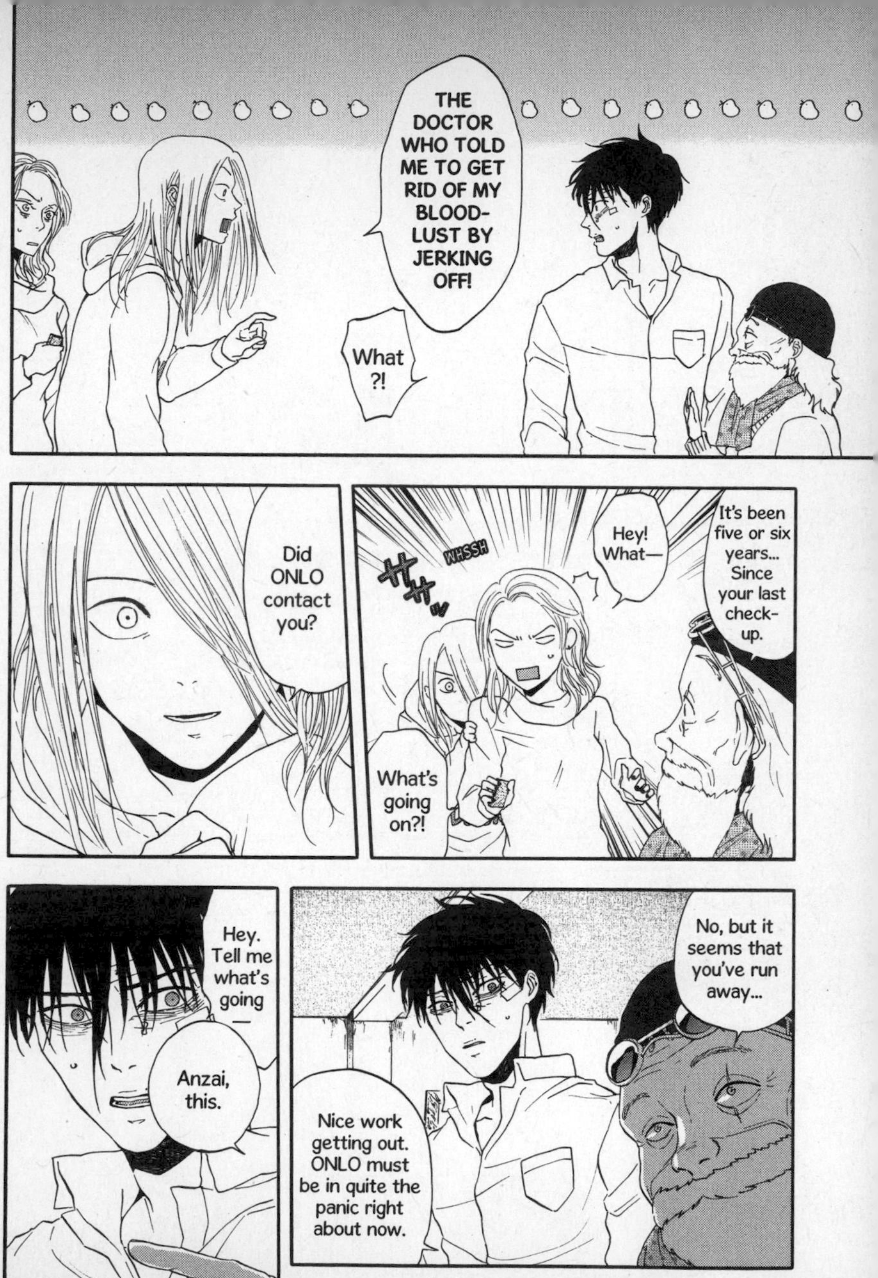
THE DOCTOR WHO TOLD ME TO GET RID OF MY BLOOD-LUST BY JERKING OFF!
What?!
It's been five or six years... Since your last check-up.
Hey! What—
WHSSH
What's going on?!
Did ONLO contact you?
No, but it seems that you've run away...
Nice work getting out. ONLO must be in quite the panic right about now.
Hey. Tell me what's going —
Anzai, this.

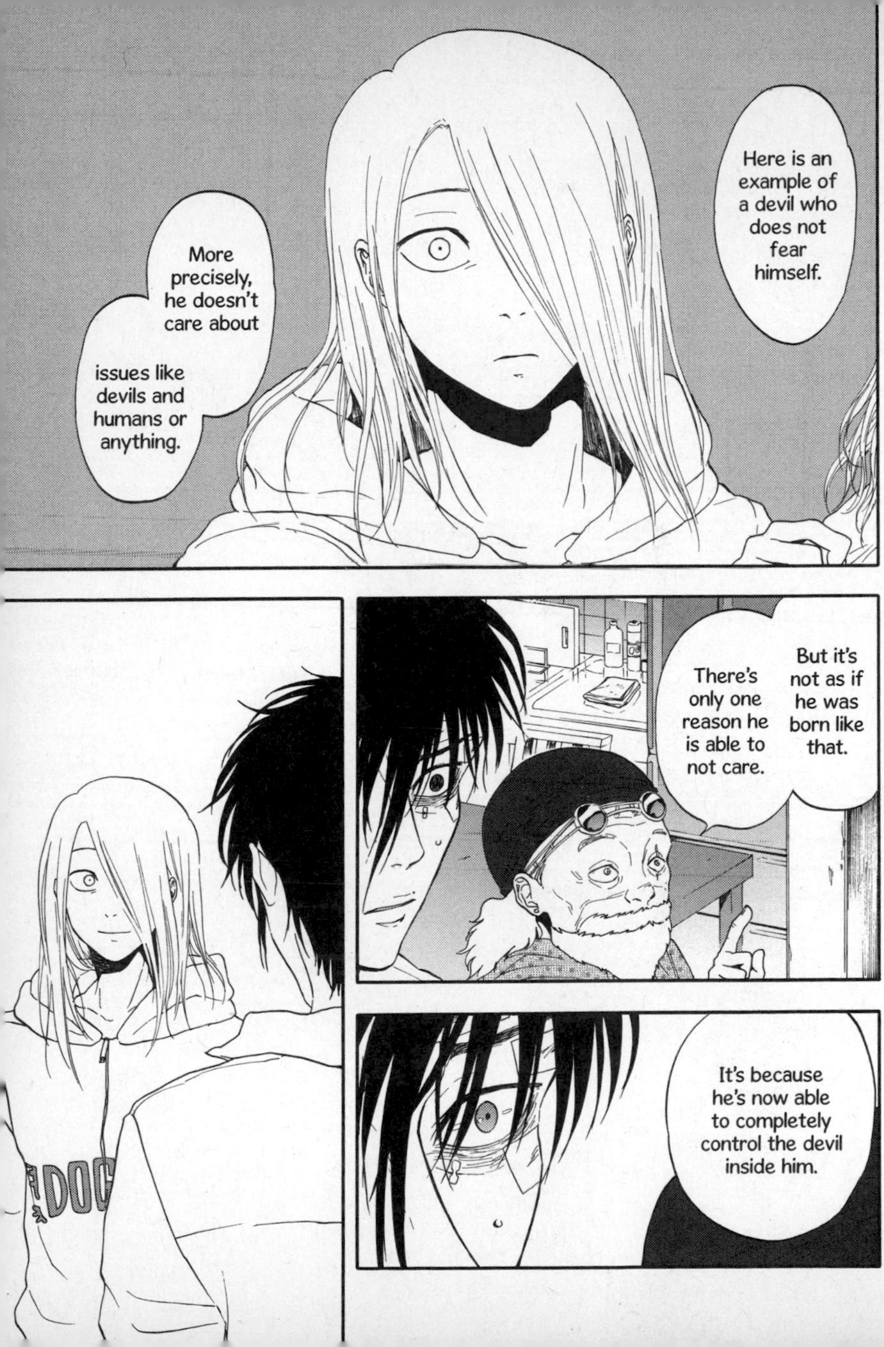
Here is an example of a devil who does not fear himself.
More precisely, he doesn't care about
issues like devils and humans or anything.
But it's not as if he was born like that.
There's only one reason he is able to not care.
It's because he's now able to completely control the devil inside him.

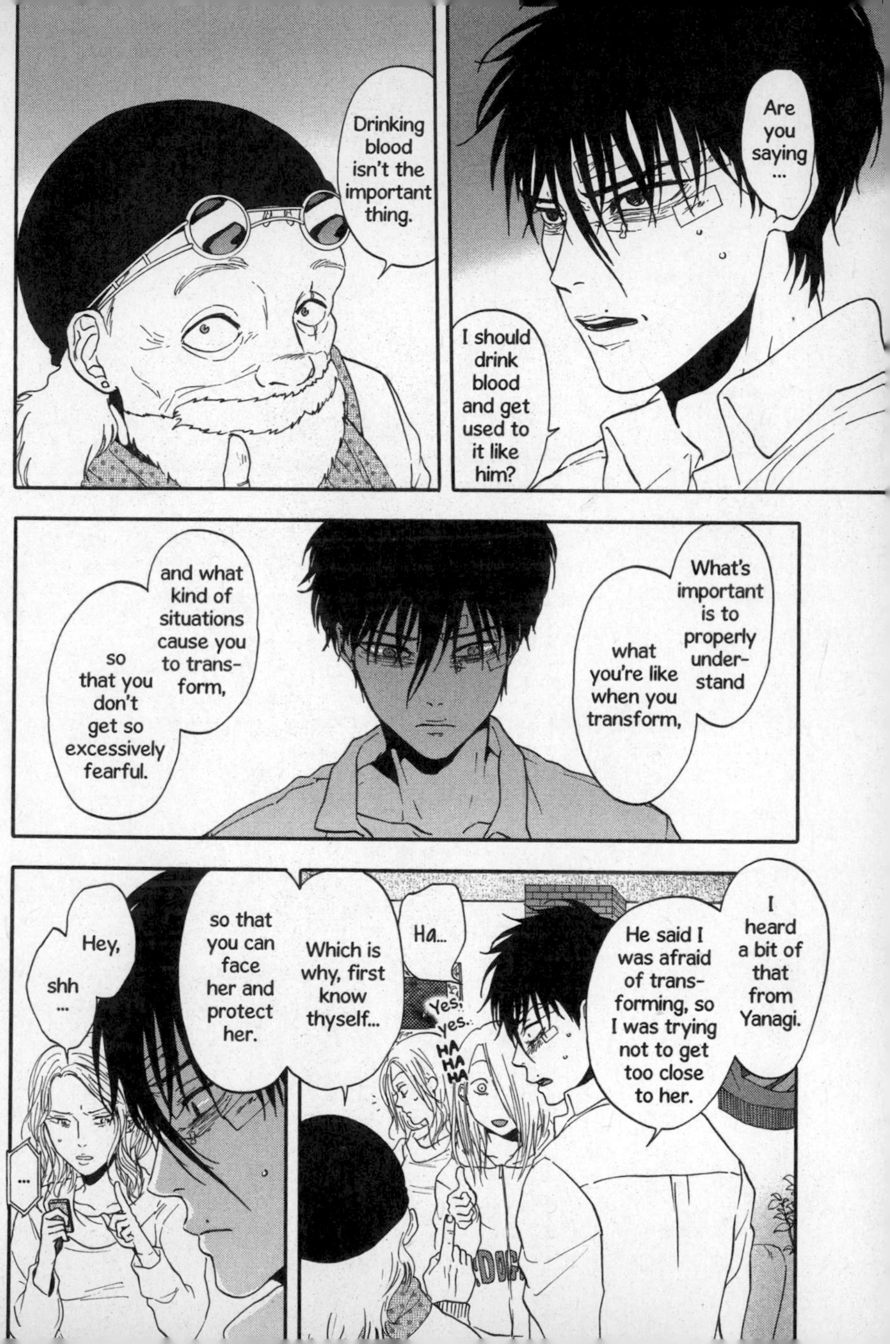
Are you saying ...
I should drink blood and get used to it like him?
Drinking blood isn't the important thing.
What's important is to properly understand what you're like when you transform,
and what kind of situations cause you to transform, so that you don't get so excessively fearful.
I heard a bit of that from Yanagi.
He said I was afraid of transforming, so I was trying not to get too close to her.
Ha...
Yes, yes.
HA HA HA
Which is why, first know thyself...
so that you can face her and protect her.
Hey, shh ...
...

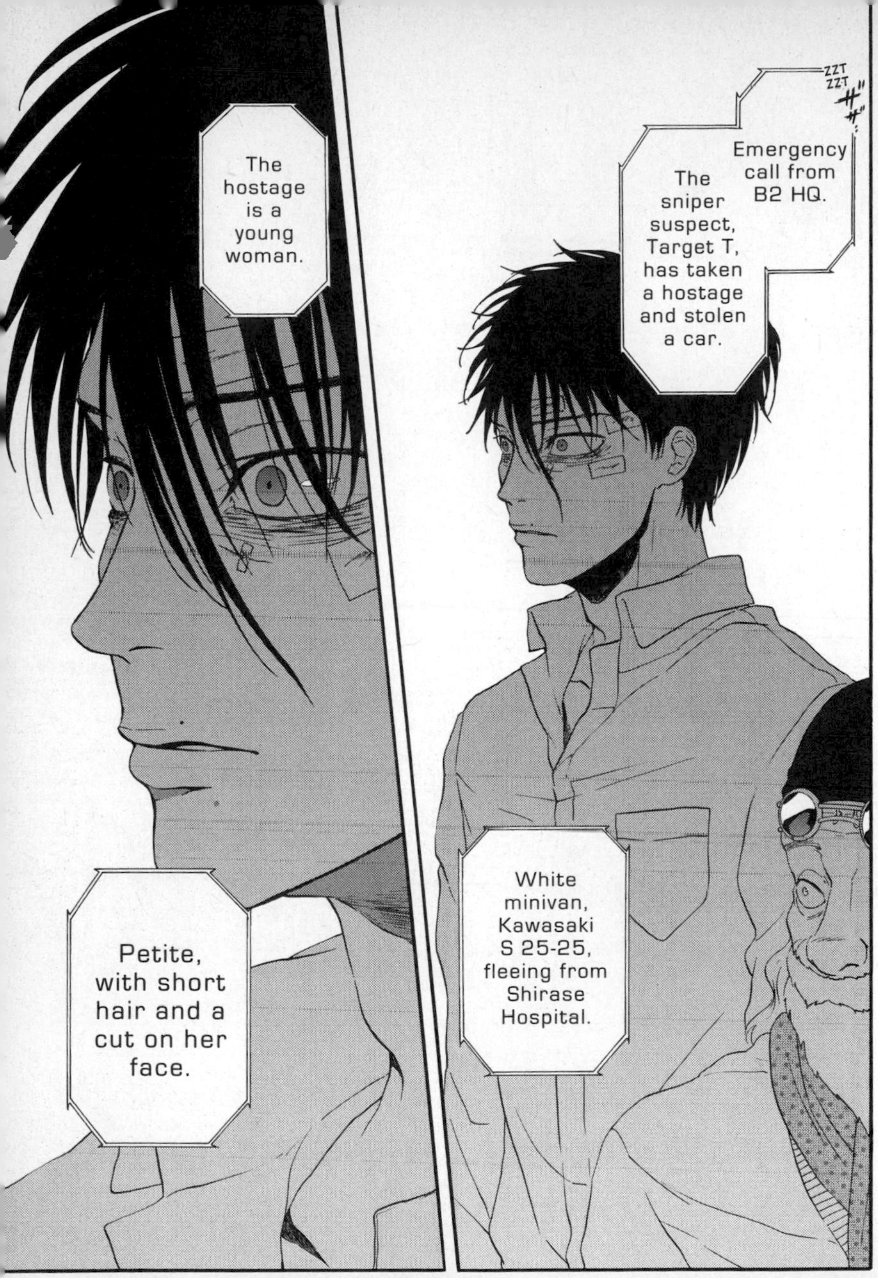
ZZT ZZT
Emergency call from B2 HQ.
The sniper suspect, Target T, has taken a hostage and stolen a car.
White minivan, Kawasaki S 25-25, fleeing from Shirase Hospital.
The hostage is a young woman.
Petite, with short hair and a cut on her face.

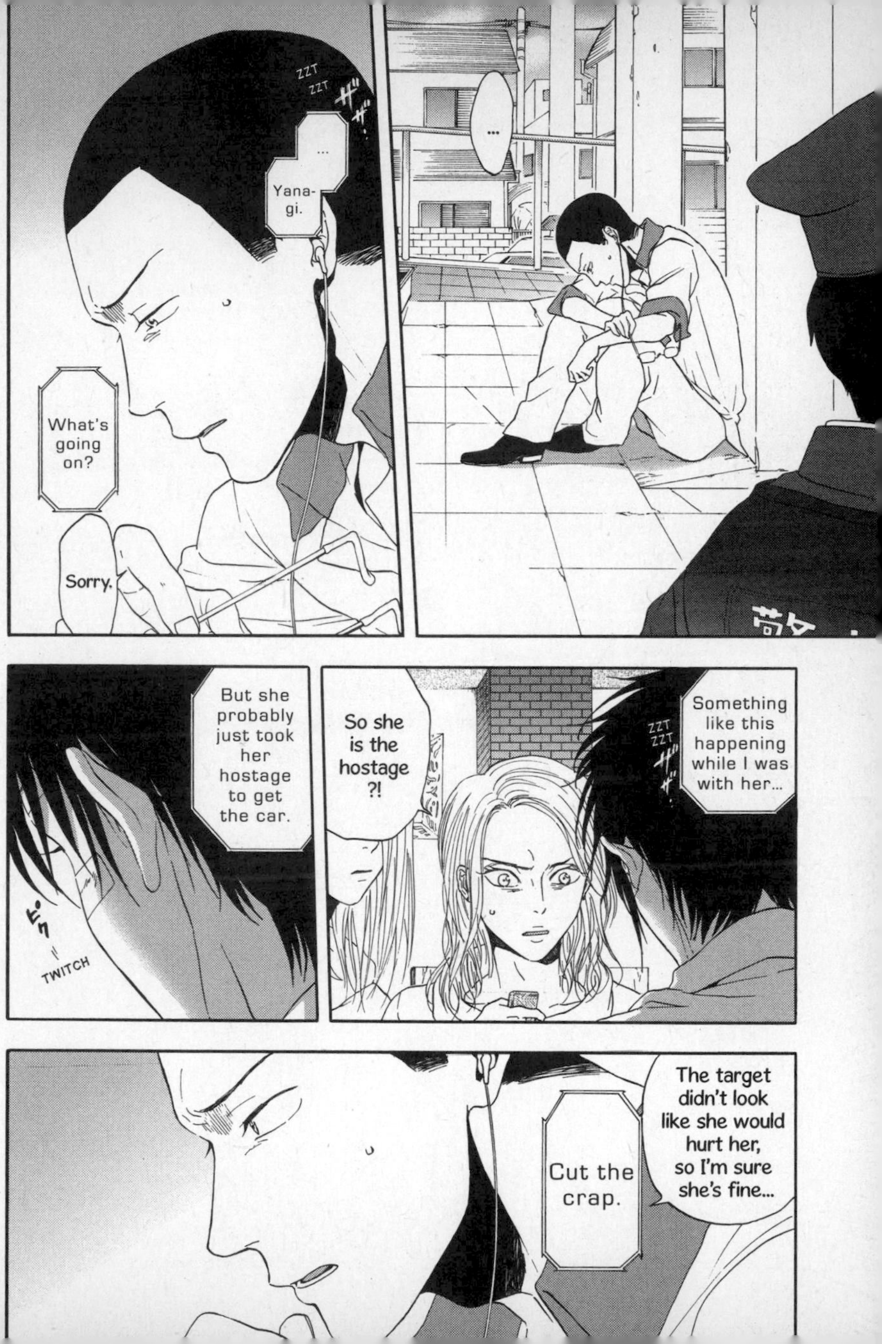
...
ZZT ZZT
...
Yana-gi.
What's going on?
Sorry.
ZZT ZZT
Something like this happening while I was with her...
So she is the hostage?!
But she probably just took her hostage to get the car.
TWITCH
The target didn't look like she would hurt her, so I'm sure she's fine...
Cut the crap.

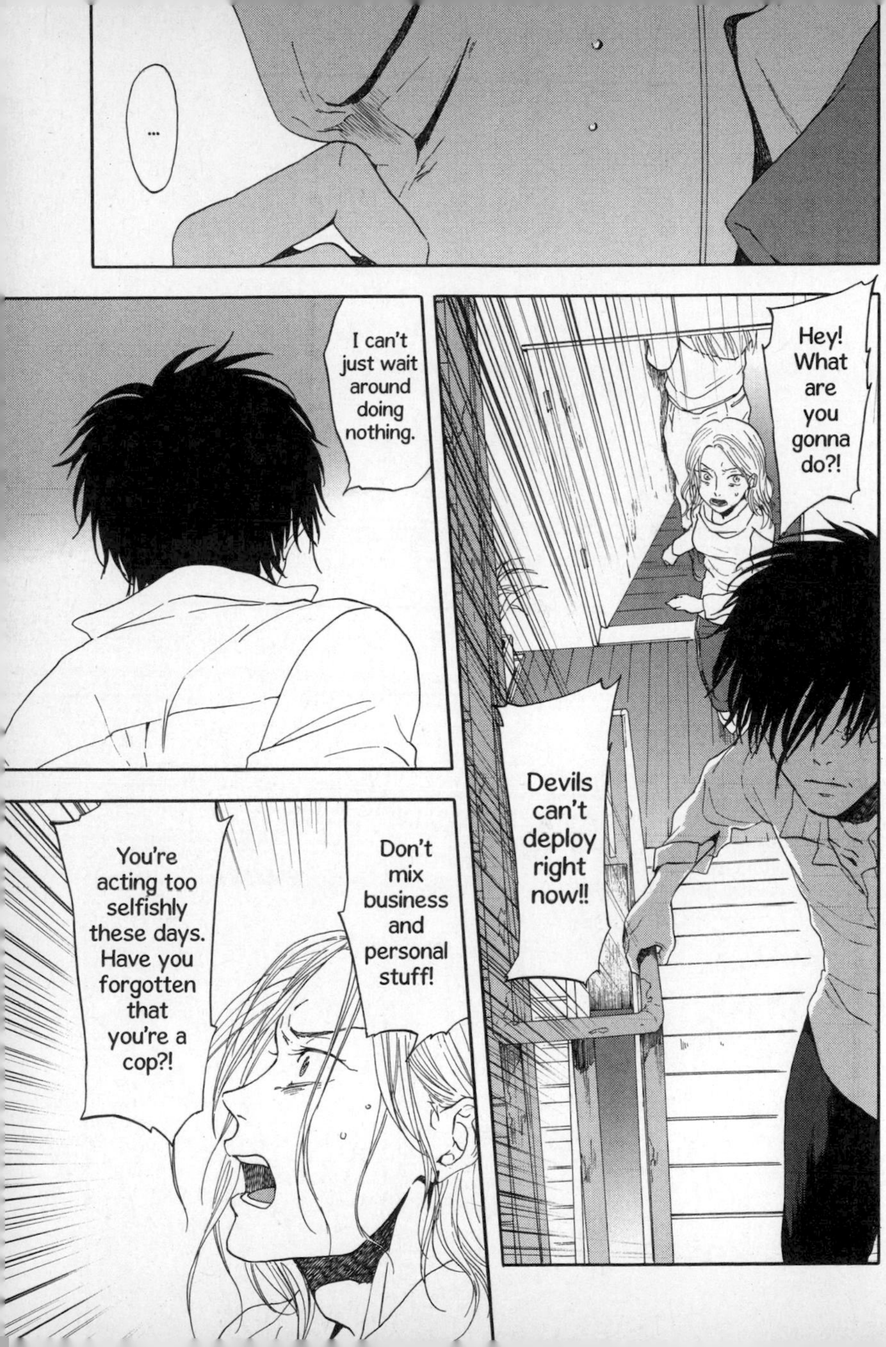
...
Hey! What are you gonna do?!
Devils can't deploy right now!!
I can't just wait around doing nothing.
Don't mix business and personal stuff!
You're acting too selfishly these days. Have you forgotten that you're a cop?!

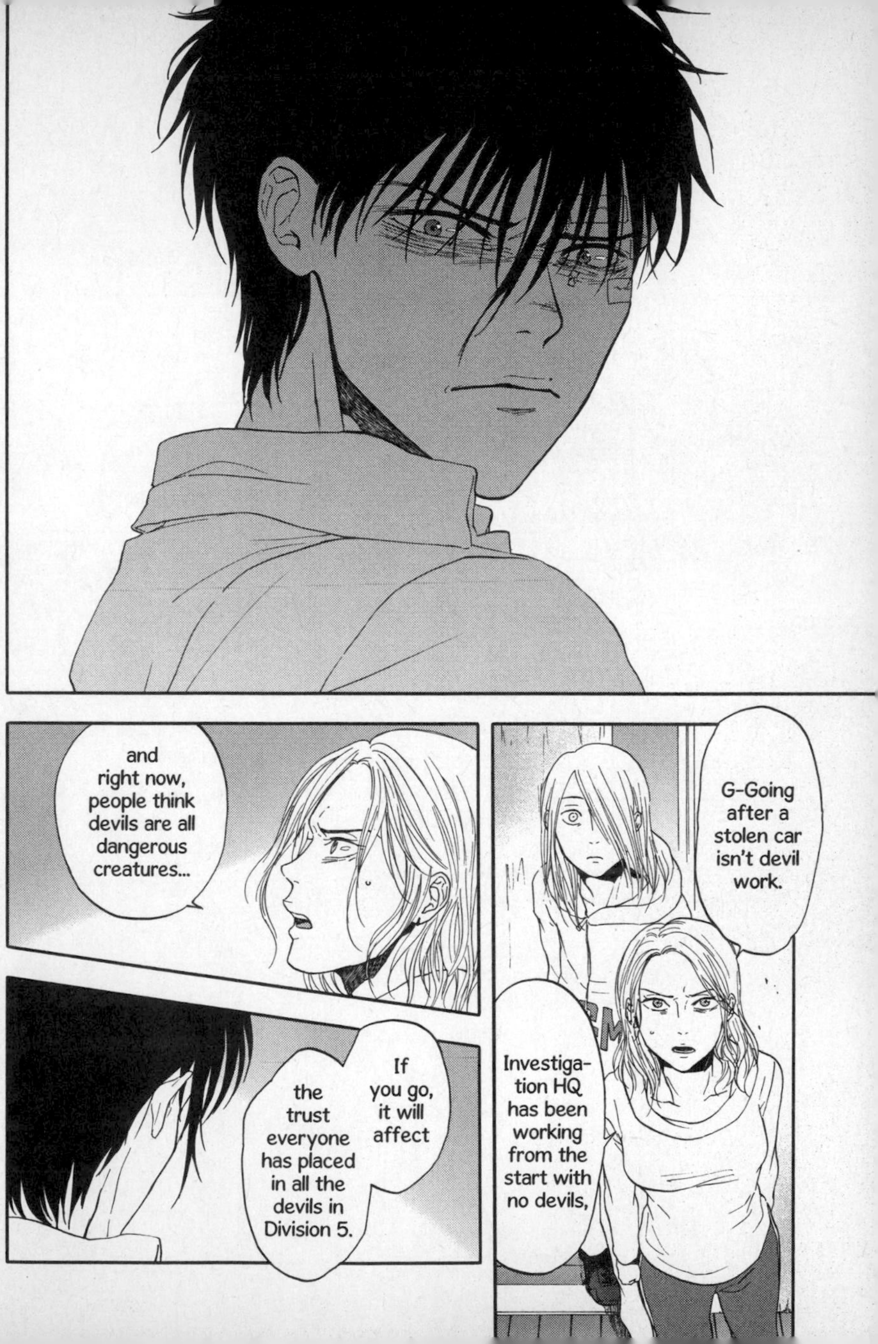
G-Going after a stolen car isn't devil work.
Investigation HQ has been working from the start with no devils,
and right now, people think devils are all dangerous creatures...
If you go, it will affect
the trust everyone has placed in all the devils in Division 5.

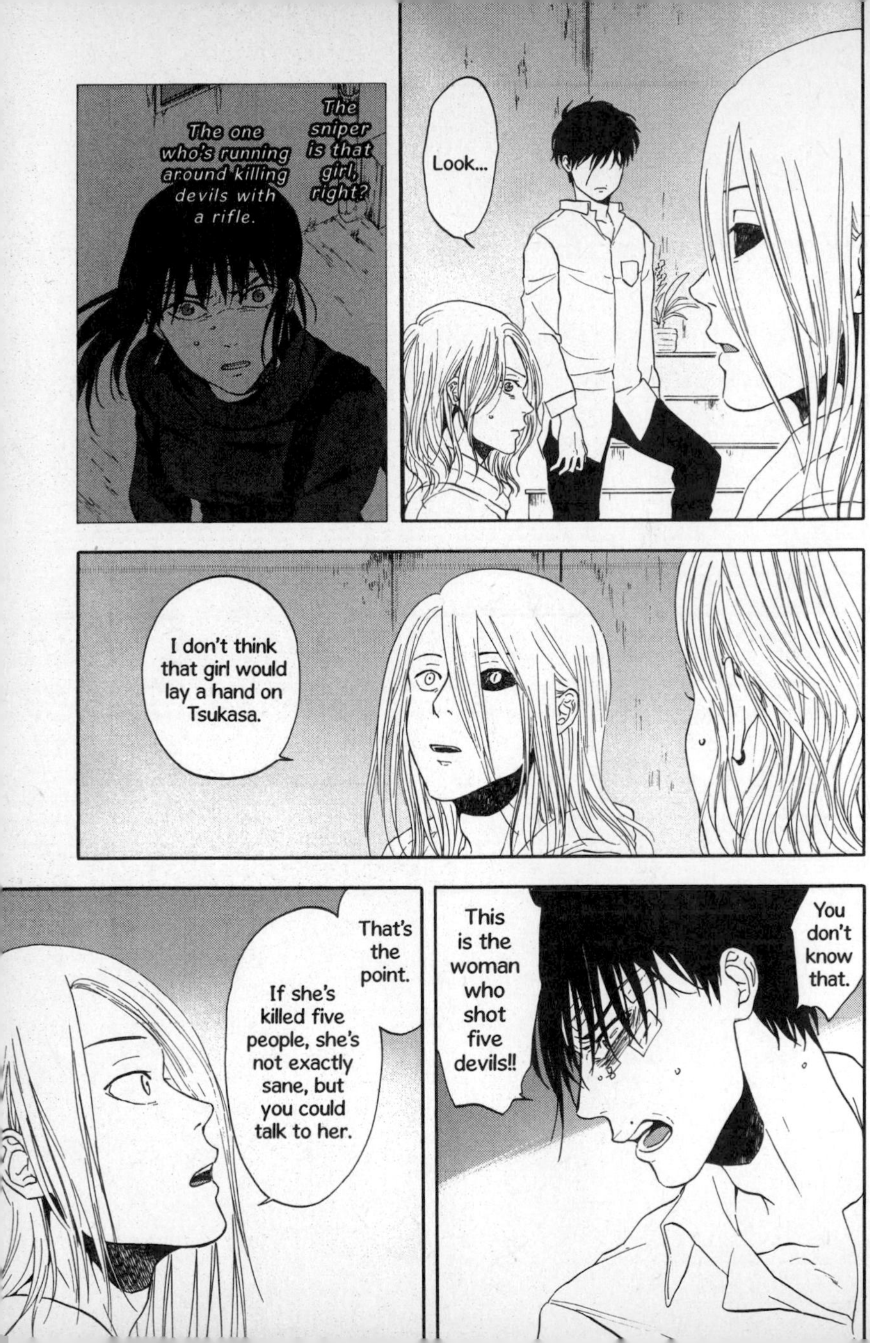
Look...
The sniper is that girl, right?
The one who's running around killing devils with a rifle.
I don't think that girl would lay a hand on Tsukasa.
You don't know that.
This is the woman who shot five devils!!
That's the point.
If she's killed five people, she's not exactly sane, but you could talk to her.

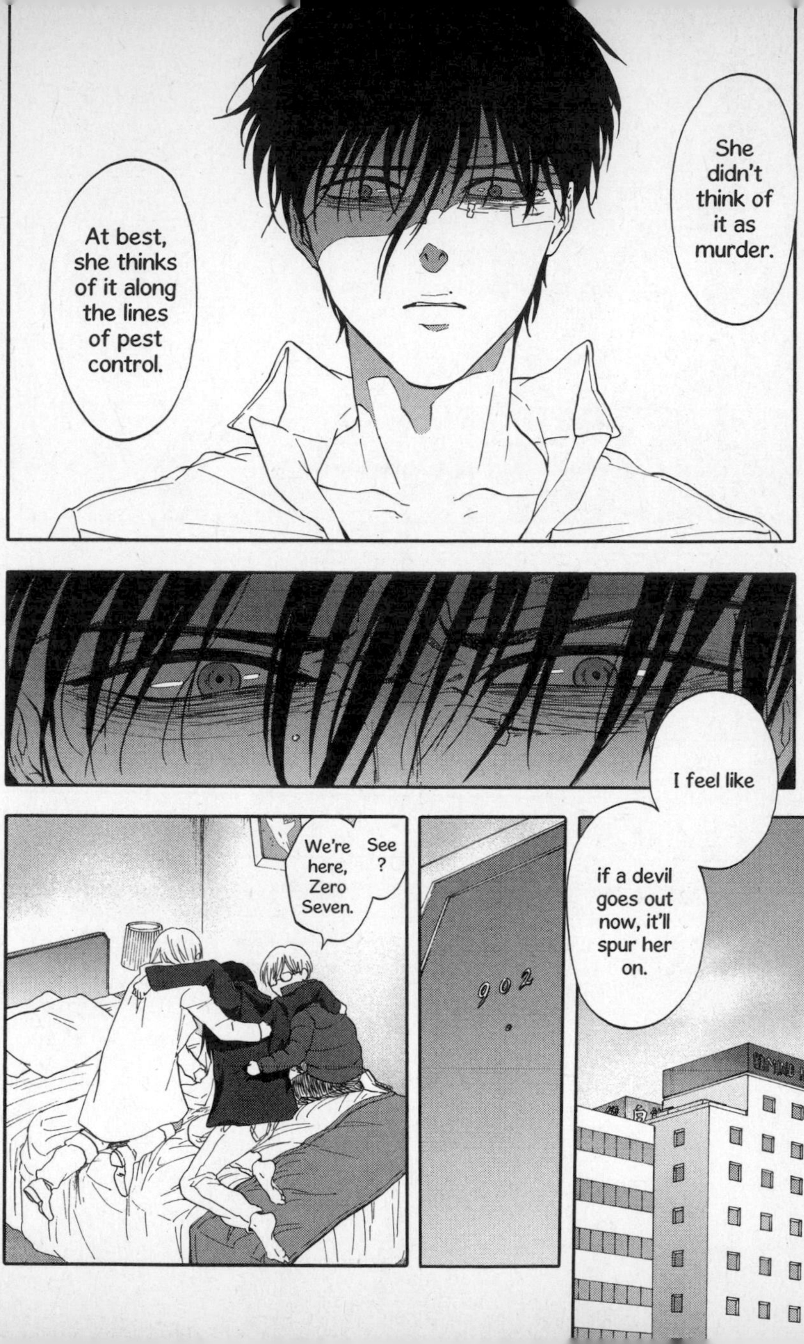
She didn't think of it as murder.
At best, she thinks of it along the lines of pest control.
I feel like
if a devil goes out now, it'll spur her on.
902
See?
We're here, Zero Seven.

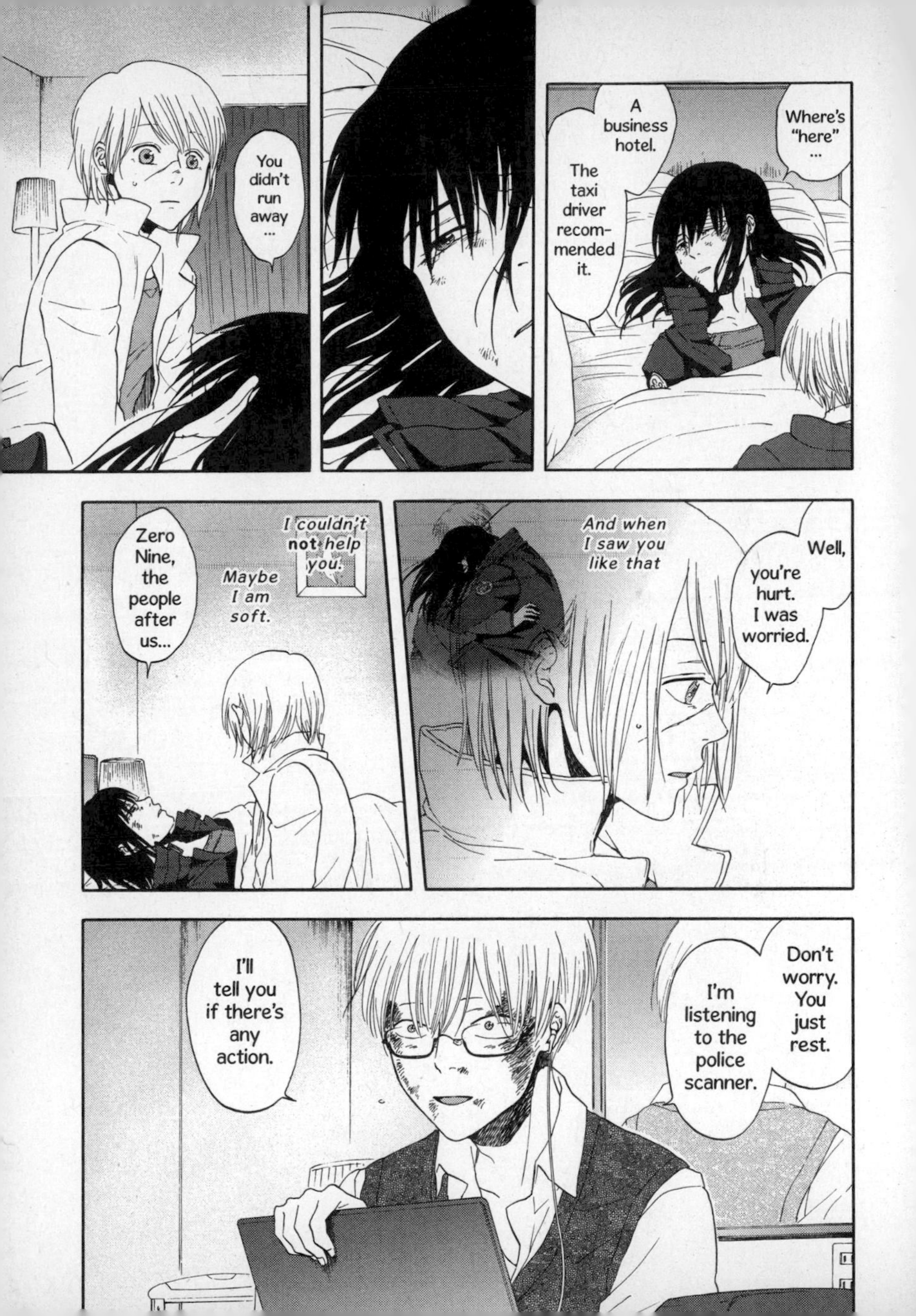
Where's "here"...
A business hotel.
The taxi driver recommended it.
You didn't run away...
Well, you're hurt. I was worried.
And when I saw you like that
I couldn't not help you.
Maybe I am soft.
Zero Nine, the people after us...
Don't worry. You just rest.
I'm listening to the police scanner.
I'll tell you if there's any action.

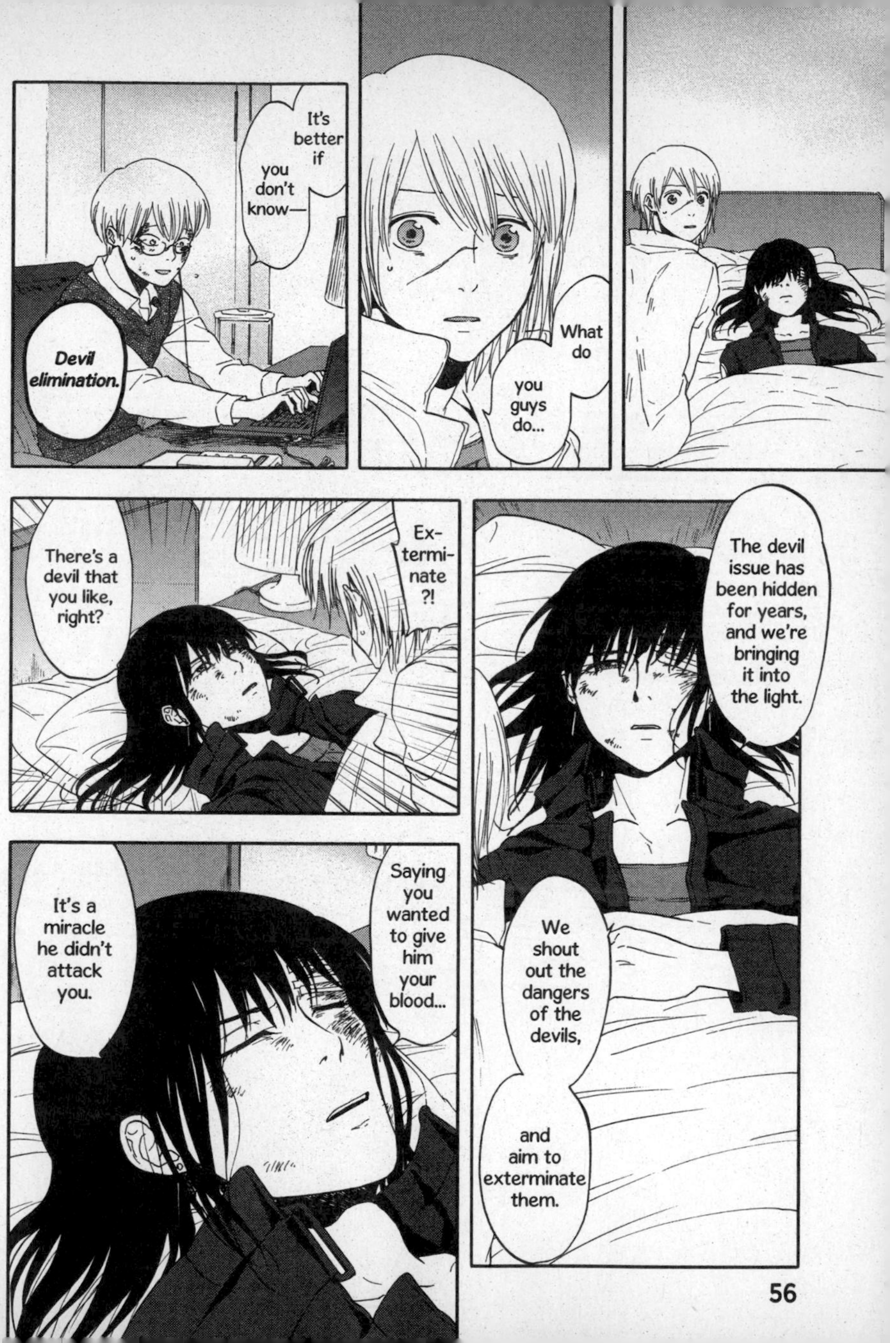
What do you guys do...
It's better if you don't know—
Devil elimination.
The devil issue has been hidden for years, and we're bringing it into the light.
We shout out the dangers of the devils,
and aim to exterminate them.
Ex-terminate?!
There's a devil that you like, right?
Saying you wanted to give him your blood...
It's a miracle he didn't attack you.

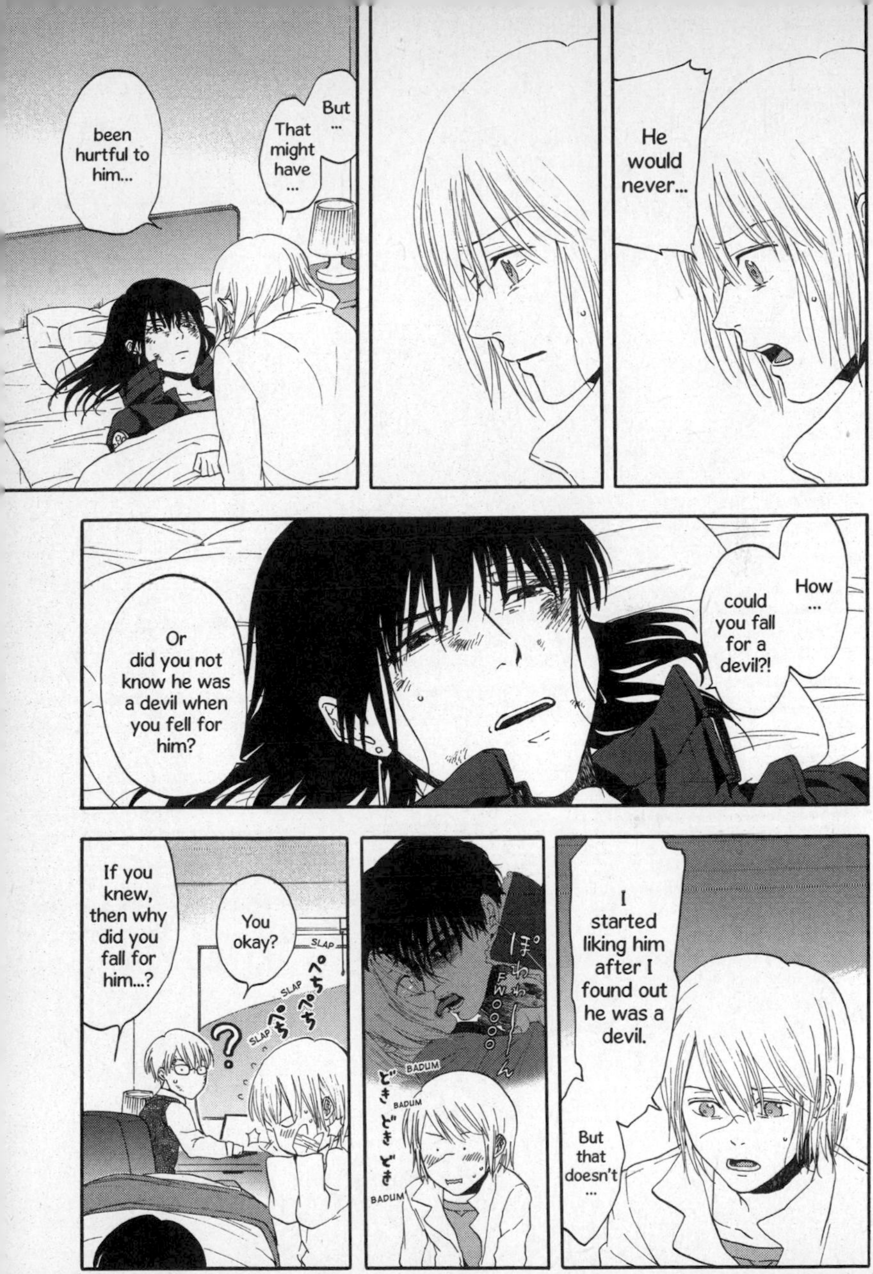
He would never...
But ...
That might have ...
been hurtful to him...
How ... could you fall for a devil?!
Or did you not know he was a devil when you fell for him?
I started liking him after I found out he was a devil.
But that doesn't ...
ぽわーーん
FWOOOOO
どき どき どき
BADUM
BADUM
BADUM
If you knew, then why did you fall for him...?
You okay?
ぺちぺち
SLAP
SLAP
ぺち
SLAP

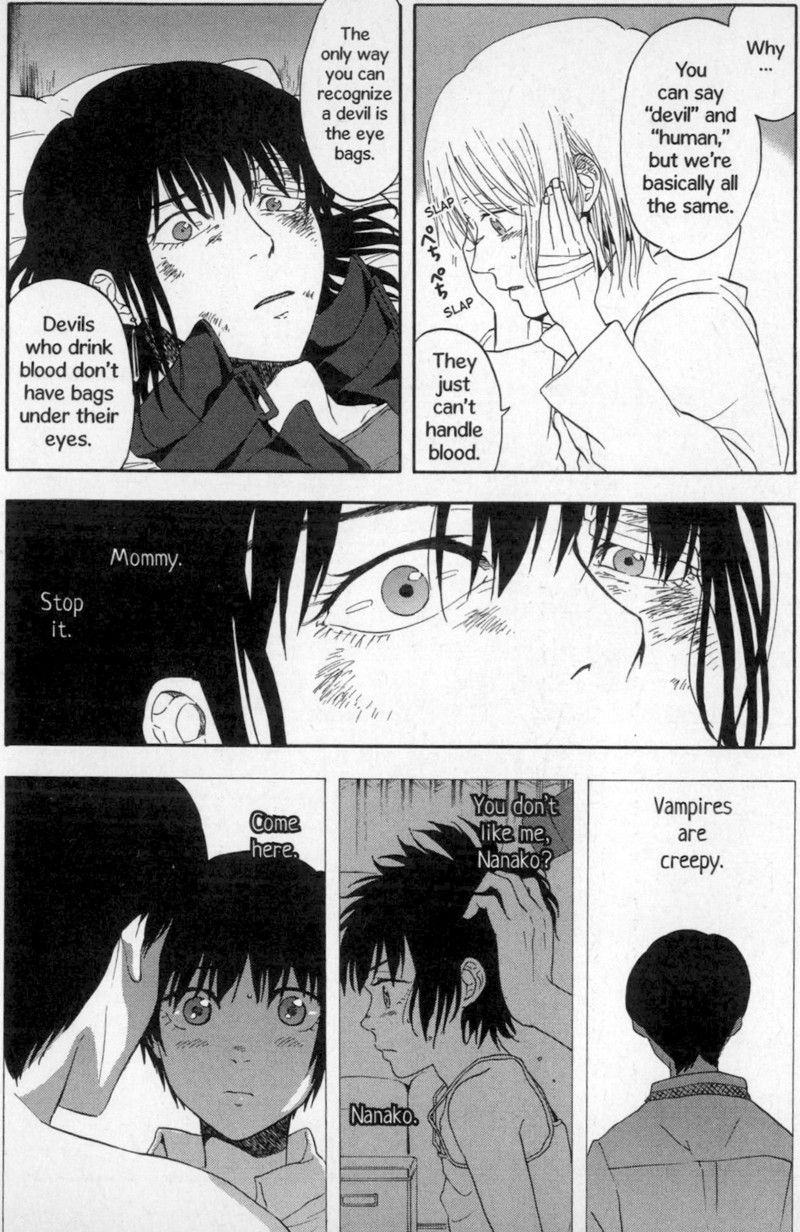
Why ...
You can say "devil" and "human," but we're basically all the same.
SLAP
ぺち ぺち
SLAP
They just can't handle blood.
The only way you can recognize a devil is the eye bags.
Devils who drink blood don't have bags under their eyes.
Mommy.
Stop it.
Vampires are creepy.
You don't like me, Nanako?
Nanako.
Come here.

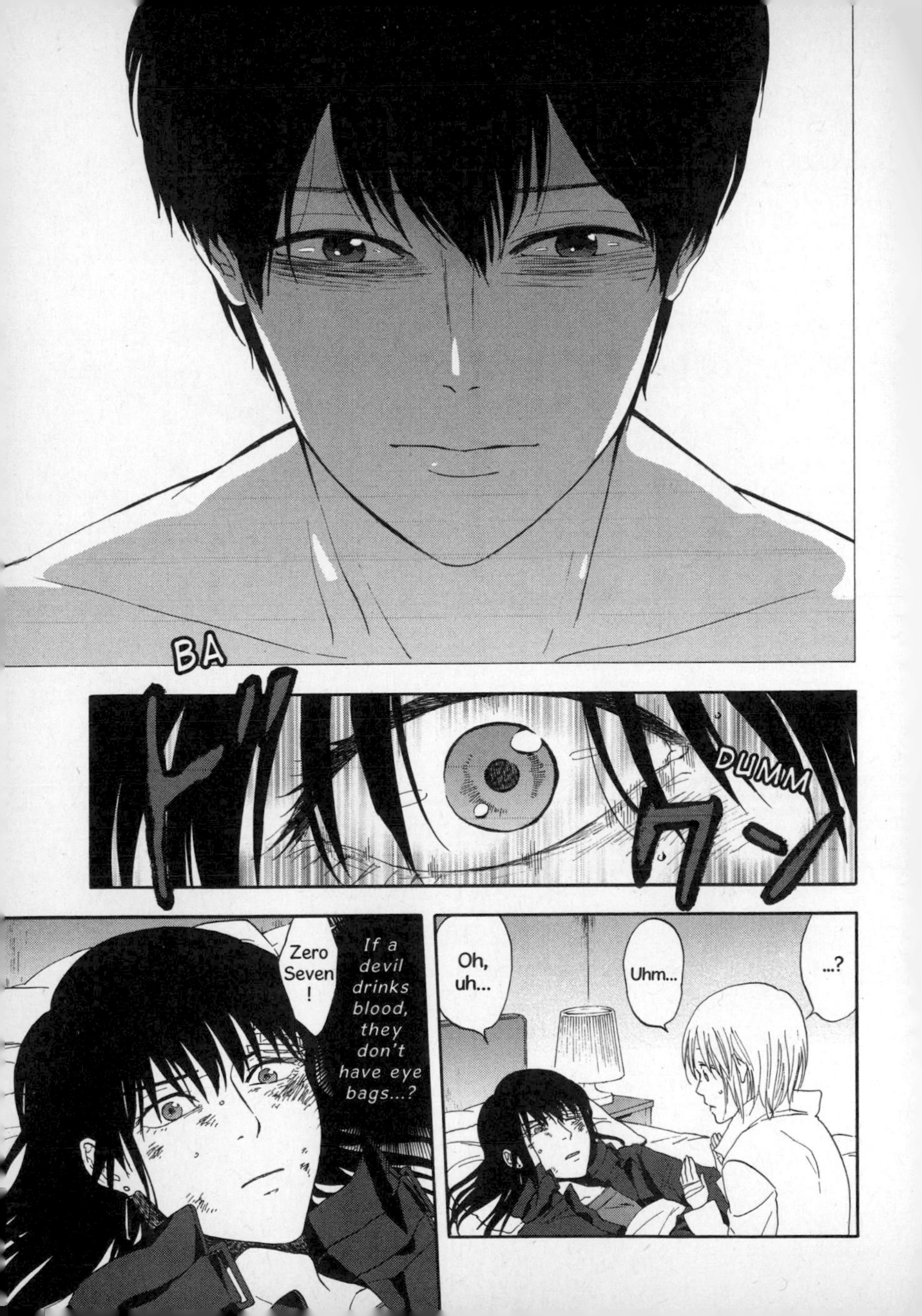
BA
DUMM
...?
Uhm...
Oh, uh...
If a devil drinks blood, they don't have eye bags...?
Zero Seven!

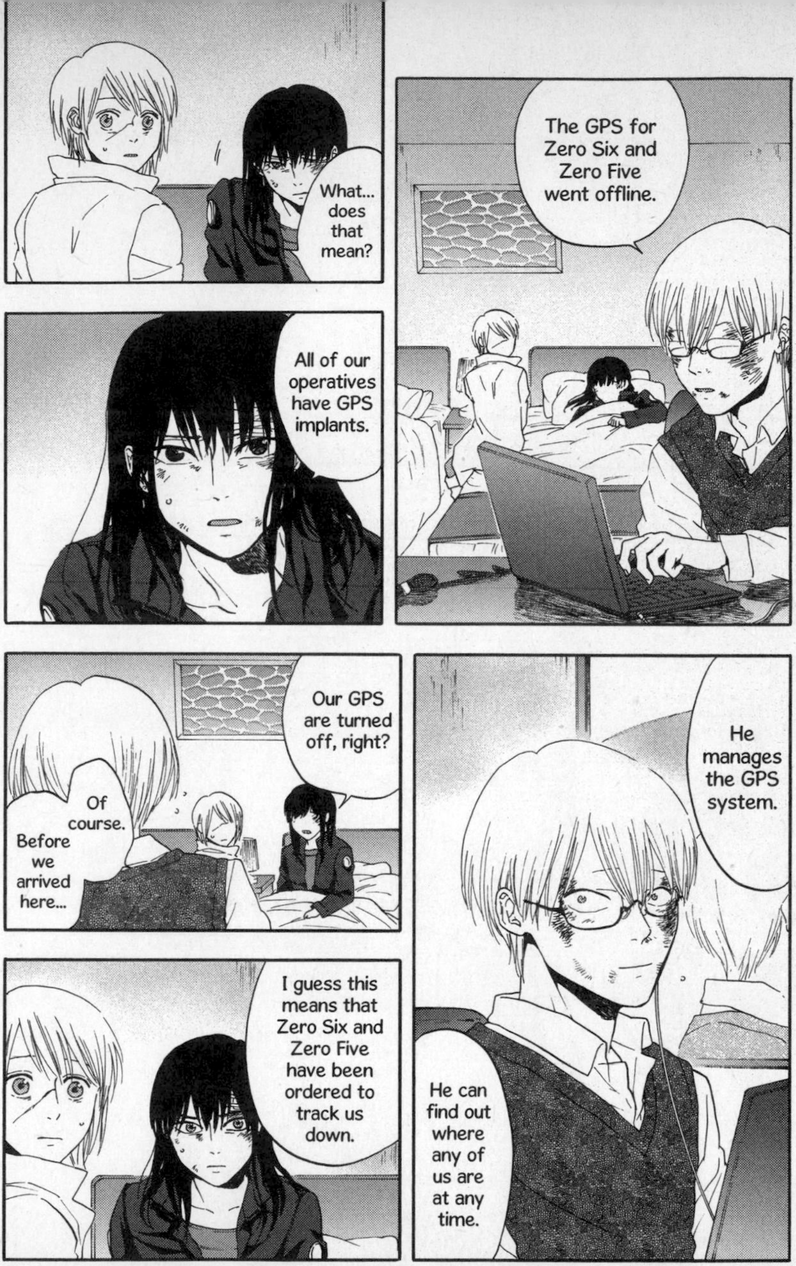

The GPS for Zero Six and Zero Five went offline.
What... does that mean?
All of our operatives have GPS implants.
He manages the GPS system.
He can find out where any of us are at any time.
Our GPS are turned off, right?
Of course. Before we arrived here...
I guess this means that Zero Six and Zero Five have been ordered to track us down.

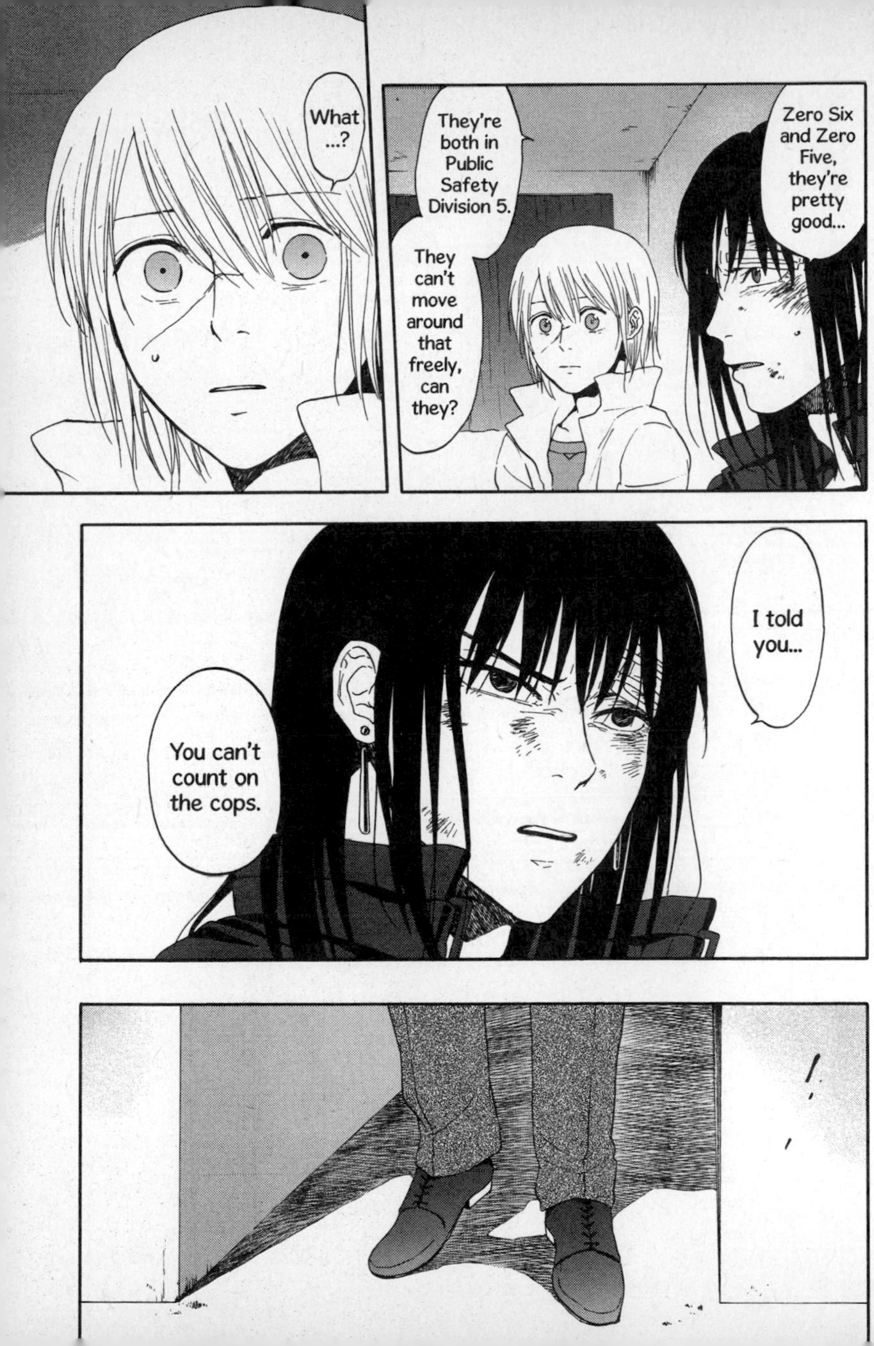
Zero Six and Zero Five, they're pretty good...
They're both in Public Safety Division 5.
They can't move around that freely, can they?
What ...?
I told you...
You can't count on the cops.
!

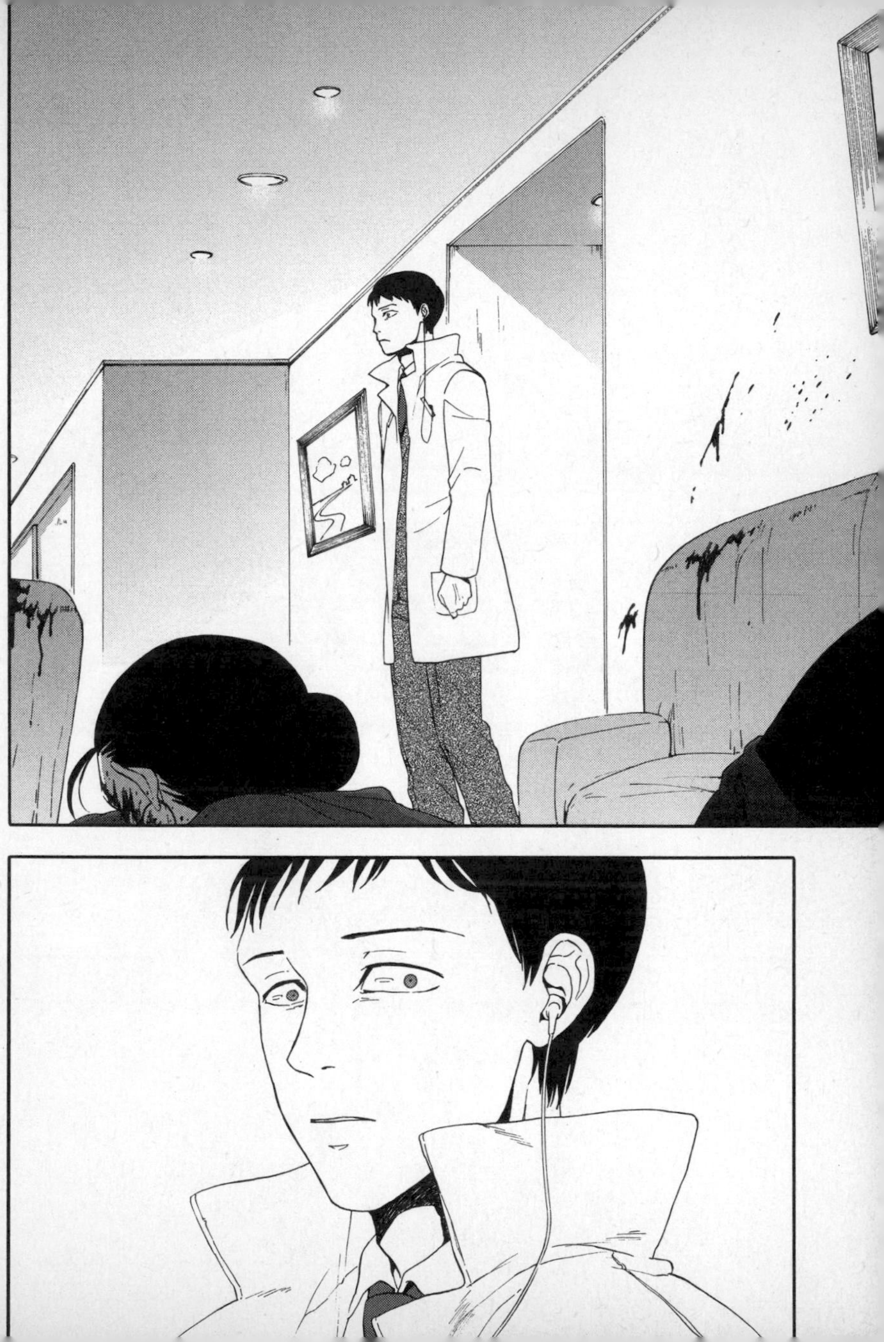

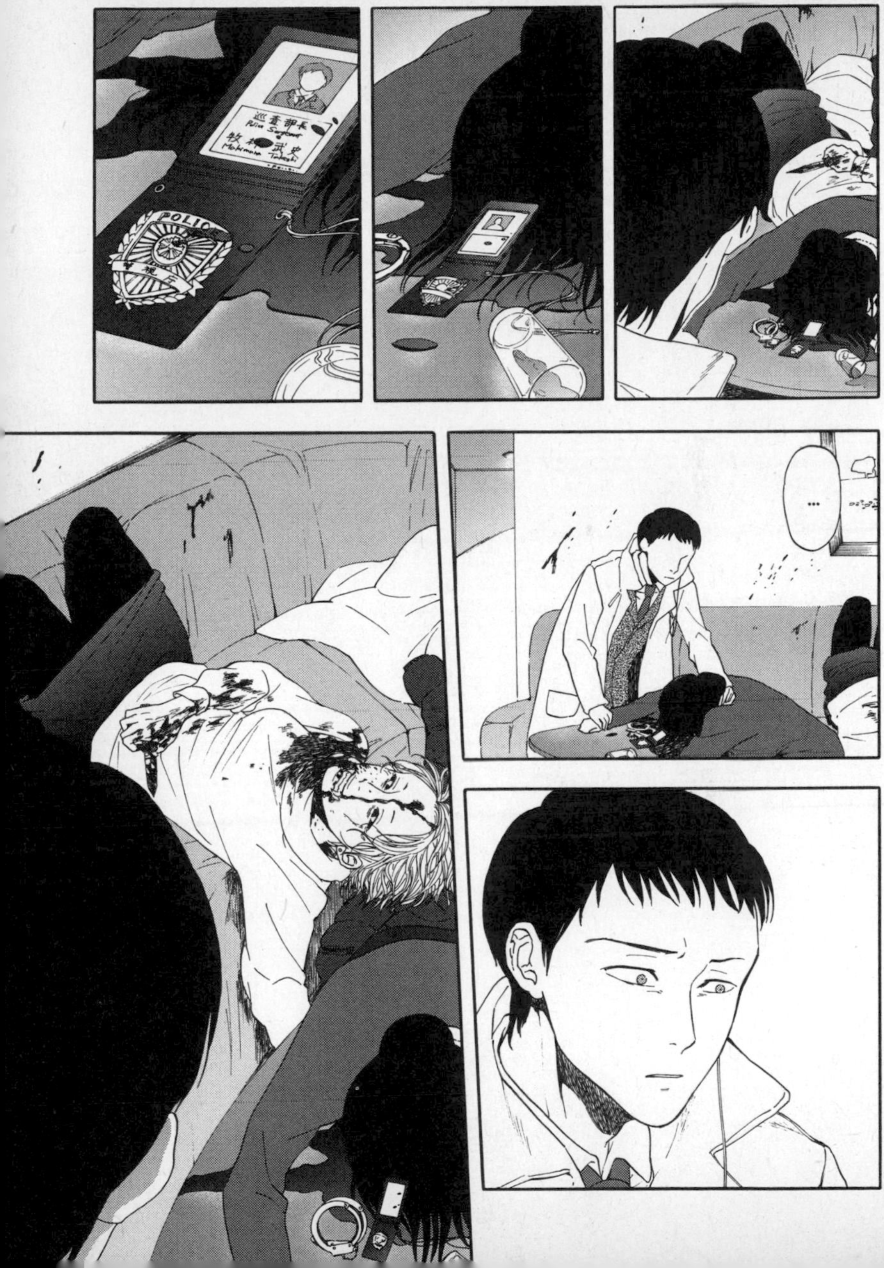
巡査部長
Police Sergeant
牧村 武史
Makimura Takeshi
…

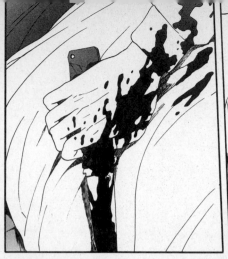

Aah...

For this
hand to
be like
that...

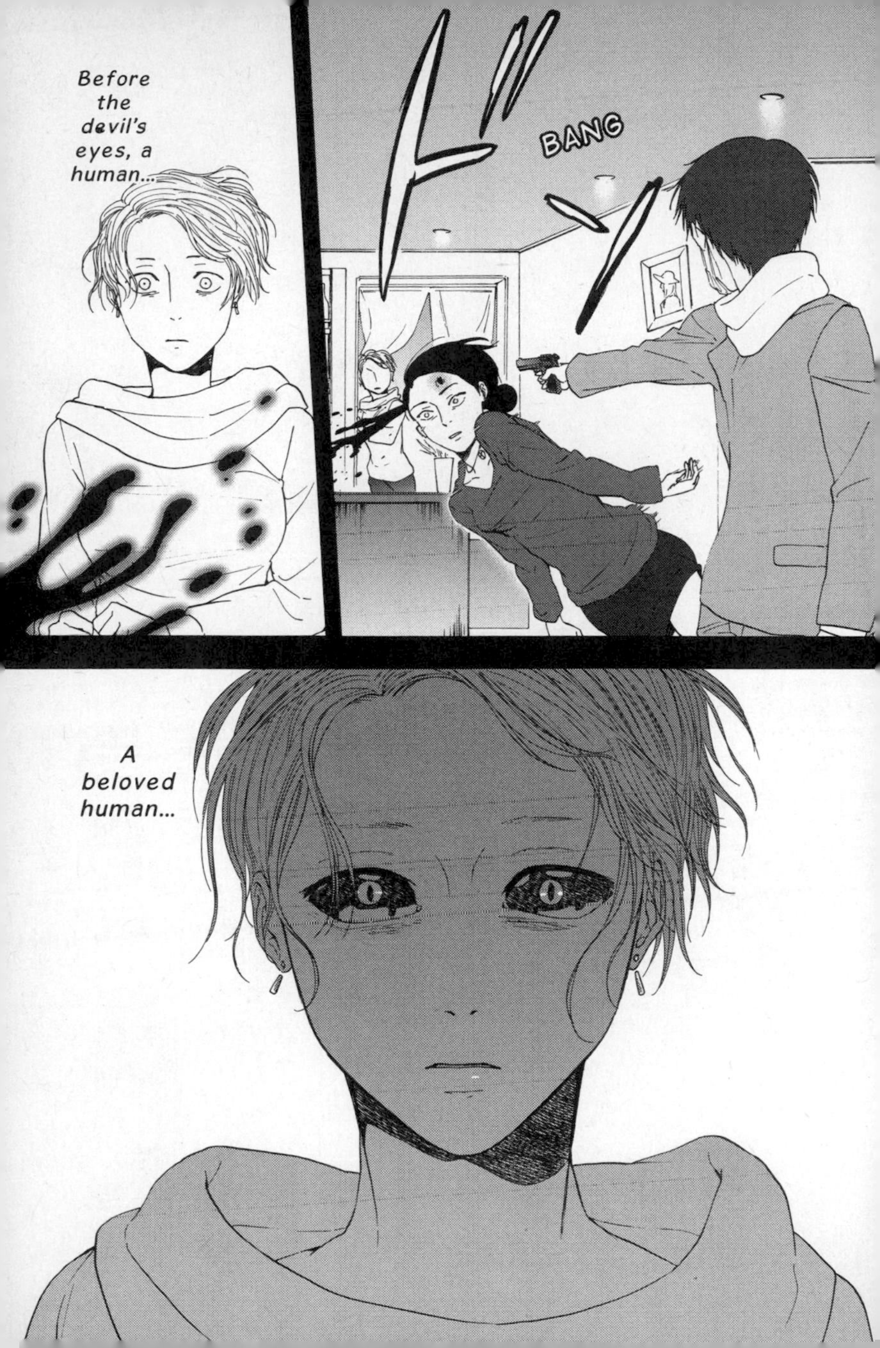
BANG
Before the devil's eyes, a human...
A beloved human...

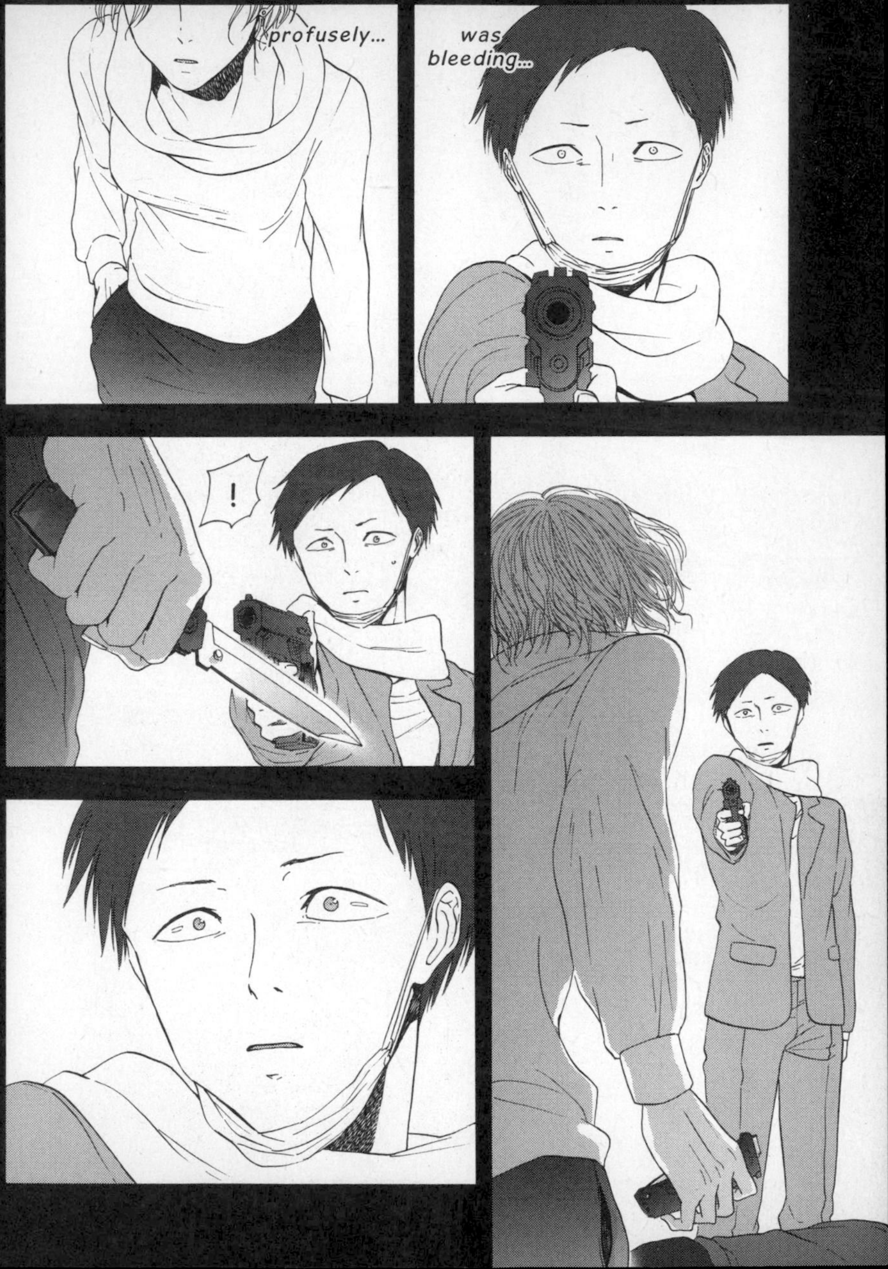
was bleeding...
profusely...
!

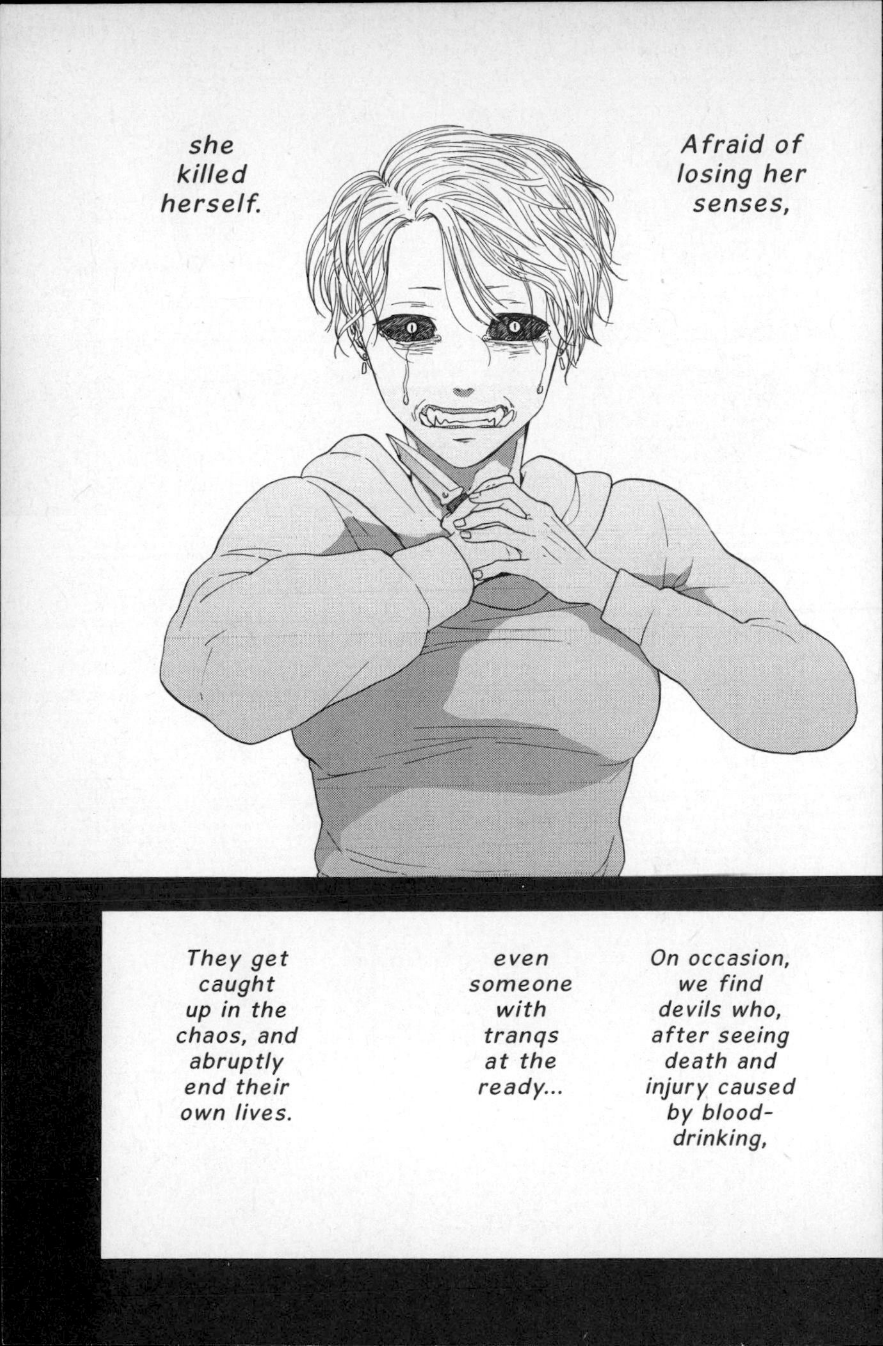
Afraid of losing her senses,
she killed herself.
On occasion, we find devils who, after seeing death and injury caused by blood-drinking,
even someone with tranqs at the ready...
They get caught up in the chaos, and abruptly end their own lives.

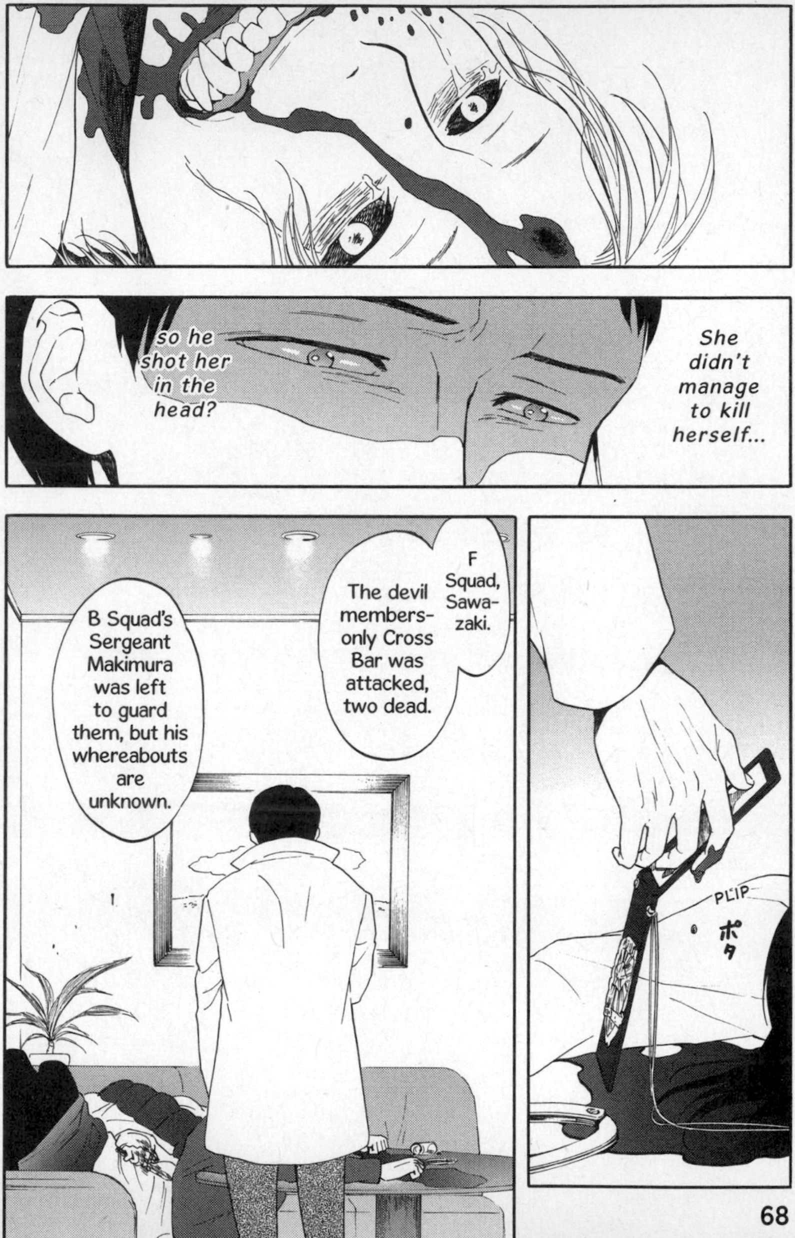
She didn't manage to kill herself...
so he shot her in the head?
PLIP
ポタ
F Squad, Sawazaki.
The devil members-only Cross Bar was attacked, two dead.
B Squad's Sergeant Makimura was left to guard them, but his whereabouts are unknown.

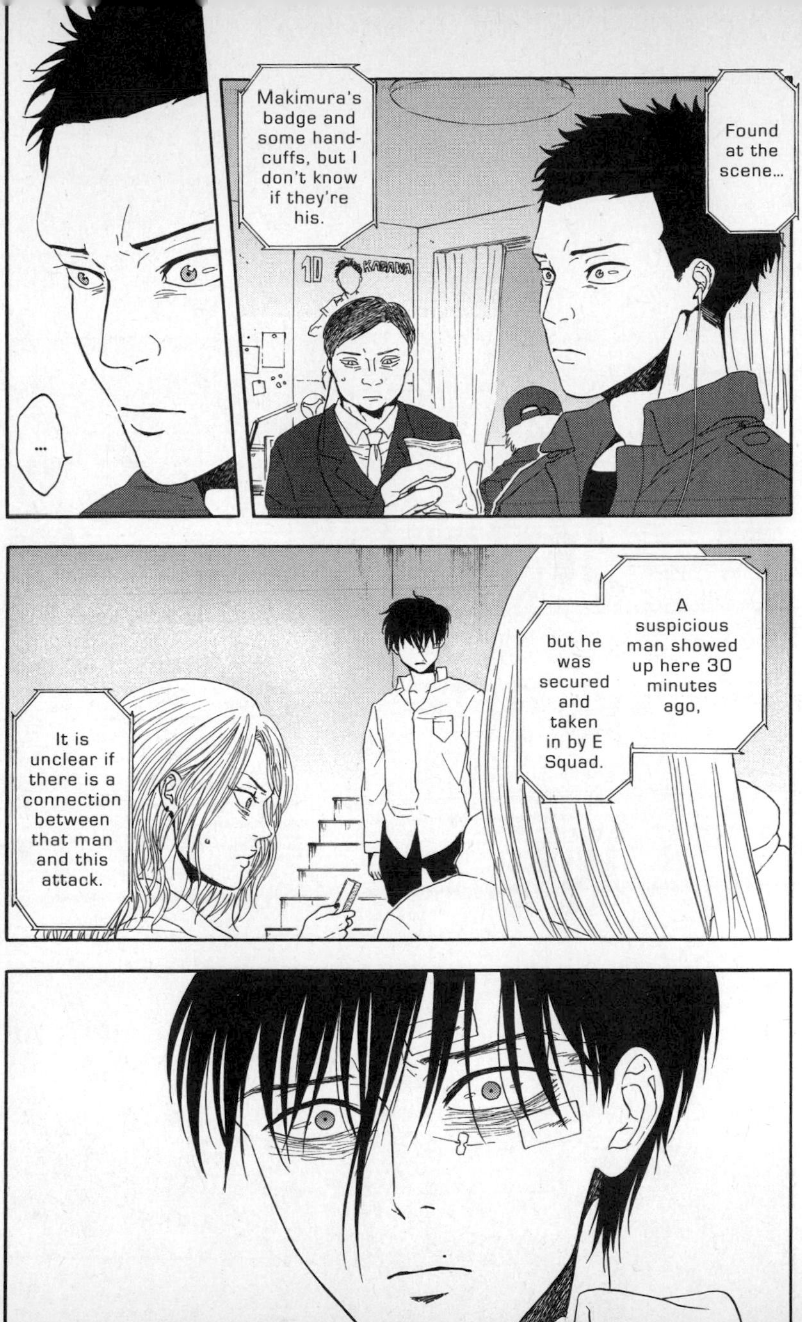
Found at the scene...
Makimura's badge and some handcuffs, but I don't know if they're his.
...
A suspicious man showed up here 30 minutes ago,
but he was secured and taken in by E Squad.
It is unclear if there is a connection between that man and this attack.

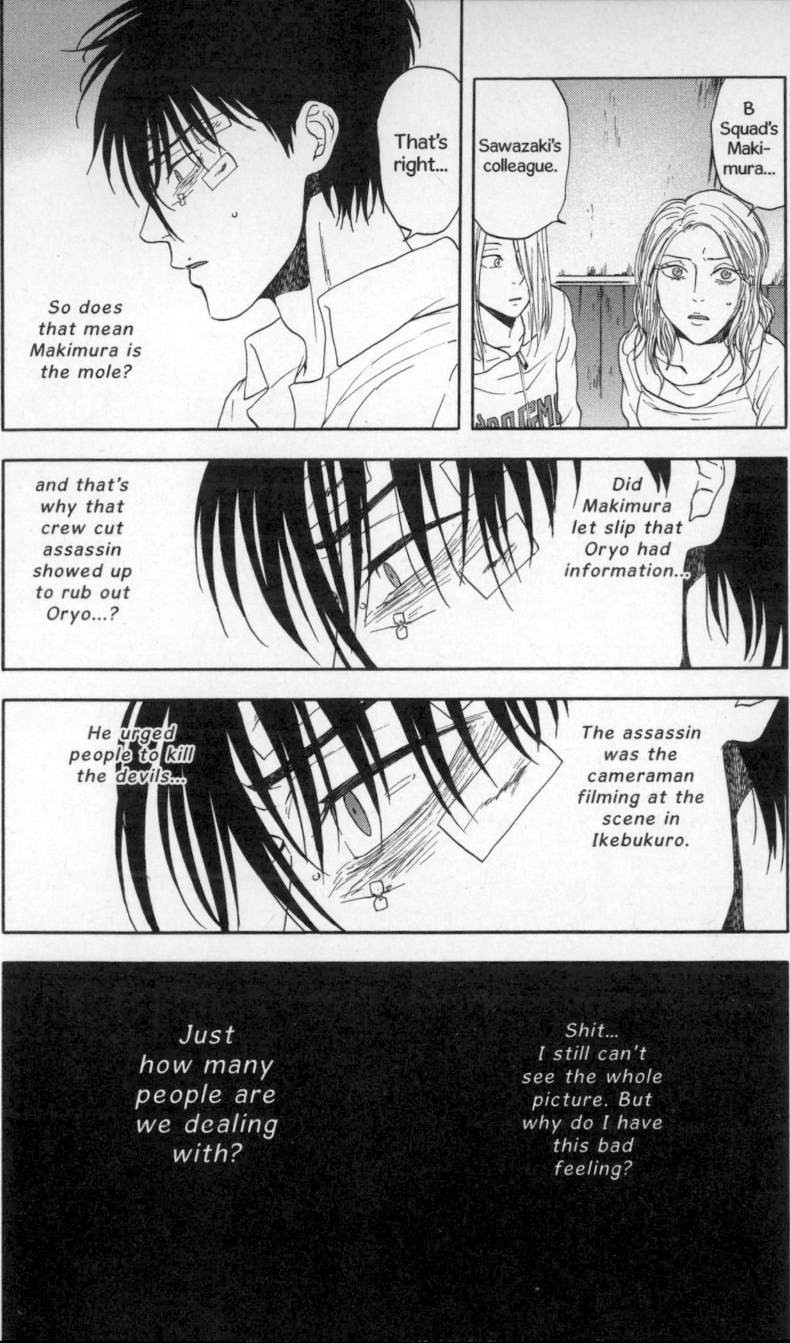
B Squad's Maki-mura...
Sawazaki's colleague.
That's right...
So does that mean Makimura is the mole?
Did Makimura let slip that Oryo had information...
and that's why that crew cut assassin showed up to rub out Oryo...?
The assassin was the cameraman filming at the scene in Ikebukuro.
He urged people to kill the devils...
Shit... I still can't see the whole picture. But why do I have this bad feeling?
Just how many people are we dealing with?

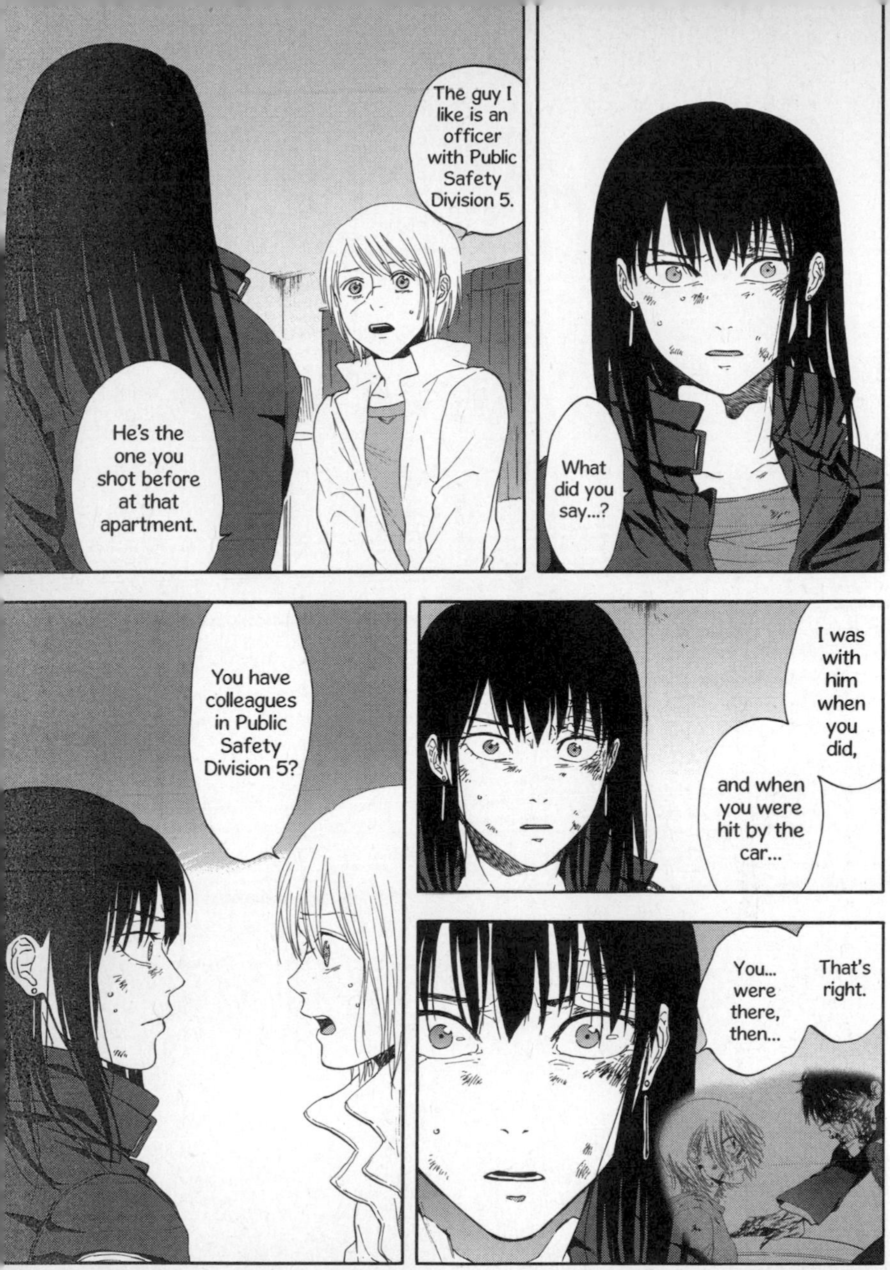
What did you say...?
The guy I like is an officer with Public Safety Division 5.
He's the one you shot before at that apartment.
I was with him when you did,
and when you were hit by the car...
That's right.
You... were there, then...
You have colleagues in Public Safety Division 5?

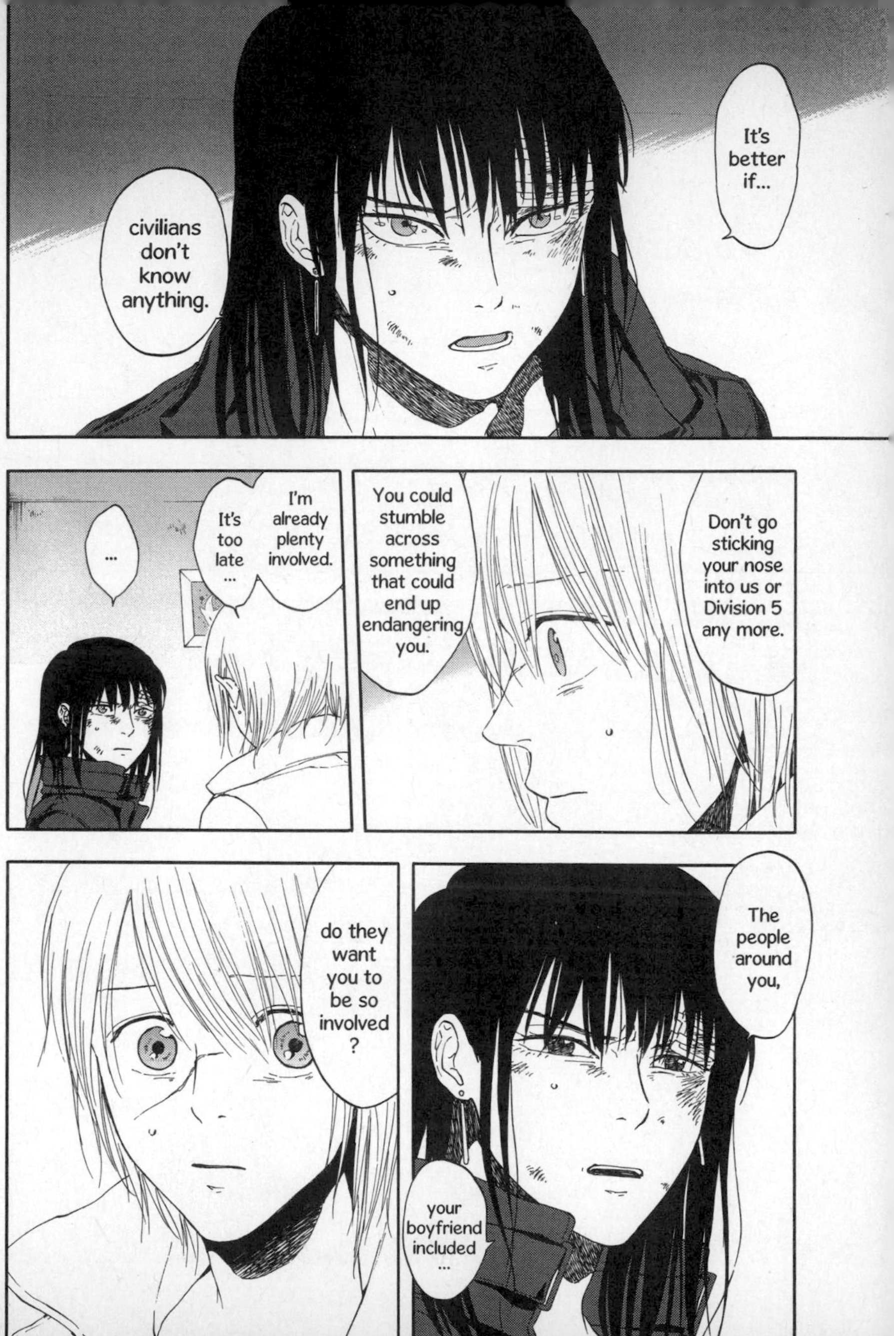
It's better if...
civilians don't know anything.
Don't go sticking your nose into us or Division 5 any more.
You could stumble across something that could end up endangering you.
I'm already plenty involved.
It's too late...
...
The people around you,
your boyfriend included...
do they want you to be so involved?

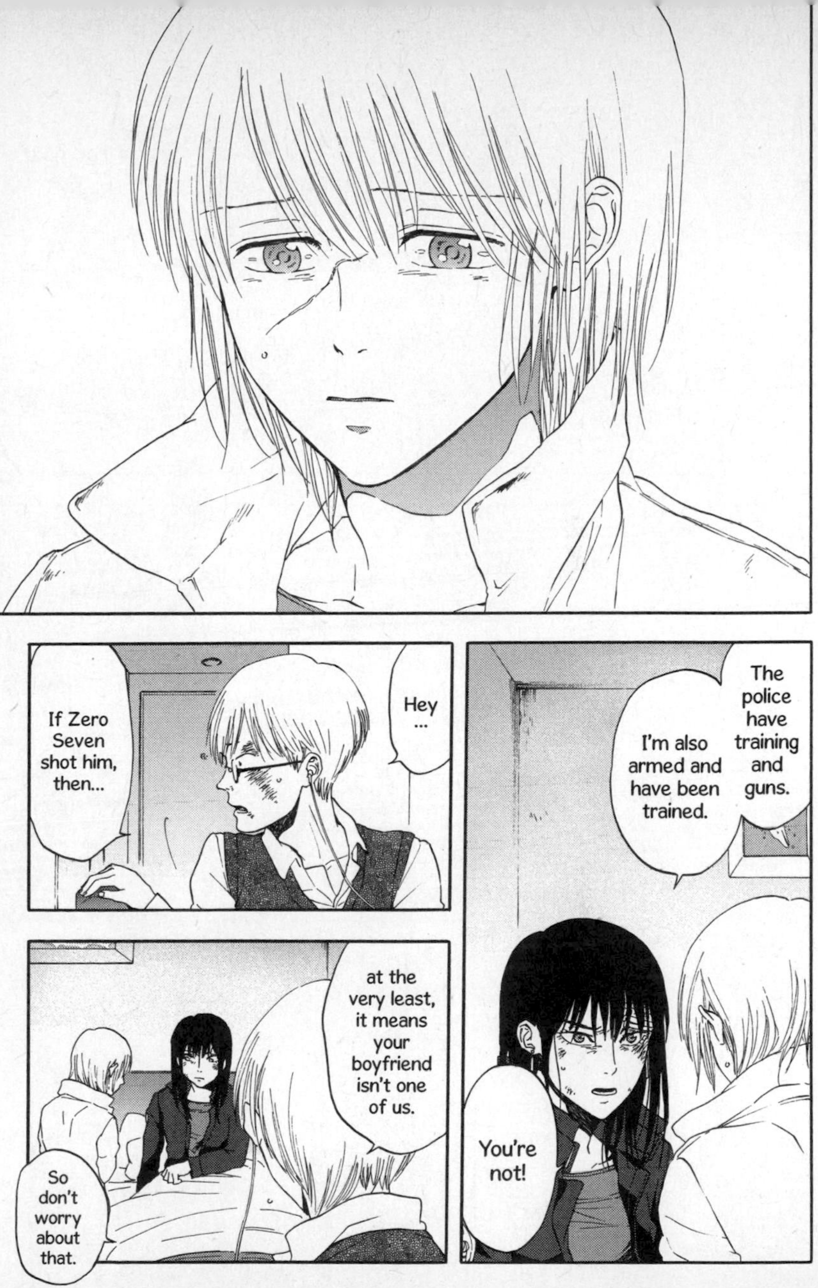
The police have training and guns.
I'm also armed and have been trained.
You're not!
Hey ...
If Zero Seven shot him, then...
at the very least, it means your boyfriend isn't one of us.
So don't worry about that.

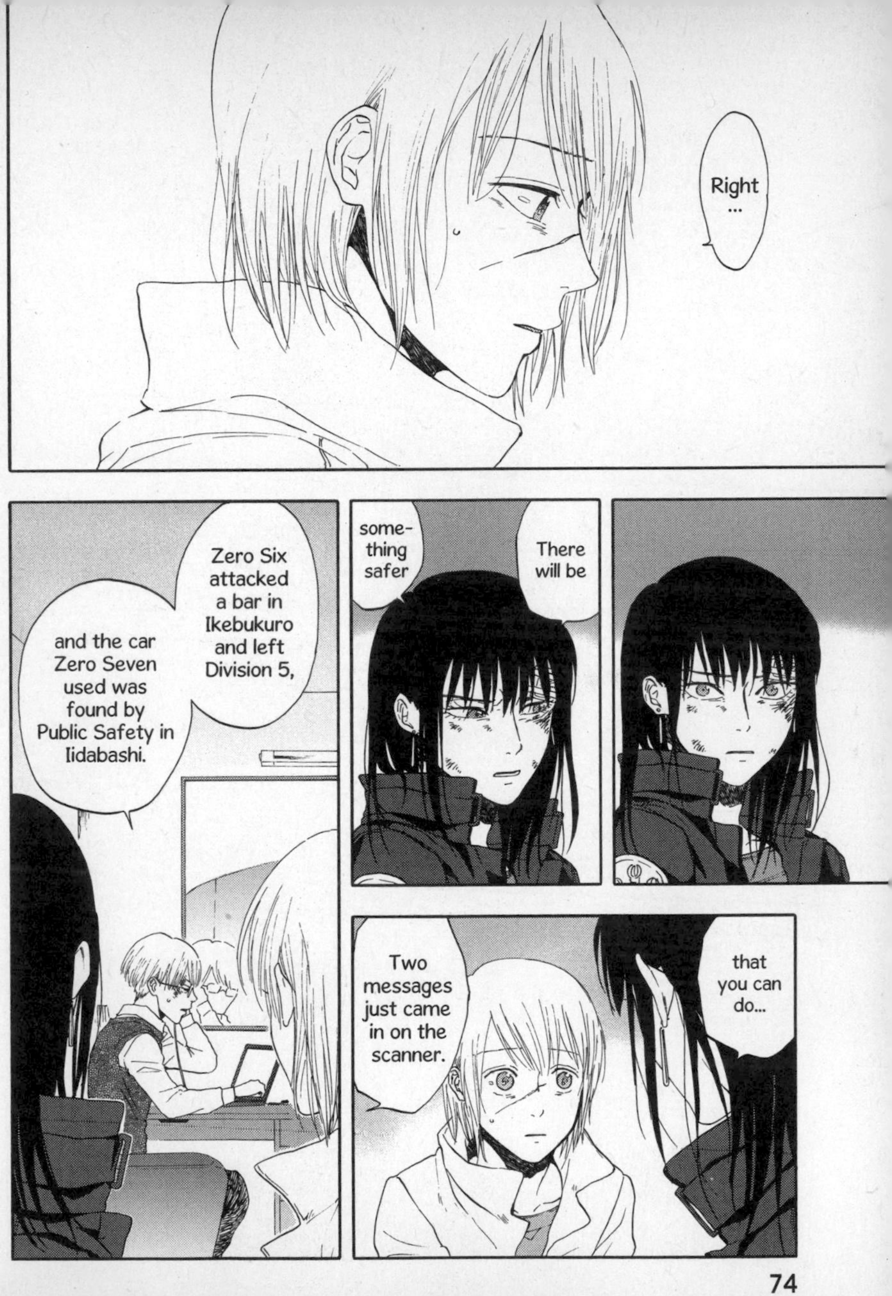
Right ...
There will be
some-thing safer
that you can do...
Two messages just came in on the scanner.
Zero Six attacked a bar in Ikebukuro and left Division 5,
and the car Zero Seven used was found by Public Safety in Iidabashi.

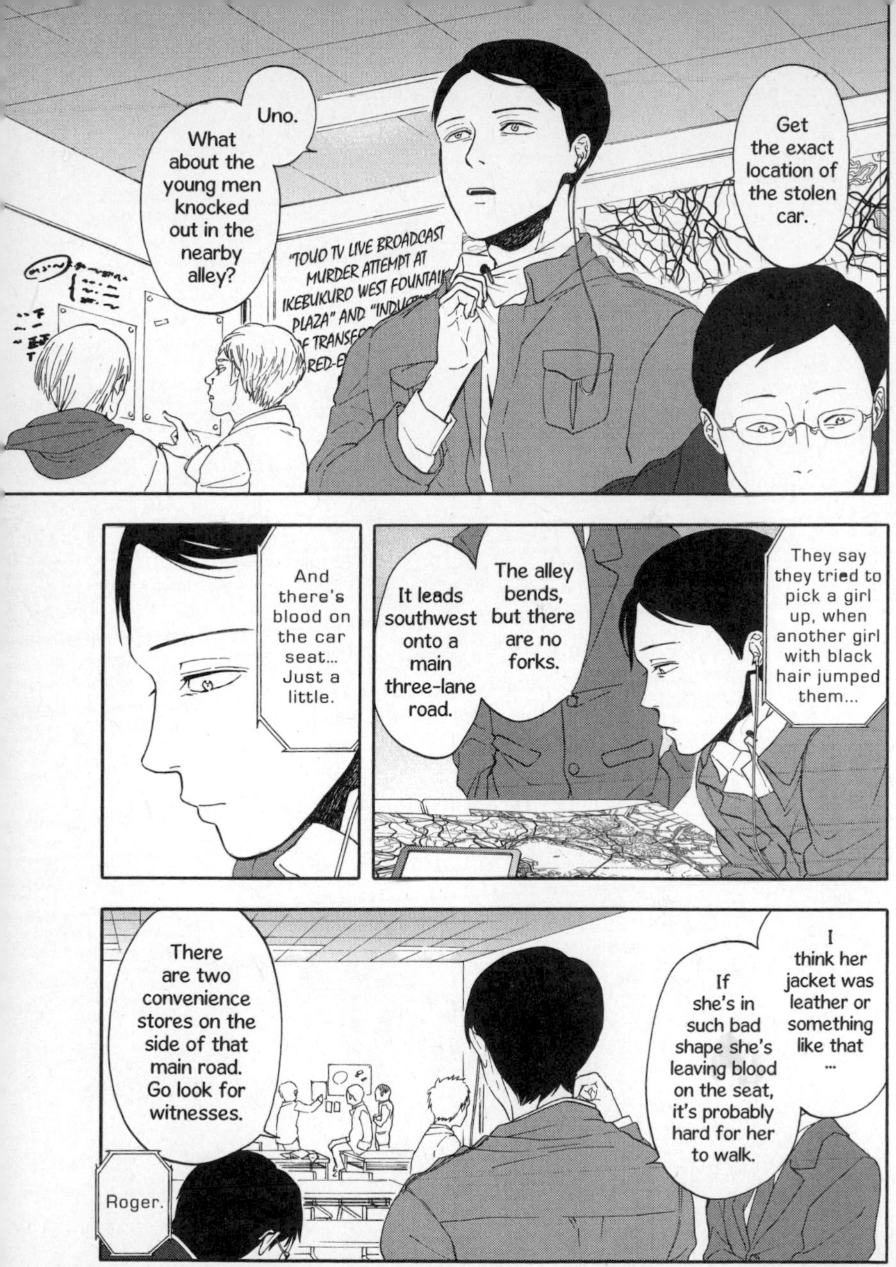
Get the exact location of the stolen car.
Uno.
What about the young men knocked out in the nearby alley?
"TOUO TV LIVE BROADCAST MURDER ATTEMPT AT IKEBUKURO WEST FOUNTAI
PLAZA" AND "INDU
They say they tried to pick a girl up, when another girl with black hair jumped them...
The alley bends, but there are no forks.
It leads southwest onto a main three-lane road.
And there's blood on the car seat... Just a little.
I think her jacket was leather or something like that ...
If she's in such bad shape she's leaving blood on the seat, it's probably hard for her to walk.
There are two convenience stores on the side of that main road. Go look for witnesses.
Roger.

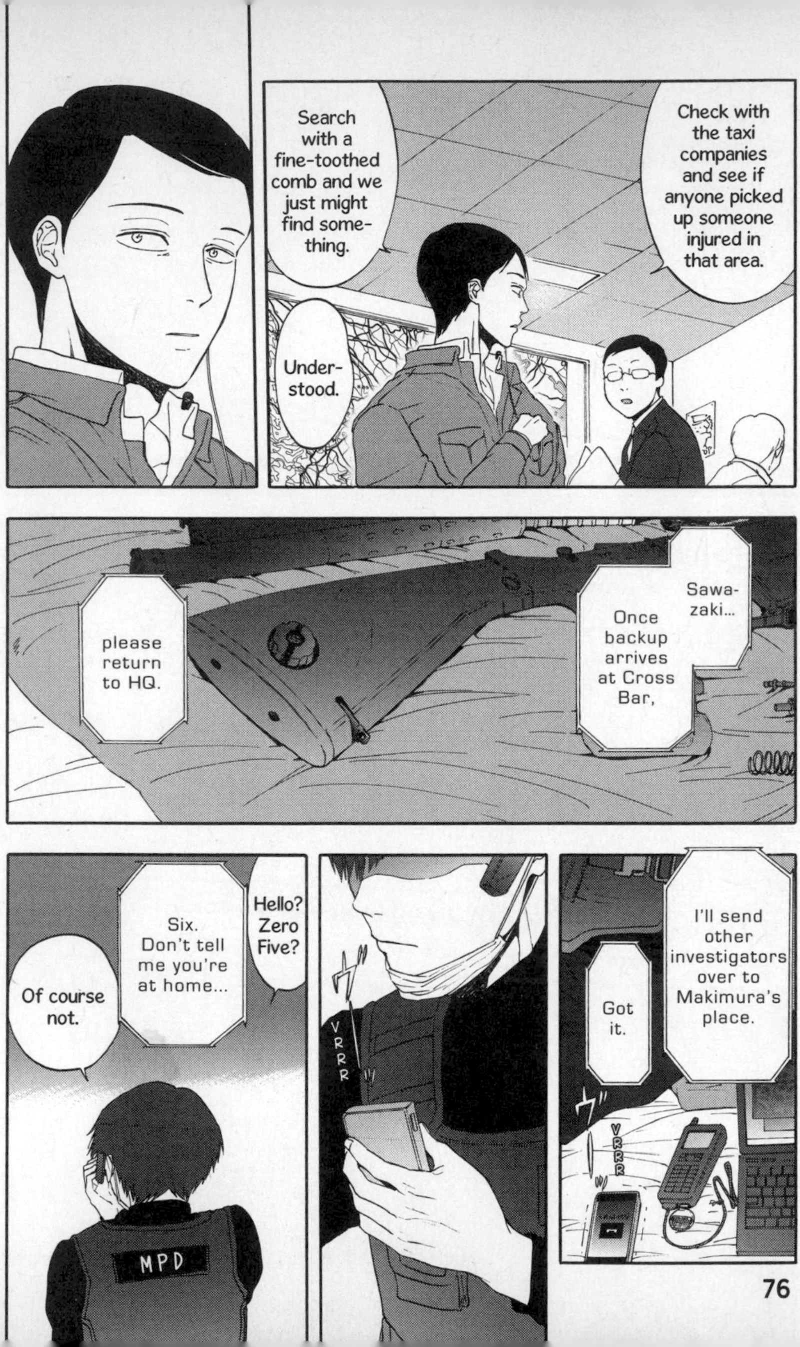
Check with the taxi companies and see if anyone picked up someone injured in that area.
Search with a fine-toothed comb and we just might find some-thing.
Under-stood.
Sawa-zaki...
Once backup arrives at Cross Bar,
please return to HQ.
I'll send other investigators over to Makimura's place.
Got it.
VRRR
VRRR
Hello? Zero Five?
Six. Don't tell me you're at home...
Of course not.
MPD

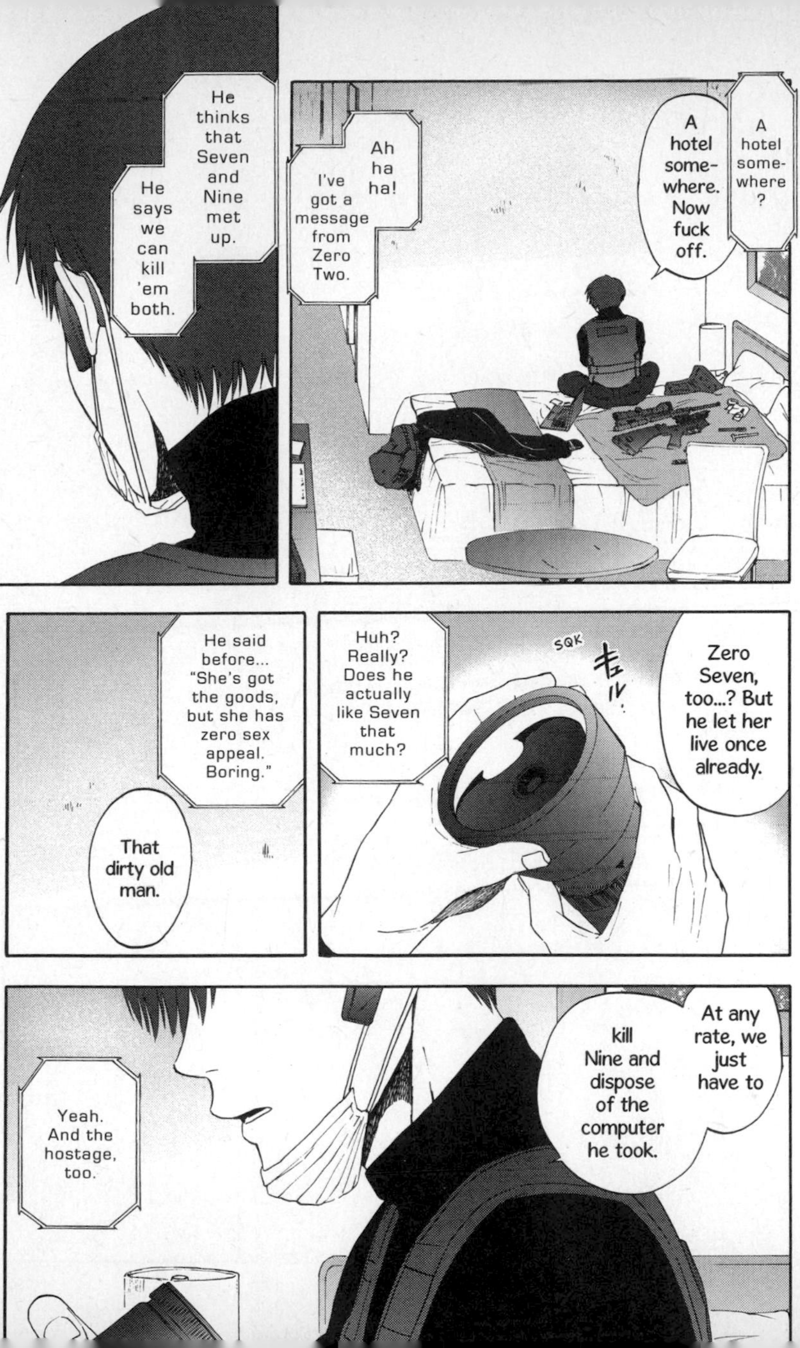
A hotel somewhere?
A hotel somewhere. Now fuck off.
Ah ha ha!
I've got a message from Zero Two.
He thinks that Seven and Nine met up.
He says we can kill 'em both.
SQK
Zero Seven, too...? But he let her live once already.
Huh? Really? Does he actually like Seven that much?
He said before... "She's got the goods, but she has zero sex appeal. Boring."
That dirty old man.
At any rate, we just have to kill Nine and dispose of the computer he took.
Yeah. And the hostage, too.

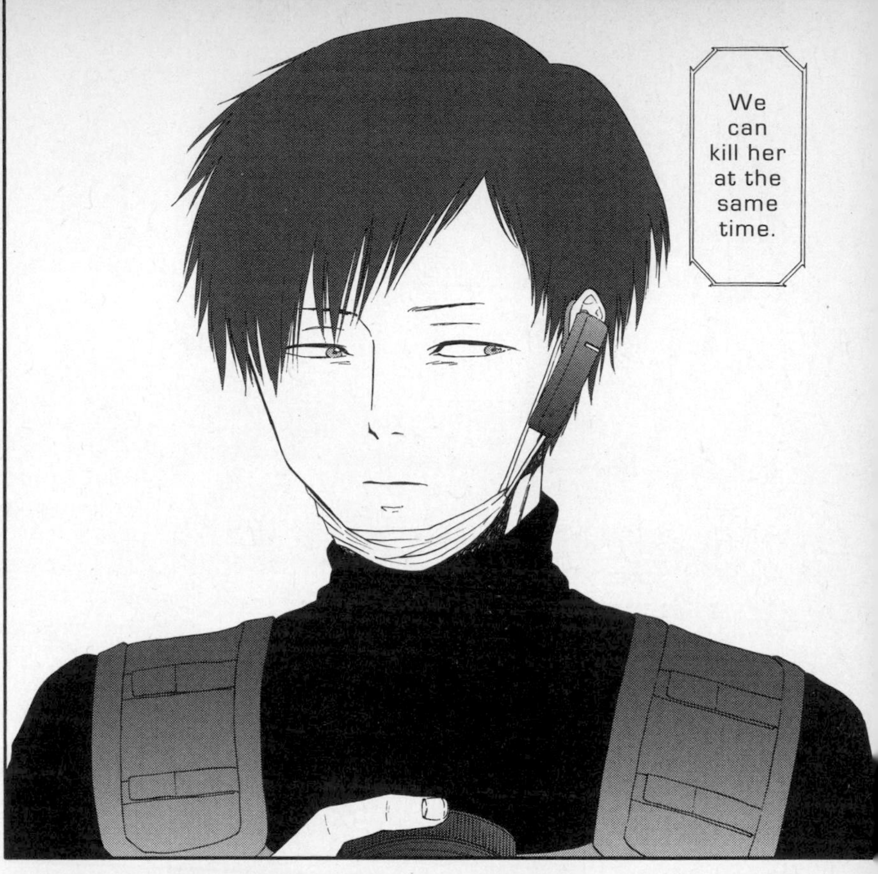
We can kill her at the same time.

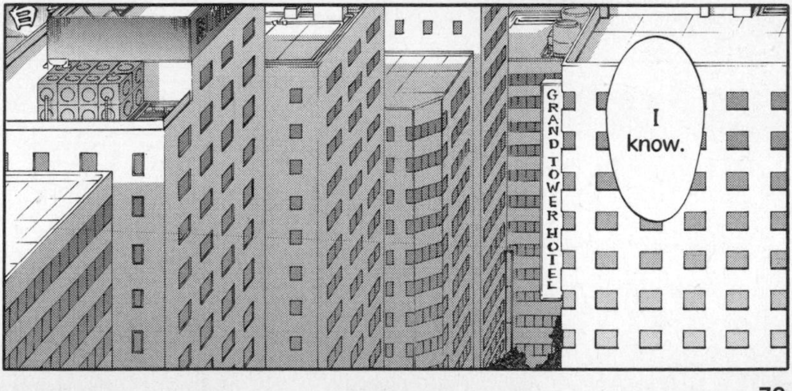
I know.
GRAND TOWER HOTEL

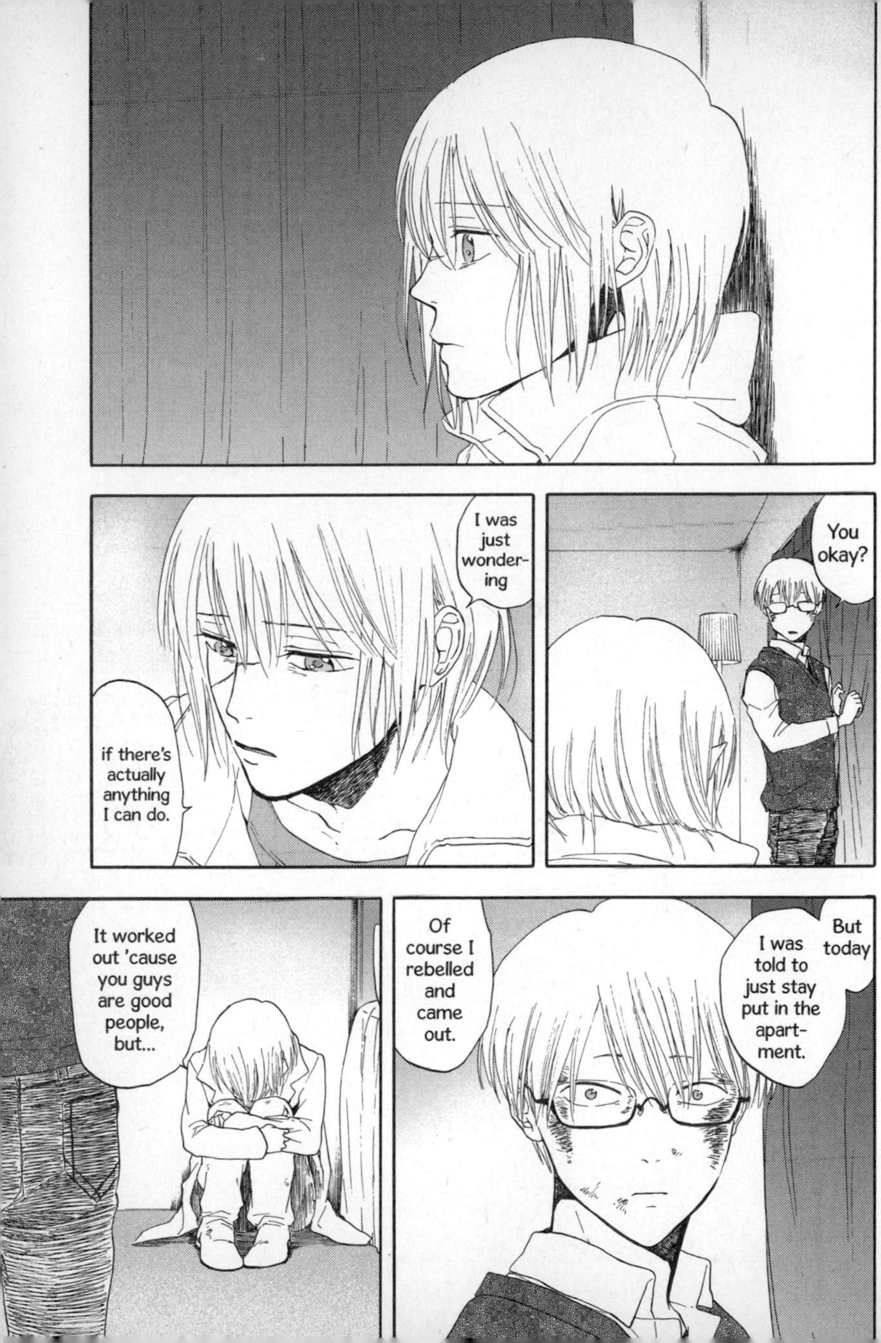
You okay?
I was just wondering
if there's actually anything I can do.
But today
I was told to just stay put in the apartment.
Of course I rebelled and came out.
It worked out 'cause you guys are good people, but...

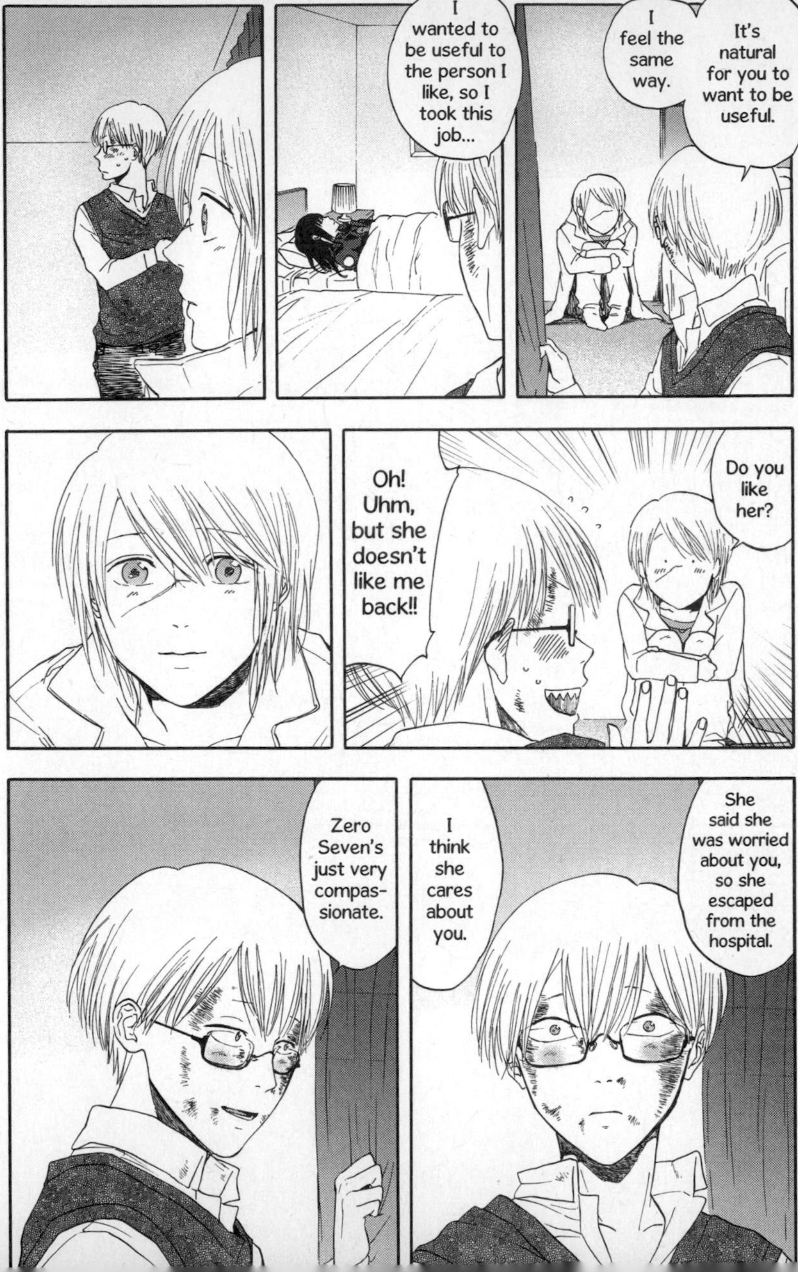

It's natural for you to want to be useful.
I feel the same way.
I wanted to be useful to the person I like, so I took this job...
Do you like her?
Oh! Uhm, but she doesn't like me back!!
She said she was worried about you, so she escaped from the hospital.
I think she cares about you.
Zero Seven's just very compassionate.

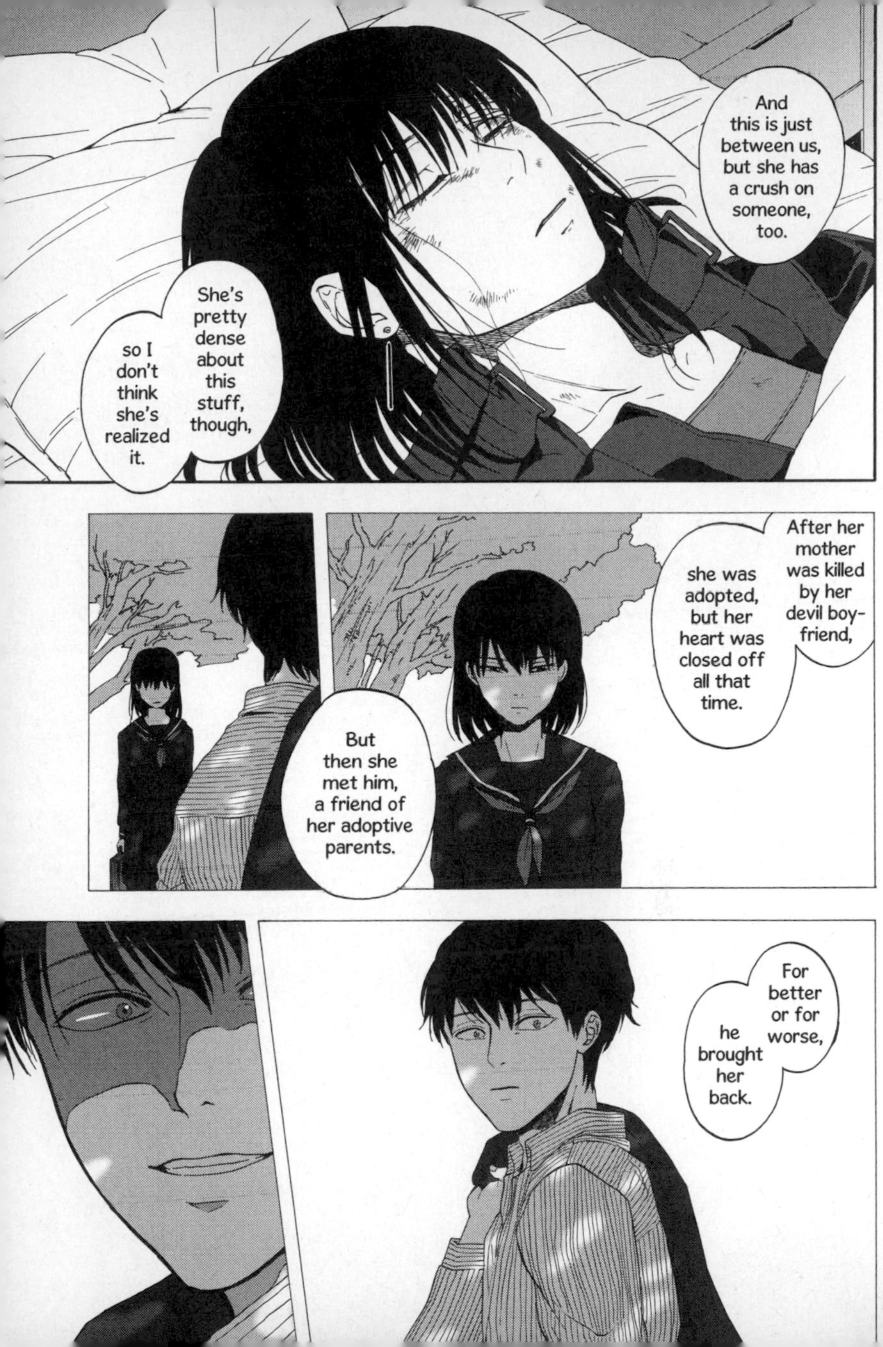
And this is just between us, but she has a crush on someone, too.
She's pretty dense about this stuff, though,
so I don't think she's realized it.
After her mother was killed by her devil boy-friend,
she was adopted, but her heart was closed off all that time.
But then she met him, a friend of her adoptive parents.
For better or for worse,
he brought her back.

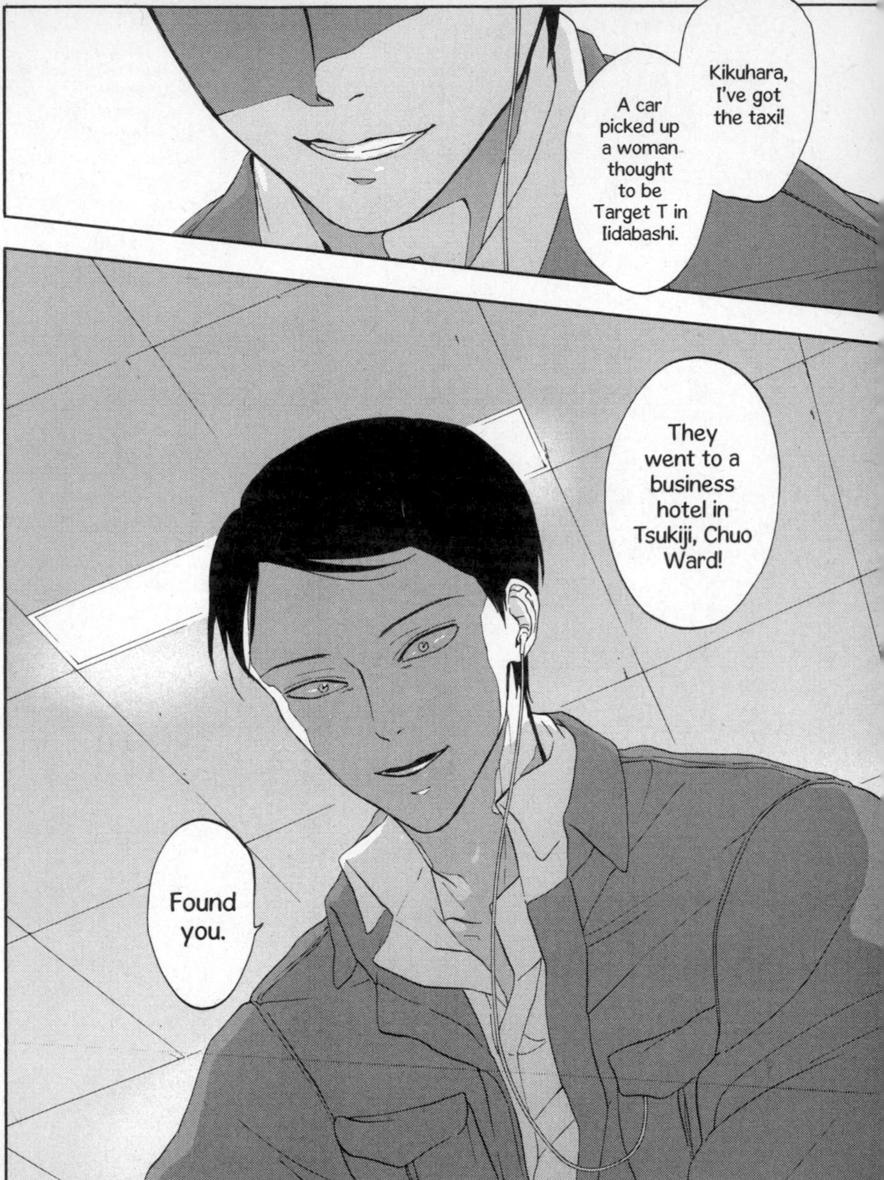
Kikuhara, I've got the taxi!
A car picked up a woman thought to be Target T in Iidabashi.
They went to a business hotel in Tsukiji, Chuo Ward!
Found you.

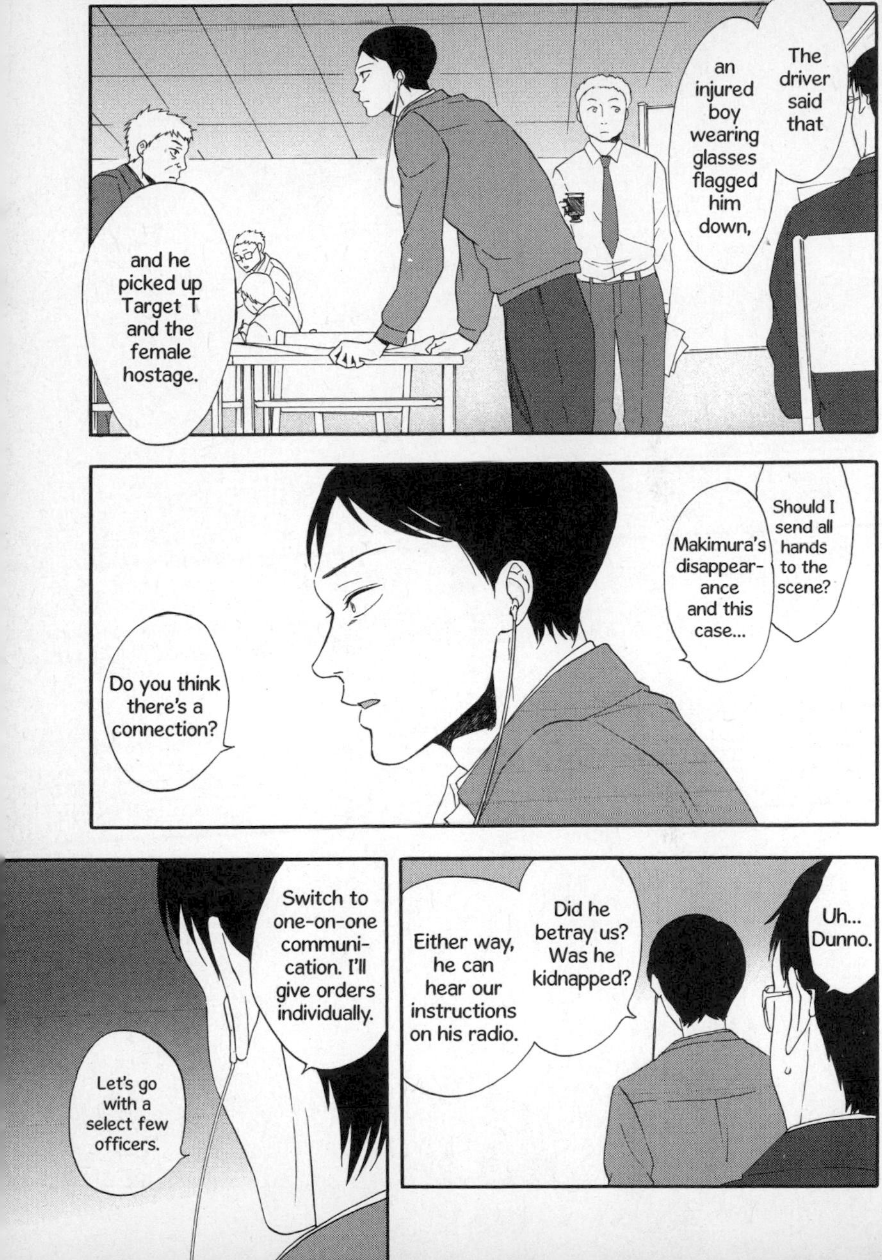
The driver said that
an injured boy wearing glasses flagged him down,
and he picked up Target T and the female hostage.
Should I send all hands to the scene?
Makimura's disappear-ance and this case...
Do you think there's a connection?
Uh... Dunno.
Did he betray us? Was he kidnapped?
Either way, he can hear our instructions on his radio.
Switch to one-on-one communi-cation. I'll give orders individually.
Let's go with a select few officers.

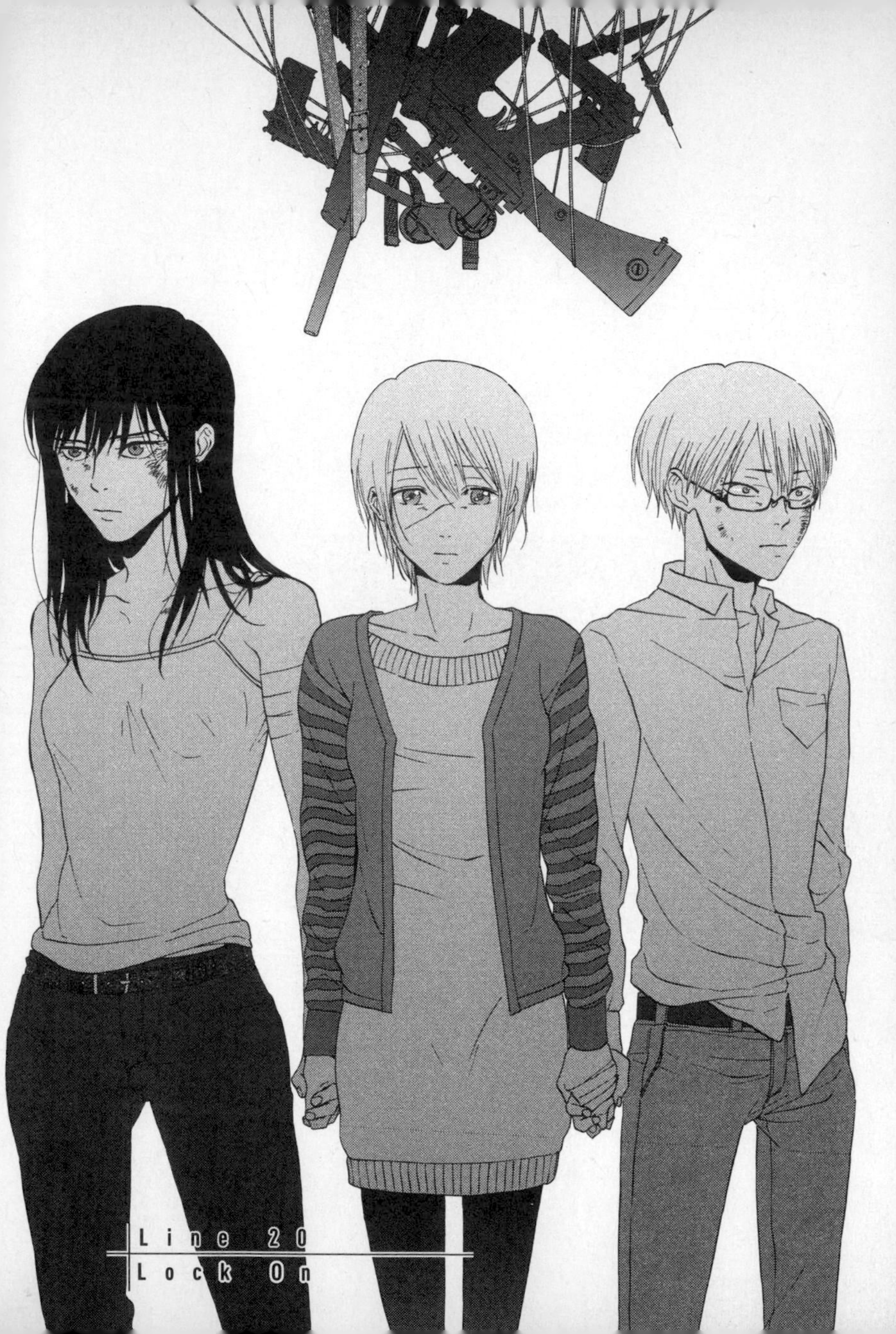

Line 20
Lock On

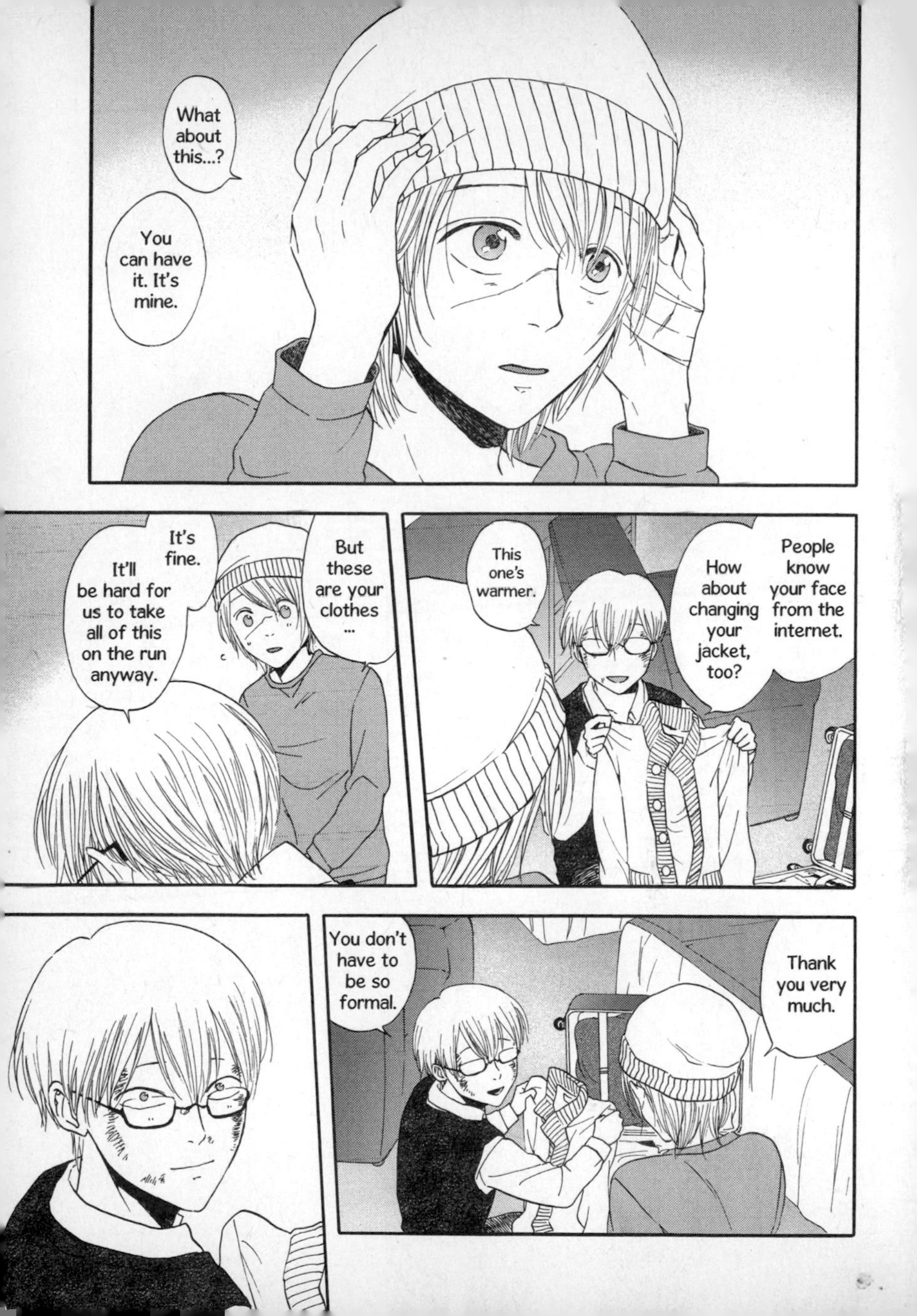
What about this...?
You can have it. It's mine.
People know your face from the internet.
How about changing your jacket, too?
This one's warmer.
But these are your clothes ...
It's fine.
It'll be hard for us to take all of this on the run anyway.
Thank you very much.
You don't have to be so formal.

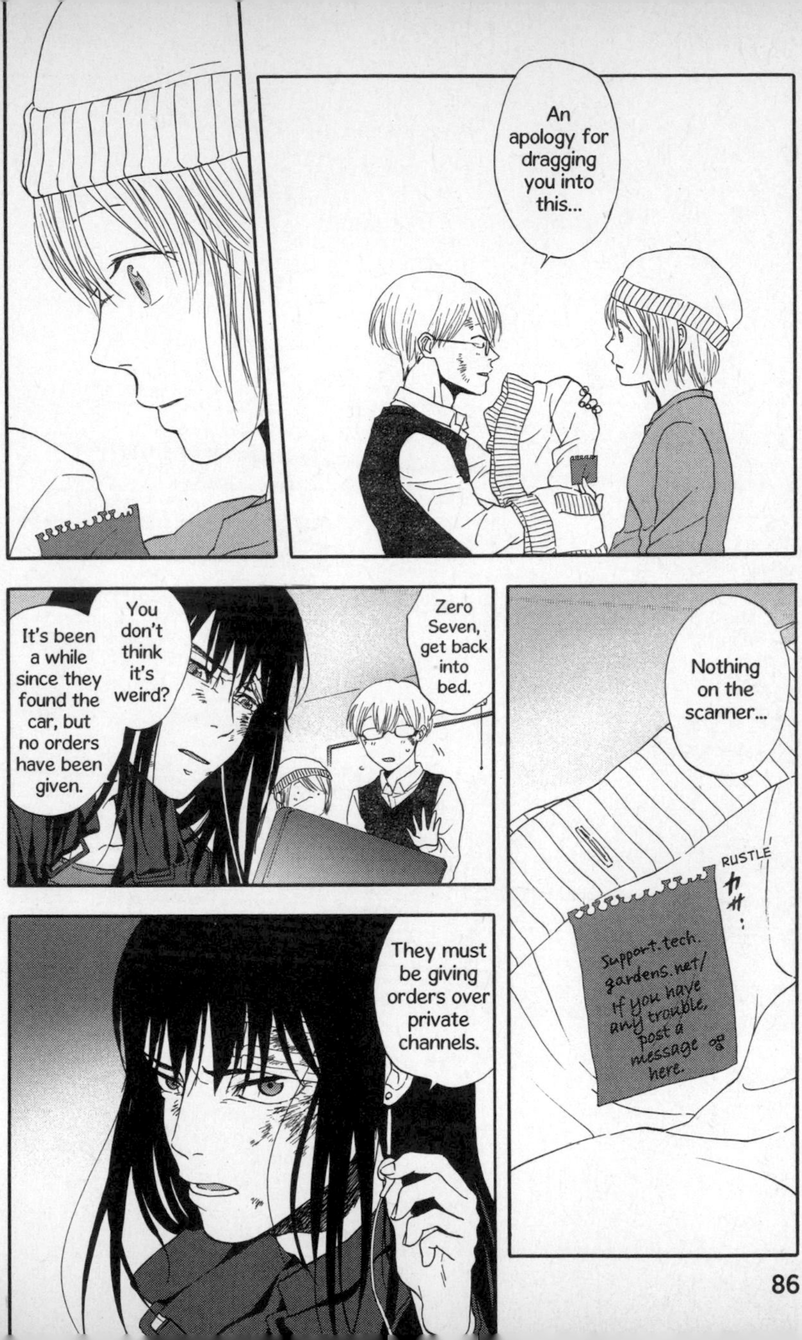

An apology for dragging you into this...
Nothing on the scanner...
RUSTLE
カサ
Support.tech.gardenS.net/ If you have any trouble, post a message here.
Zero Seven, get back into bed.
You don't think it's weird?
It's been a while since they found the car, but no orders have been given.
They must be giving orders over private channels.

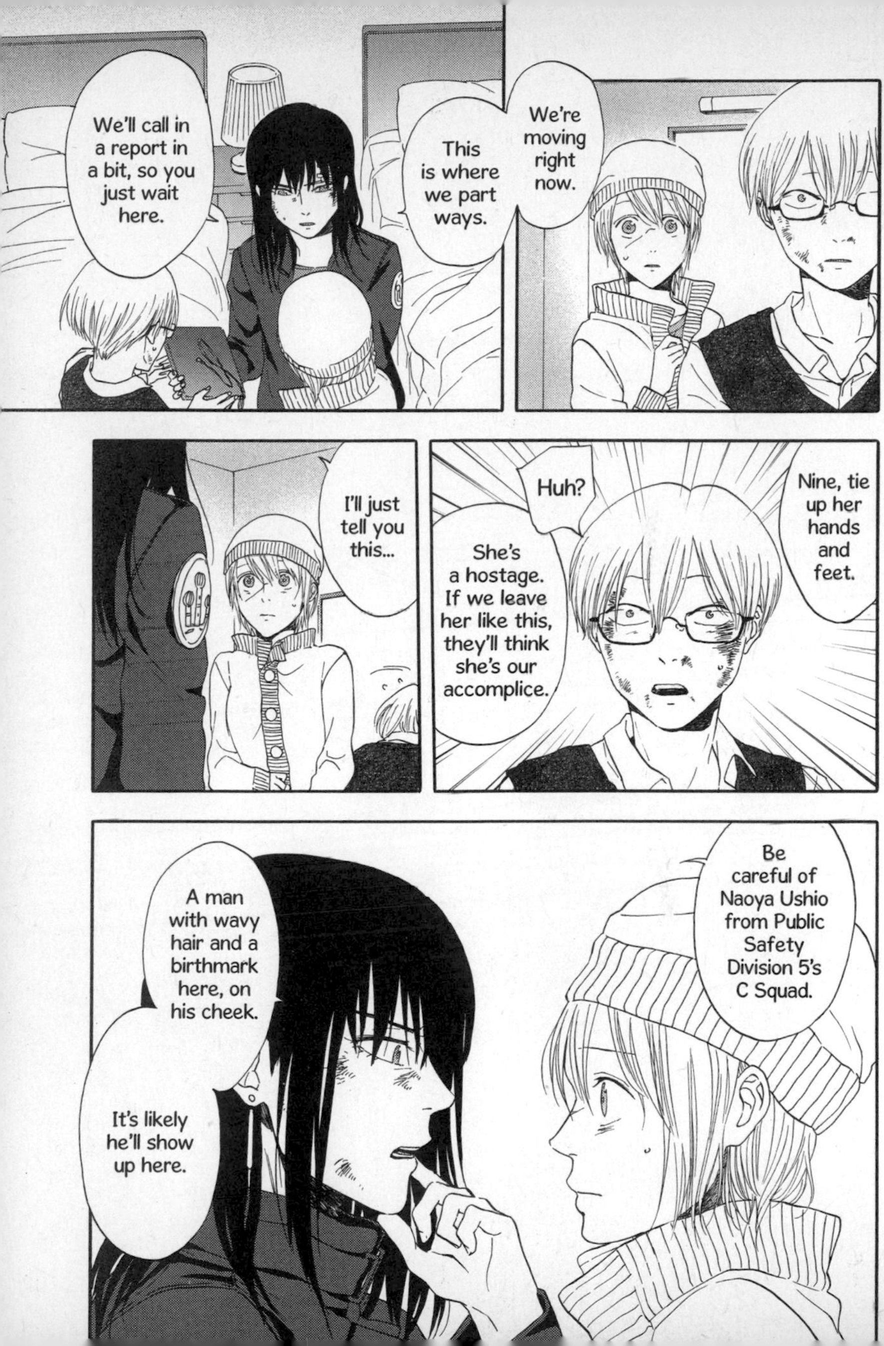
We're moving right now.
This is where we part ways.
We'll call in a report in a bit, so you just wait here.
Nine, tie up her hands and feet.
Huh?
She's a hostage. If we leave her like this, they'll think she's our accomplice.
I'll just tell you this...
Be careful of Naoya Ushio from Public Safety Division 5's C Squad.
A man with wavy hair and a birthmark here, on his cheek.
It's likely he'll show up here.

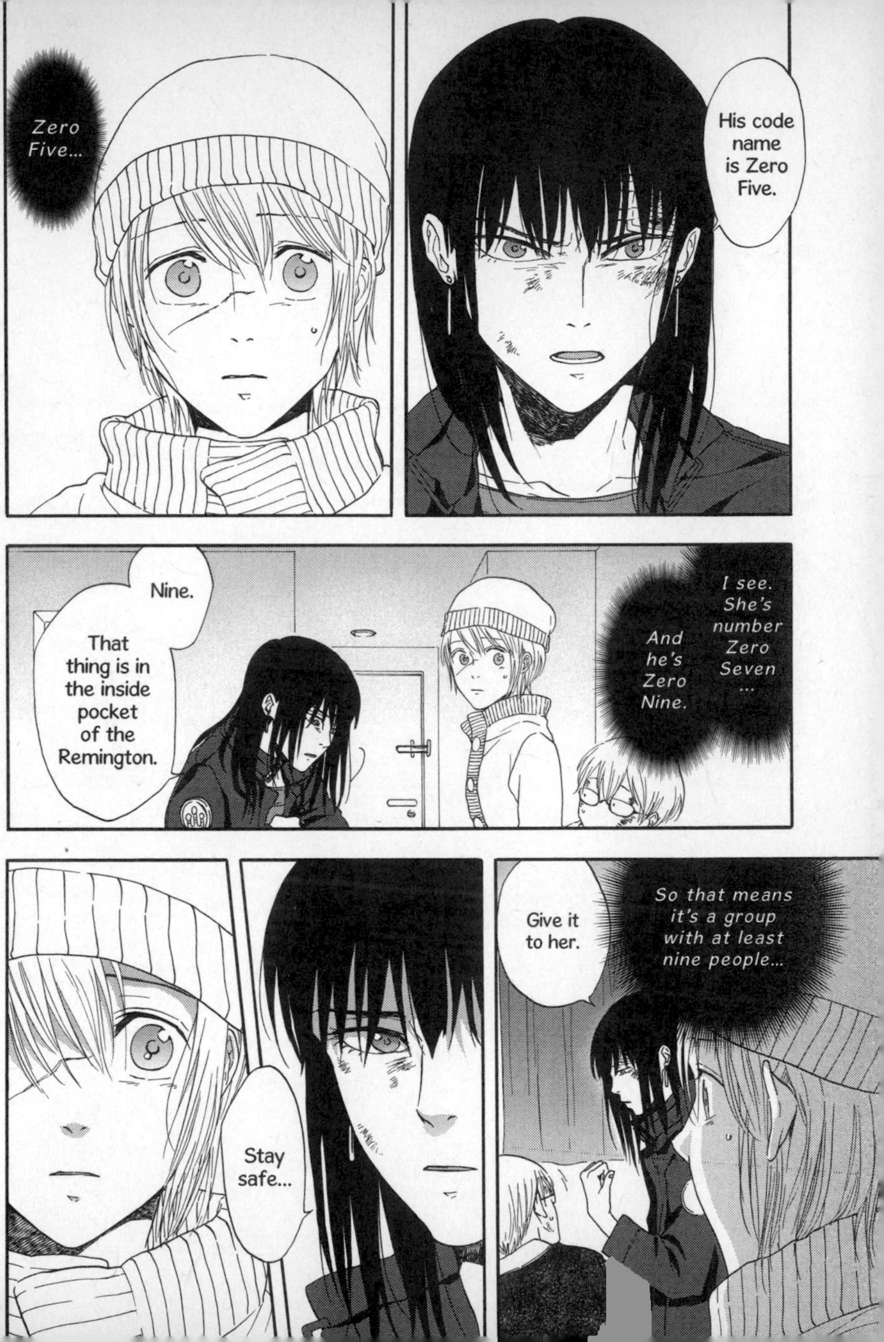
His code name is Zero Five.
Zero Five...
I see. She's number Zero Seven...
And he's Zero Nine.
Nine.
That thing is in the inside pocket of the Remington.
So that means it's a group with at least nine people...
Give it to her.
Stay safe...

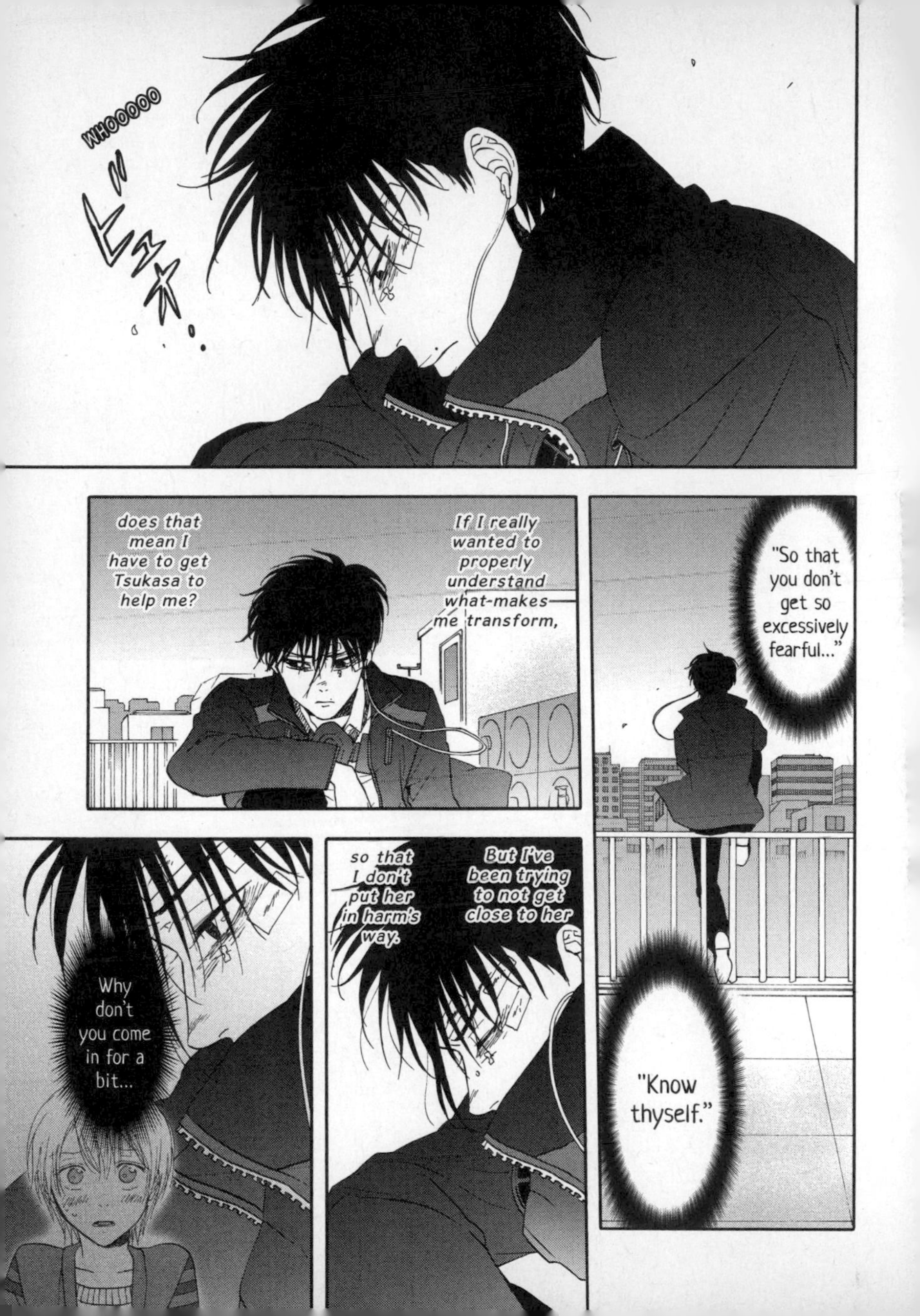
WHOOOOO
"So that you don't get so excessively fearful..."
"Know thyself."
If I really wanted to properly understand what-makes me transform,
does that mean I have to get Tsukasa to help me?
But I've been trying to not get close to her
so that I don't put her in harm's way.
Why don't you come in for a bit...

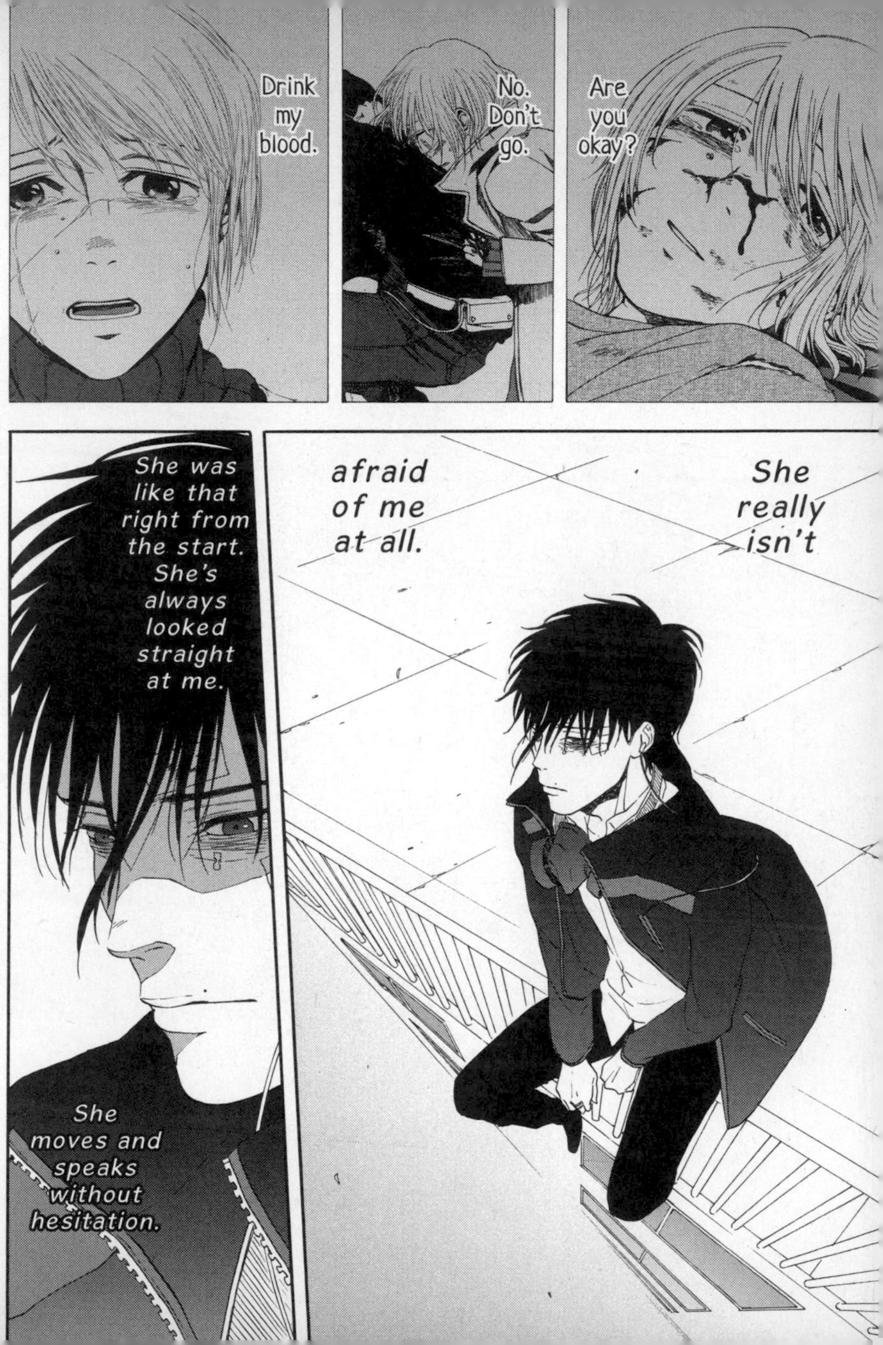
Are you okay?
No. Don't go.
Drink my blood.
She really isn't
afraid of me at all.
She was like that right from the start. She's always looked straight at me.
She moves and speaks without hesitation.

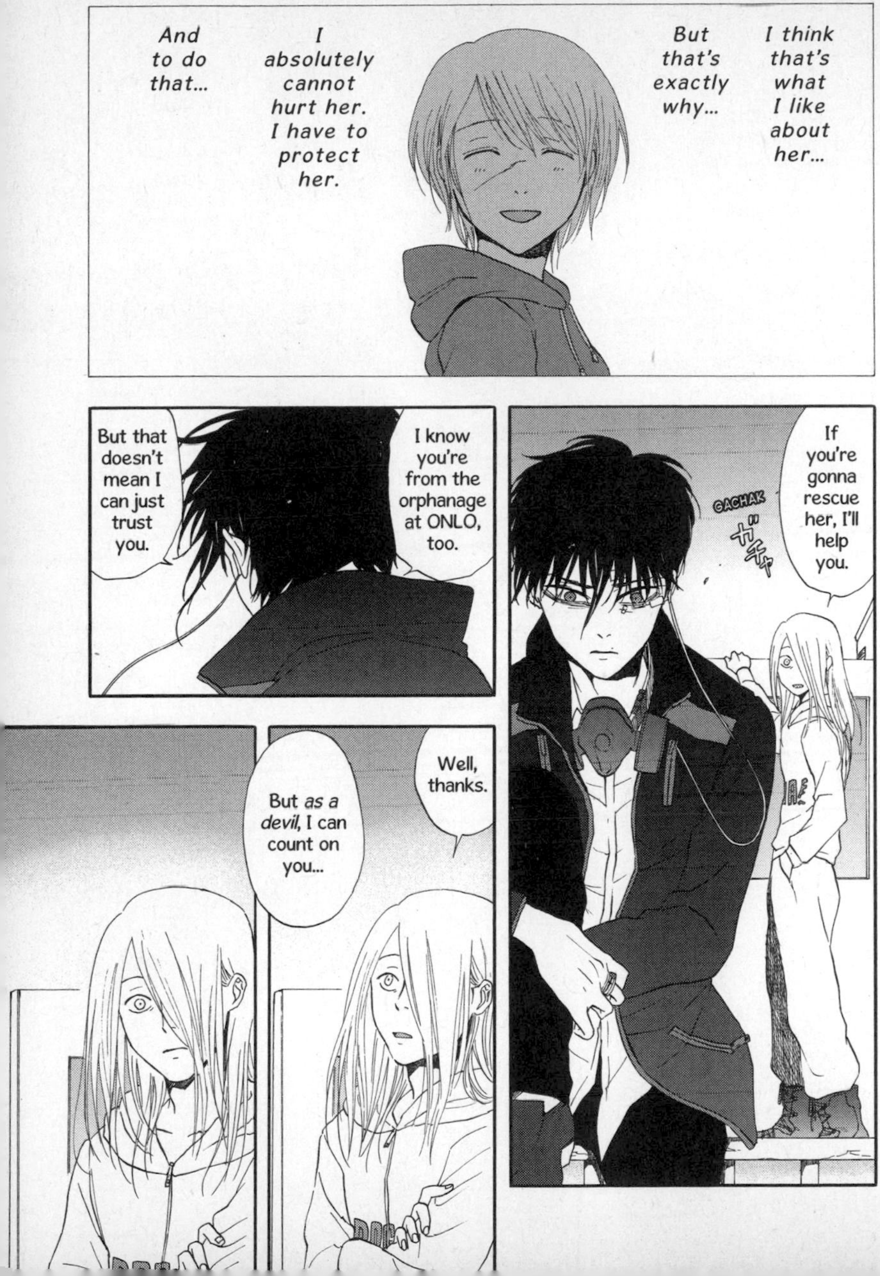
I think that's what I like about her...
But that's exactly why...
I absolutely cannot hurt her. I have to protect her.
And to do that...
If you're gonna rescue her, I'll help you.
GACHAK
I know you're from the orphanage at ONLO, too.
But that doesn't mean I can just trust you.
Well, thanks.
But *as a devil*, I can count on you...

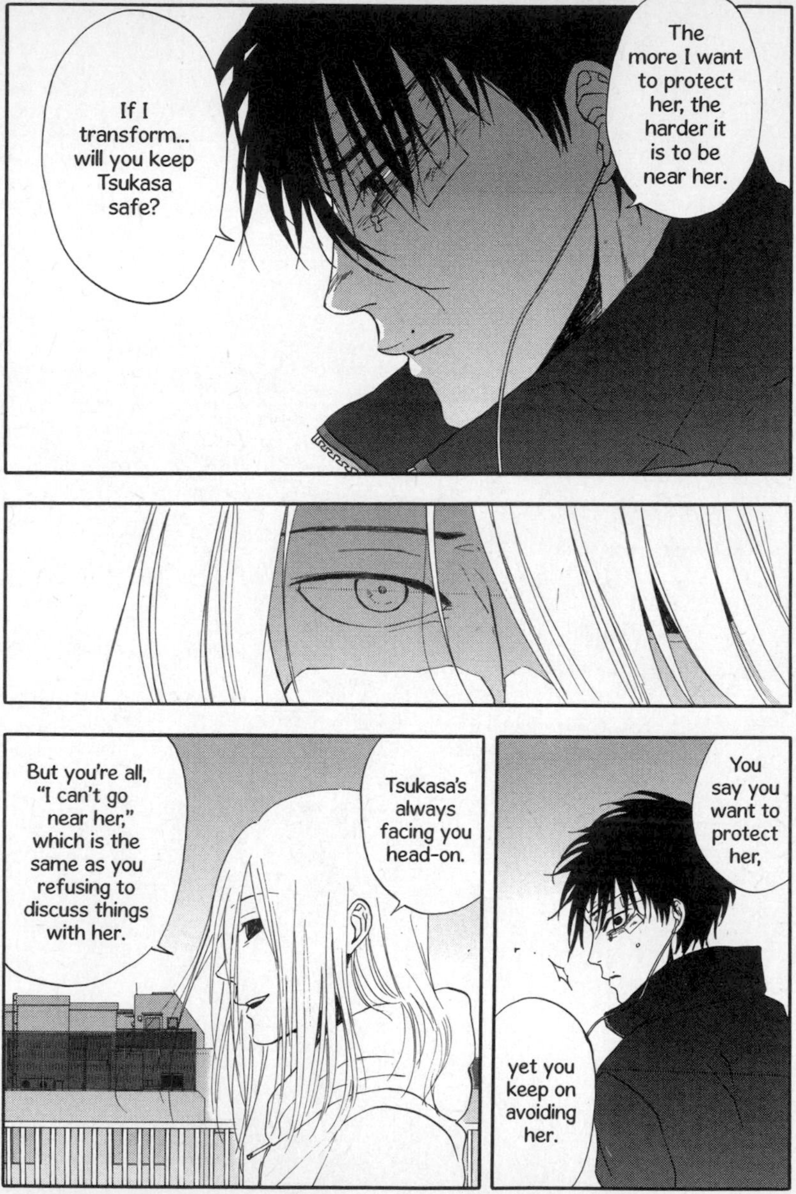
The more I want to protect her, the harder it is to be near her.
If I transform... will you keep Tsukasa safe?
You say you want to protect her,
yet you keep on avoiding her.
Tsukasa's always facing you head-on.
But you're all, "I can't go near her," which is the same as you refusing to discuss things with her.

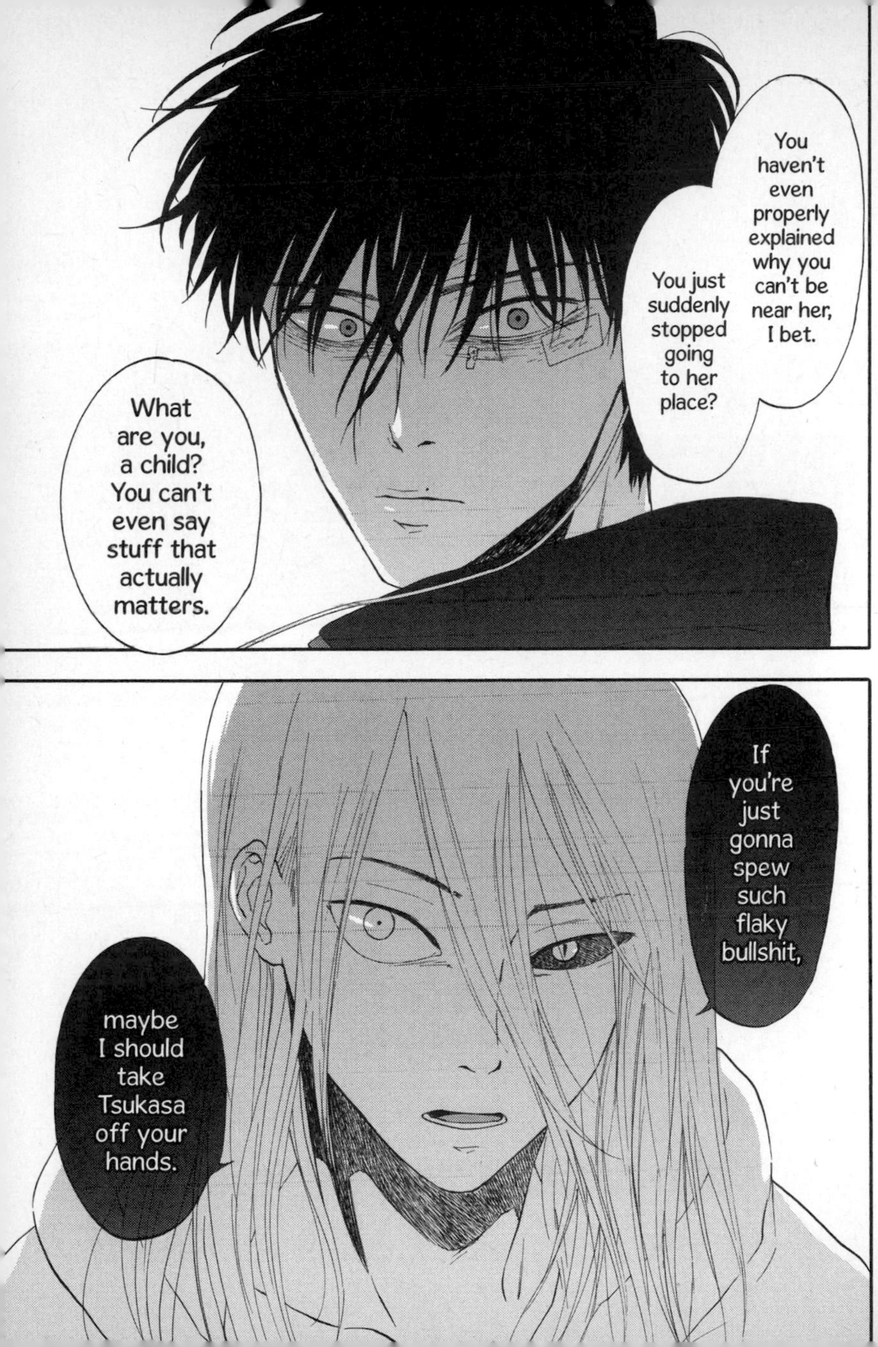
You haven't even properly explained why you can't be near her, I bet.
You just suddenly stopped going to her place?
What are you, a child? You can't even say stuff that actually matters.
If you're just gonna spew such flaky bullshit,
maybe I should take Tsukasa off your hands.

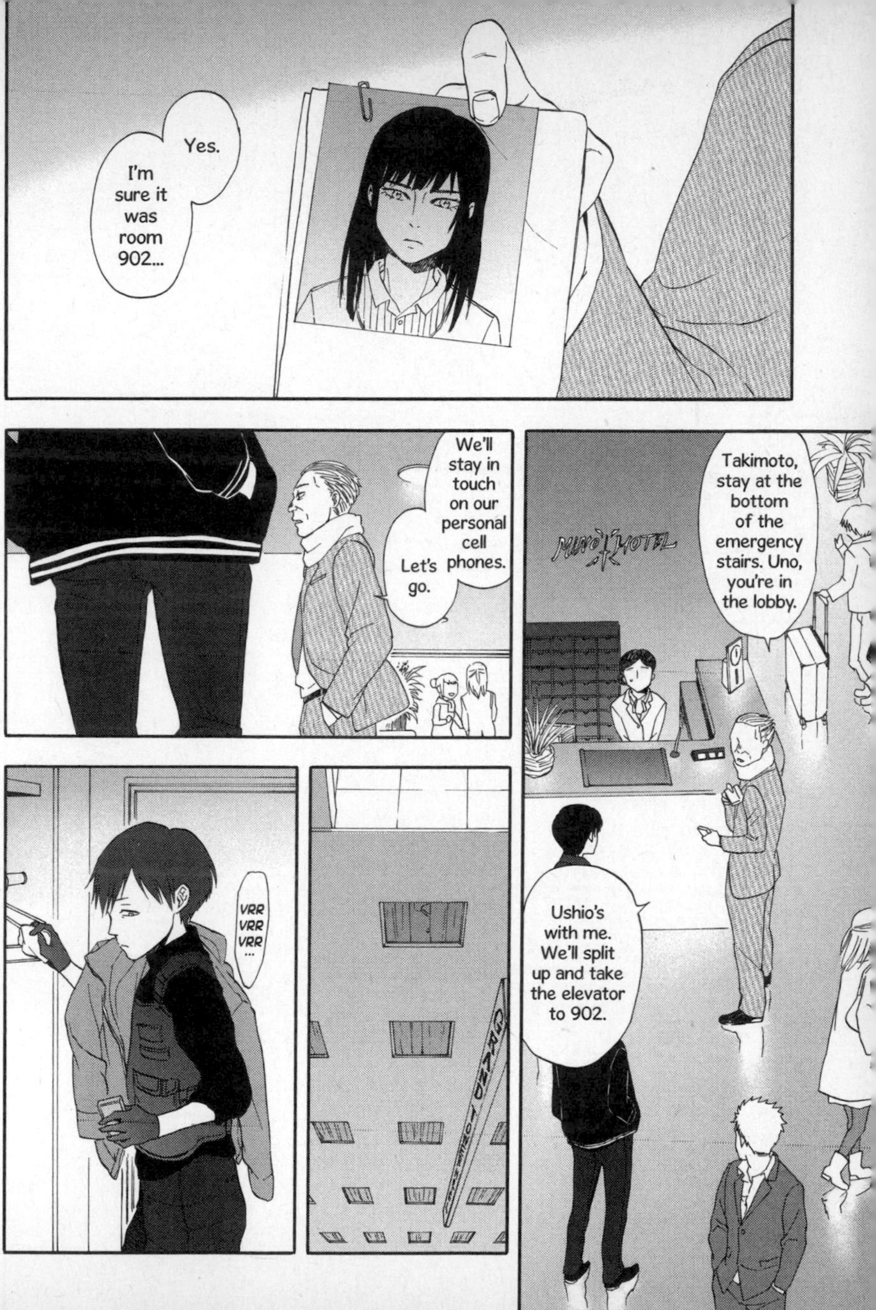
Yes.
I'm sure it was room 902...
Takimoto, stay at the bottom of the emergency stairs. Uno, you're in the lobby.
Ushio's with me. We'll split up and take the elevator to 902.
We'll stay in touch on our personal cell phones.
Let's go.
VRR VRR VRR ...

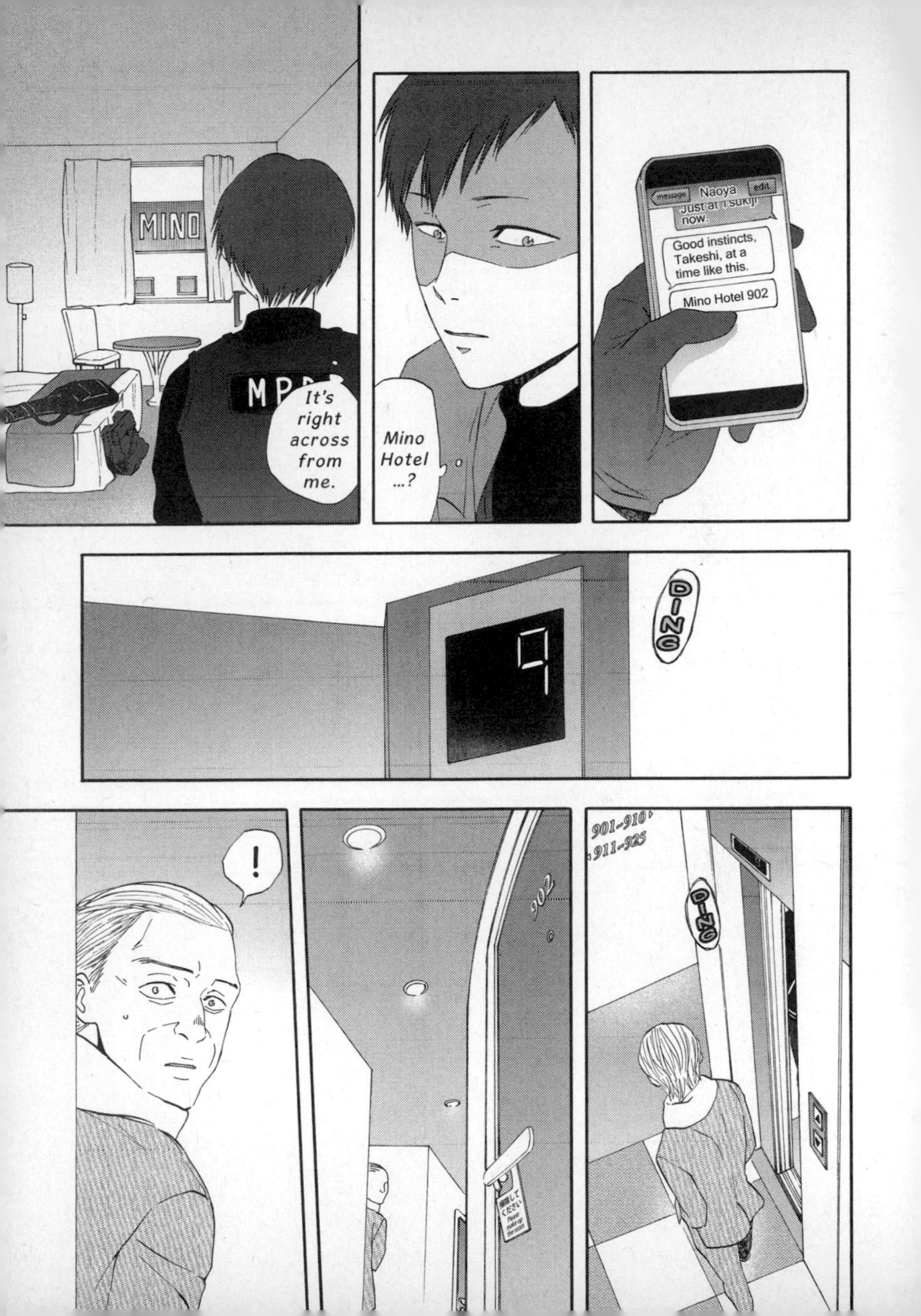
message
Naoya
edit
Just at Tsukiji now.
Good instincts, Takeshi, at a time like this.
Mino Hotel 902
Mino Hotel ...?
MPD
MINO
It's right across from me.
DING
9
901-910
911-925
DING
902
掃除してください
Please make up the room
!

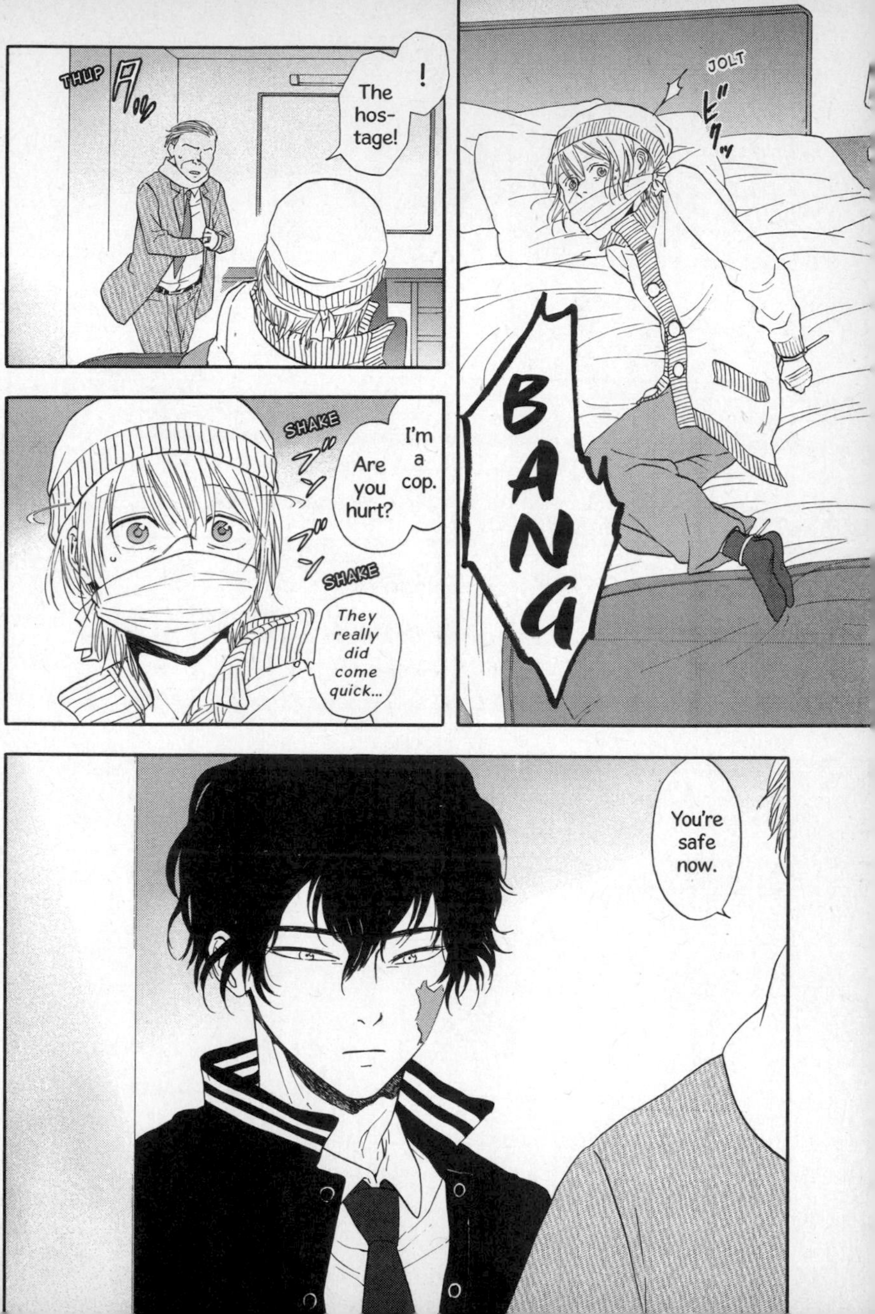
JOLT
BANG
THUP
! The hostage!
I'm a cop.
Are you hurt?
SHAKE
SHAKE
They really did come quick...
You're safe now.

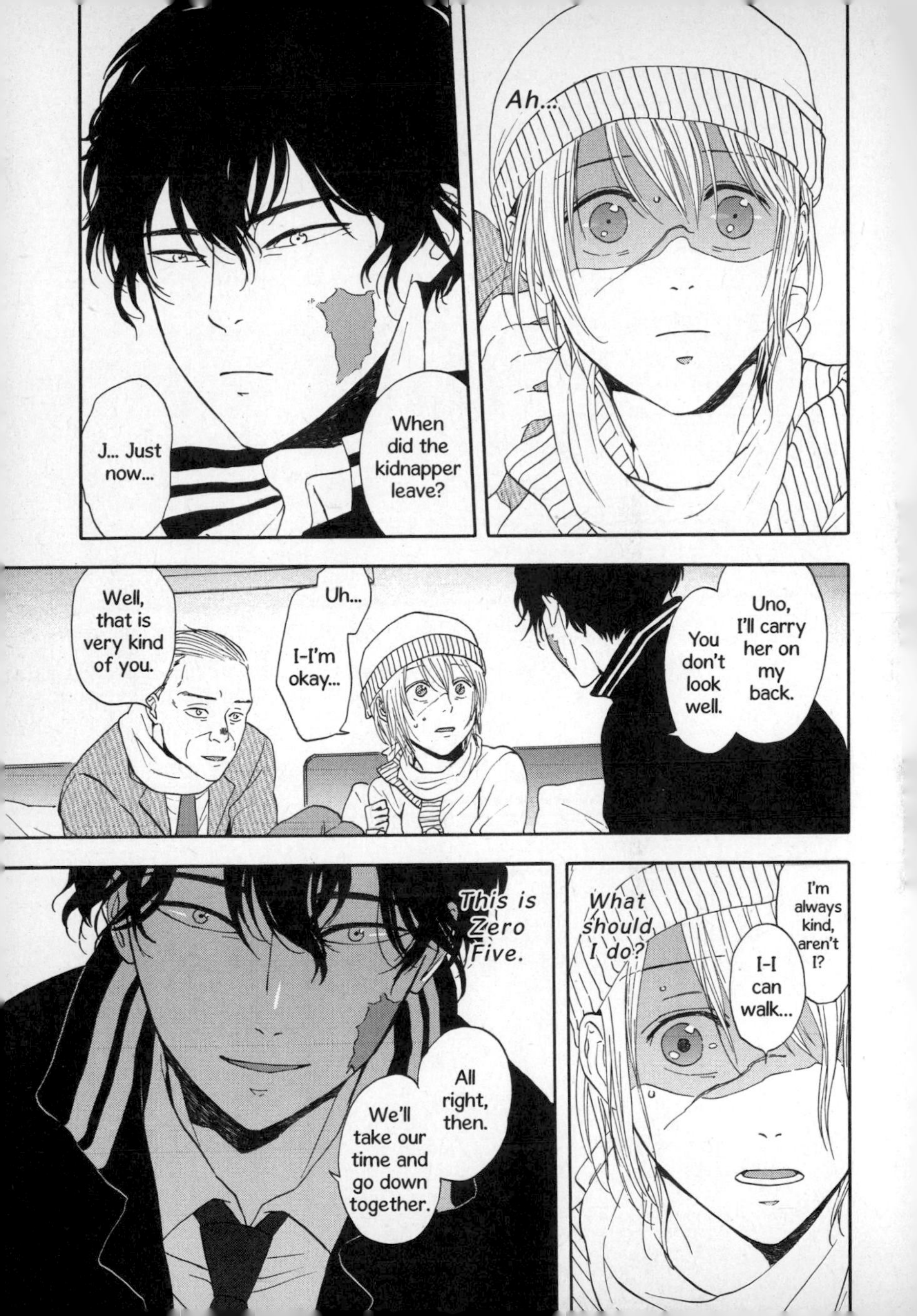
Ah...
When did the kidnapper leave?
J... Just now...
Uno, I'll carry her on my back.
You don't look well.
Uh...
I-I'm okay...
Well, that is very kind of you.
I'm always kind, aren't I?
What should I do?
I-I can walk...
This is Zero Five.
All right, then.
We'll take our time and go down together.

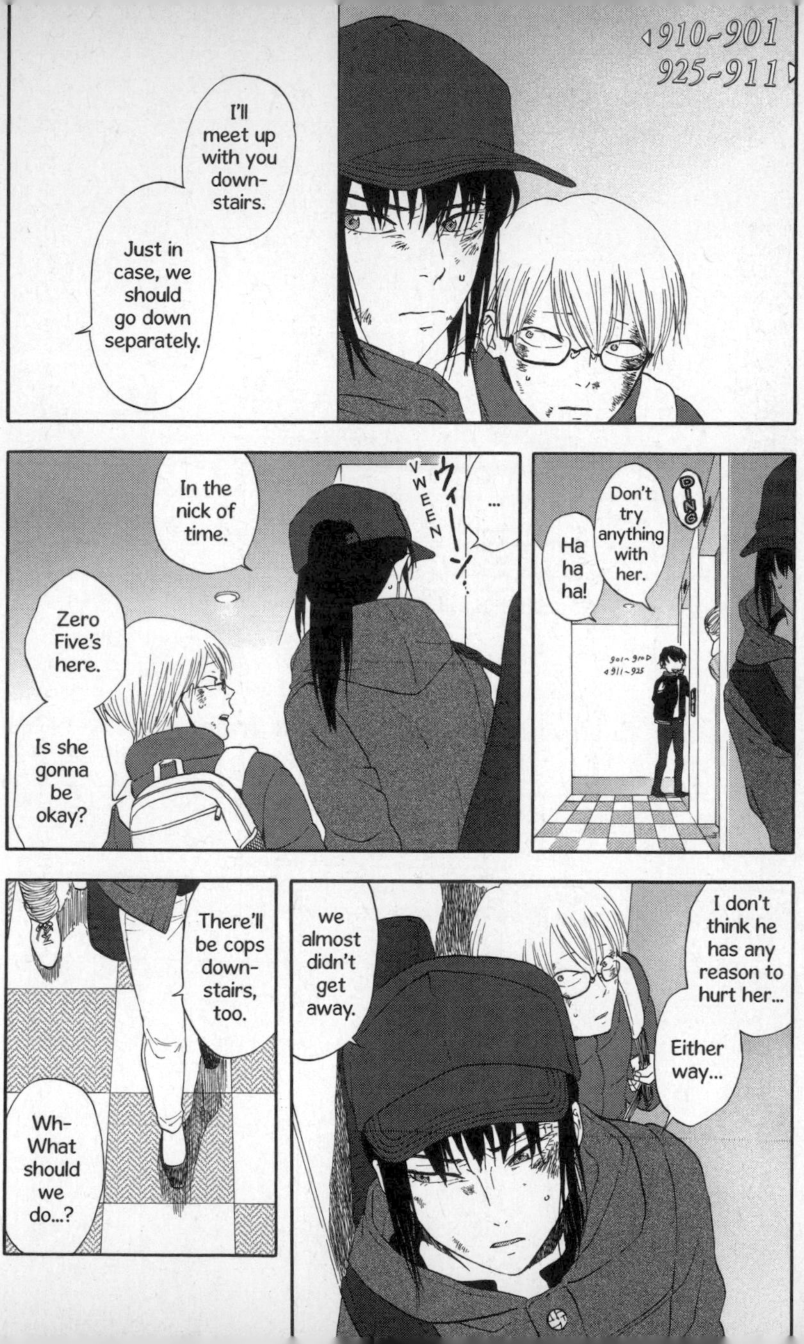
910~901
925~911
I'll meet up with you downstairs.
Just in case, we should go down separately.
DING
Don't try anything with her.
Ha ha ha!
901~910
911~925
VWEEN
...
In the nick of time.
Zero Five's here.
Is she gonna be okay?
I don't think he has any reason to hurt her...
Either way...
we almost didn't get away.
There'll be cops downstairs, too.
Wh- What should we do...?

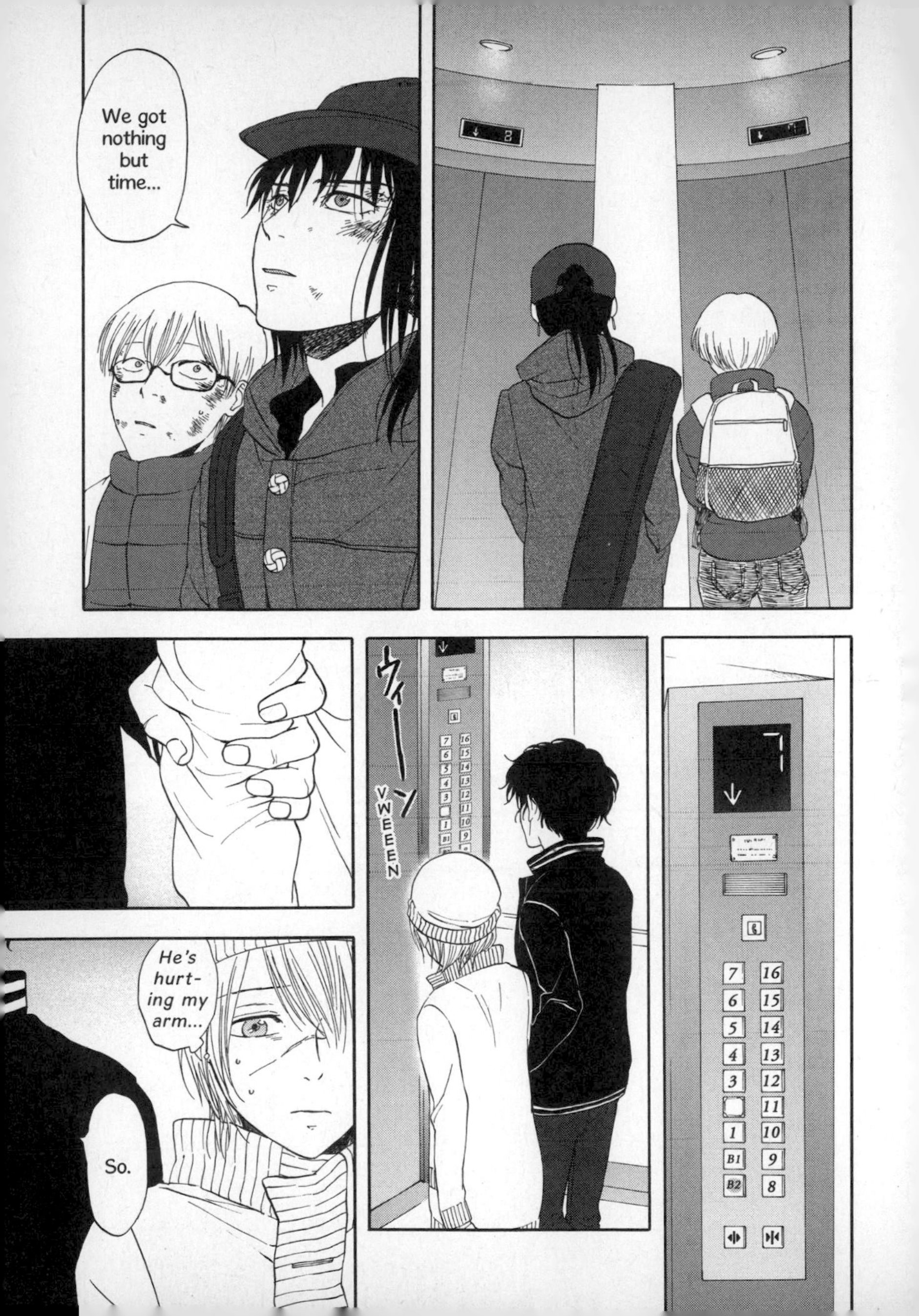
We got nothing but time...
VWEEEN
He's hurting my arm...
So.

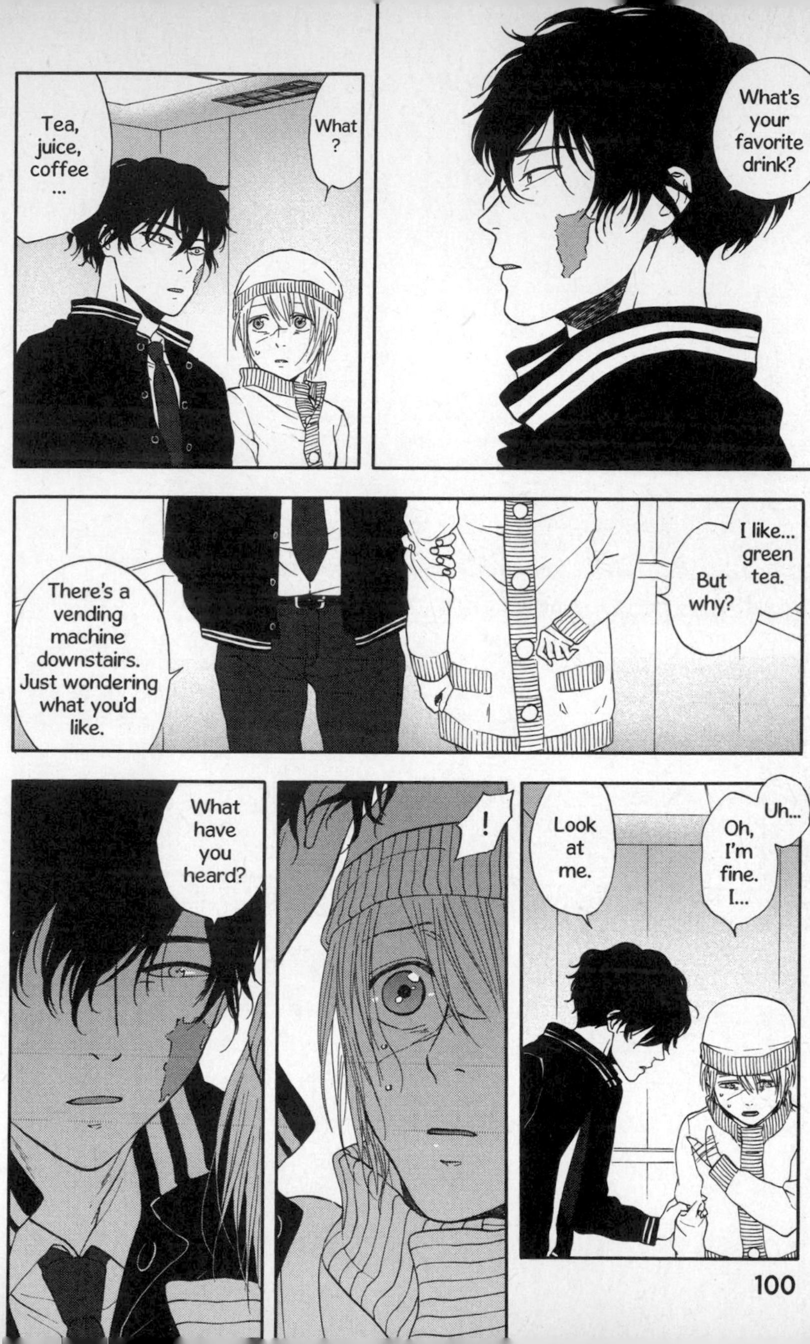
What's your favorite drink?
What ?
Tea, juice, coffee ...
I like... green tea.
But why?
There's a vending machine downstairs. Just wondering what you'd like.
Uh...
Oh, I'm fine. I...
Look at me.
!
What have you heard?

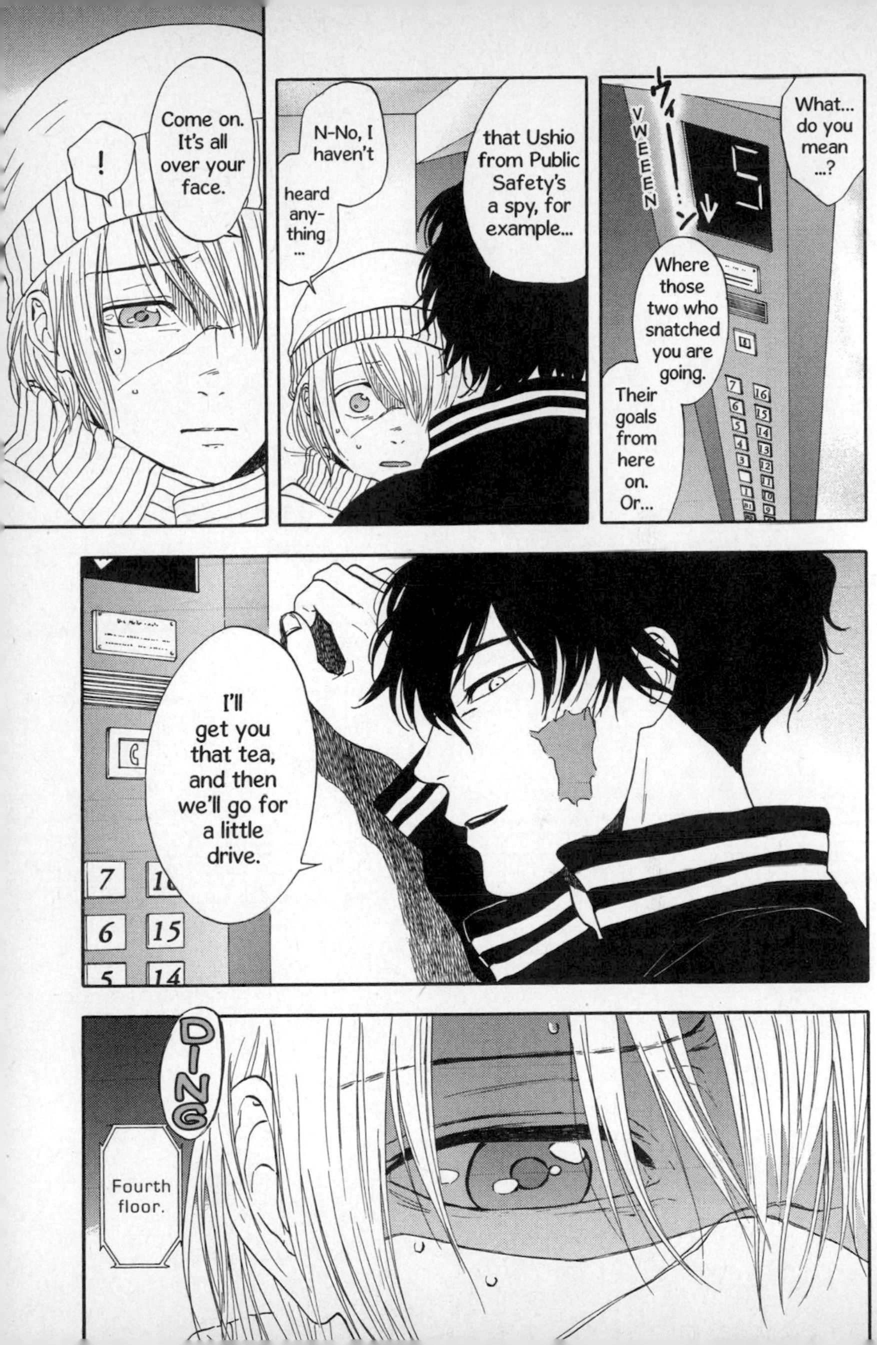
What... do you mean ...?
VWEEEN
Where those two who snatched you are going.
Their goals from here on. Or...
that Ushio from Public Safety's a spy, for example...
N-No, I haven't heard anything ...
Come on. It's all over your face.
!
I'll get you that tea, and then we'll go for a little drive.
DING
Fourth floor.

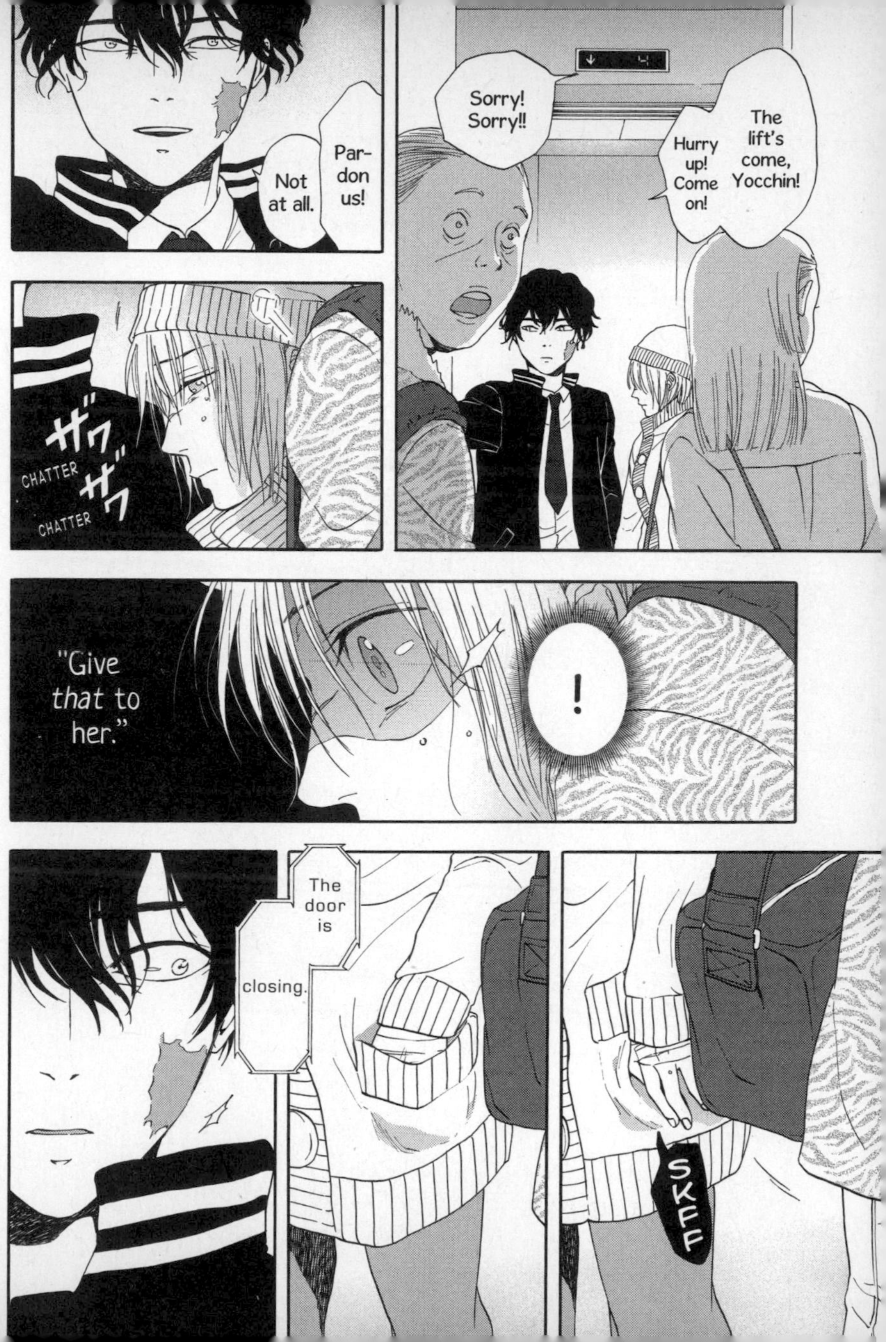
The lift's come, Yocchin!
Hurry up! Come on!
Sorry! Sorry!!
Pardon us!
Not at all.
CHATTER
CHATTER
!
"Give that to her."
SKFF
The door is closing.

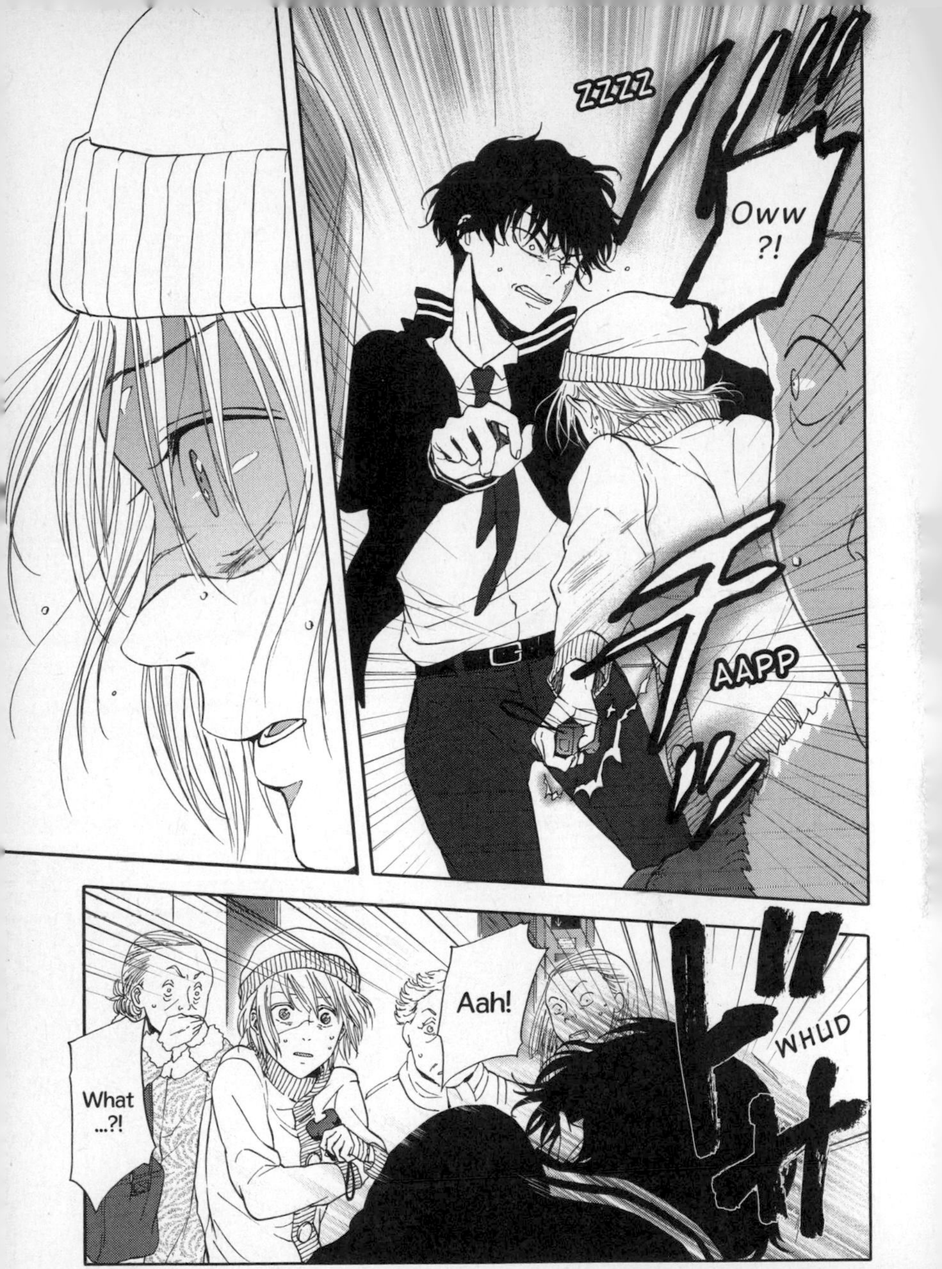
ZZZZ
Oww ?!
AAPP
WHUD
Aah!
What ...?!

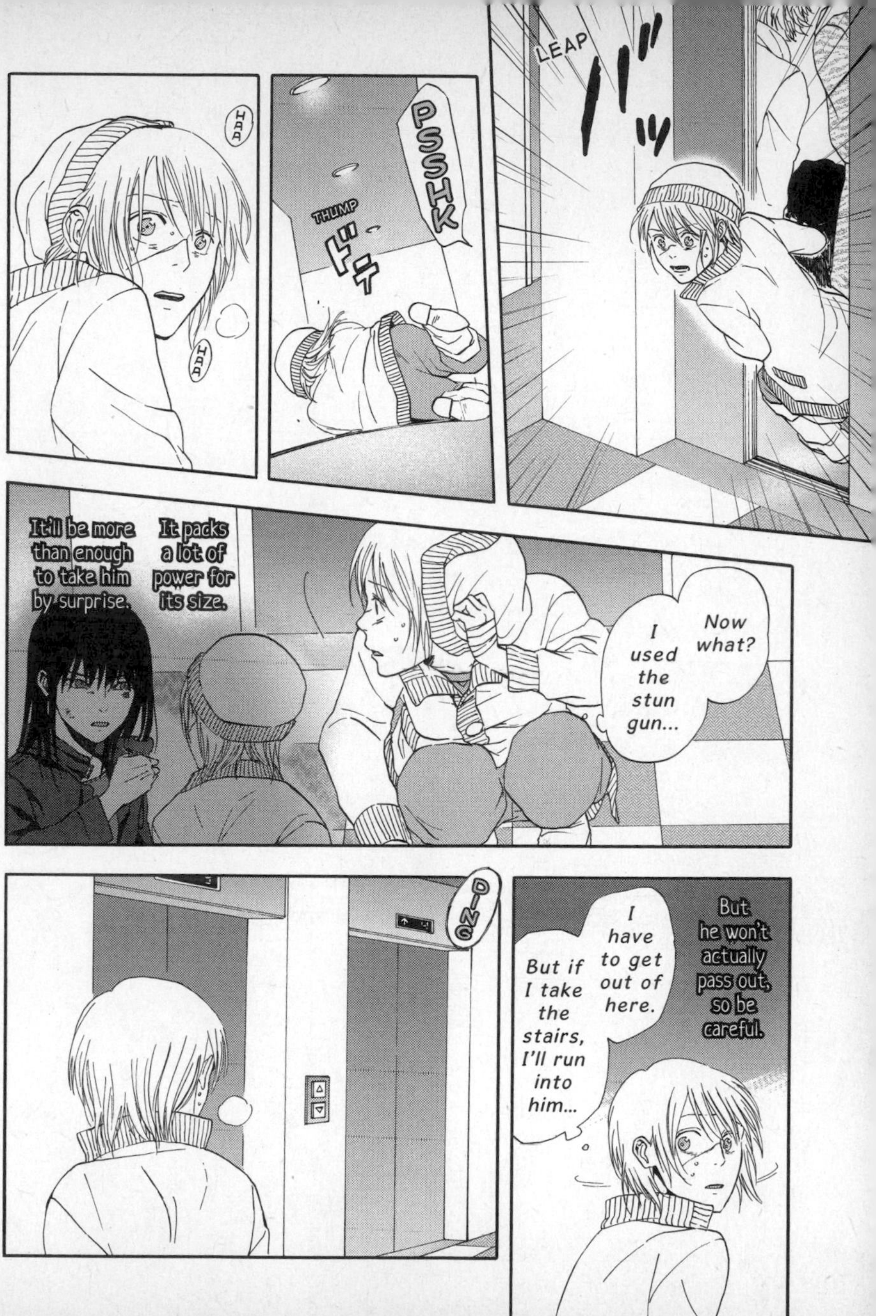
LEAP
PSSHK
THUMP
HAA
HAA
Now what?
I used the stun gun...
It packs a lot of power for its size.
It'll be more than enough to take him by surprise.
But he won't actually pass out, so be careful.
I have to get out of here.
But if I take the stairs, I'll run into him...
DING

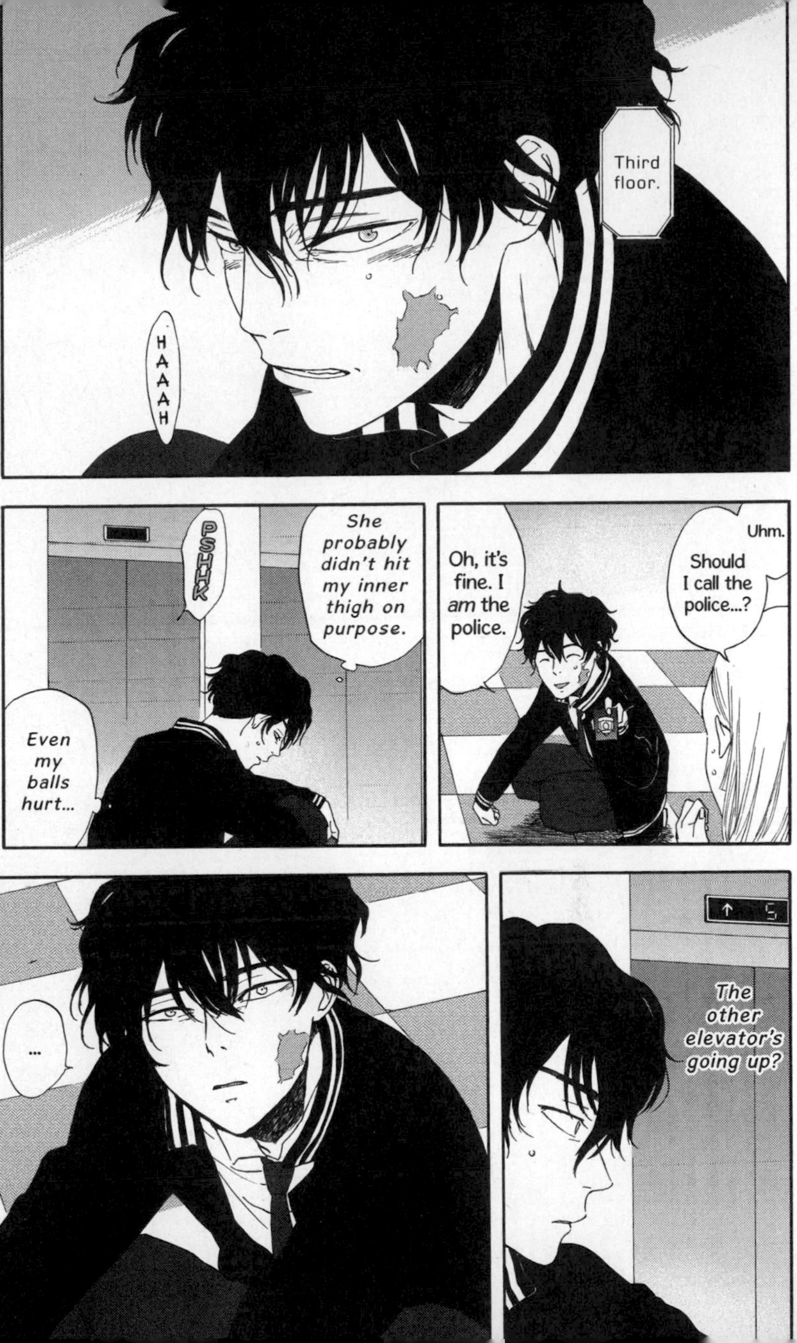
Third floor.
HAAAH
Uhm.
Should I call the police...?
Oh, it's fine. I *am* the police.
She probably didn't hit my inner thigh on purpose.
PSHHK
Even my balls hurt...
The other elevator's going up?
...

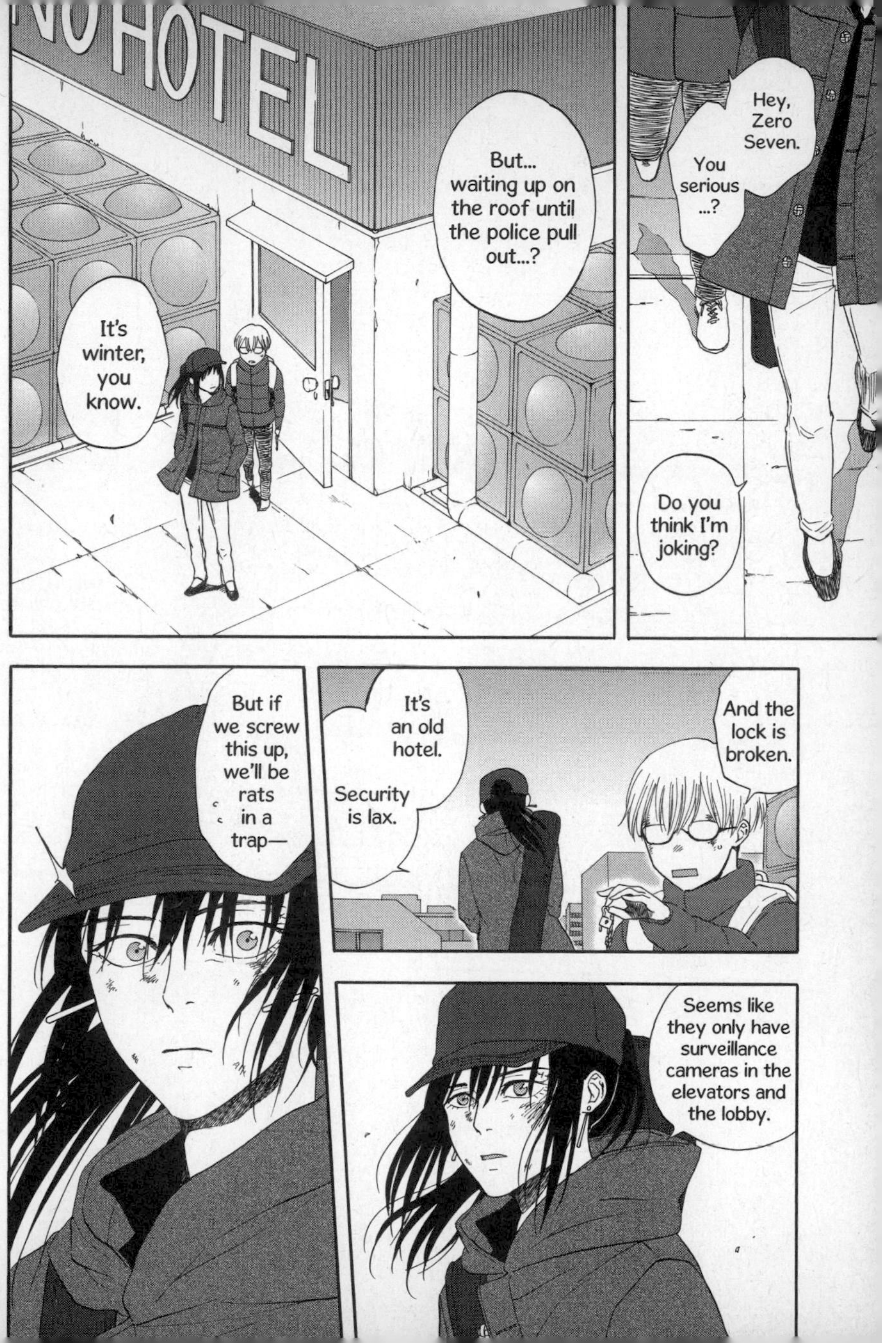
Hey, Zero Seven.
You serious ...?
Do you think I'm joking?
HOTEL
But... waiting up on the roof until the police pull out...?
It's winter, you know.
And the lock is broken.
It's an old hotel.
Security is lax.
Seems like they only have surveillance cameras in the elevators and the lobby.
But if we screw this up, we'll be rats in a trap—

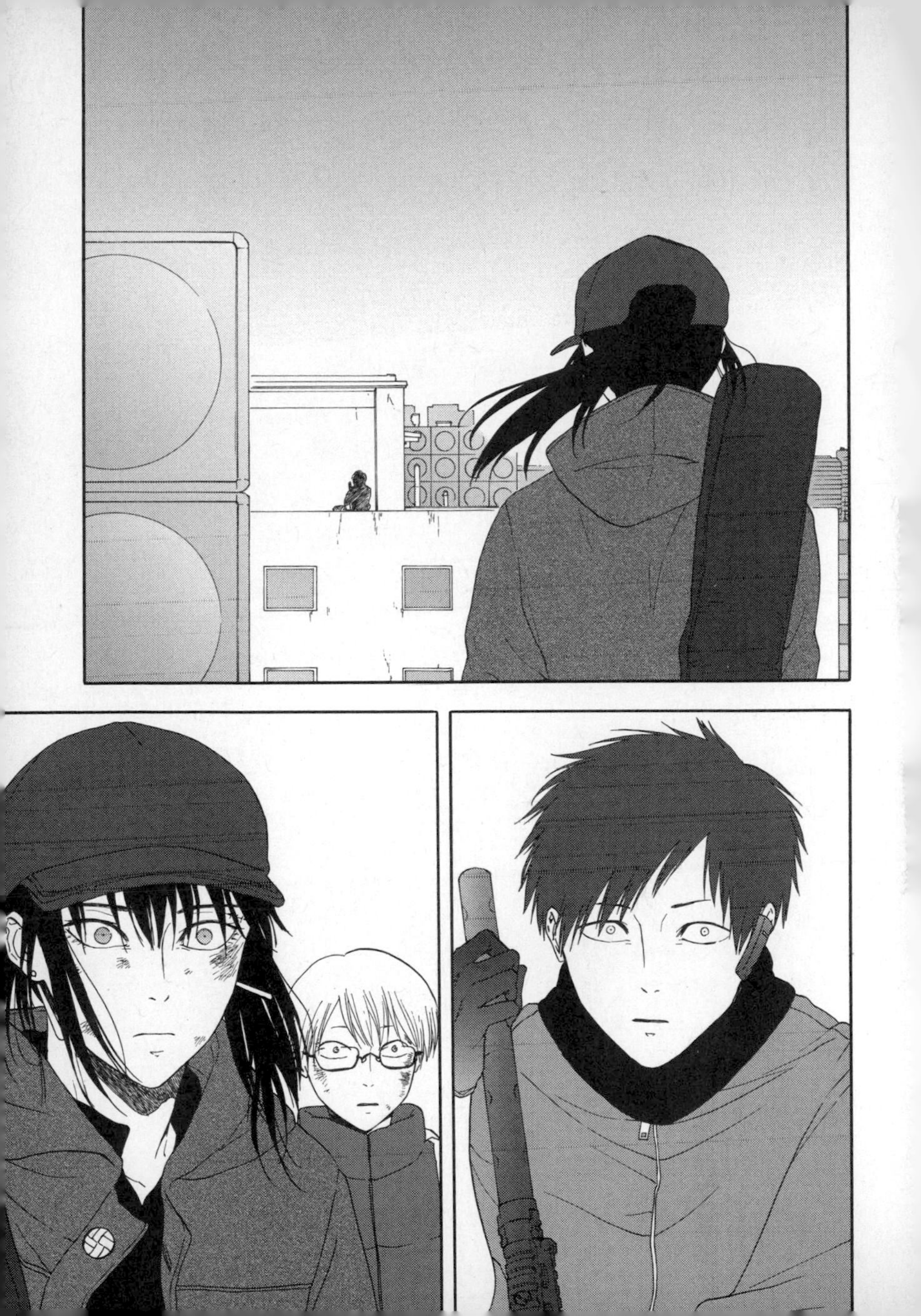

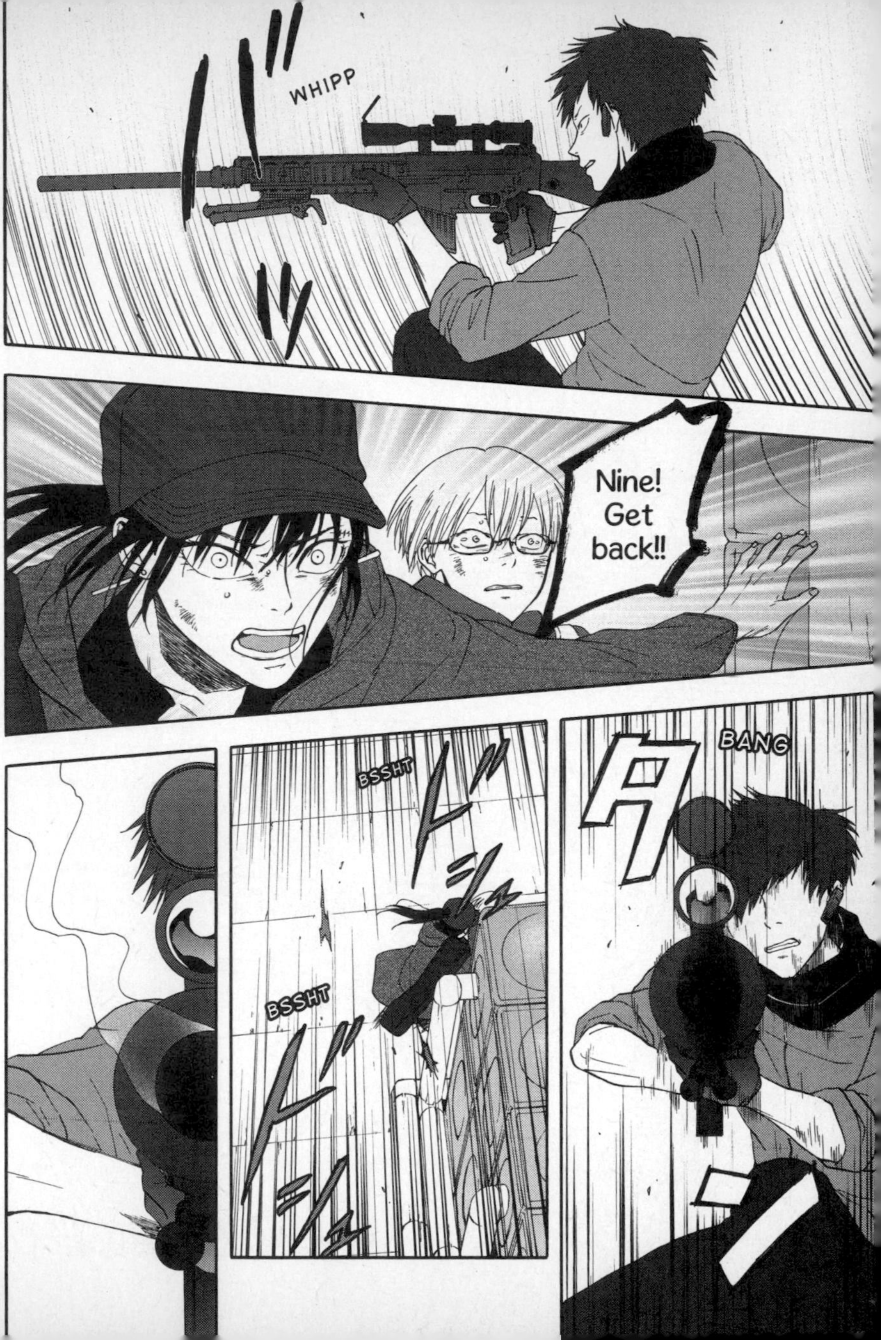
WHIPP
Nine! Get back!!
BANG
BSSHT
BSSHT

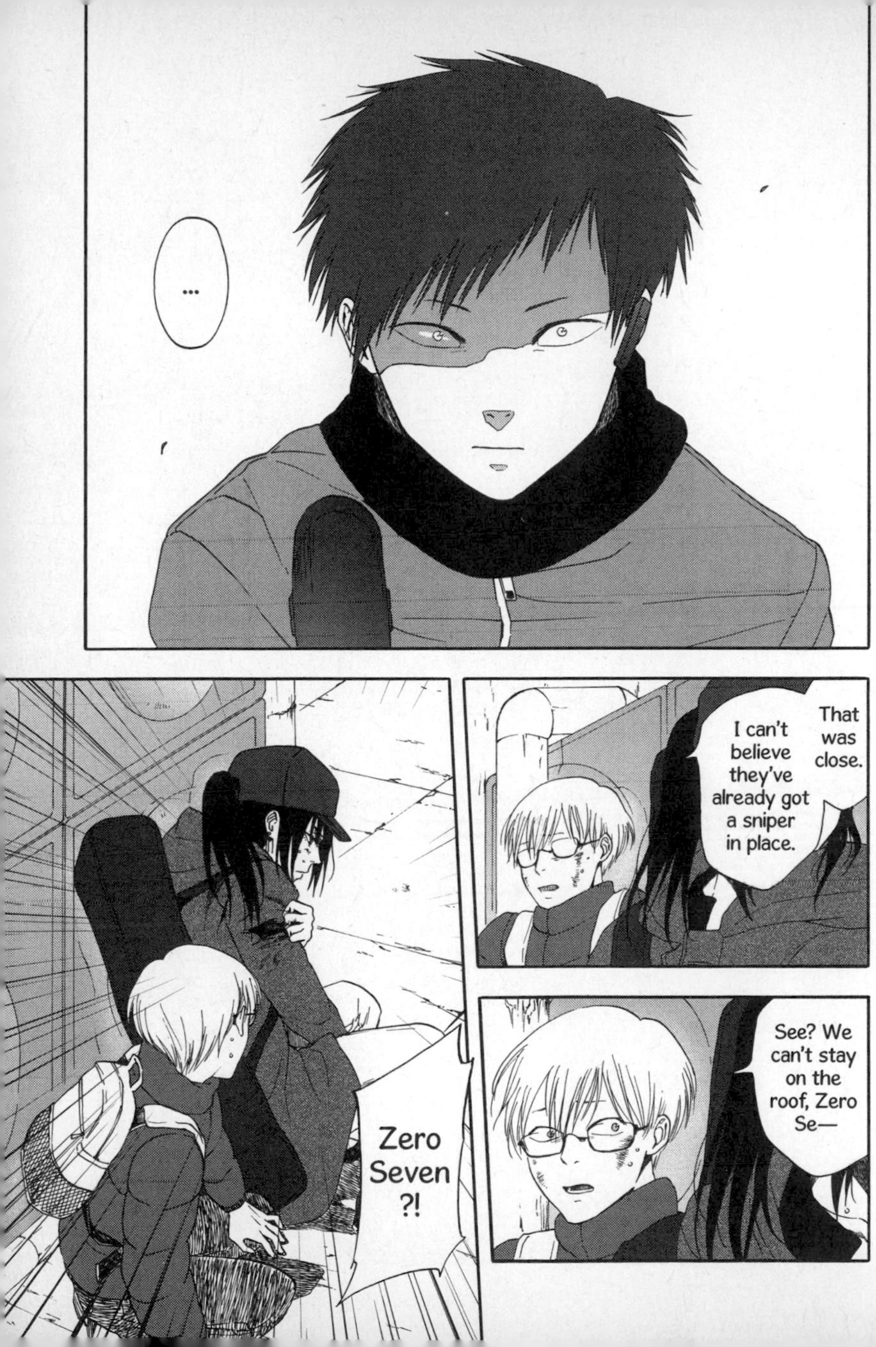
...
That was close.
I can't believe they've already got a sniper in place.
See? We can't stay on the roof, Zero Se—
Zero Seven ?!

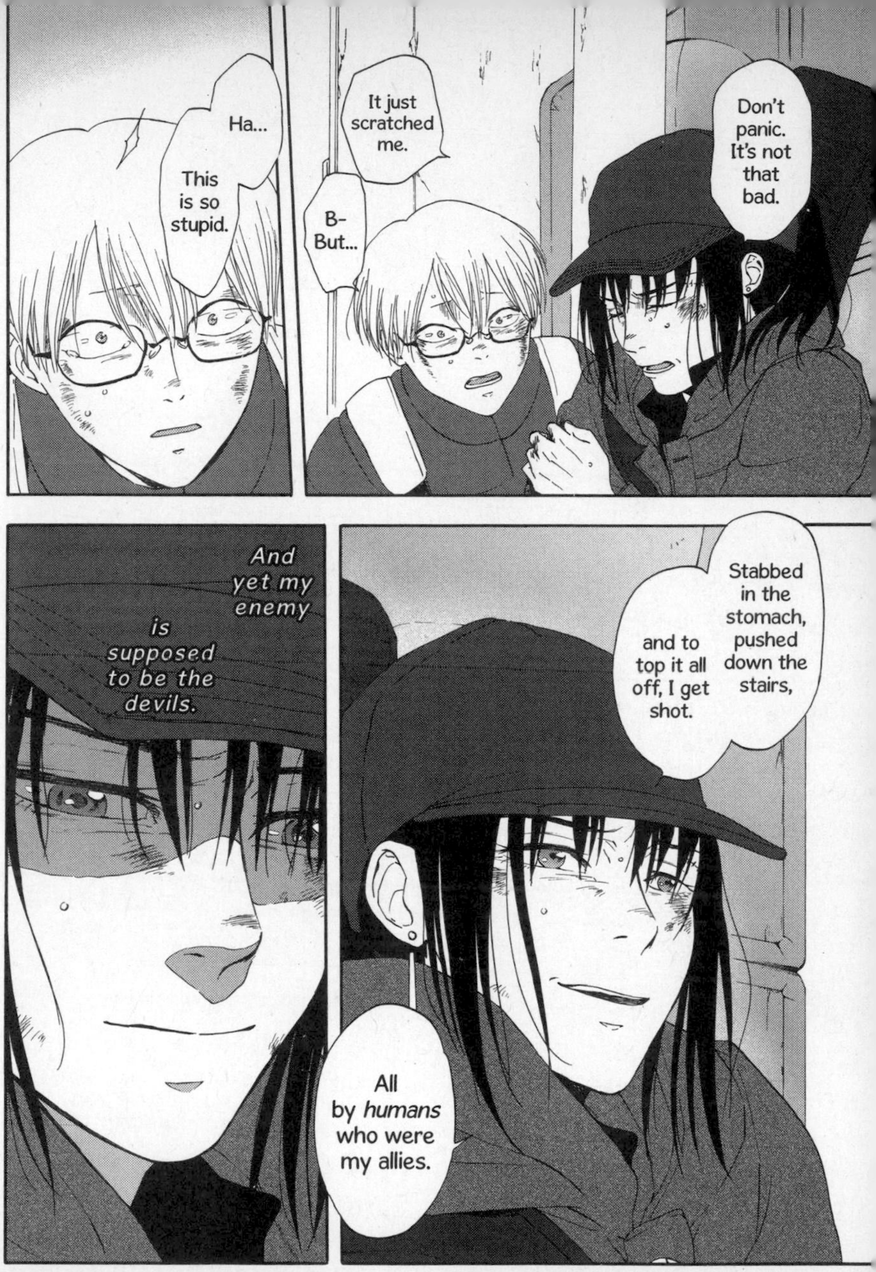
Don't panic. It's not that bad.
It just scratched me.
B- But...
Ha...
This is so stupid.
Stabbed in the stomach, pushed down the stairs,
and to top it all off, I get shot.
All by *humans* who were my allies.
And yet my enemy is supposed to be the devils.

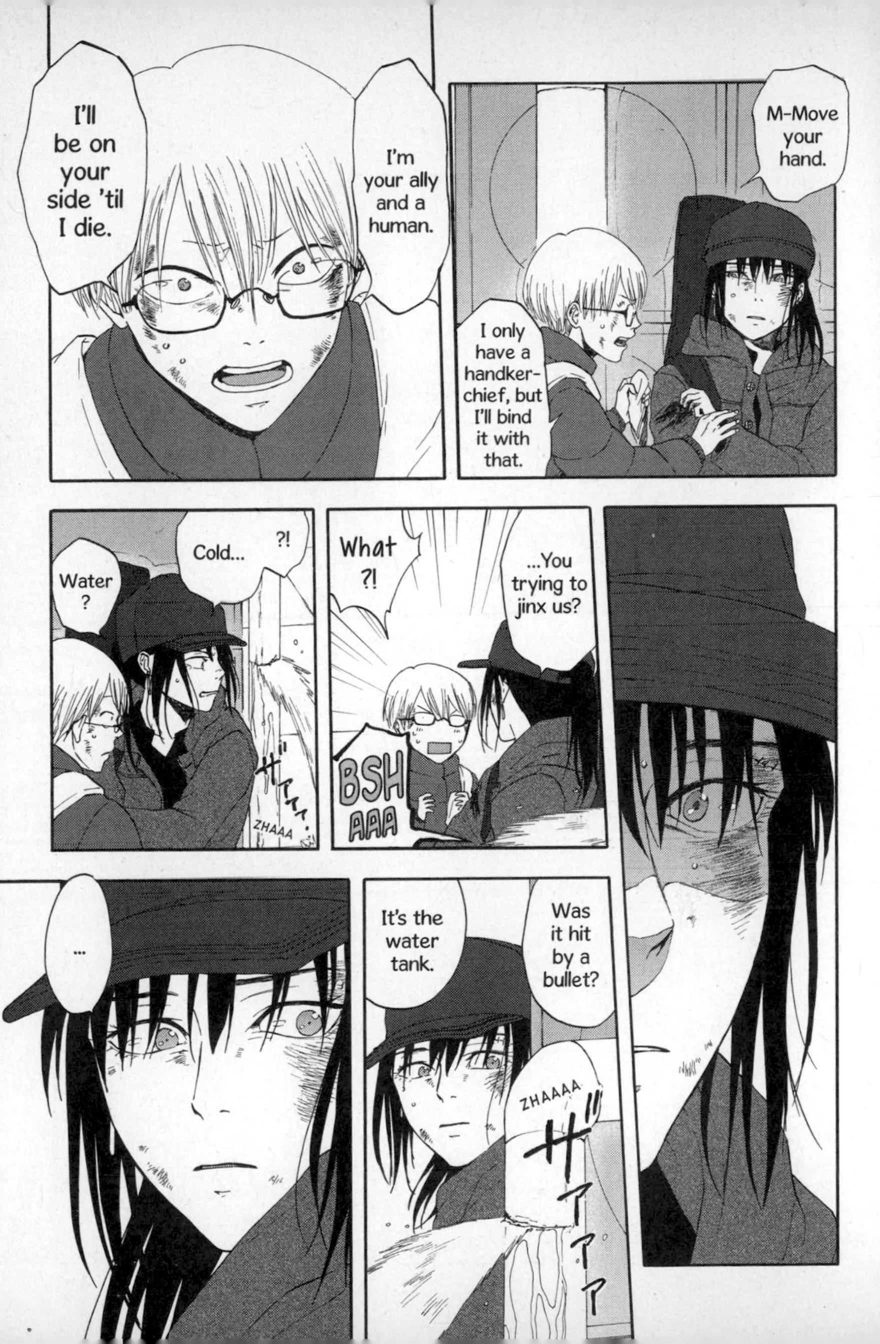
M-Move your hand.
I only have a handkerchief, but I'll bind it with that.
I'm your ally and a human.
I'll be on your side 'til I die.
...You trying to jinx us?
What ?!
BSH AAA
?!
Cold...
Water ?
ZHAAA
Was it hit by a bullet?
It's the water tank.
ZHAAAA
...

What am I doing...

SLUMP

I don't know Anzai's number.

Or Sakaki's...

Sakaki...?

I don't know Sawazaki's either.

Or Jill's, or Yanagi's.

VWEEEEN

HAA

HAA

BAR SAKAKI

CLOSED

HAA

HAA

13:27

Bar Sakaki B

| Bunkyo Ward | Brunch | Book |
| Post | Brilliant | Before |

In

QWERT...
ASDFNGHJK
ZXCVBL
123 M P Space Return

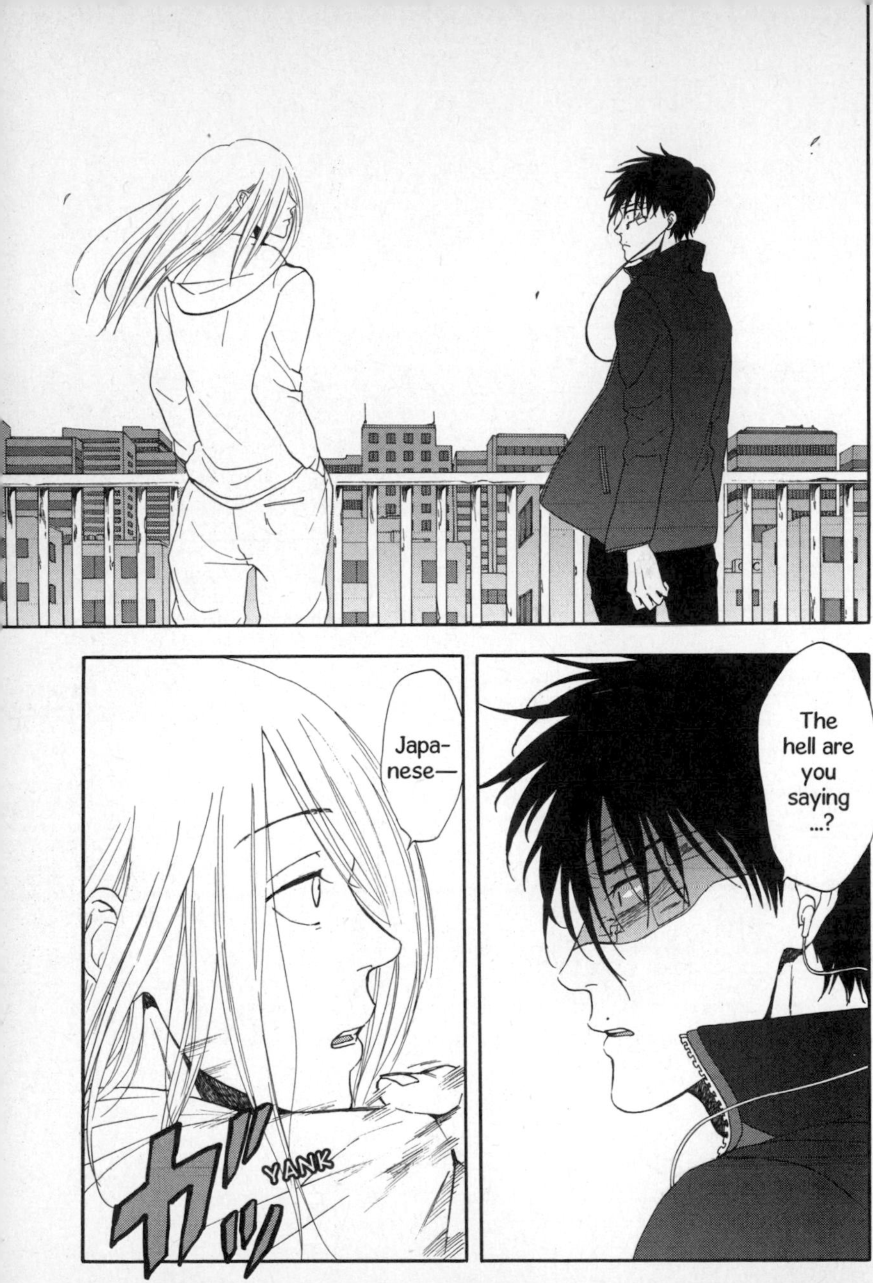
The hell are you saying ...?
Japa-nese—
YANK

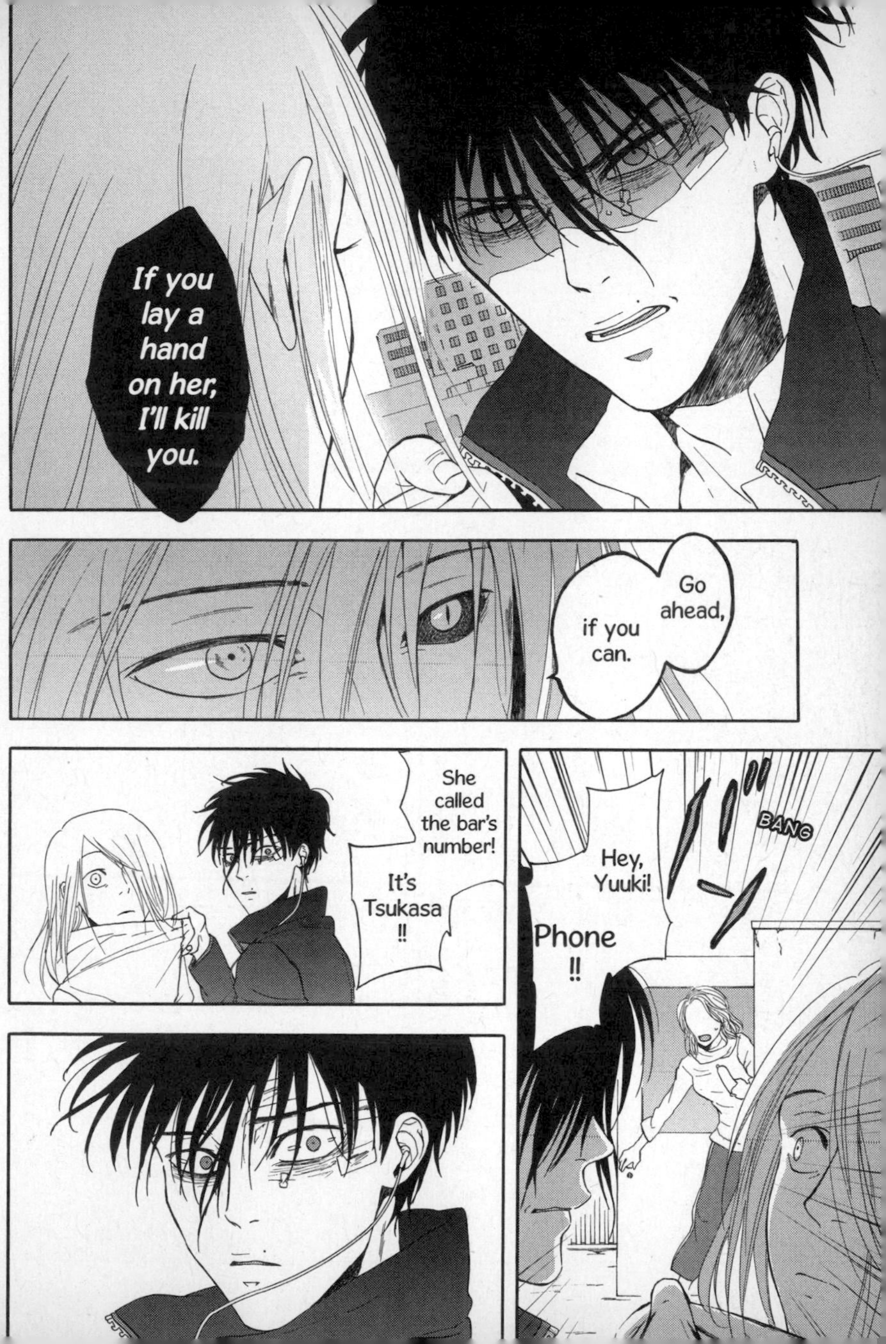
If you lay a hand on her, I'll kill you.
Go ahead, if you can.
BANG
Hey, Yuuki!
Phone !!
She called the bar's number!
It's Tsukasa !!

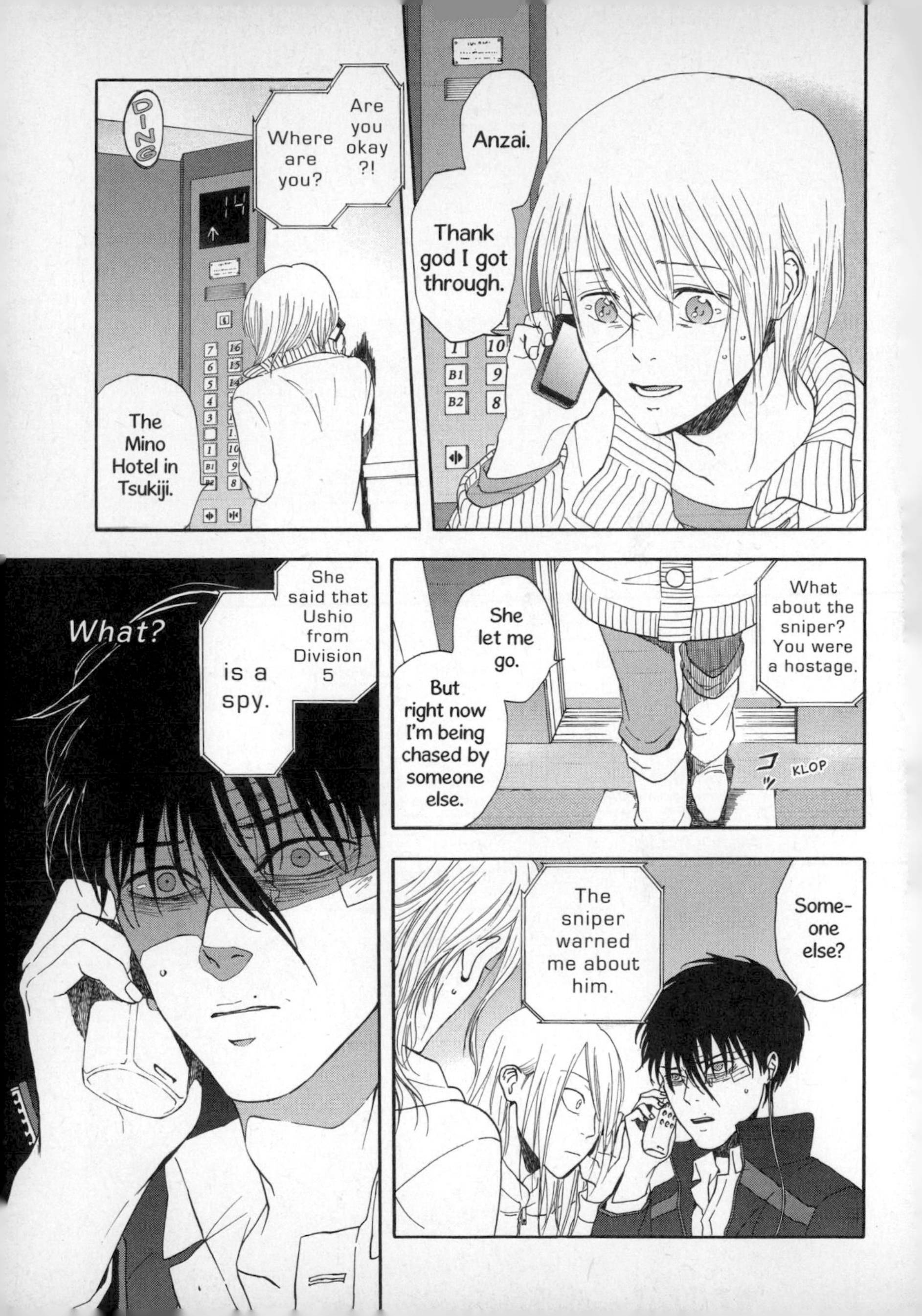
Anzai.
Thank god I got through.
Are you okay ?! Where are you?
DING
The Mino Hotel in Tsukiji.
What about the sniper? You were a hostage.
She let me go.
But right now I'm being chased by someone else.
KLOP
Some-one else?
The sniper warned me about him.
What?
She said that Ushio from Division 5 is a spy.

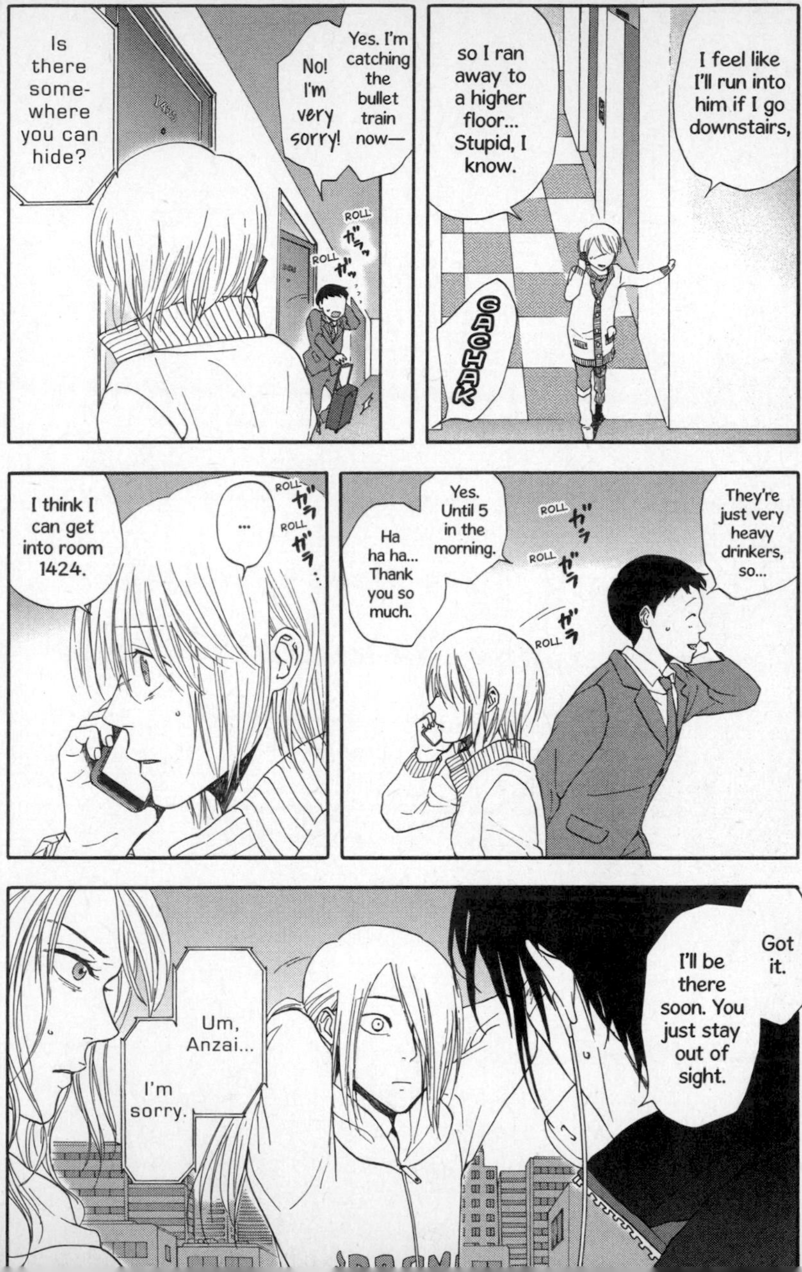
I feel like I'll run into him if I go downstairs,
so I ran away to a higher floor... Stupid, I know.
GACHAK
Yes. I'm catching the bullet train now—
No! I'm very sorry!
ROLL
ROLL
Is there somewhere you can hide?
They're just very heavy drinkers, so...
ROLL
ROLL
ROLL
Yes. Until 5 in the morning.
Ha ha ha... Thank you so much.
ROLL
ROLL
...
I think I can get into room 1424.
Got it.
I'll be there soon. You just stay out of sight.
Um, Anzai...
I'm sorry.

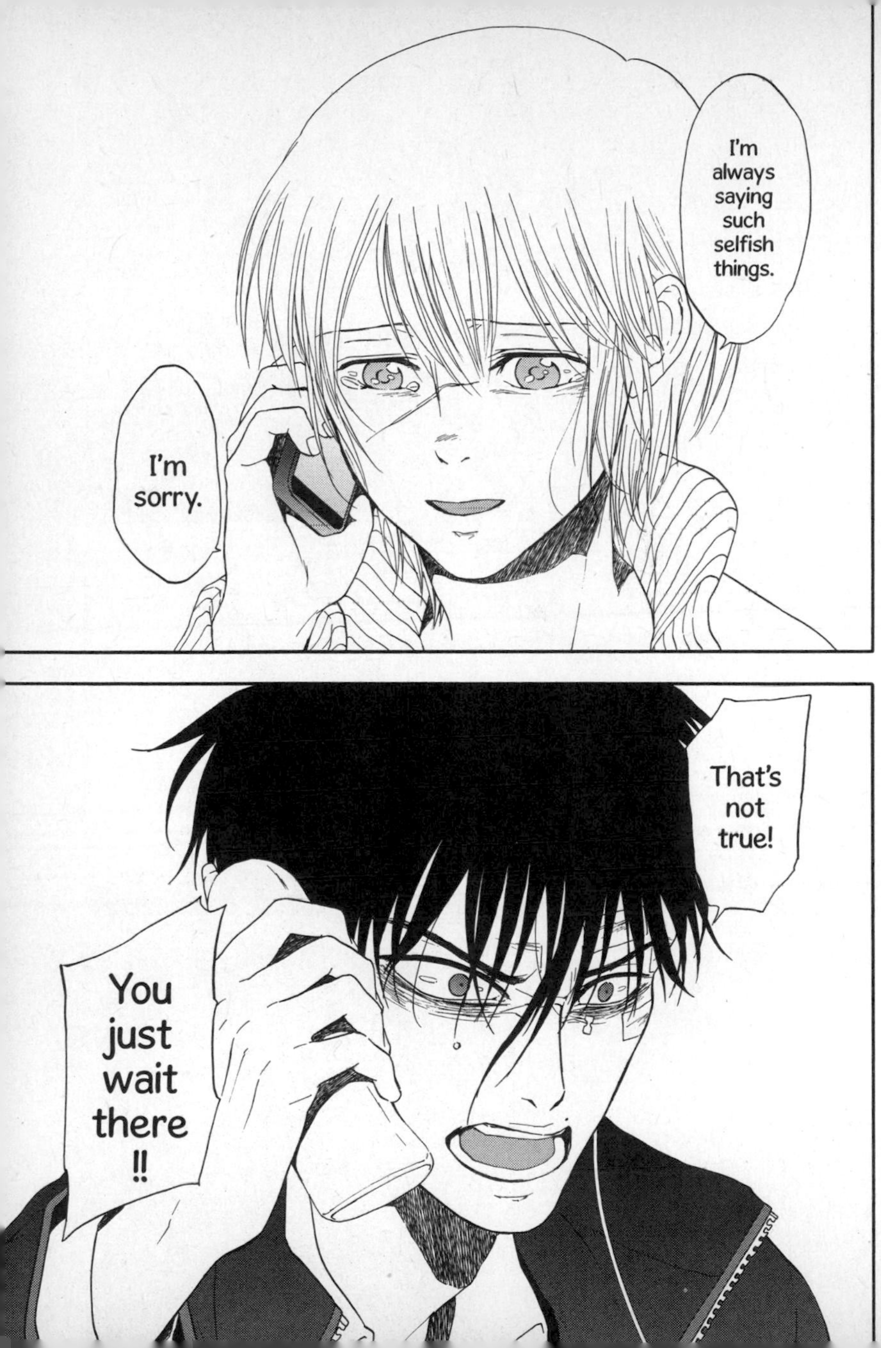
I'm always saying such selfish things.
I'm sorry.
That's not true!
You just wait there !!

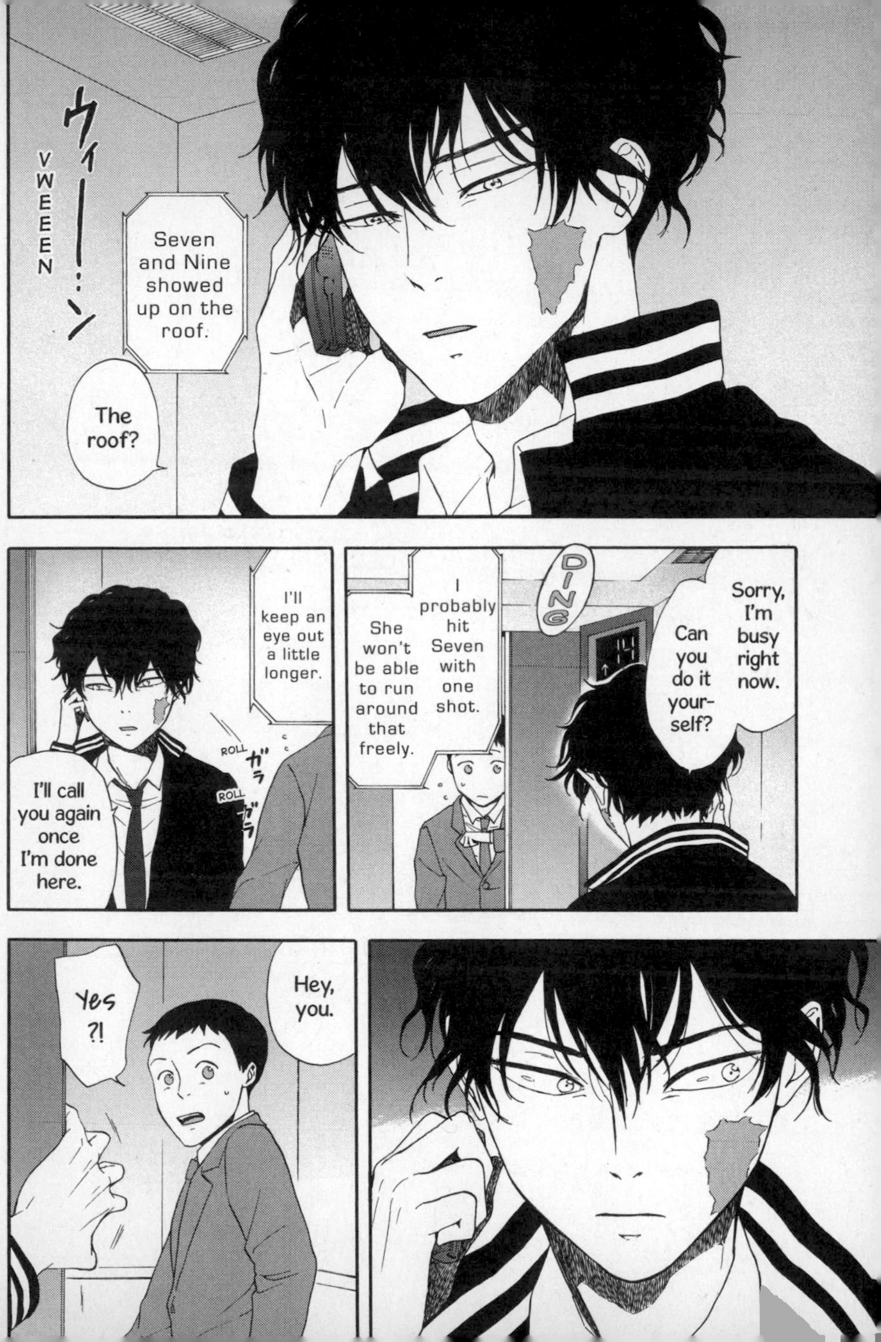
Seven and Nine showed up on the roof.
ウィーーン
VWEEEN
The roof?
DING
Sorry, I'm busy right now.
Can you do it yourself?
I probably hit Seven with one shot.
She won't be able to run around that freely.
I'll keep an eye out a little longer.
ROLL ガラ
ROLL ガラ
I'll call you again once I'm done here.
Hey, you.
Yes ?!

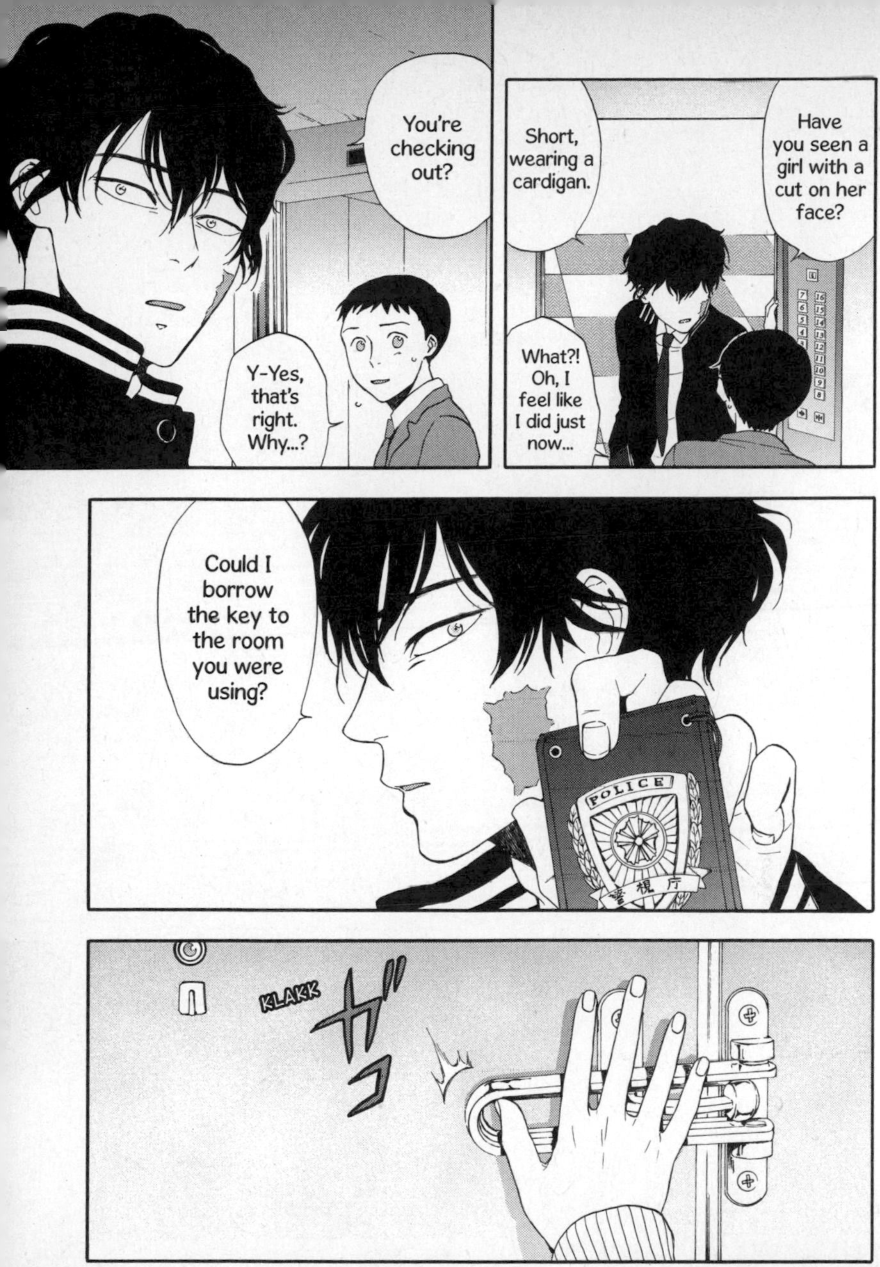
Have you seen a girl with a cut on her face?
Short, wearing a cardigan.
What?! Oh, I feel like I did just now...
You're checking out?
Y-Yes, that's right. Why...?
Could I borrow the key to the room you were using?
POLICE
警視庁
ガコ
KLAKK

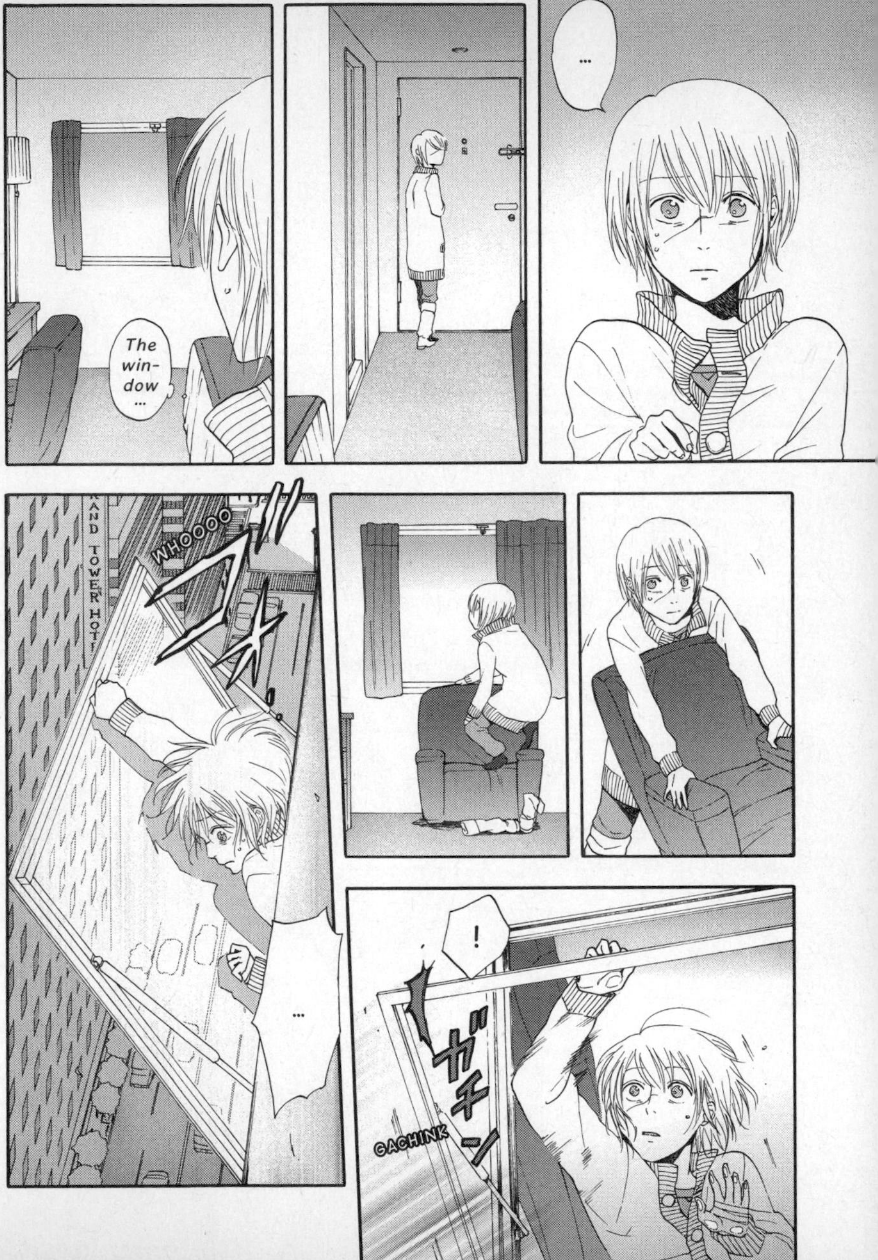
...
The win-
dow
...
!
ガチーン
GACHINK
ゴォ
WHOOOO
...

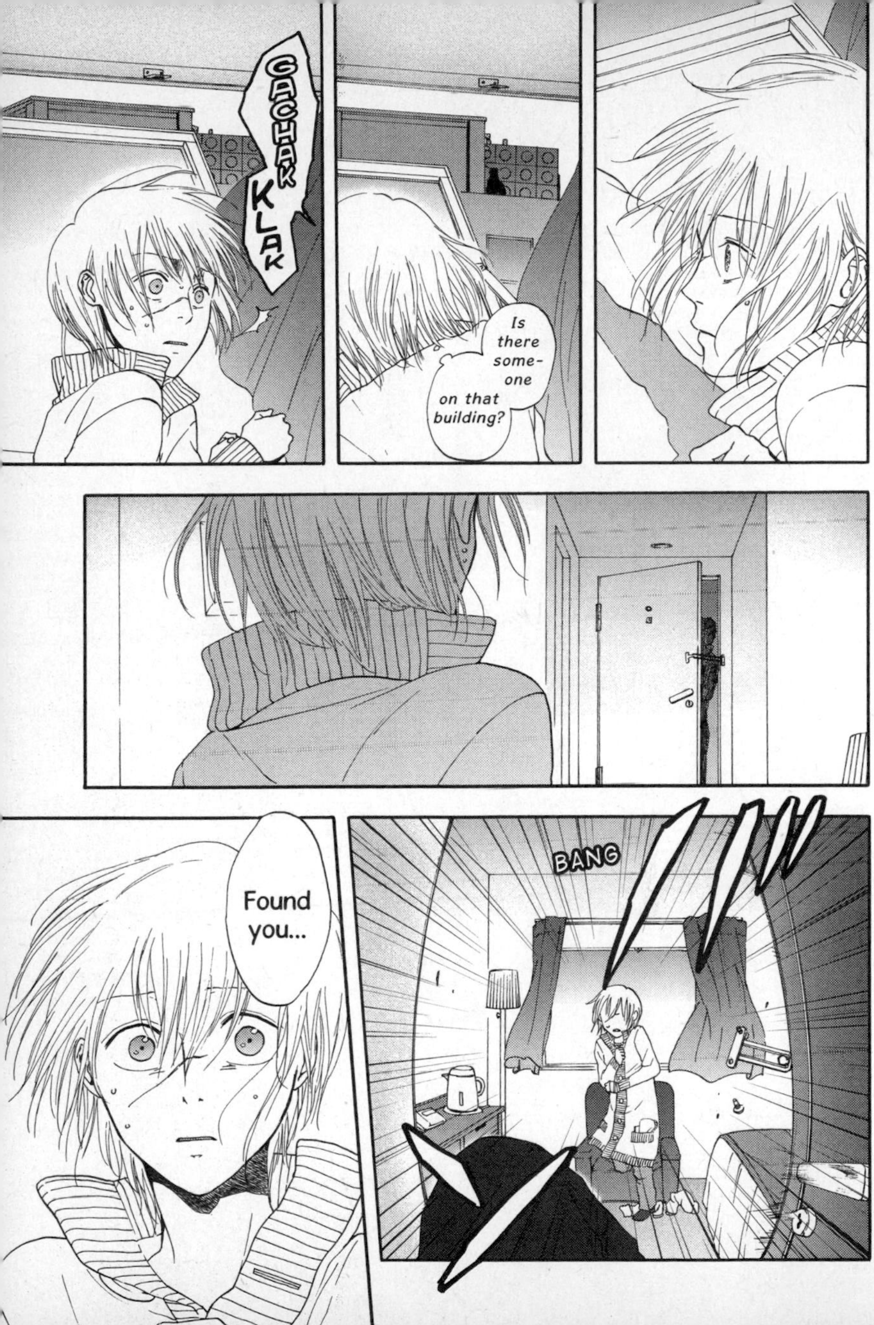
Is there some-one on that building?
GACHAK
KLAK
BANG
Found you...

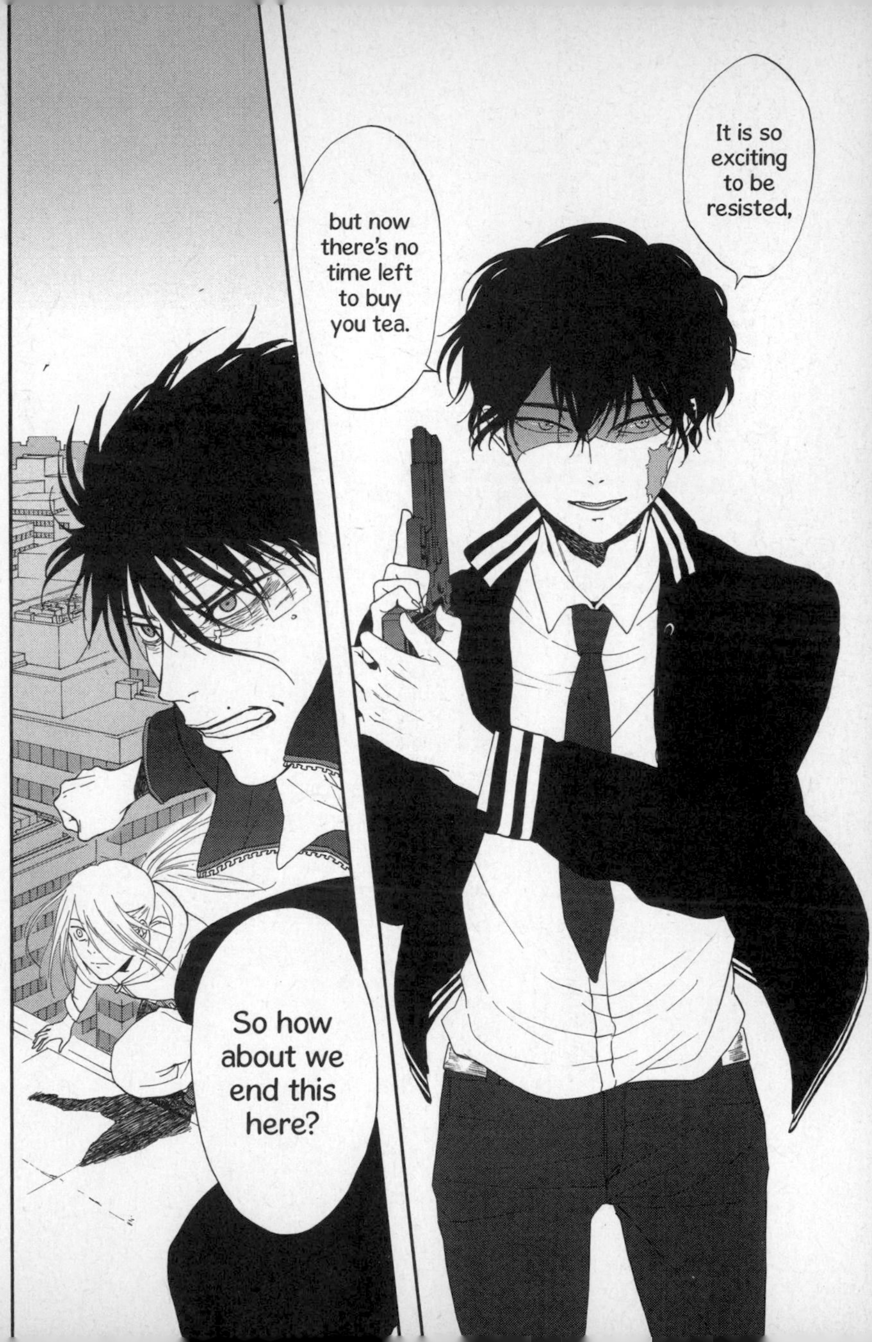
It is so exciting to be resisted,
but now there's no time left to buy you tea.
So how about we end this here?

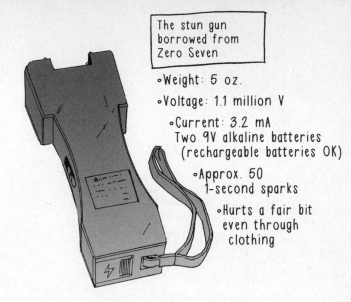

The stun gun
borrowed from
Zero Seven

○Weight: 5 oz.

○Voltage: 1.1 million V

○Current: 3.2 mA
Two 9V alkaline batteries
(rechargeable batteries OK)

○Approx. 50
1-second sparks

○Hurts a fair bit
even through
clothing

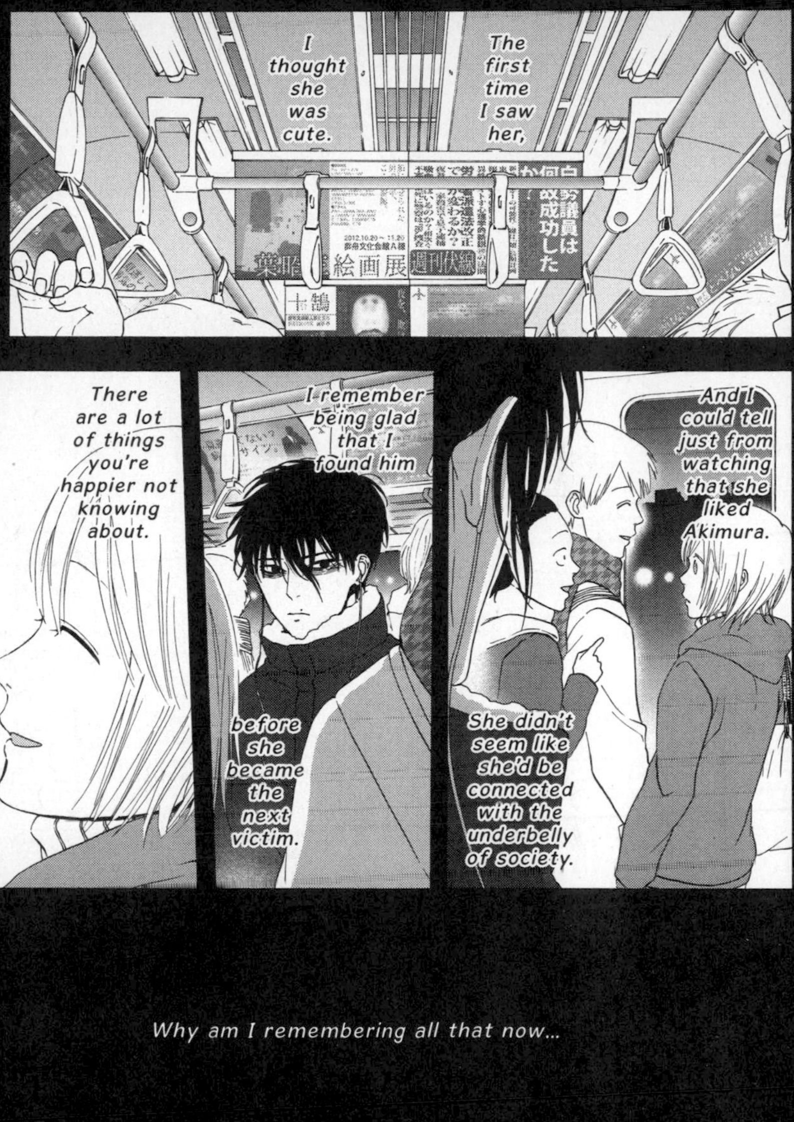
The first time I saw her,
I thought she was cute.
And I could tell just from watching that she liked Akimura.
She didn't seem like she'd be connected with the underbelly of society.
I remember being glad that I found him
before she became the next victim.
There are a lot of things you're happier not knowing about.
Why am I remembering all that now...

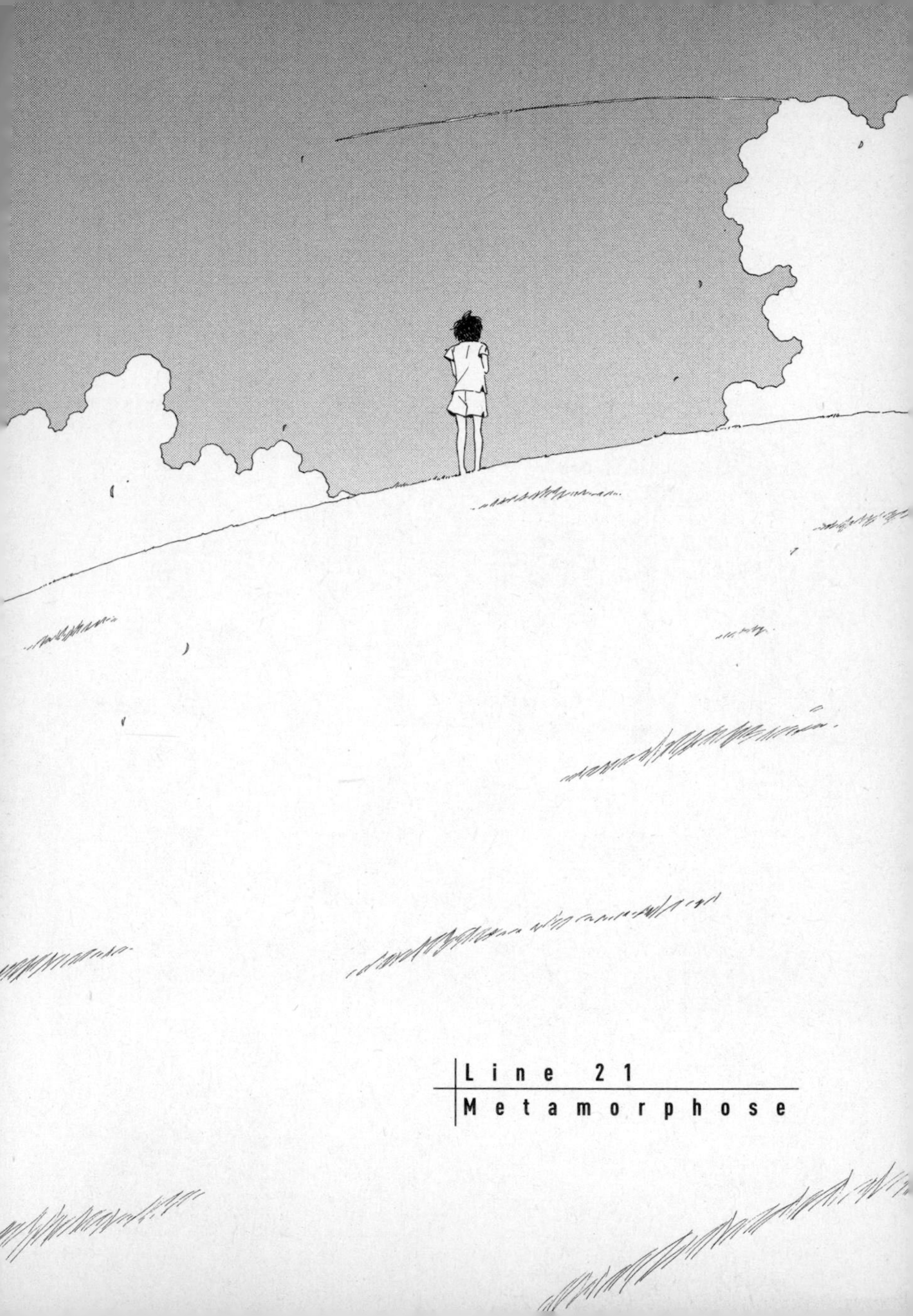
Line 21
Metamorphose

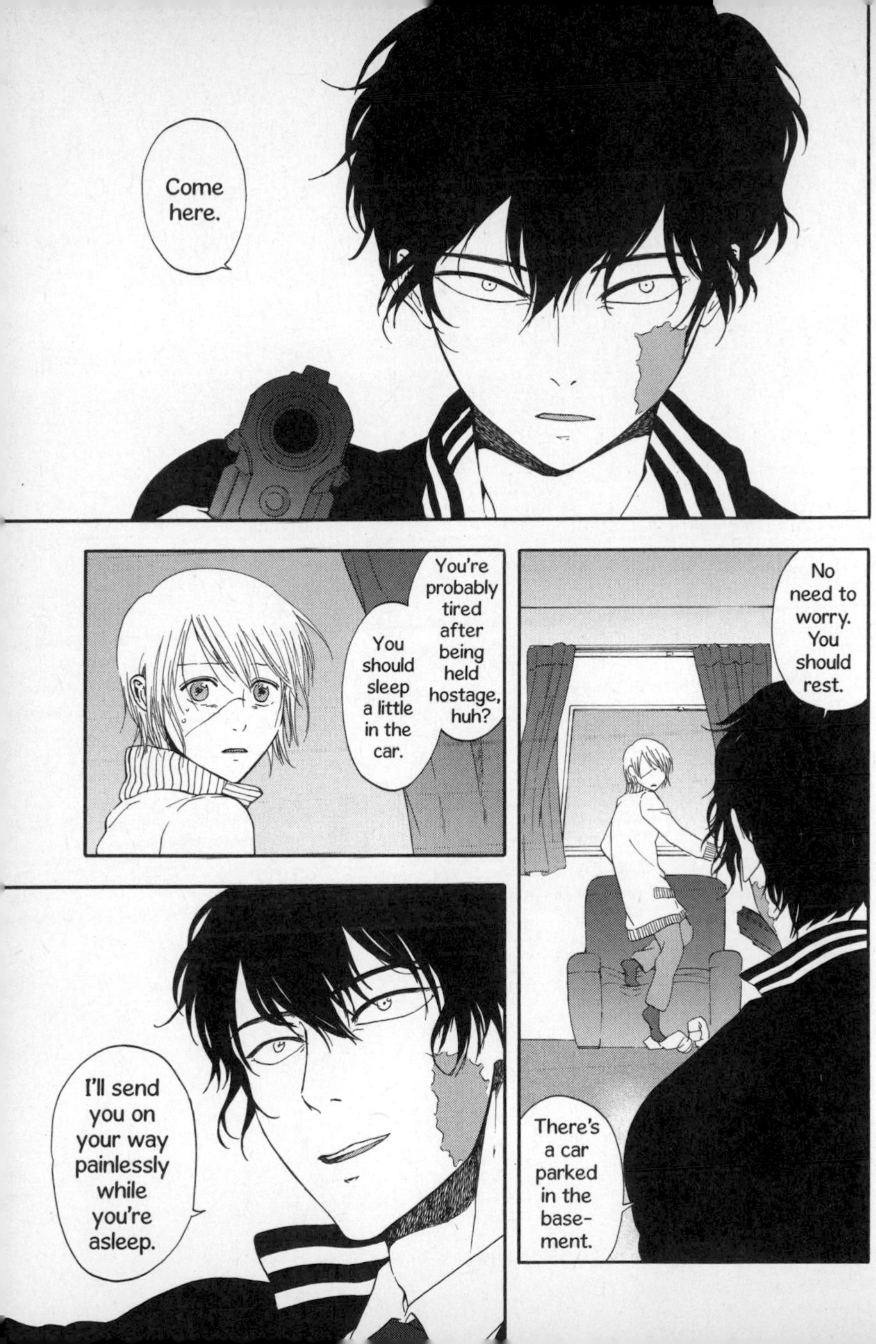
Come here.
No need to worry. You should rest.
There's a car parked in the base-ment.
You're probably tired after being held hostage, huh?
You should sleep a little in the car.
I'll send you on your way painlessly while you're asleep.

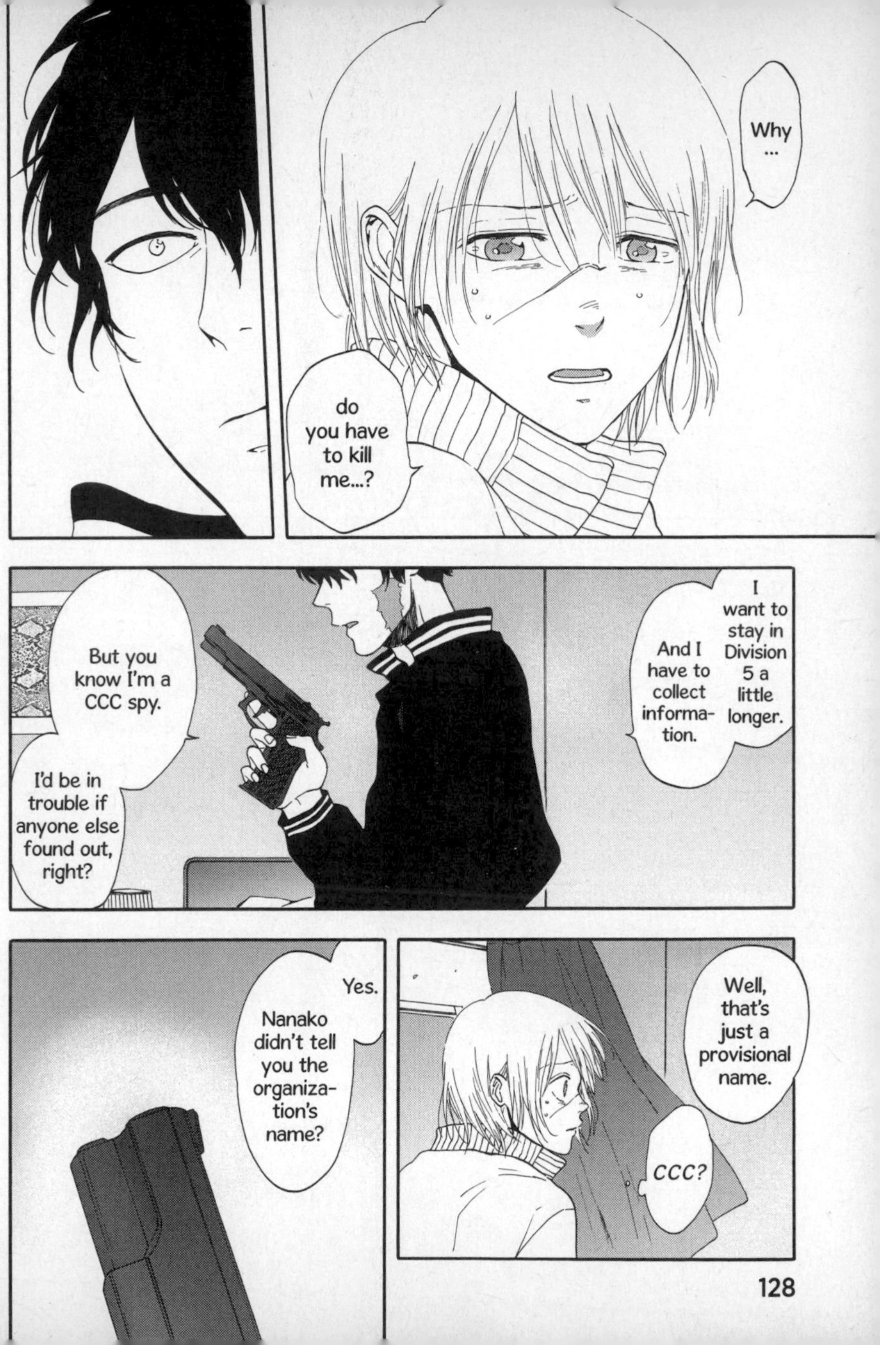
Why ...
do you have to kill me...?
I want to stay in Division 5 a little longer.
And I have to collect information.
But you know I'm a CCC spy.
I'd be in trouble if anyone else found out, right?
Well, that's just a provisional name.
CCC?
Yes.
Nanako didn't tell you the organization's name?

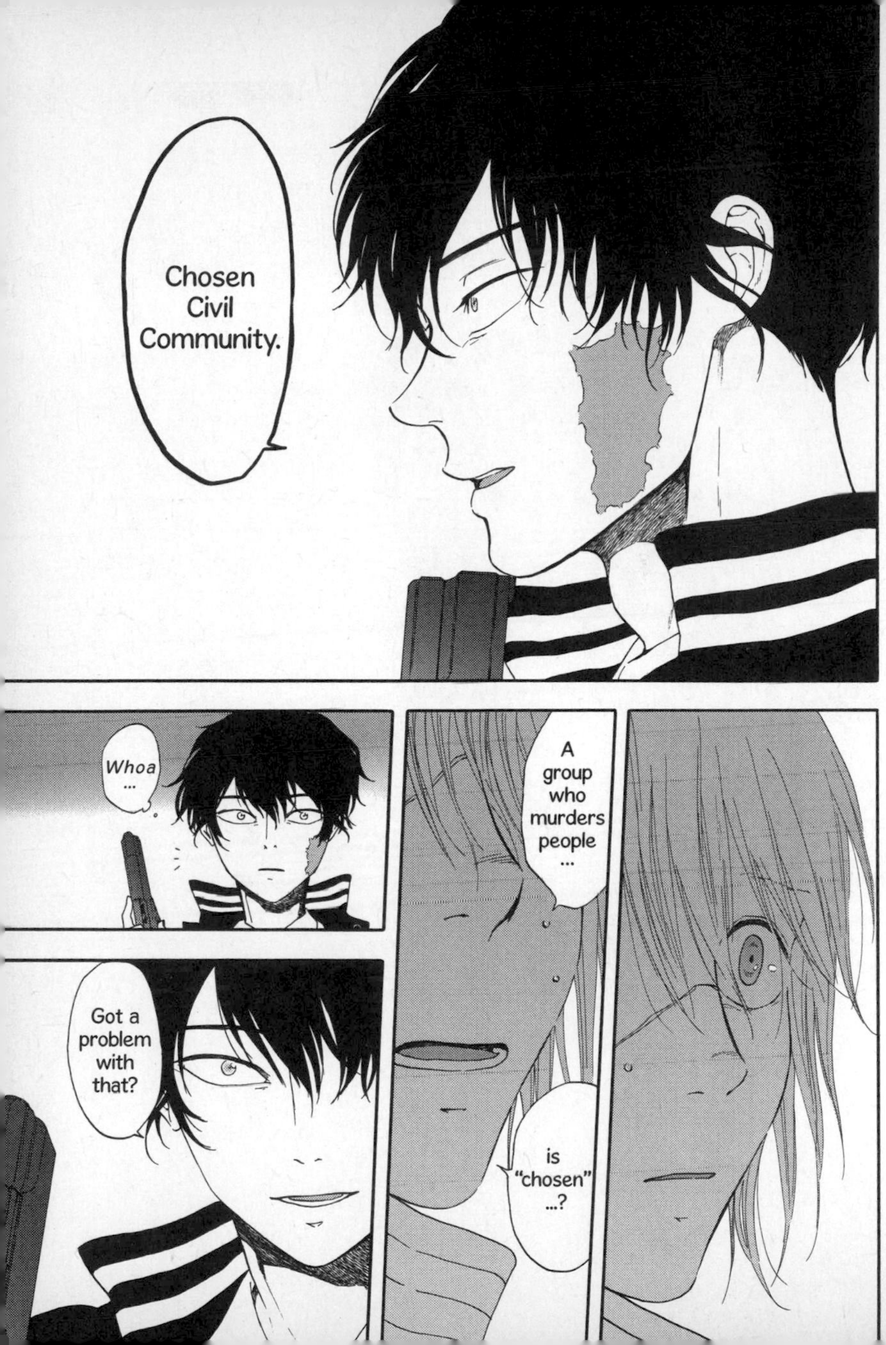
Chosen Civil Community.
A group who murders people ...
is "chosen" ...?
Whoa ...
Got a problem with that?

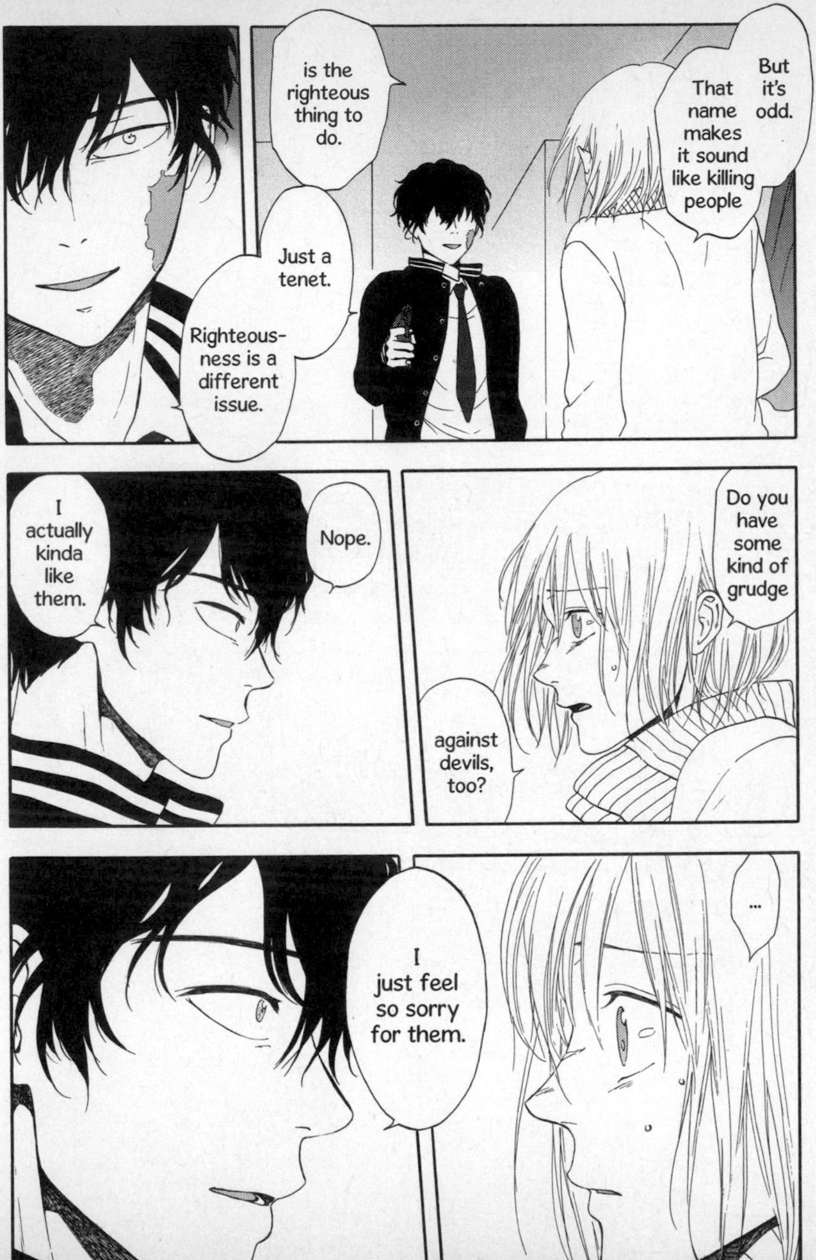
But it's odd.
That name makes it sound like killing people
is the righteous thing to do.
Just a tenet.
Righteousness is a different issue.
Do you have some kind of grudge
against devils, too?
Nope.
I actually kinda like them.
...
I just feel so sorry for them.

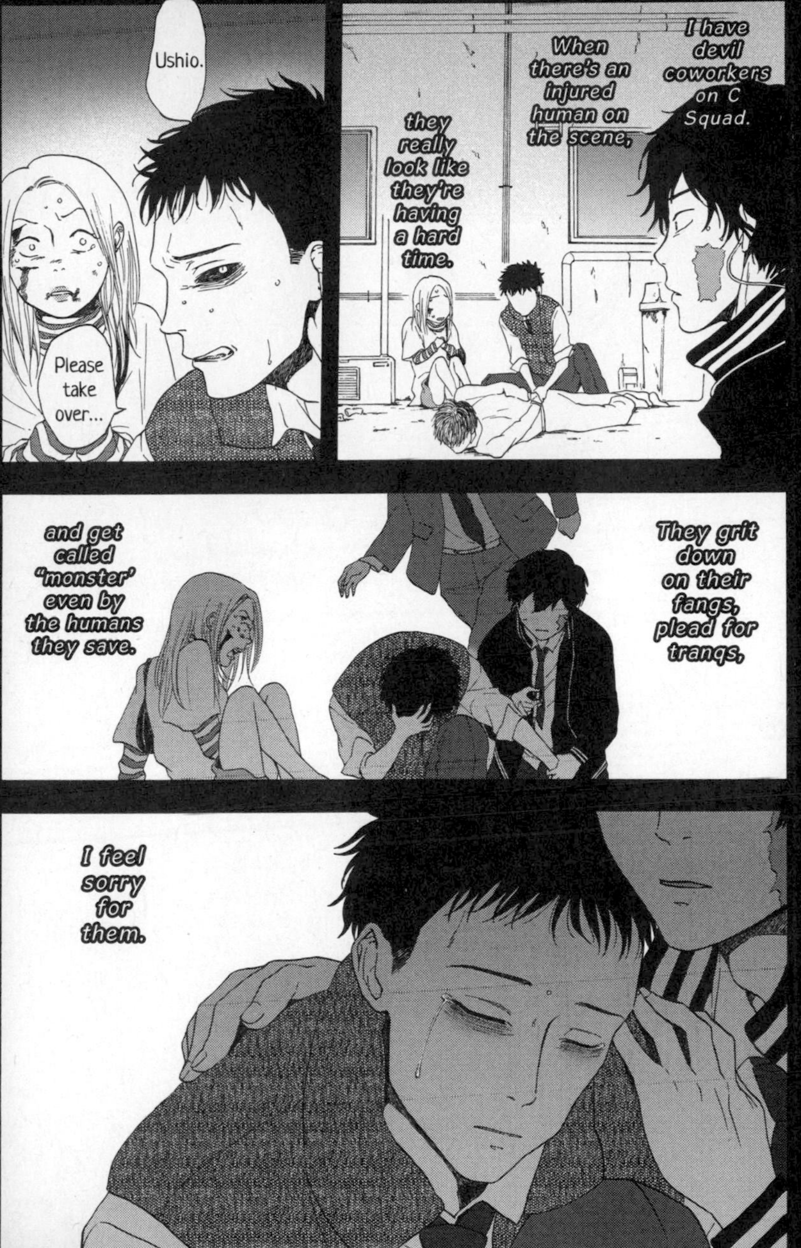
I have devil coworkers on C Squad.
When there's an injured human on the scene,
they really look like they're having a hard time.
Ushio.
Please take over...
They grit down on their fangs, plead for tranqs,
and get called "monster" even by the humans they save.
I feel sorry for them.

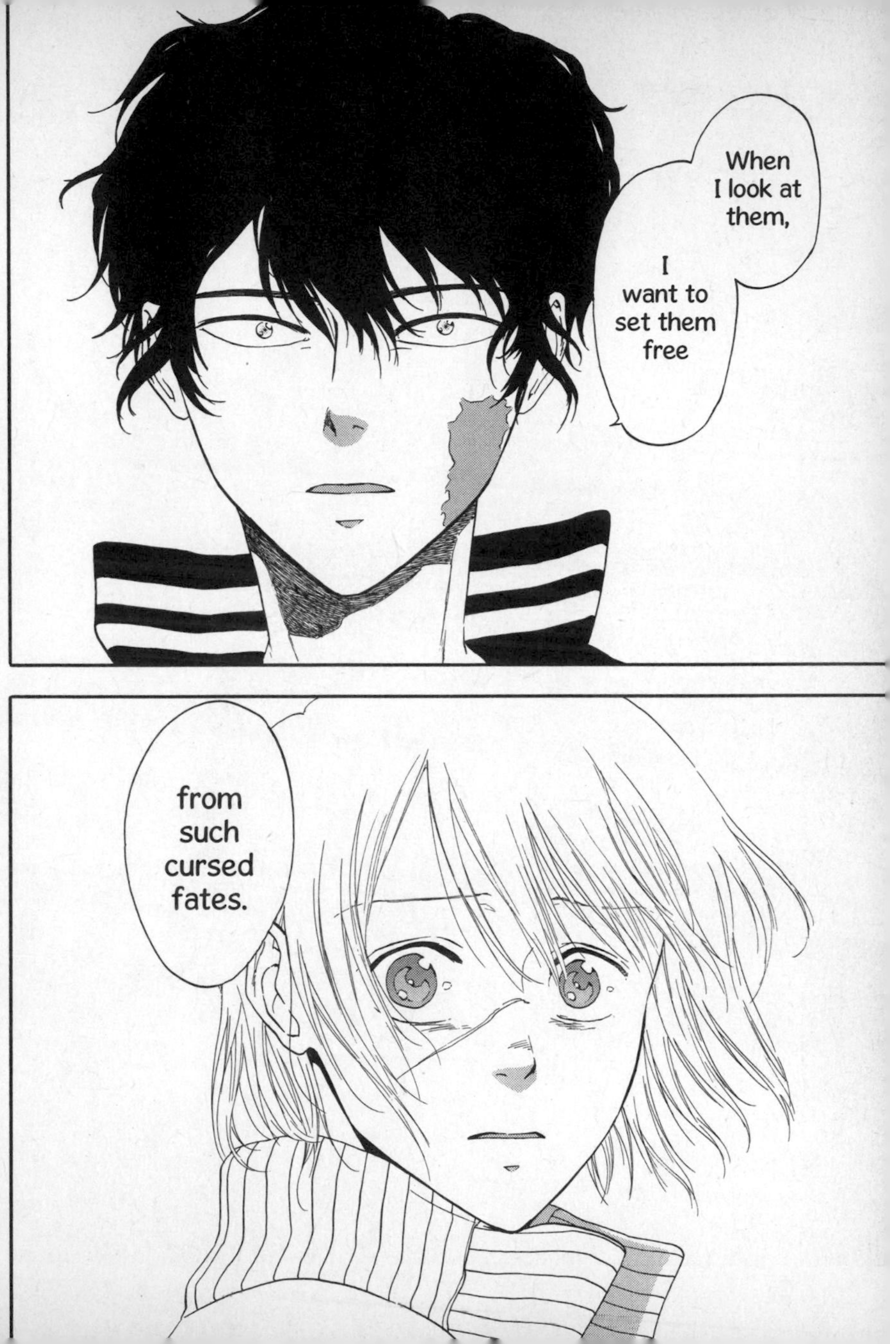
When I look at them,
I want to set them free
from such cursed fates.

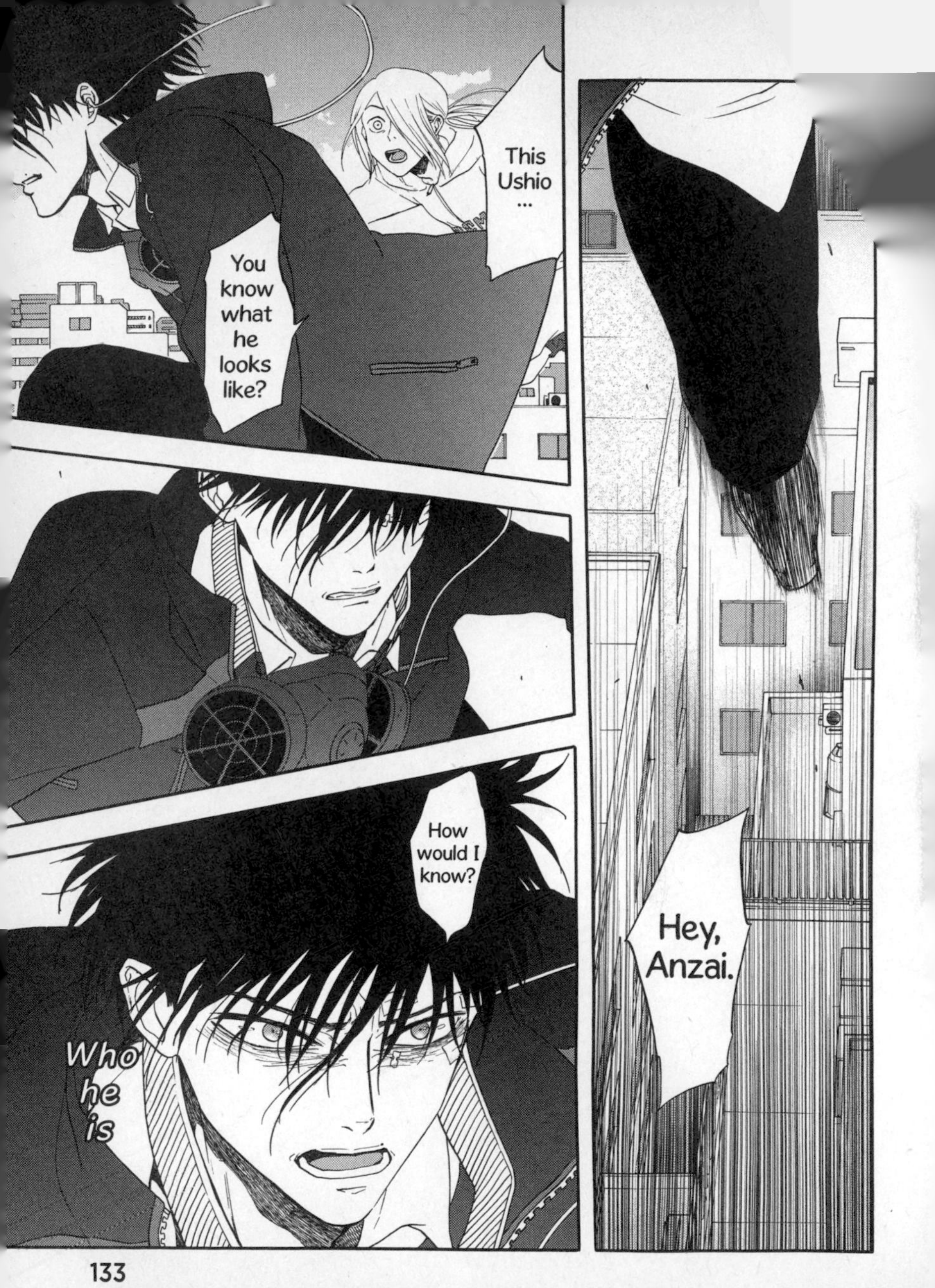
Hey, Anzai.
This Ushio ...
You know what he looks like?
How would I know?
Who he is

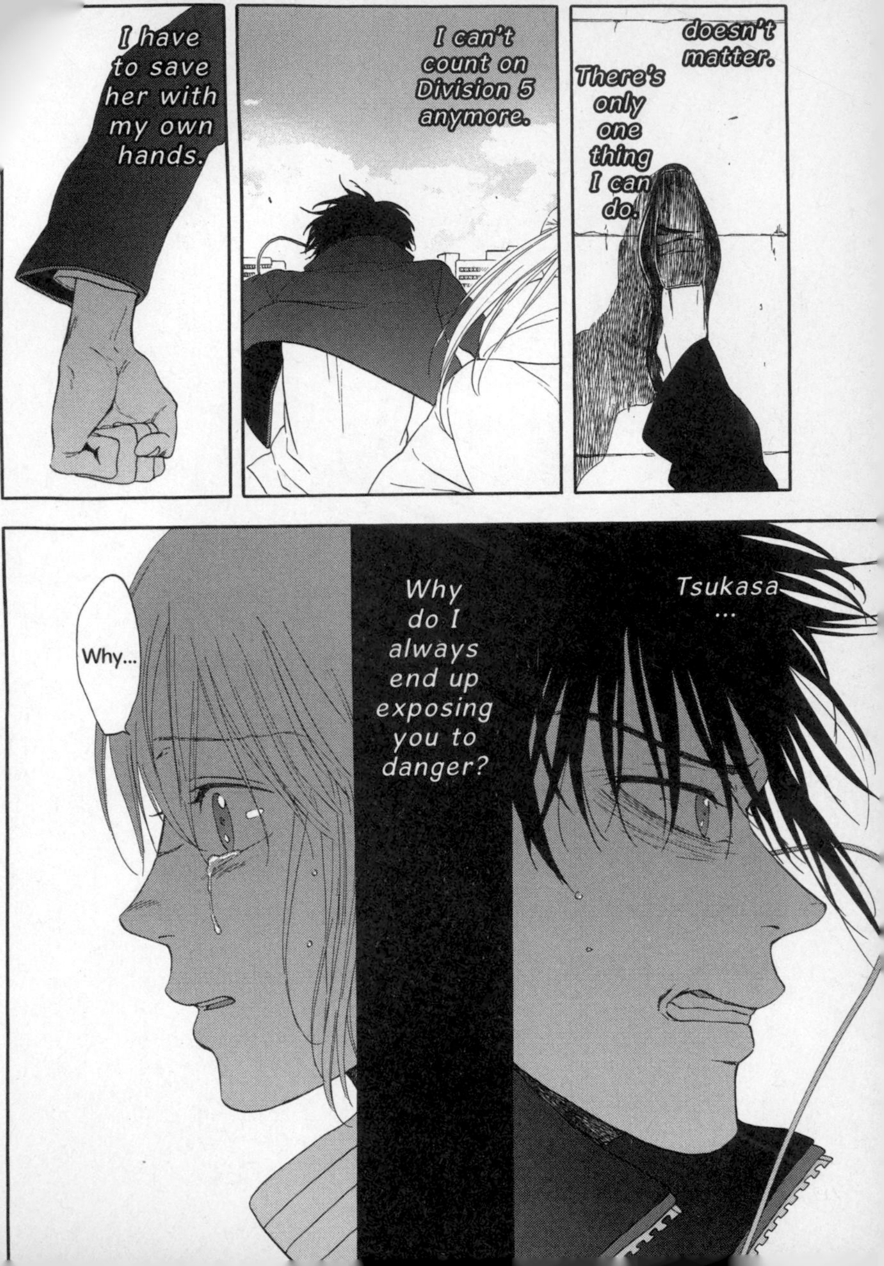
doesn't matter.
There's only one thing I can do.
I can't count on Division 5 anymore.
I have to save her with my own hands.
Tsukasa...
Why do I always end up exposing you to danger?
Why...

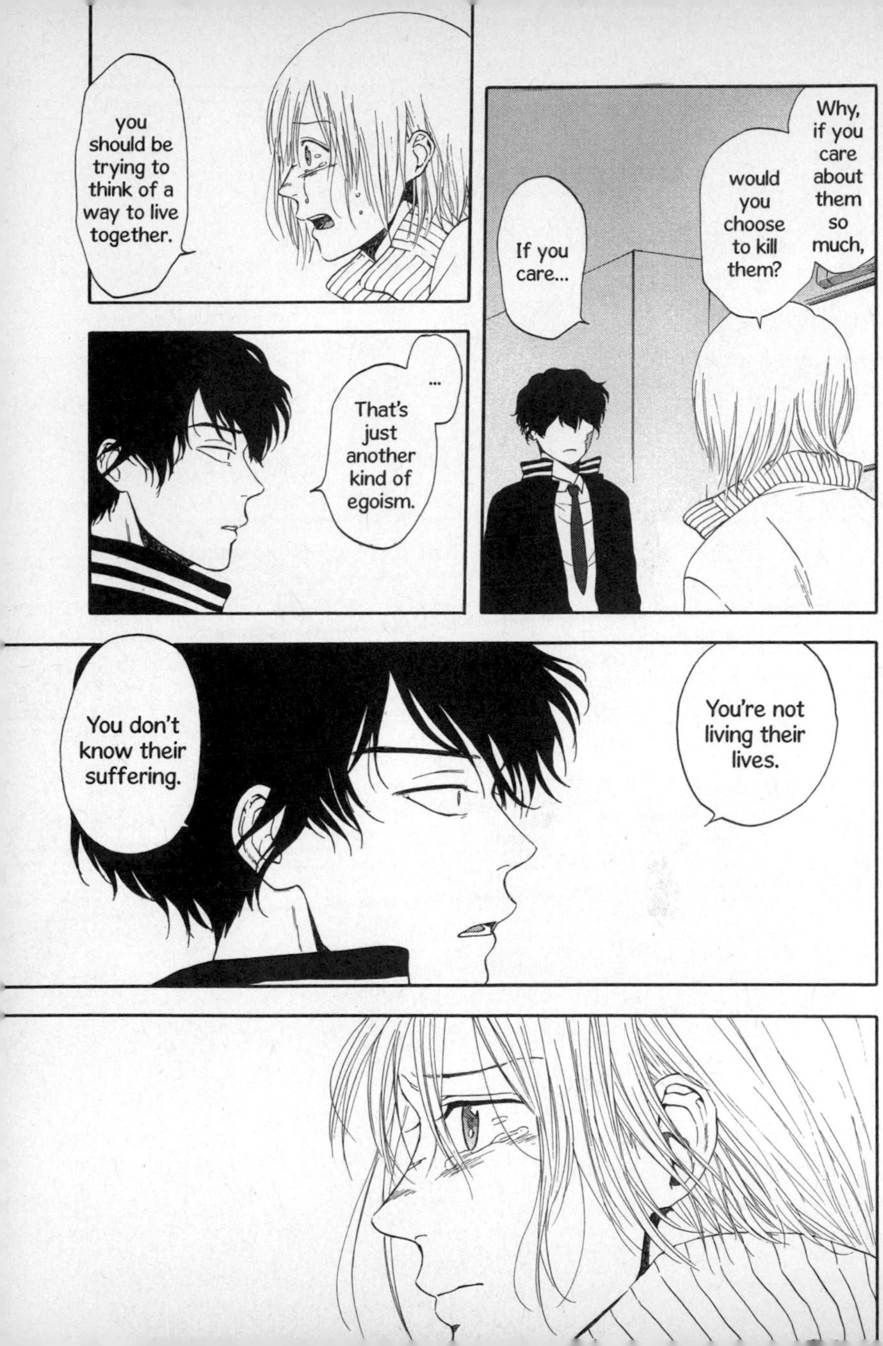
you should be trying to think of a way to live together.
Why, if you care about them so much,
would you choose to kill them?
If you care...
... That's just another kind of egoism.
You're not living their lives.
You don't know their suffering.

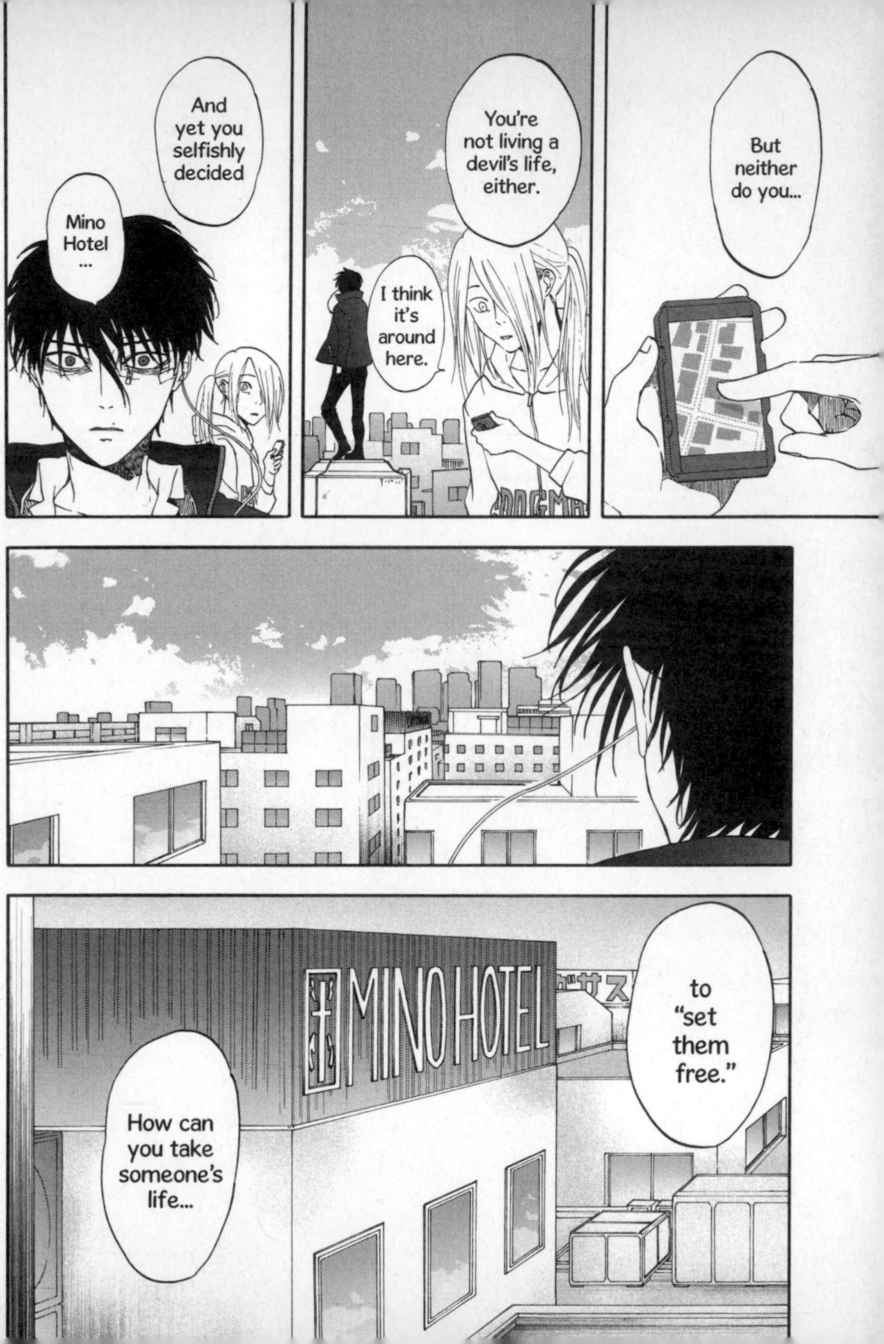

But neither do you...
You're not living a devil's life, either.
I think it's around here.
And yet you selfishly decided
Mino Hotel ...
MINO HOTEL
to "set them free."
How can you take someone's life...

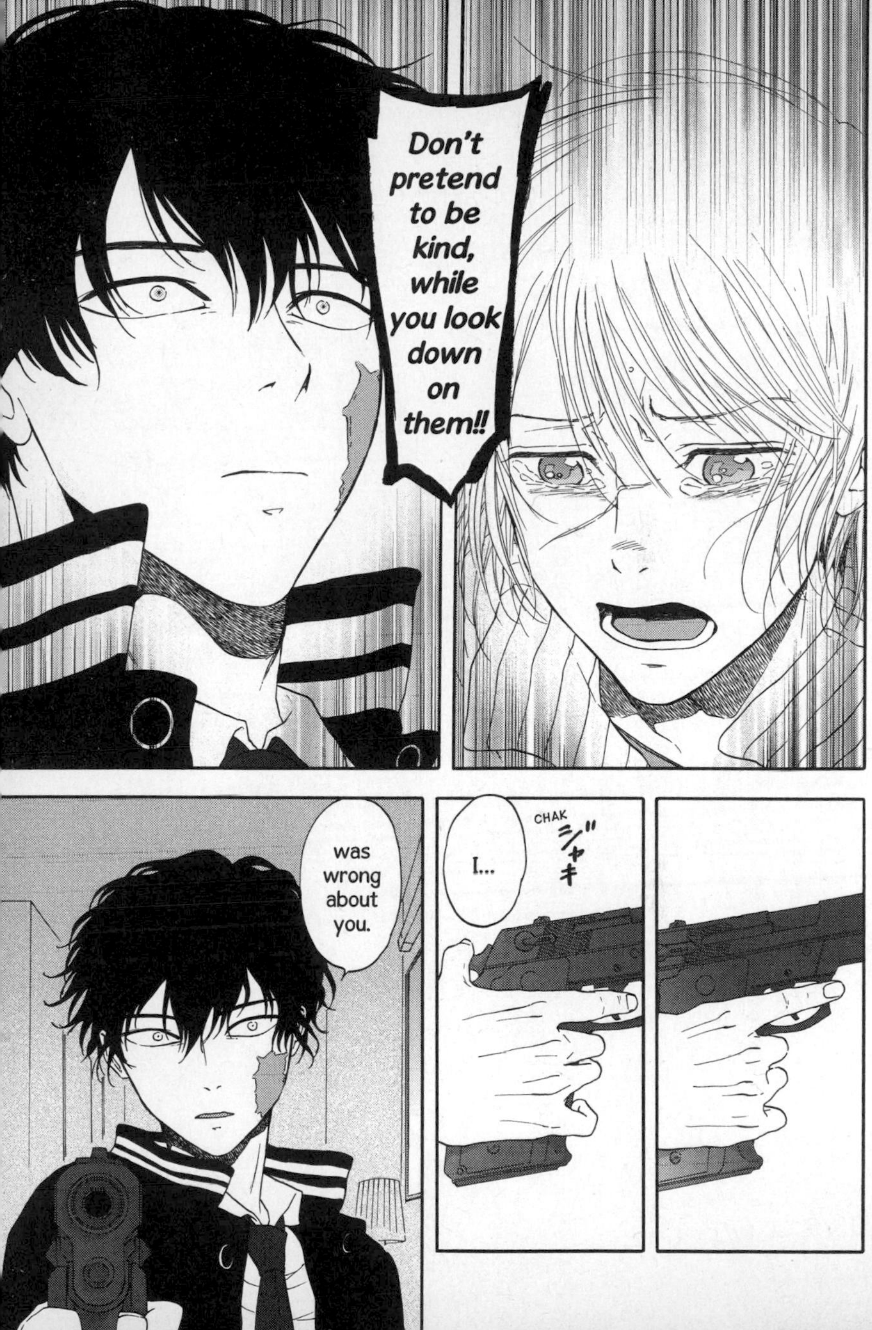
Don't pretend to be kind, while you look down on them!!
CHAK
ジャキ
I...
was wrong about you.

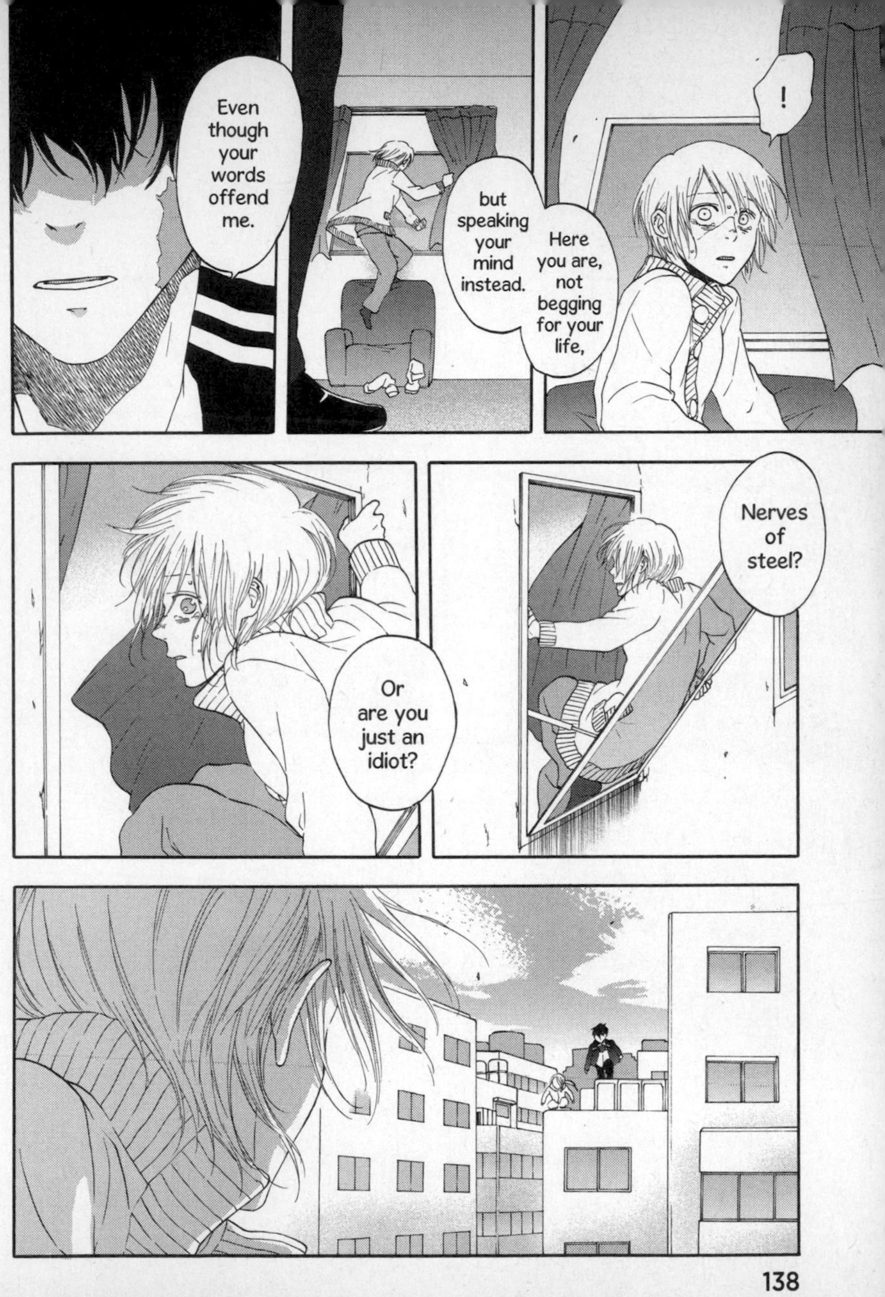
!
Here you are, not begging for your life,
but speaking your mind instead.
Even though your words offend me.
Nerves of steel?
Or are you just an idiot?

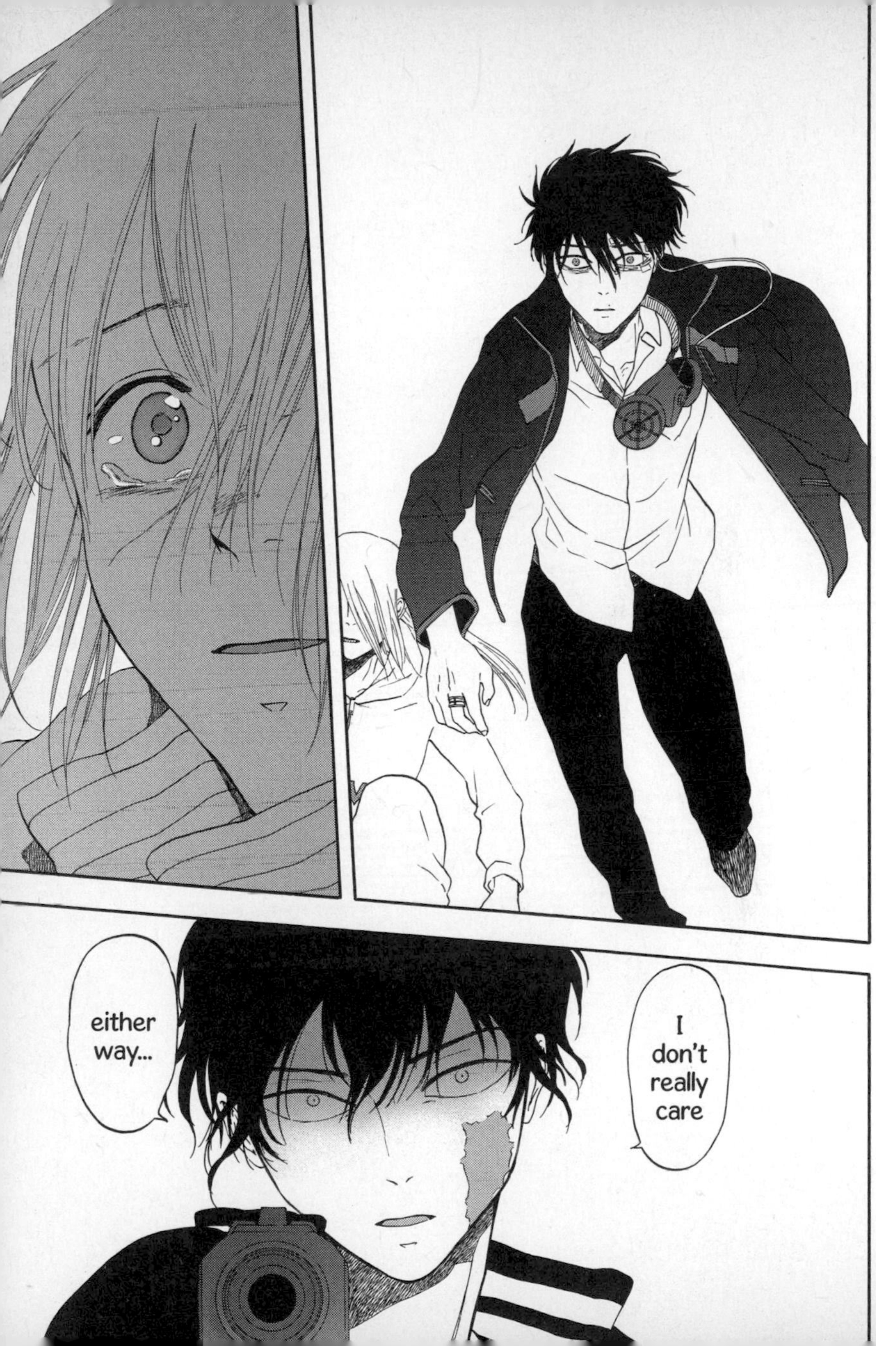
I don't really care
either way...

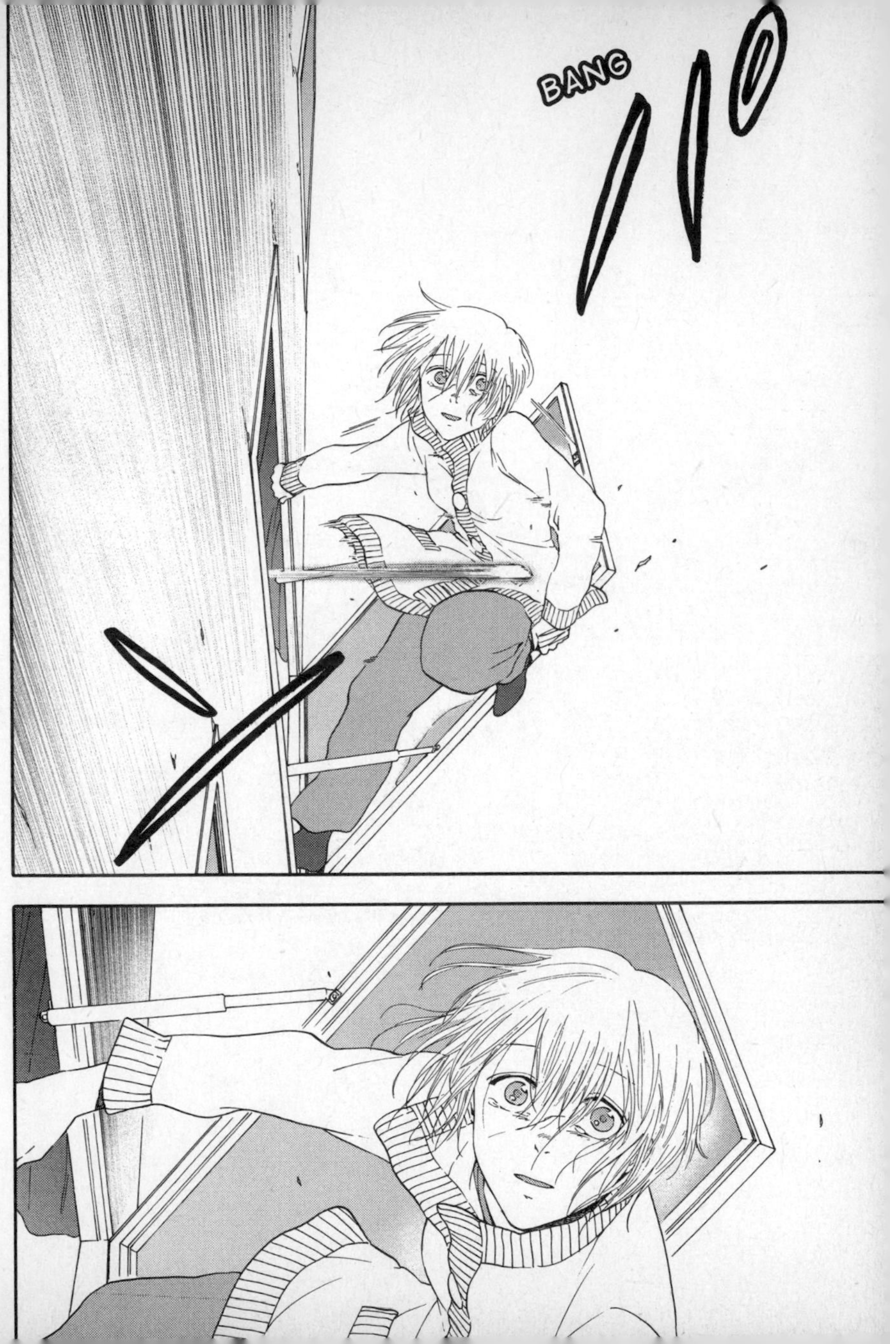
BANG

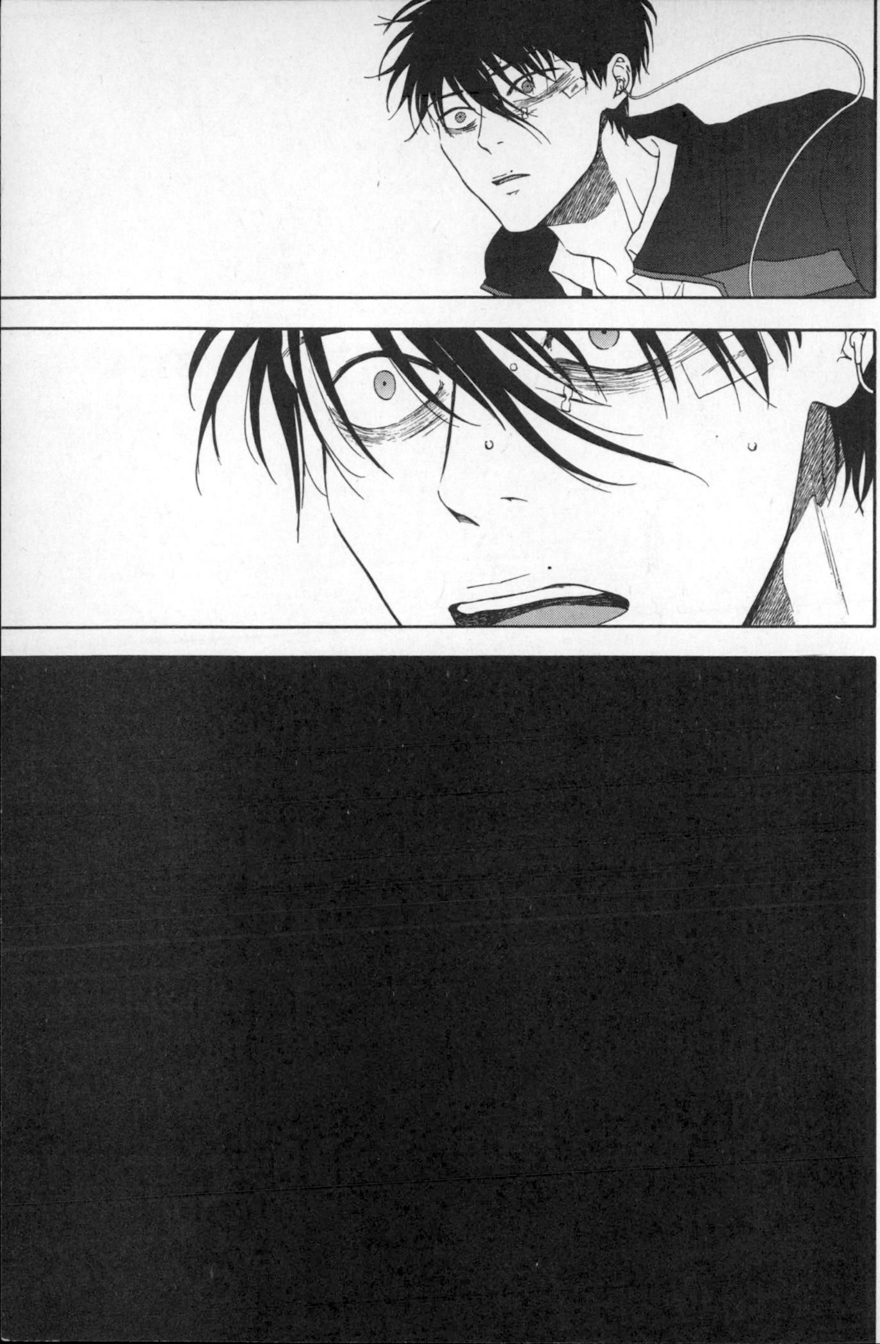

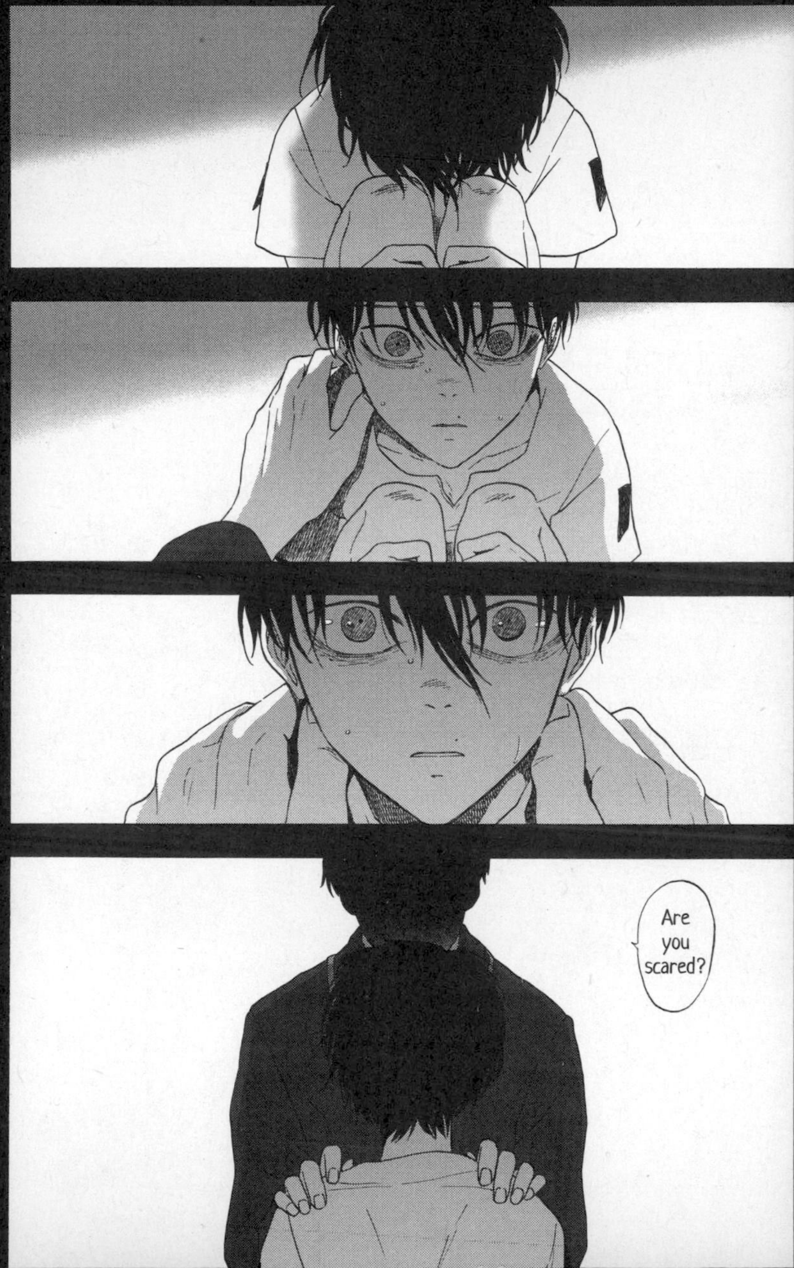
Are you scared?

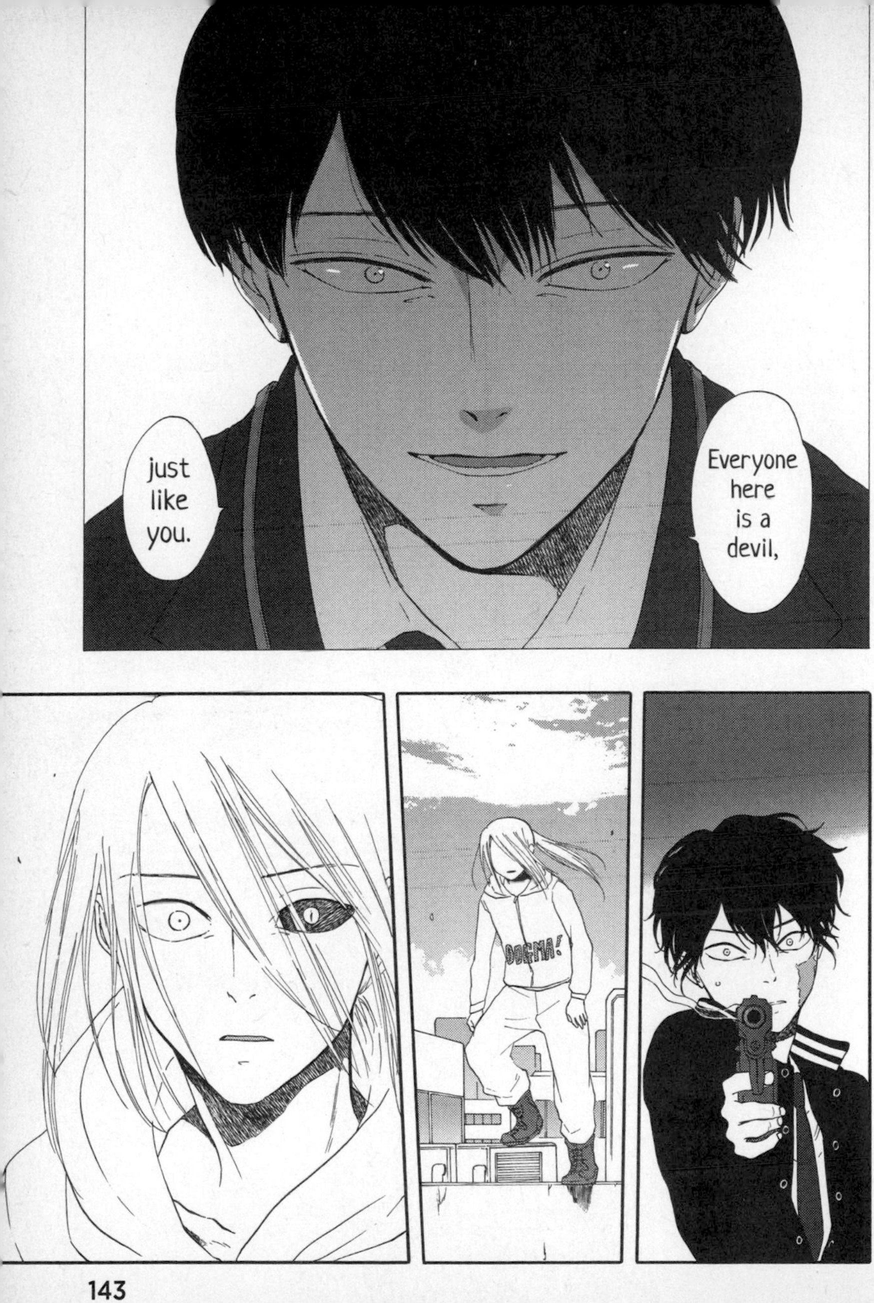
Everyone here is a devil,
just like you.
DOGMA!

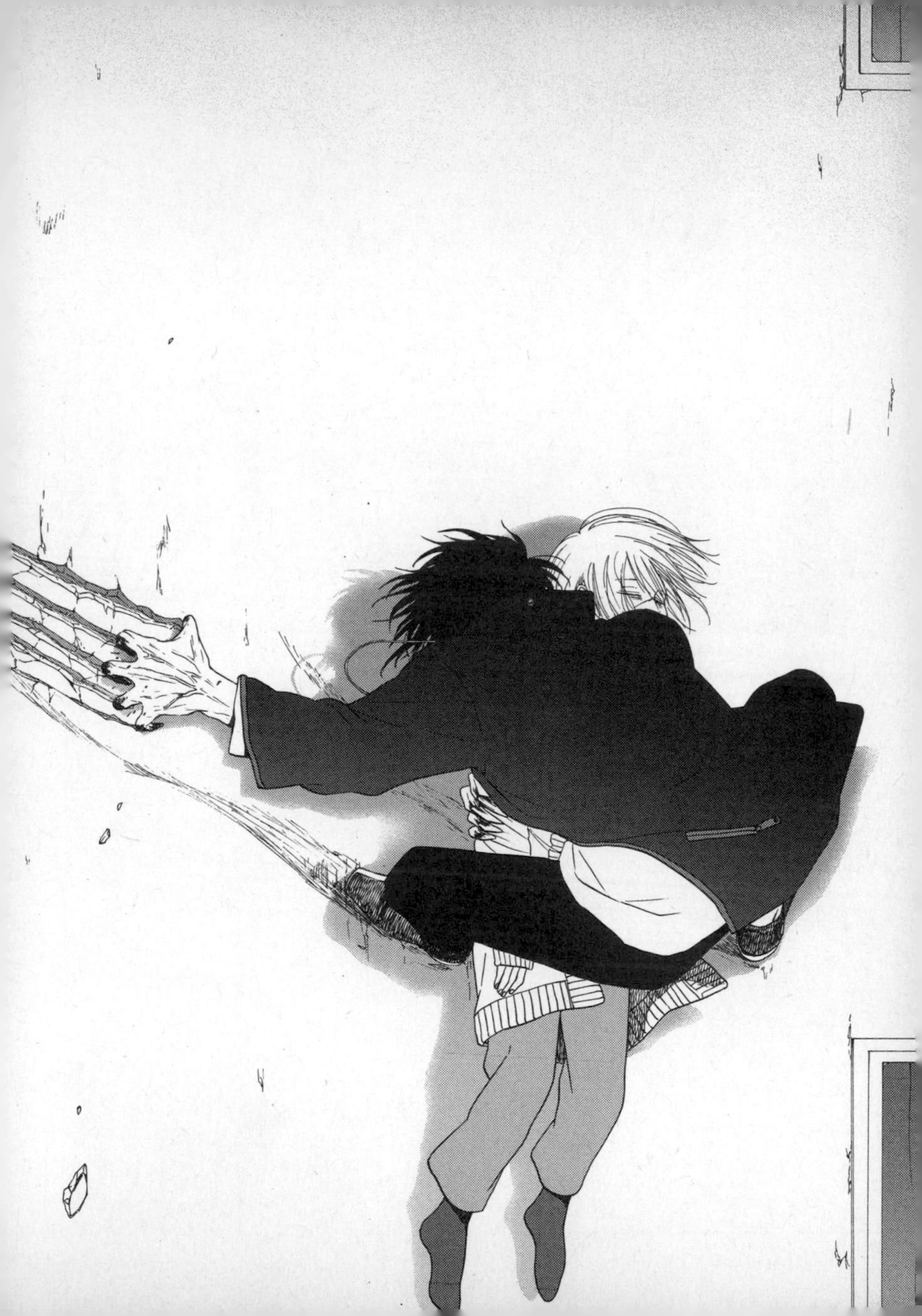

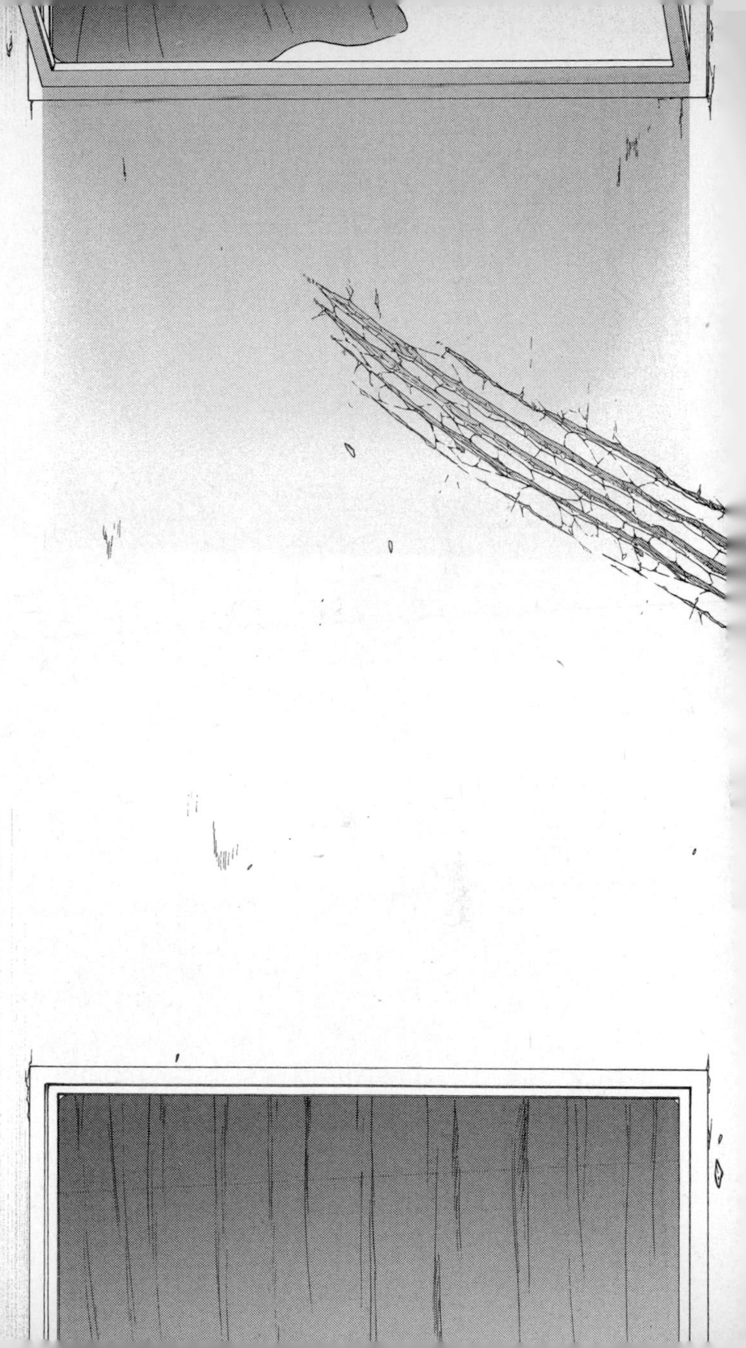

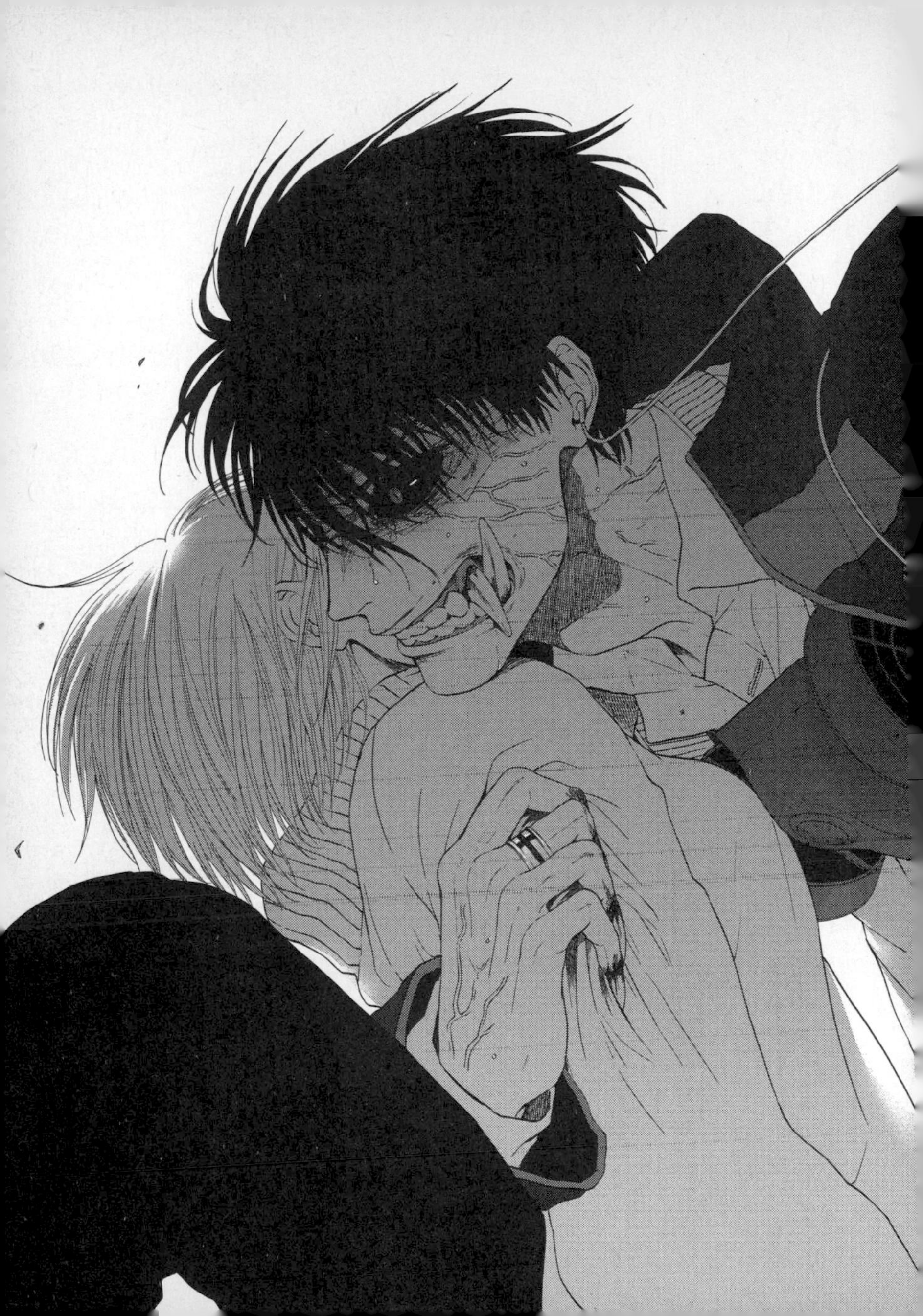

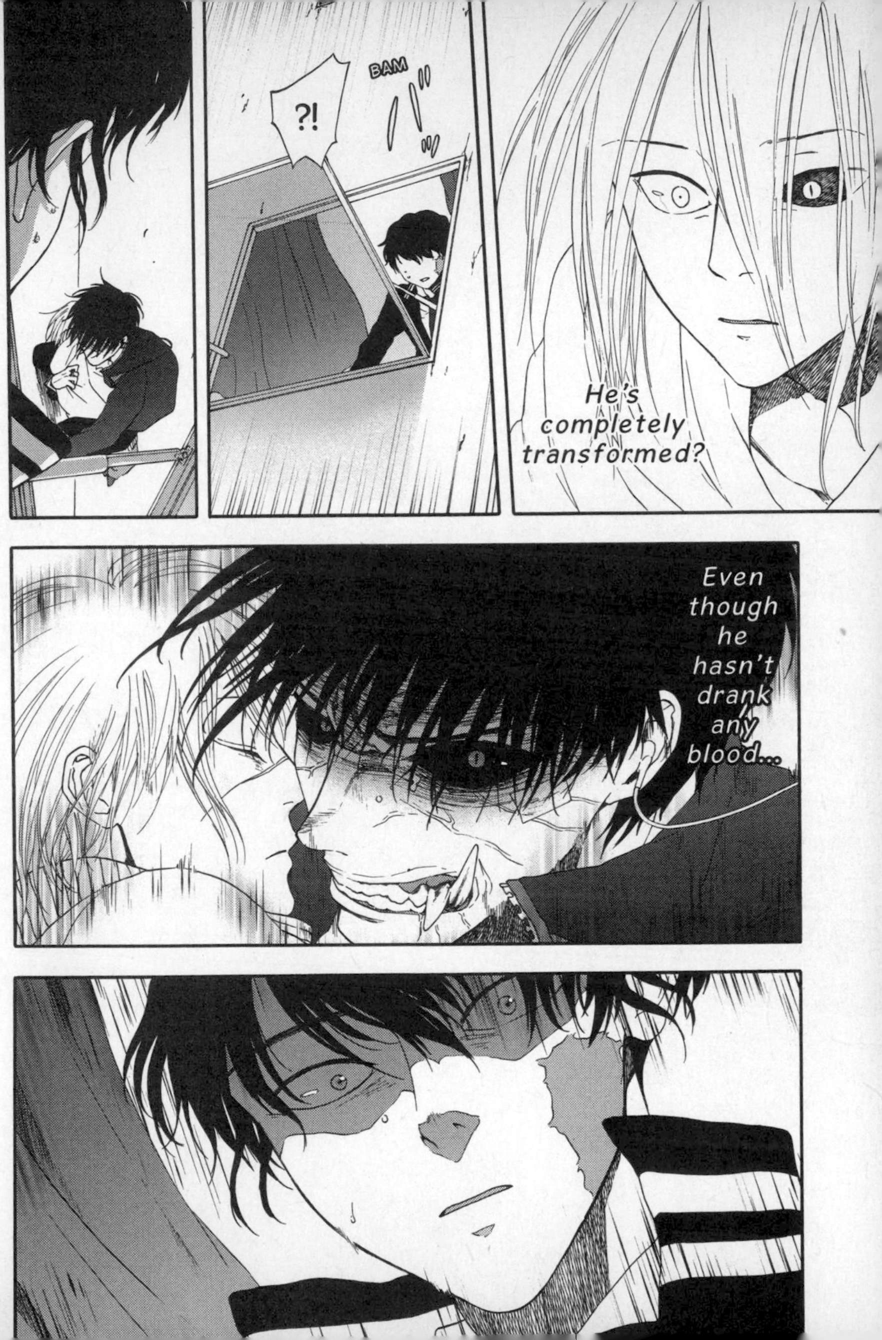
He's completely transformed?
BAM
?!
Even though he hasn't drank any blood...

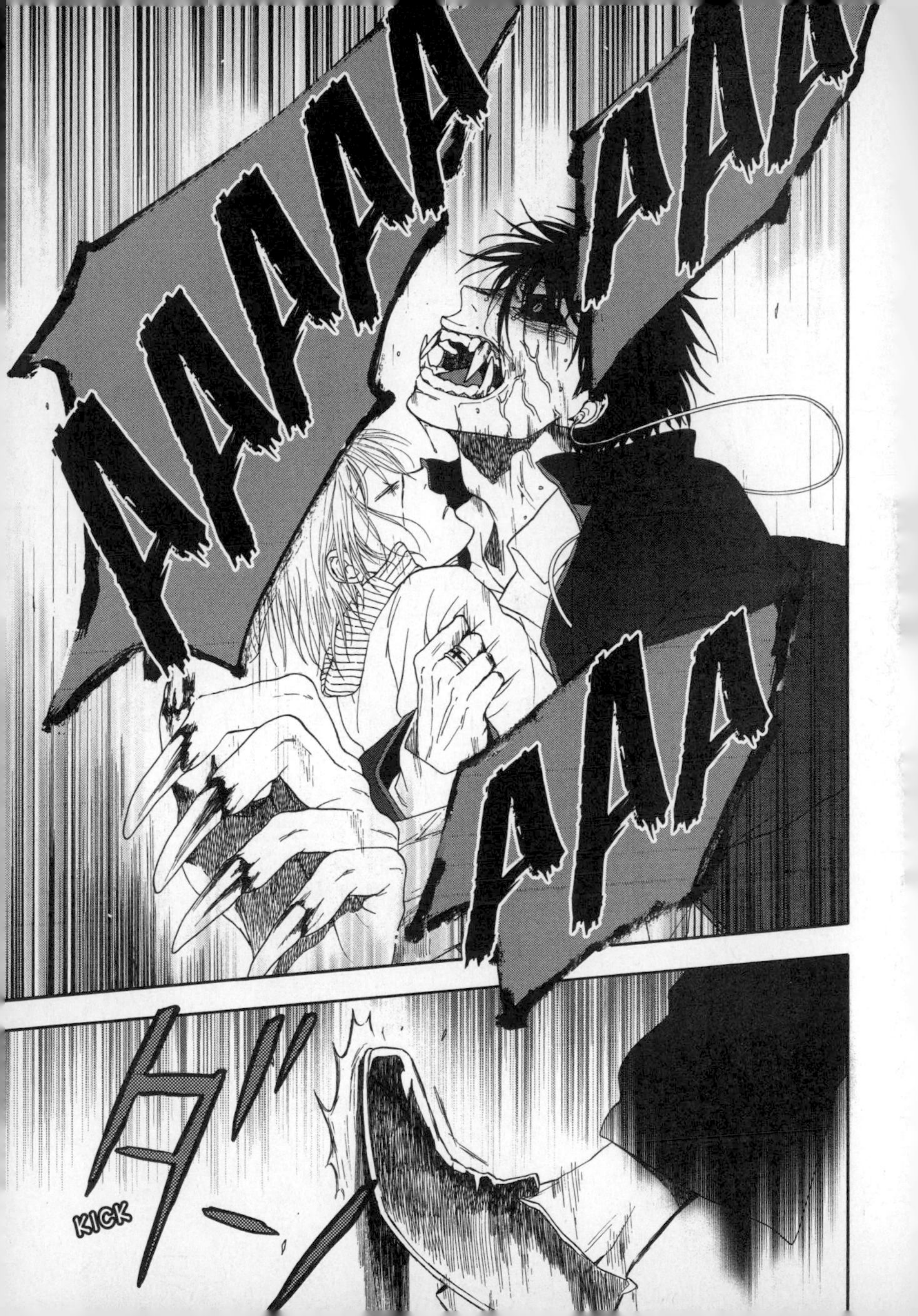
AAAAAA
AAAAA
AAA
KICK

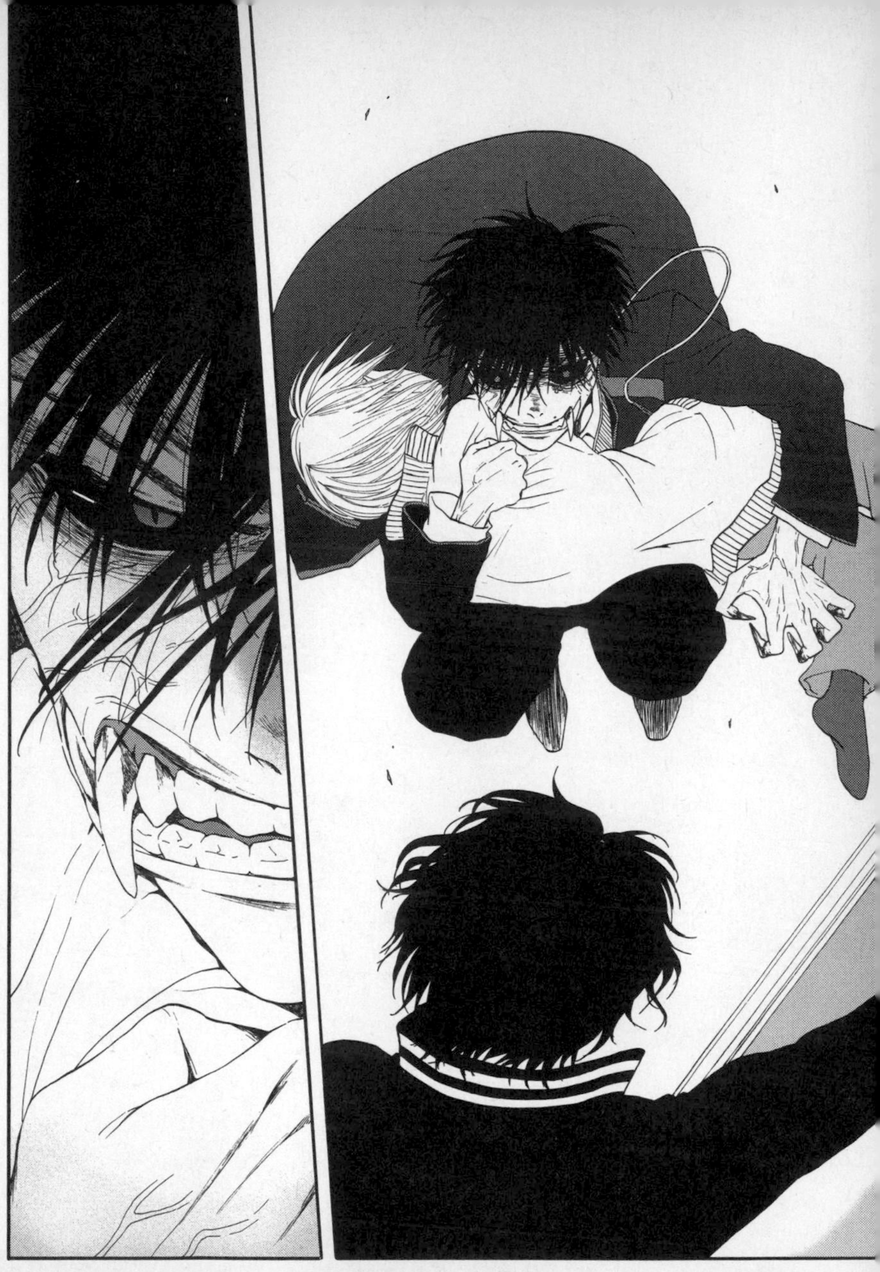

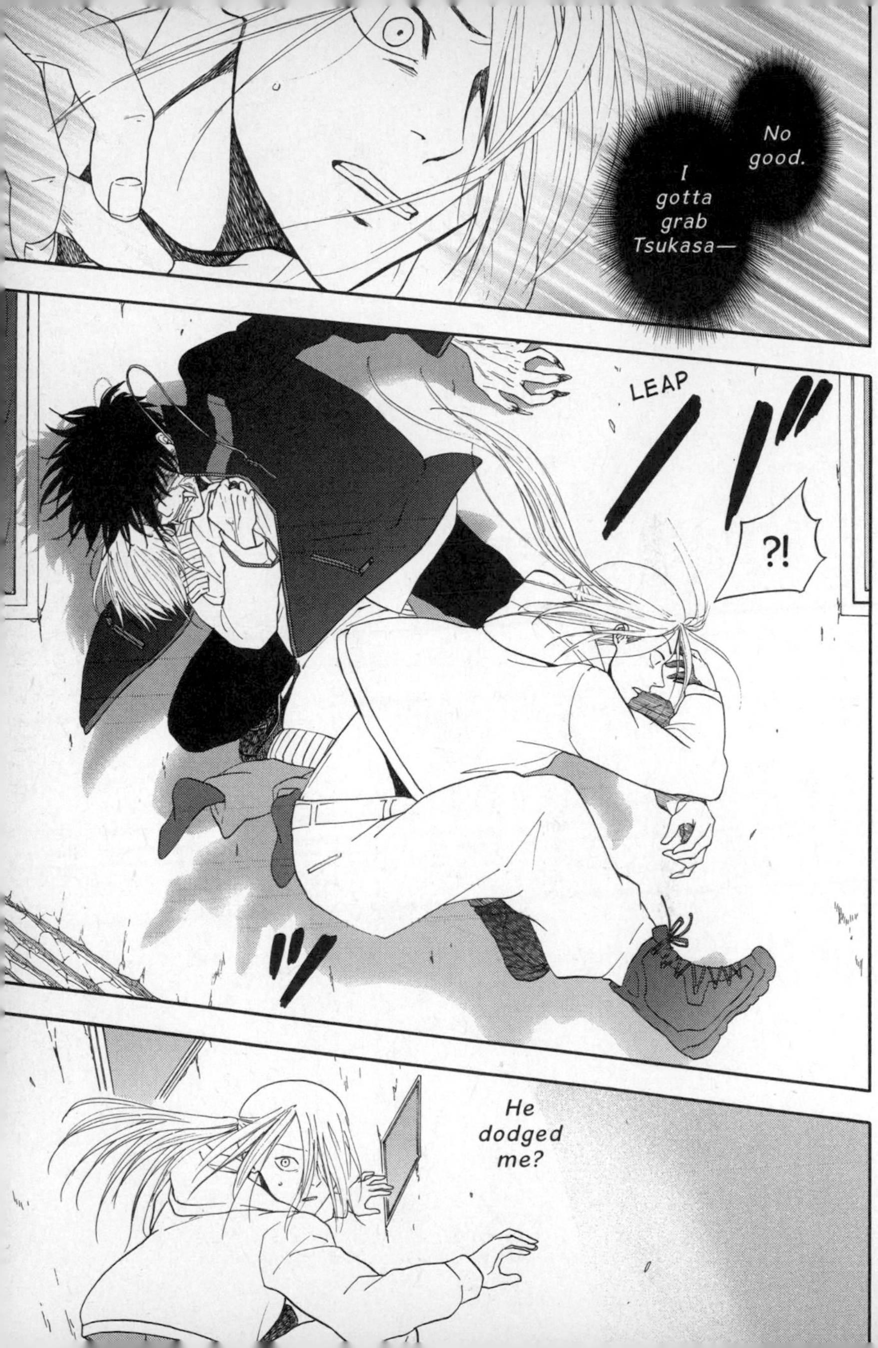
No good.
I gotta grab Tsukasa—
LEAP
?!
He dodged me?

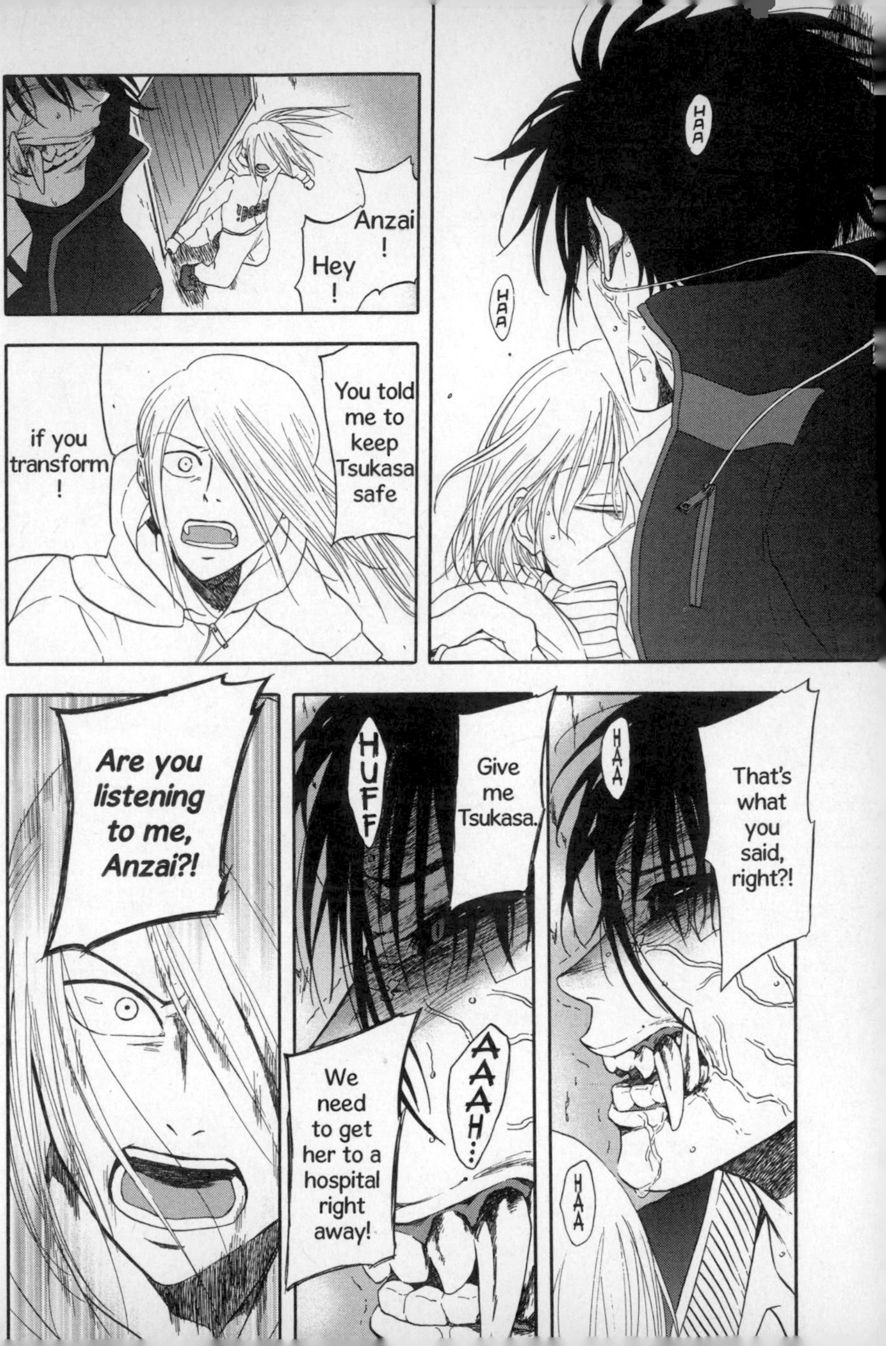
HAA
HAA
Anzai!
Hey!
You told me to keep Tsukasa safe
if you transform!
HAA
That's what you said, right?!
HAA
Give me Tsukasa.
HUFF
AAAH...
We need to get her to a hospital right away!
Are you listening to me, Anzai?!

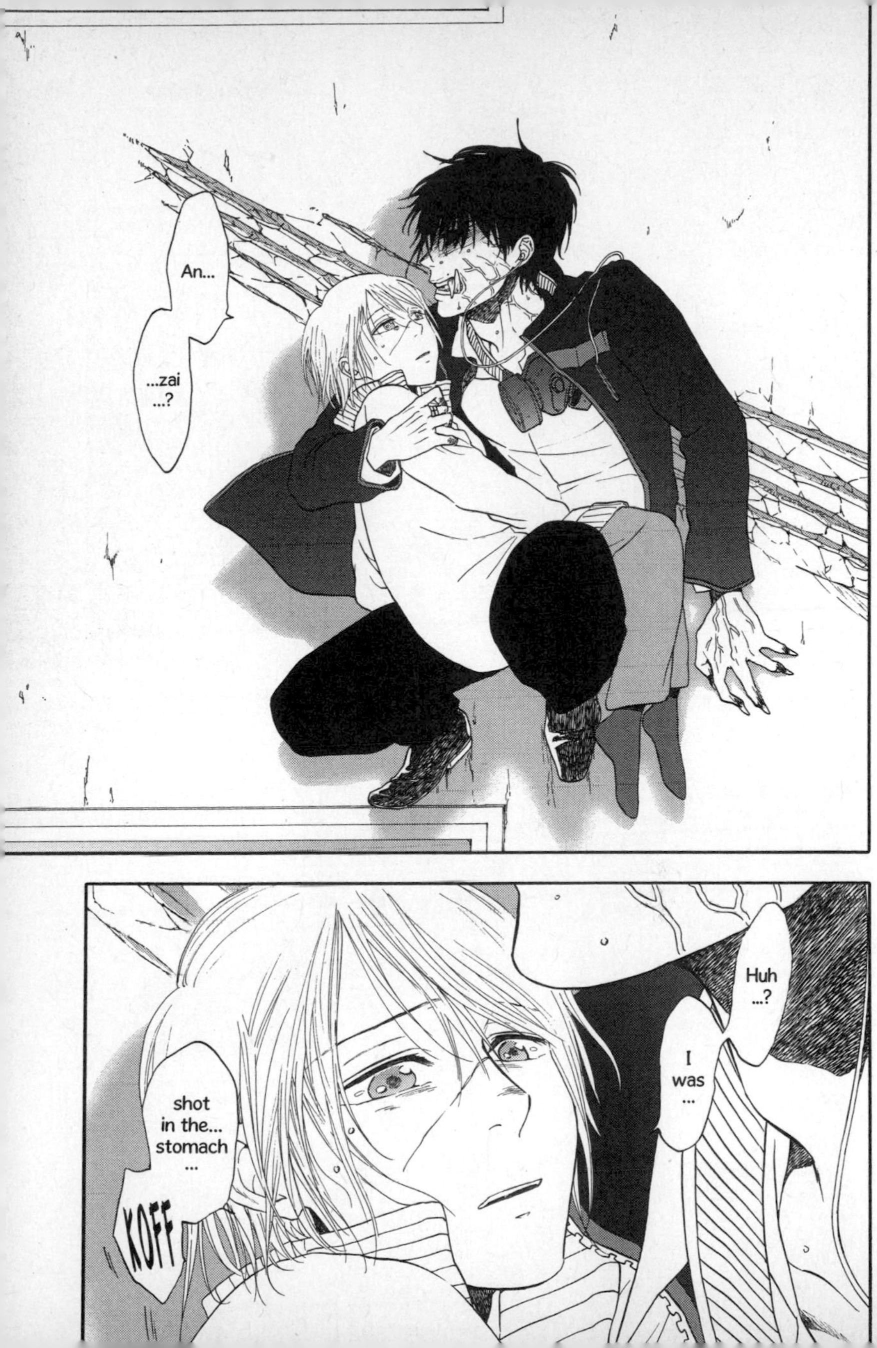
An...
...zai ...?
Huh ...?
I was ...
shot in the... stomach ...
KOFF

Huh...?

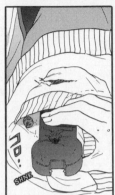

...An
...

zai...

bullet
was
stopped.

The

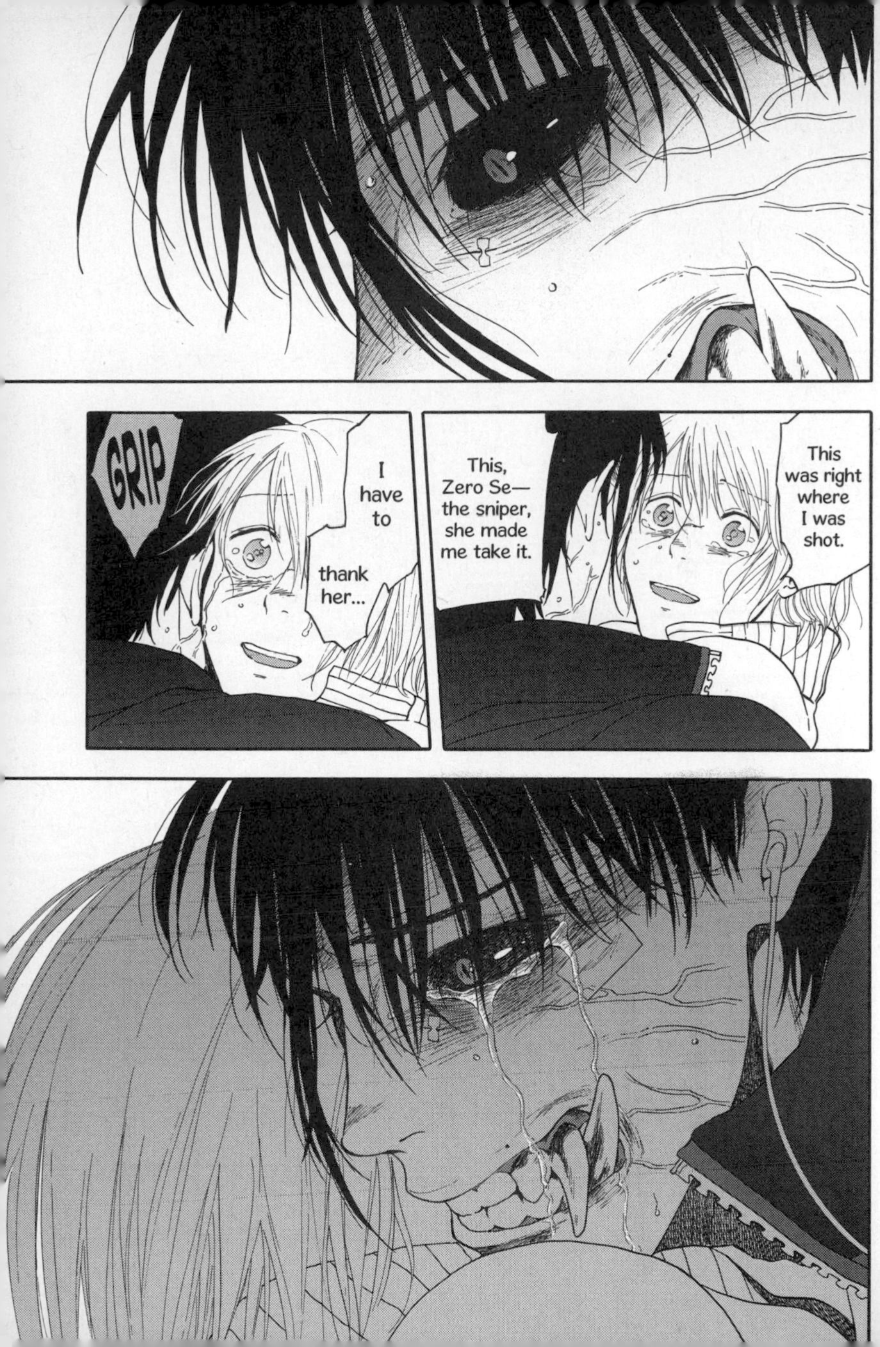
This was right where I was shot.
This, Zero Se— the sniper, she made me take it.
I have to thank her...
GRIP

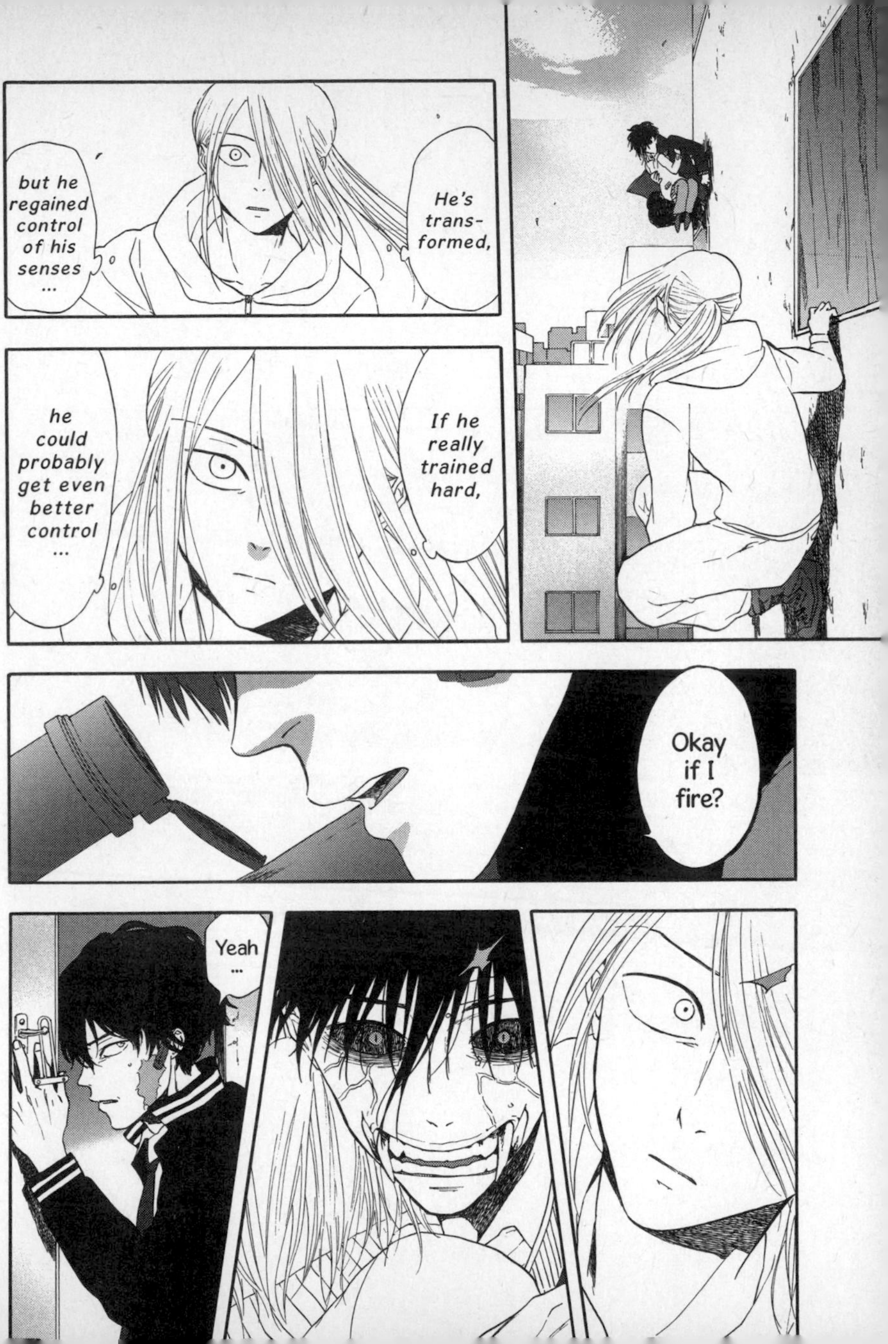
He's transformed,
but he regained control of his senses ...
If he really trained hard,
he could probably get even better control ...
Okay if I fire?
Yeah ...

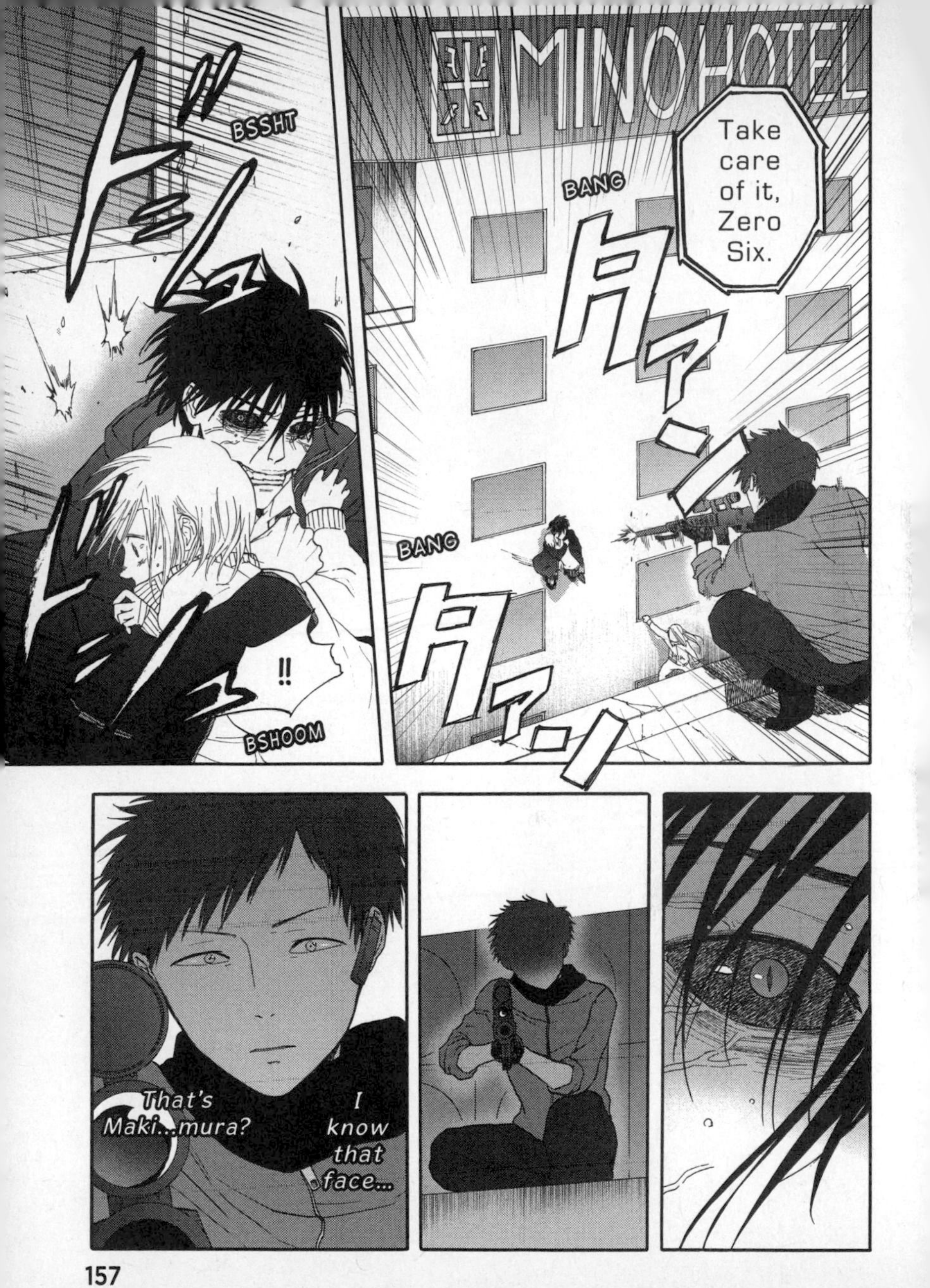
Take care of it, Zero Six.
BANG
タァーン
BANG
タァーン
BSSHT
!!
BSHOOM
I know that face...
That's Maki...mura?

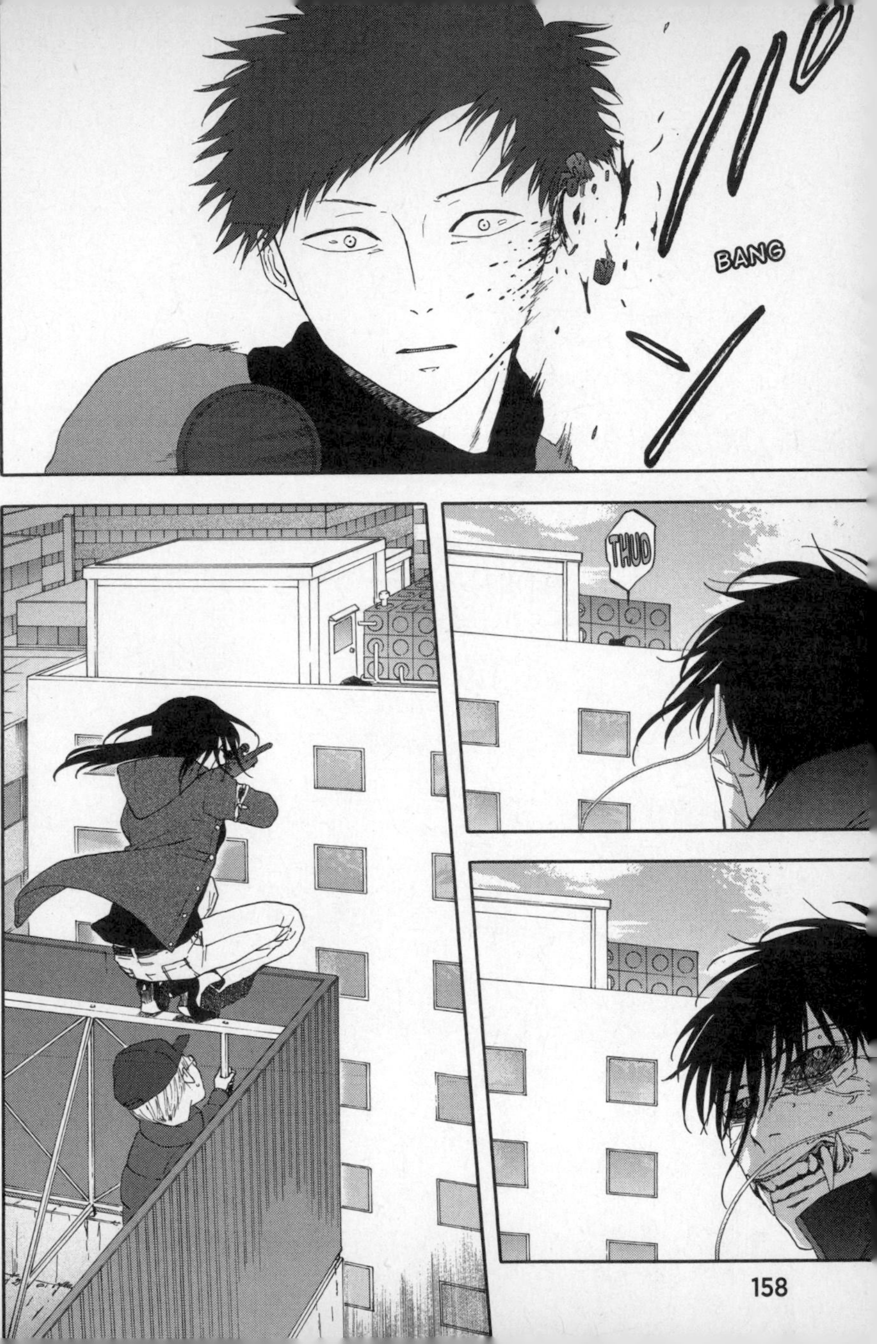
BANG
THUD

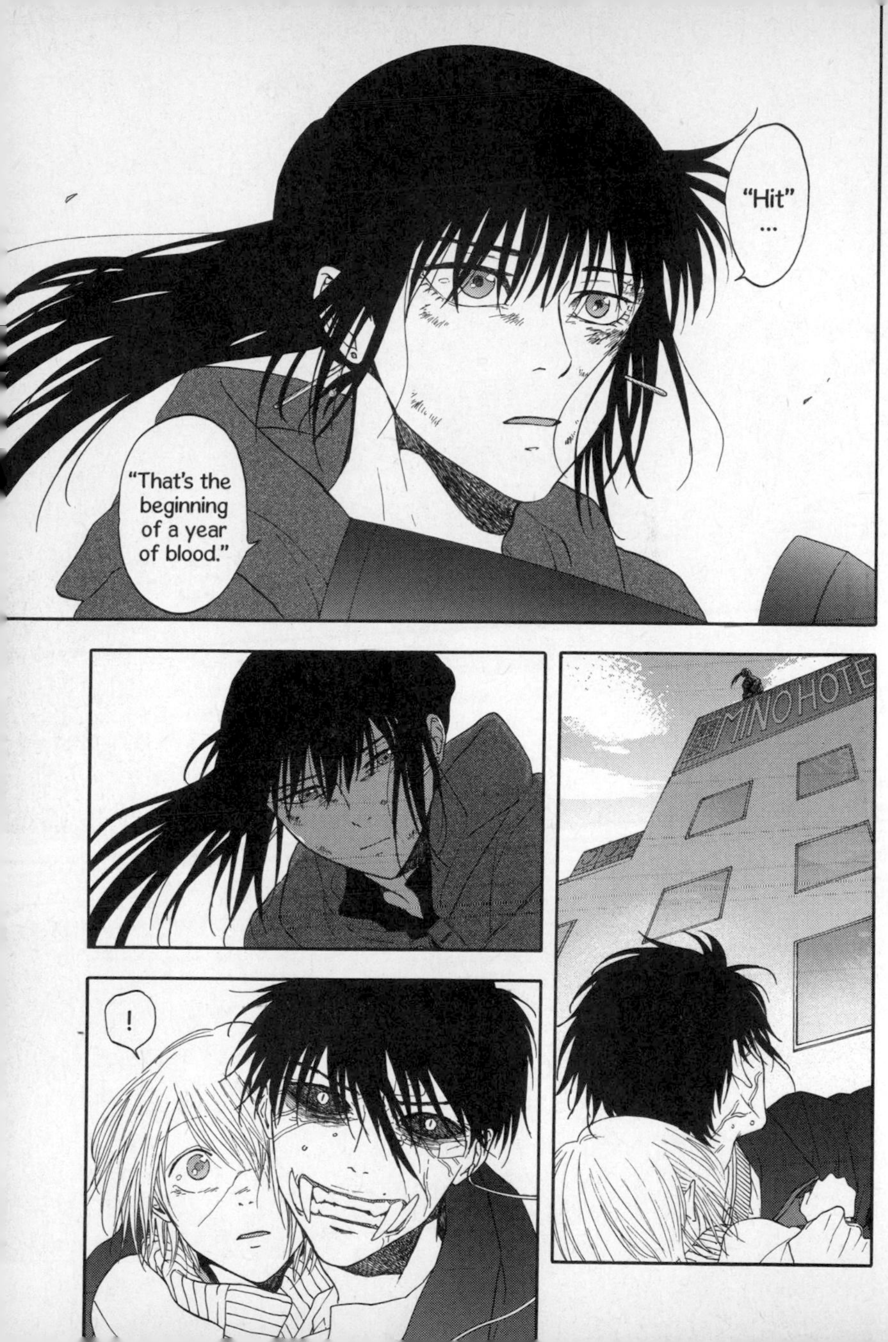
"Hit" …
"That's the beginning of a year of blood."
MINOHOTE
!

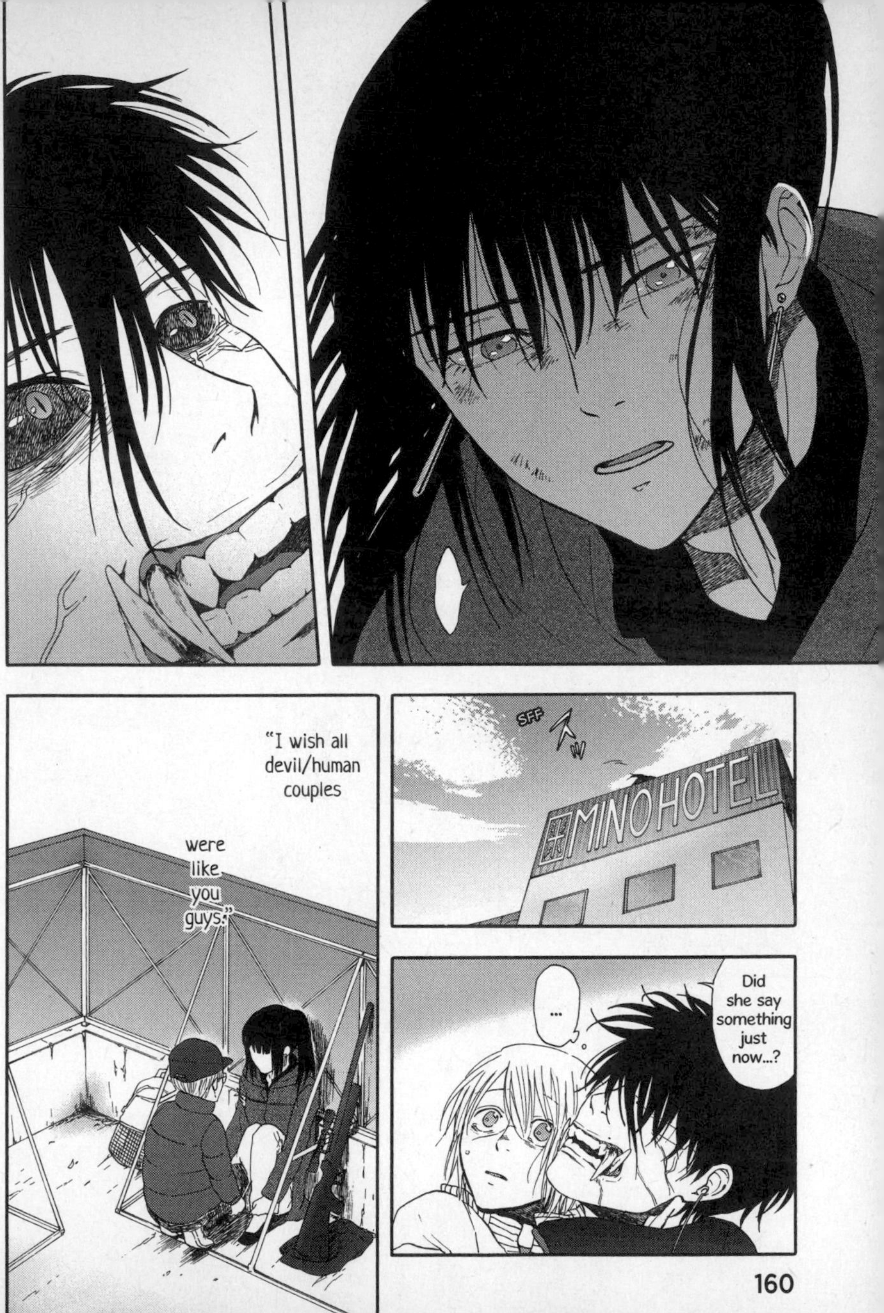
SFF
MINOHOTEL
Did she say something just now...?
...
"I wish all devil/human couples were like you guys."

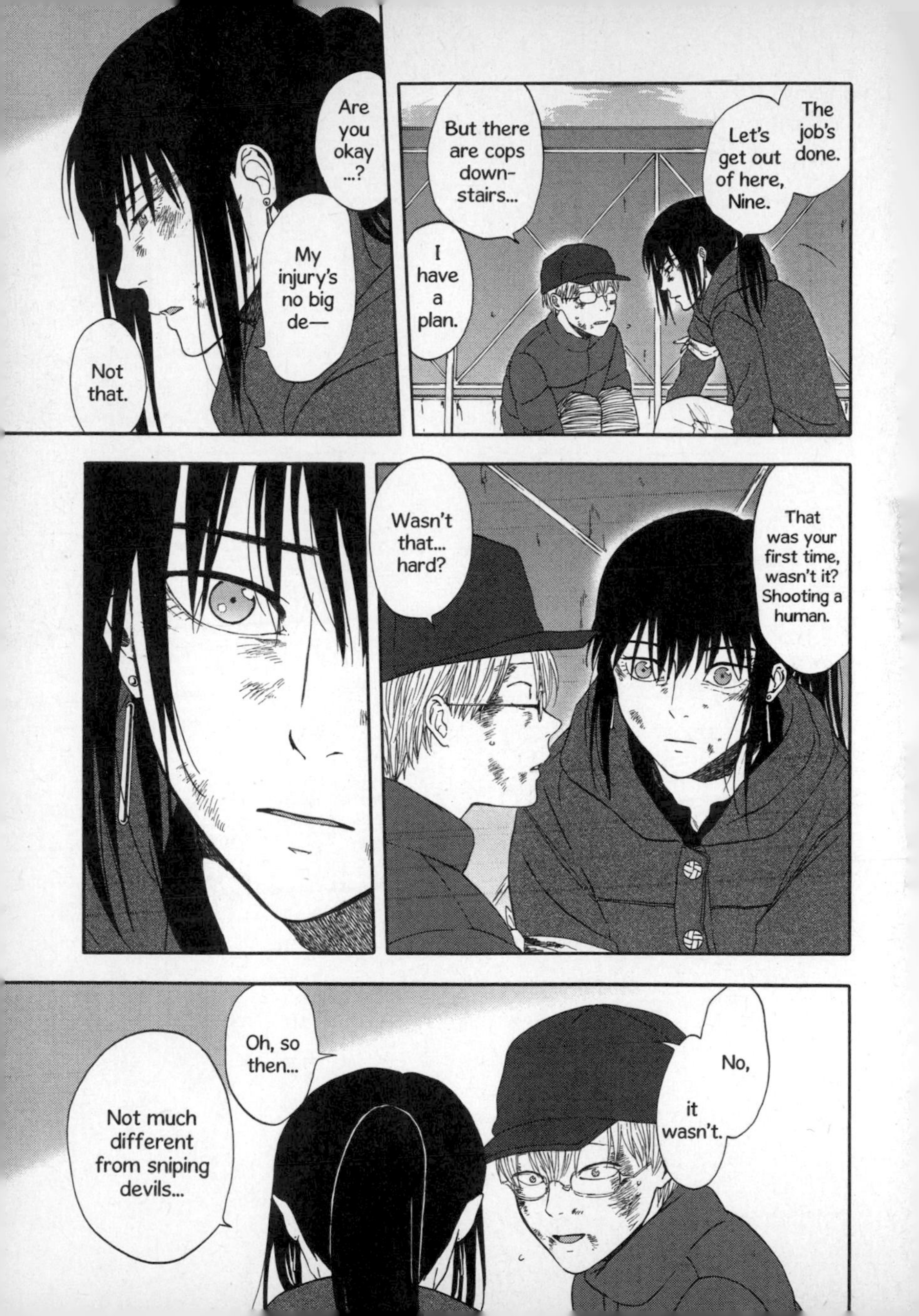
The job's done.
Let's get out of here, Nine.
But there are cops down-stairs...
I have a plan.
Are you okay ...?
My injury's no big de—
Not that.
That was your first time, wasn't it? Shooting a human.
Wasn't that... hard?
No,
it wasn't.
Oh, so then...
Not much different from sniping devils...

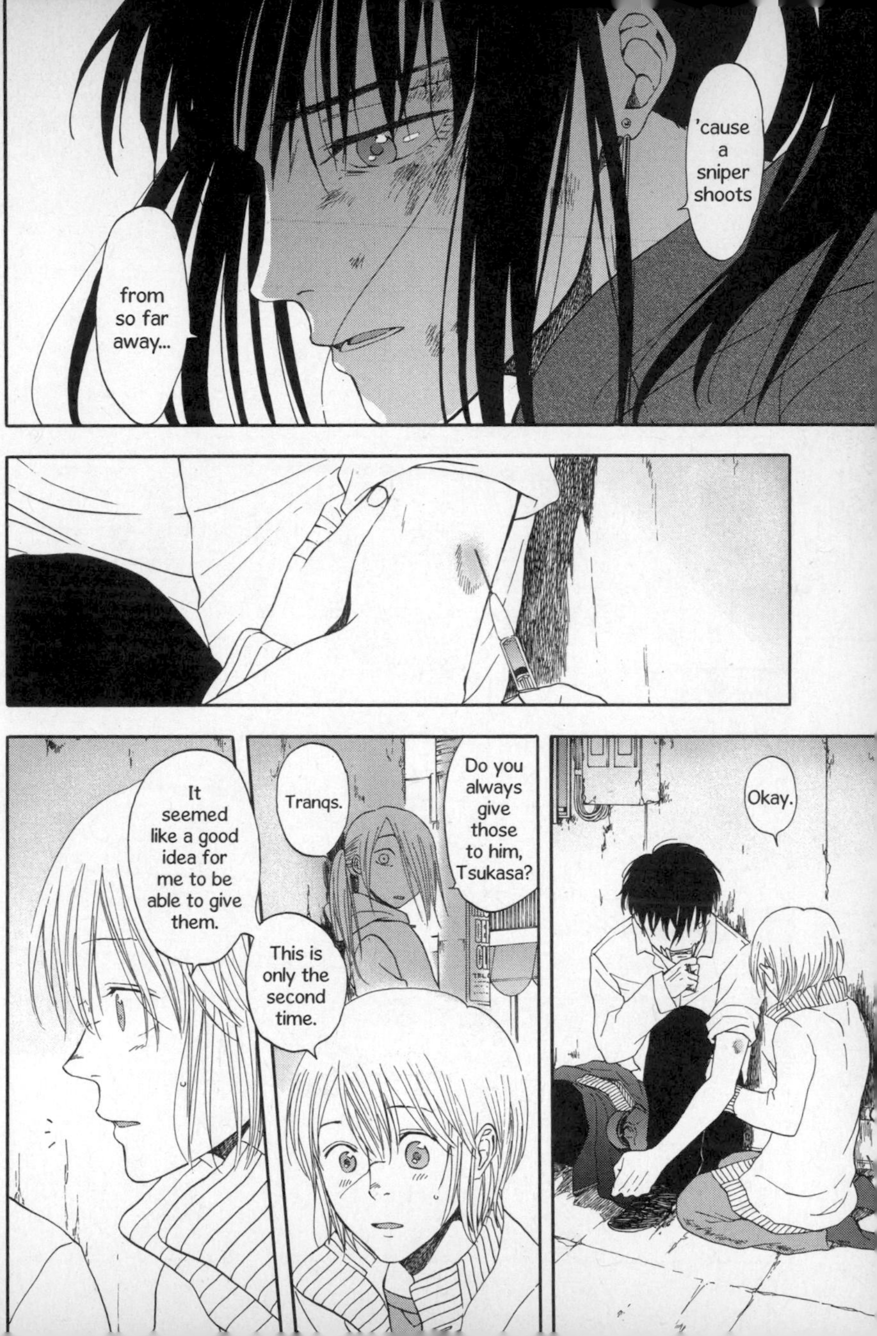
'cause a sniper shoots
from so far away...
Okay.
Do you always give those to him, Tsukasa?
Tranqs.
This is only the second time.
It seemed like a good idea for me to be able to give them.

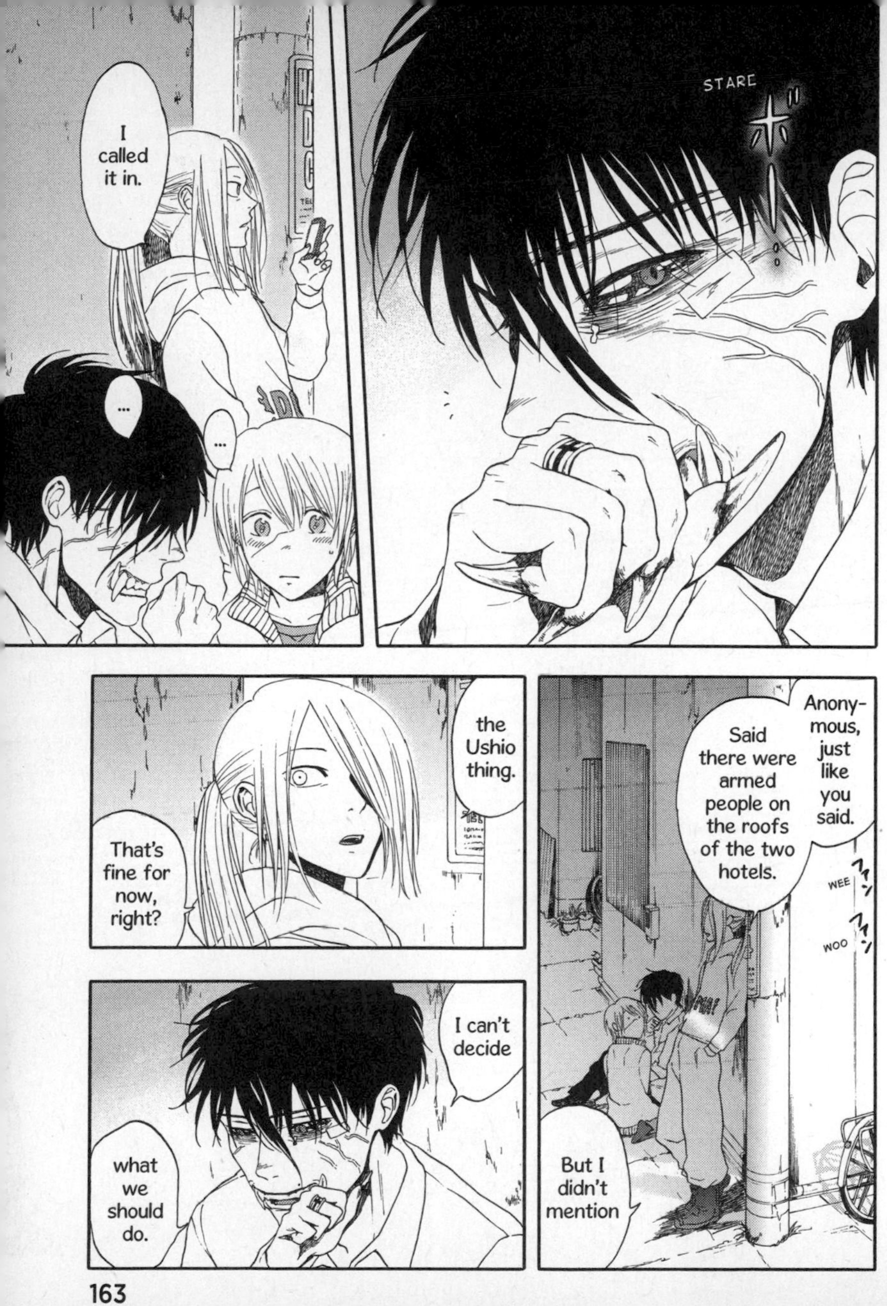
STARE
I called it in.
...
...
Anony-mous, just like you said.
Said there were armed people on the roofs of the two hotels.
WEE
WOO
But I didn't mention
the Ushio thing.
That's fine for now, right?
I can't decide
what we should do.

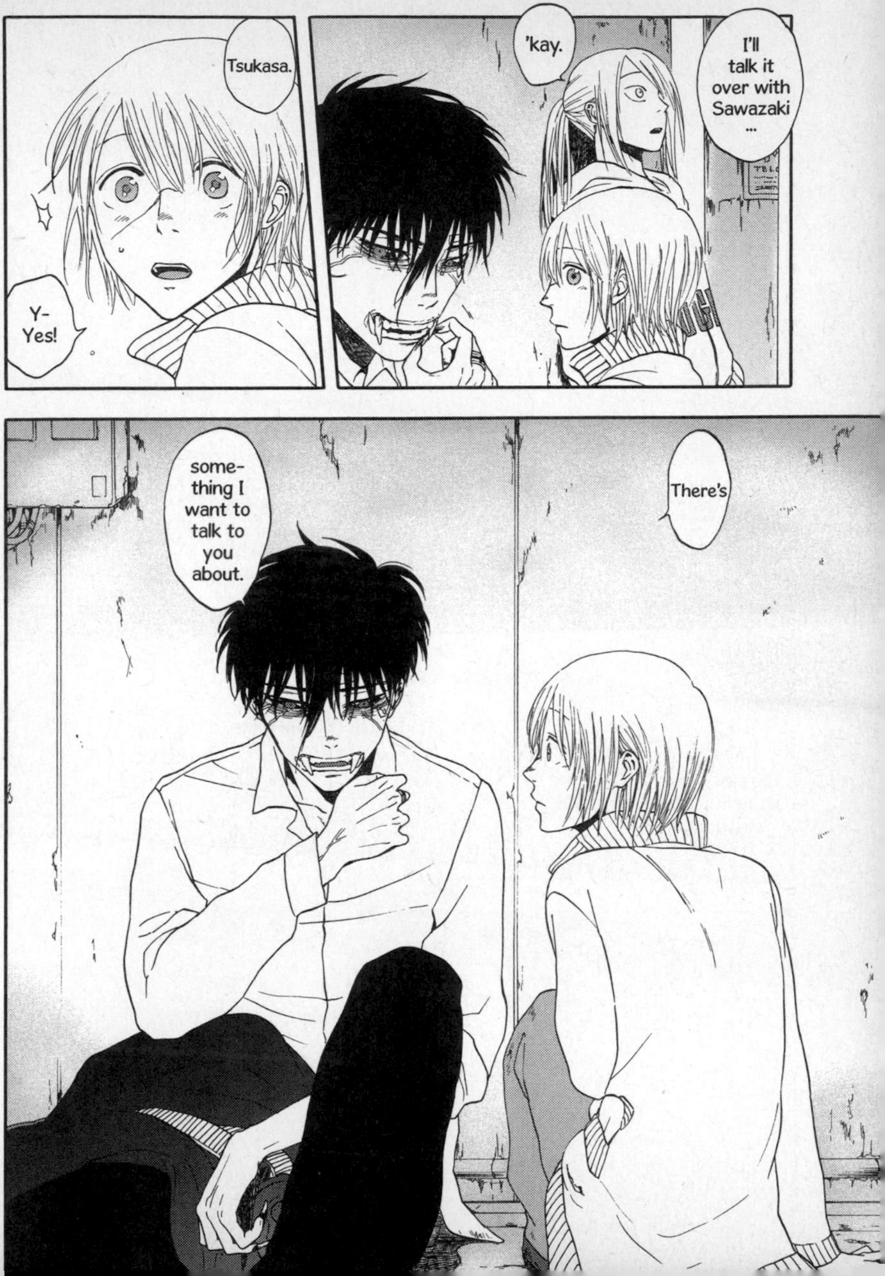
I'll talk it over with Sawazaki ...
'kay.
Tsukasa.
Y-Yes!
There's
something I want to talk to you about.

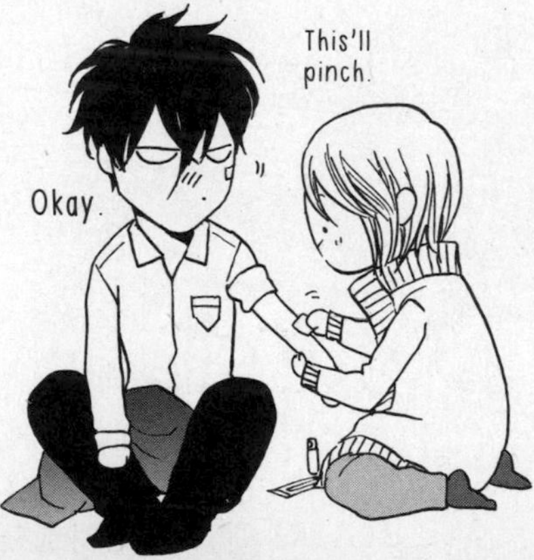
This'll pinch.
Okay.

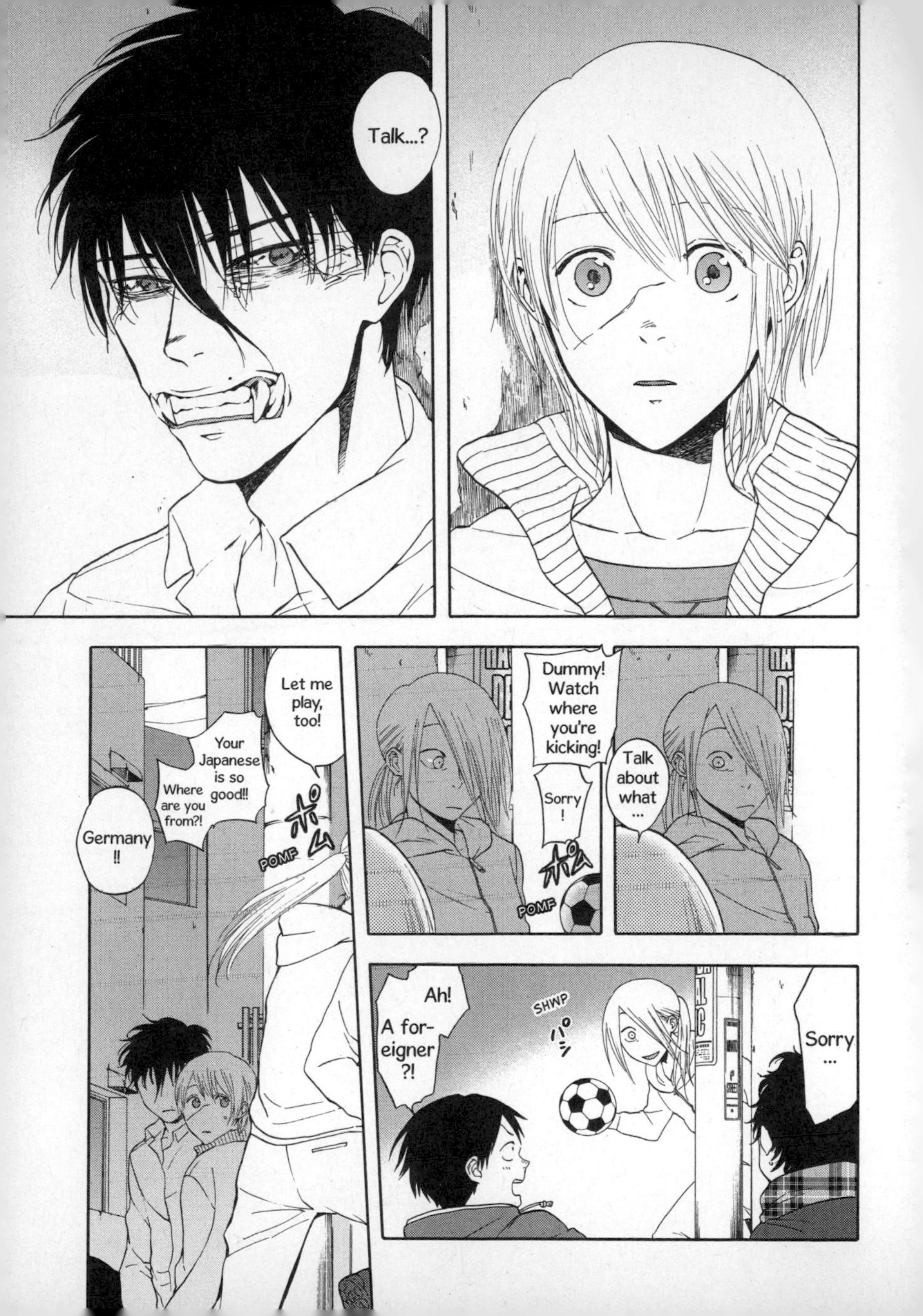
Talk...?
Talk about what...
Dummy! Watch where you're kicking!
Sorry!
POMF
Sorry...
SHWP
Ah! A foreigner?!
Let me play, too!
POMF
Your Japanese is so good!!
Where are you from?!
Germany!!

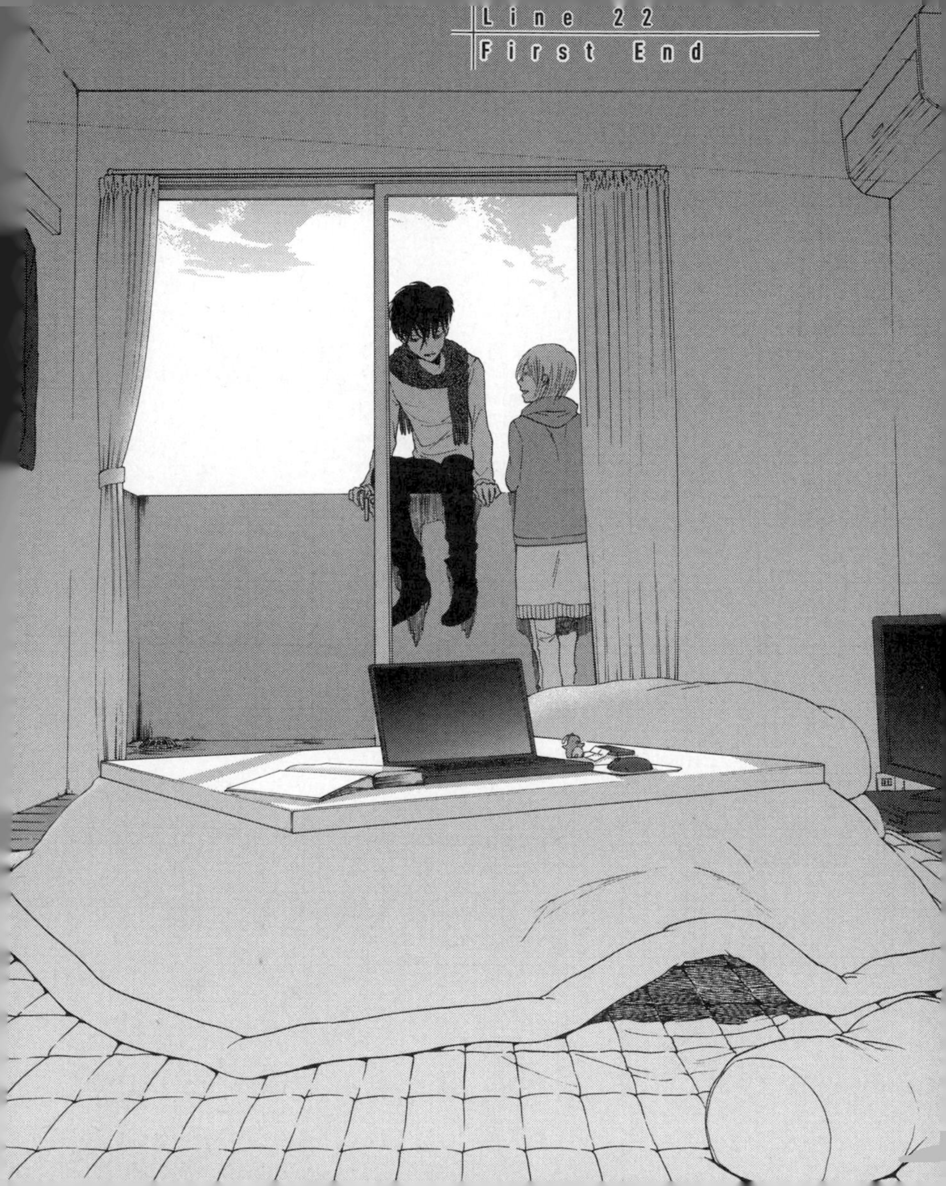
Line 22
First End

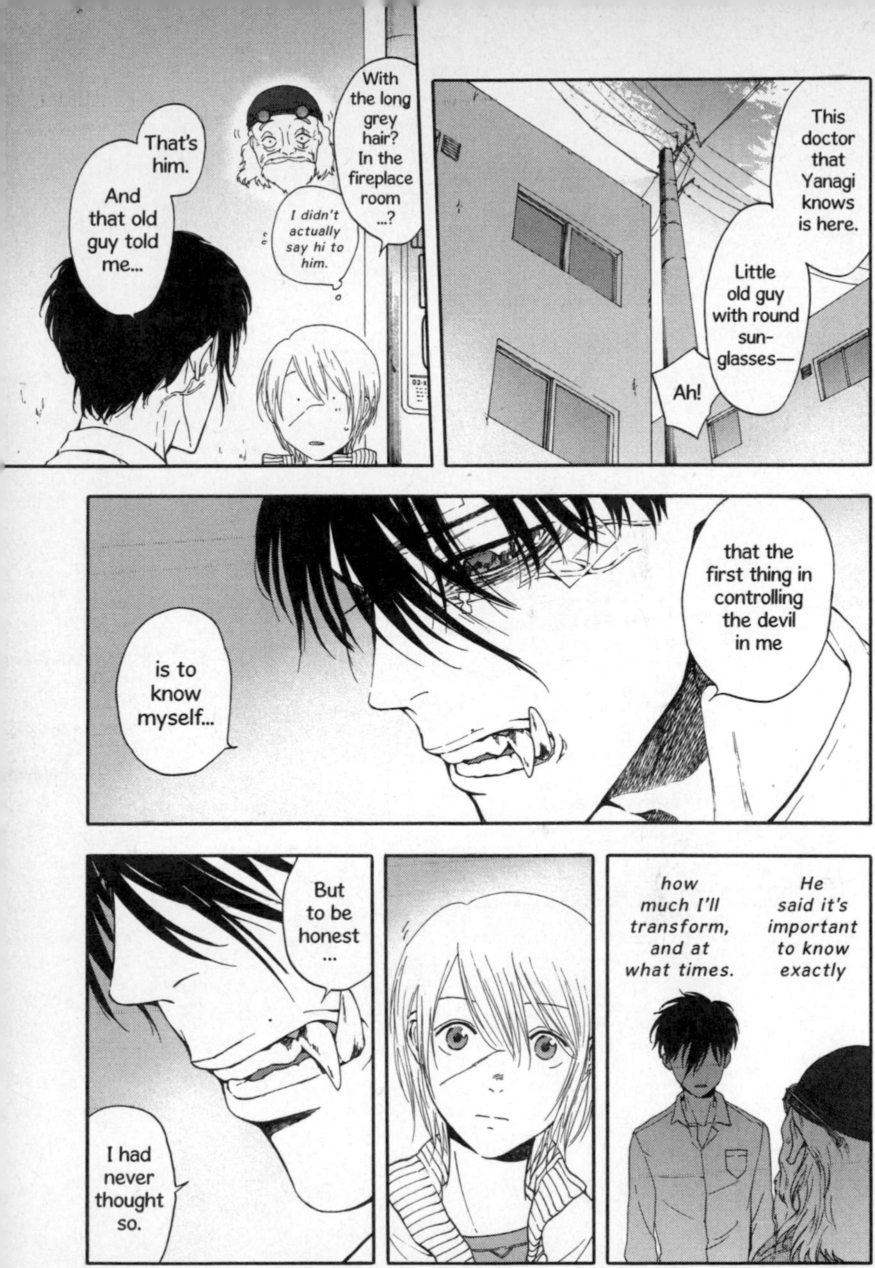
This doctor that Yanagi knows is here.
Little old guy with round sunglasses—
Ah!
With the long grey hair? In the fireplace room ...?
I didn't actually say hi to him.
That's him.
And that old guy told me...
that the first thing in controlling the devil in me
is to know myself...
He said it's important to know exactly
how much I'll transform, and at what times.
But to be honest ...
I had never thought so.

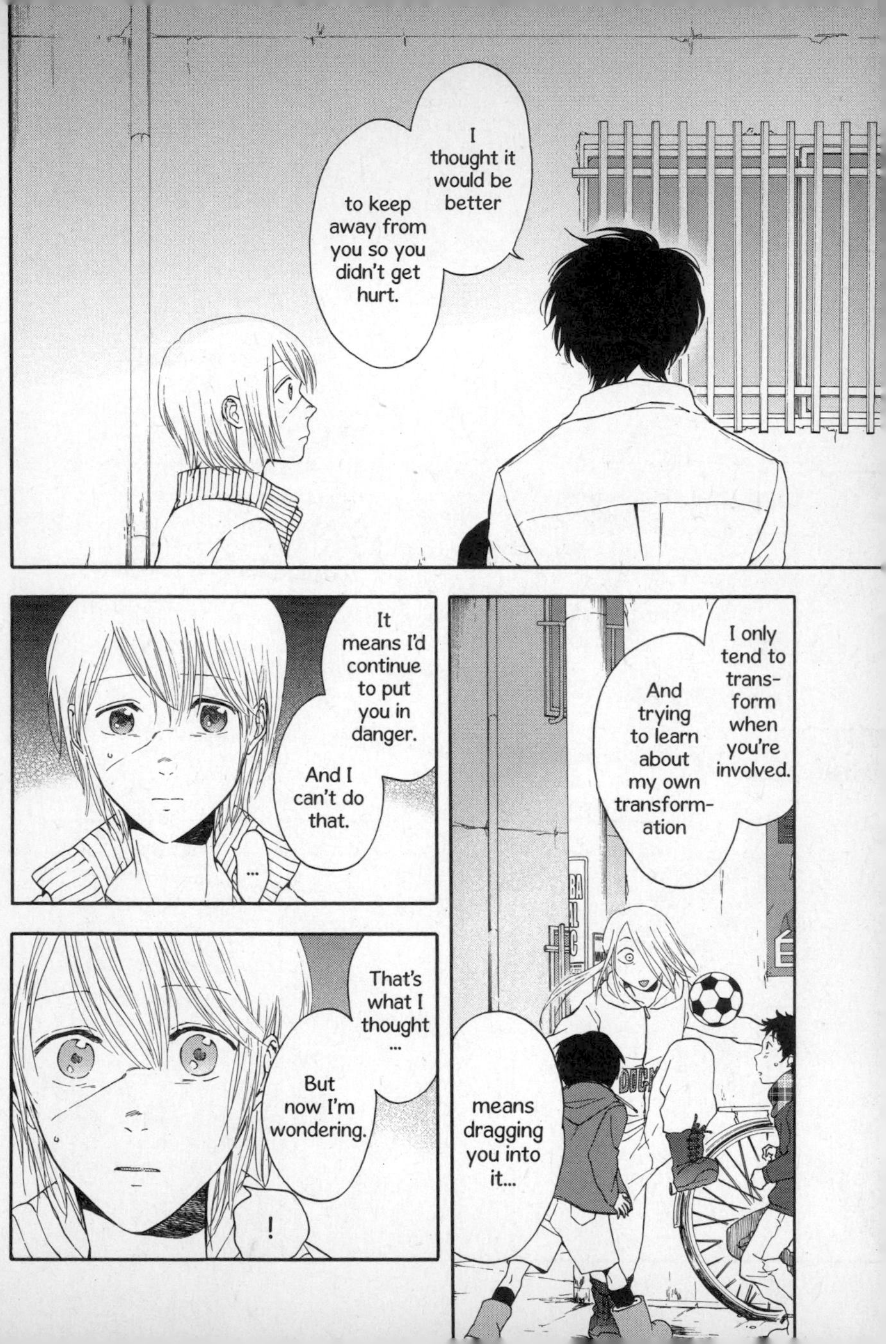
I thought it would be better to keep away from you so you didn't get hurt.
I only tend to transform when you're involved.
And trying to learn about my own transformation
means dragging you into it...
It means I'd continue to put you in danger.
And I can't do that.
...
That's what I thought...
But now I'm wondering.
!

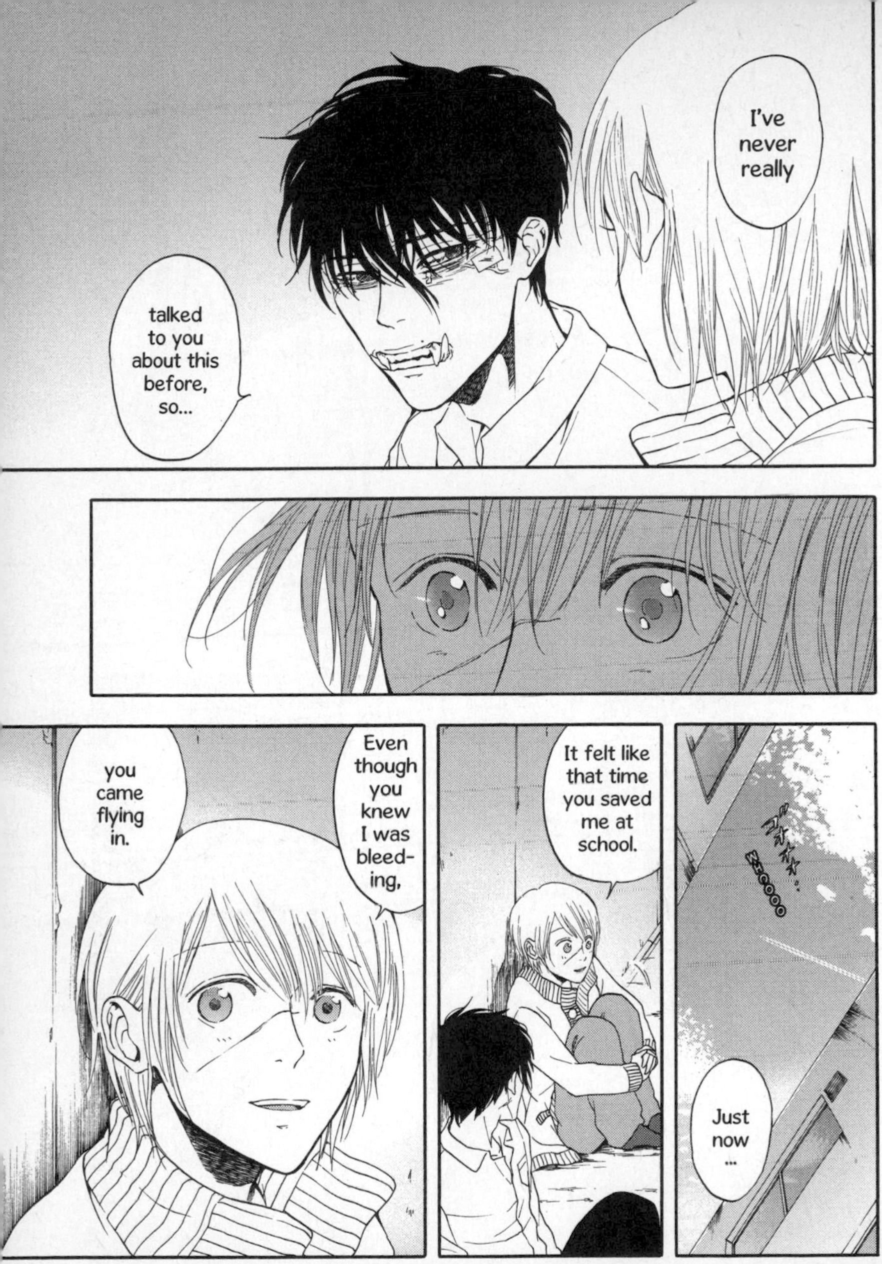
I've never really
talked to you about this before, so...
WHOOOO
Just now...
It felt like that time you saved me at school.
Even though you knew I was bleed-ing,
you came flying in.

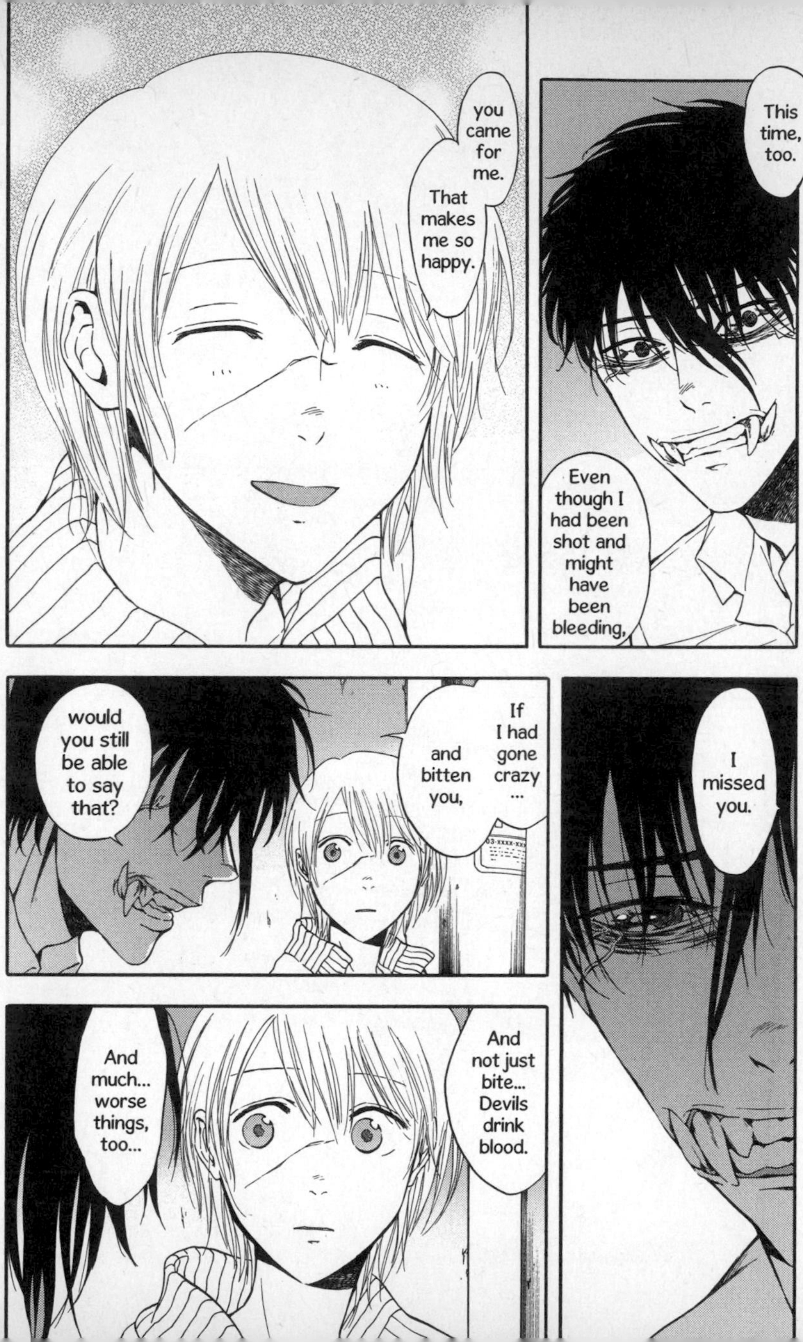
This time, too.
Even though I had been shot and might have been bleeding,
you came for me.
That makes me so happy.
I missed you.
If I had gone crazy...
and bitten you,
would you still be able to say that?
And not just bite... Devils drink blood.
And much... worse things, too...

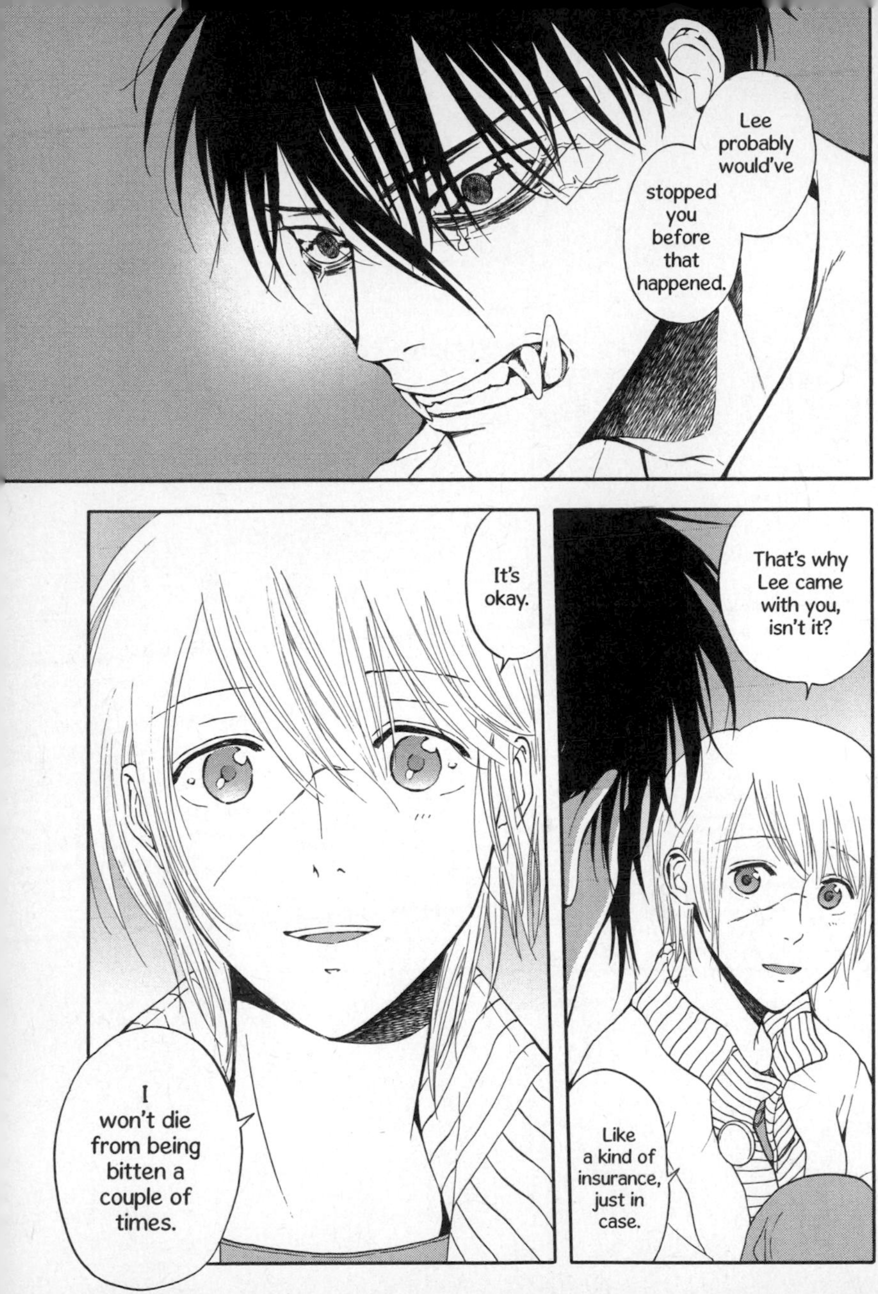
Lee probably would've stopped you before that happened.
That's why Lee came with you, isn't it?
Like a kind of insurance, just in case.
It's okay.
I won't die from being bitten a couple of times.

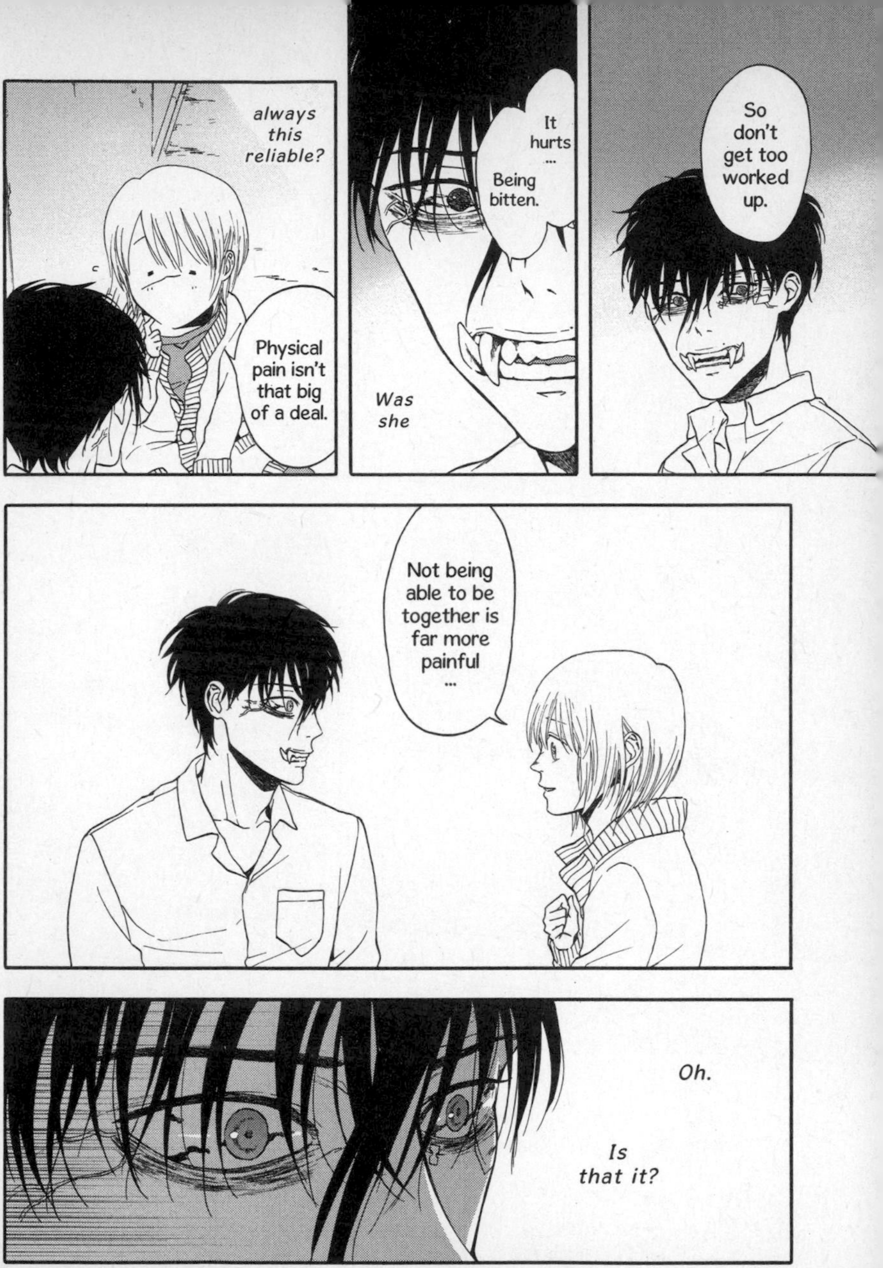
So don't get too worked up.
It hurts ... Being bitten.
Was she
always this reliable?
Physical pain isn't that big of a deal.
Not being able to be together is far more painful ...
Oh.
Is that it?

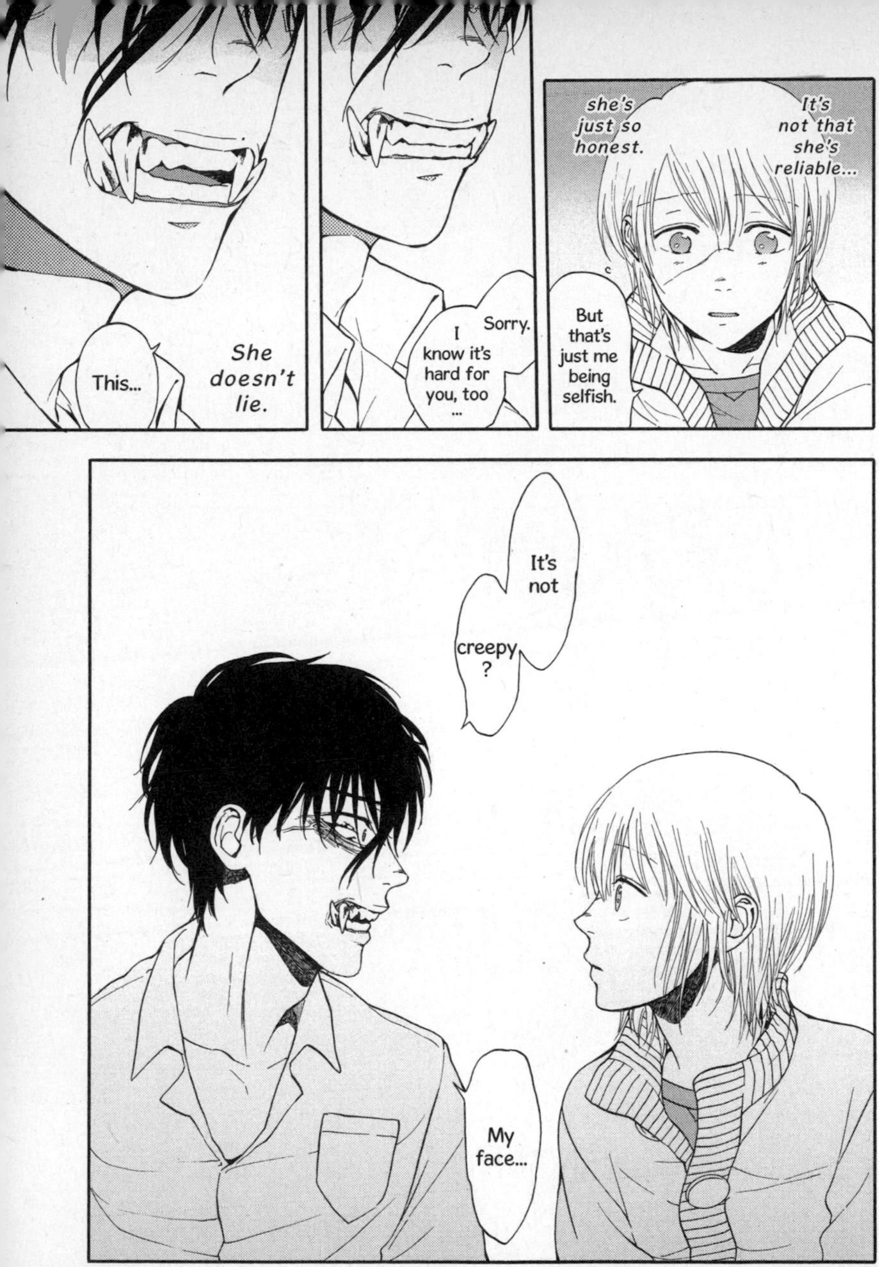
It's not that she's reliable...
she's just so honest.
But that's just me being selfish.
Sorry.
I know it's hard for you, too ...
She doesn't lie.
This...
It's not
creepy ?
My face...

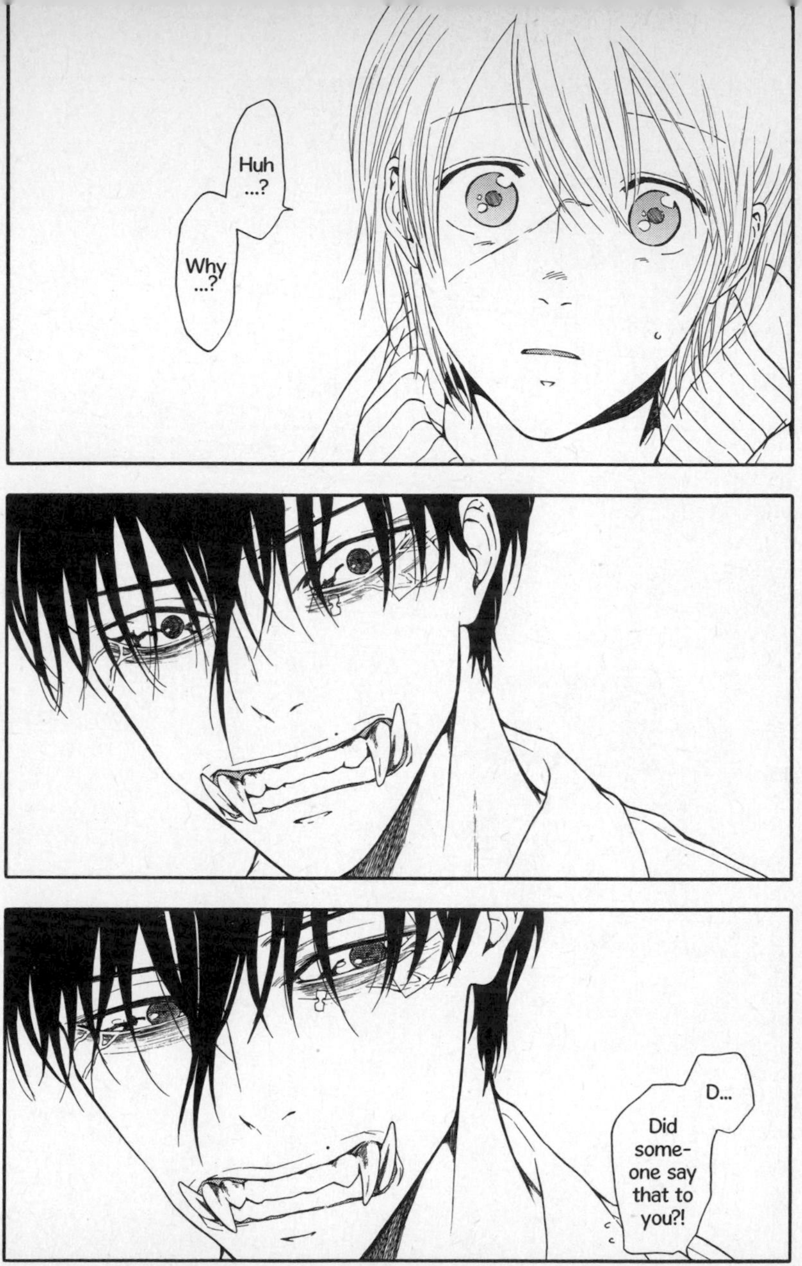
Huh ...?
Why ...?
D...
Did some-one say that to you?!

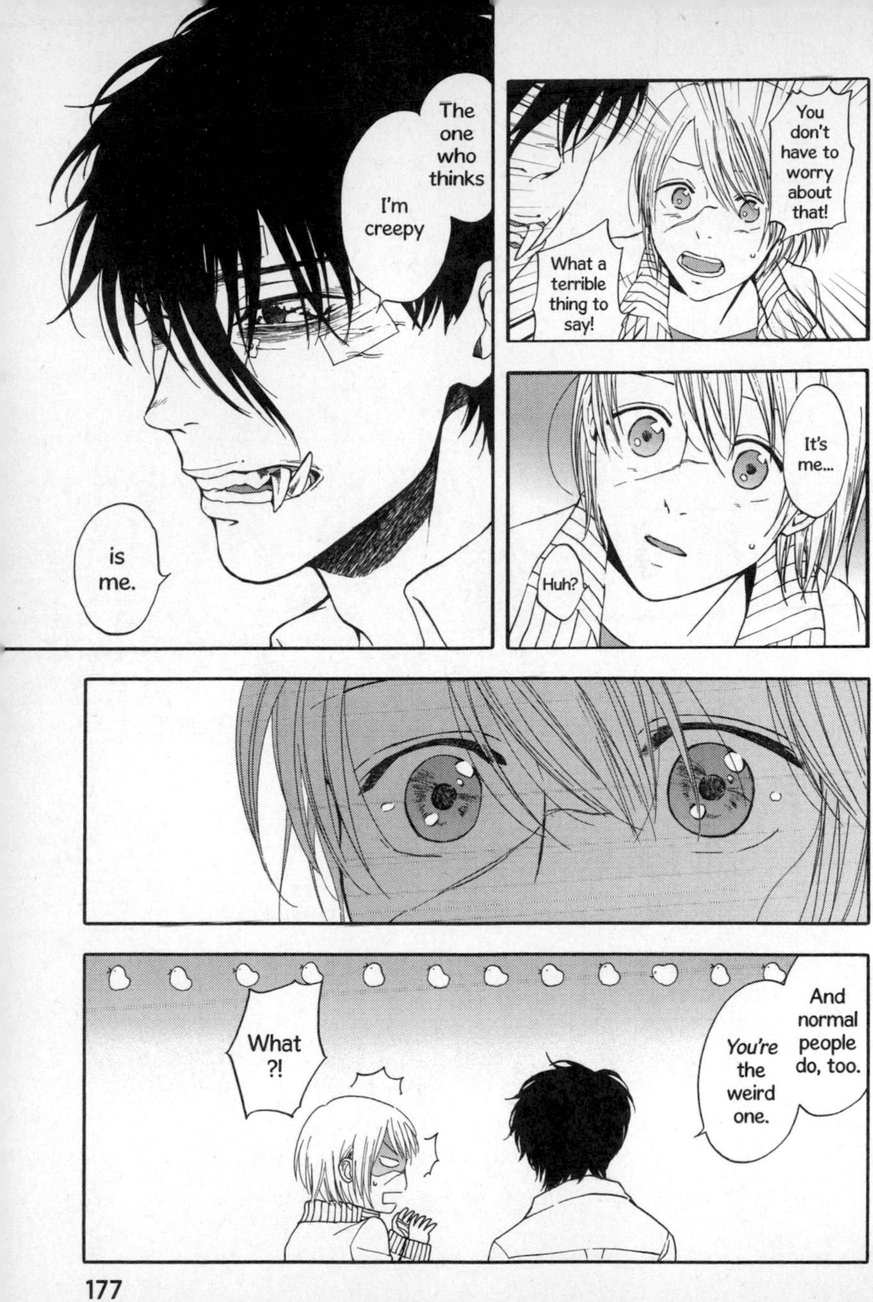
You don't have to worry about that!
What a terrible thing to say!
It's me...
Huh?
The one who thinks I'm creepy
is me.
And normal people do, too.
You're the weird one.
What ?!

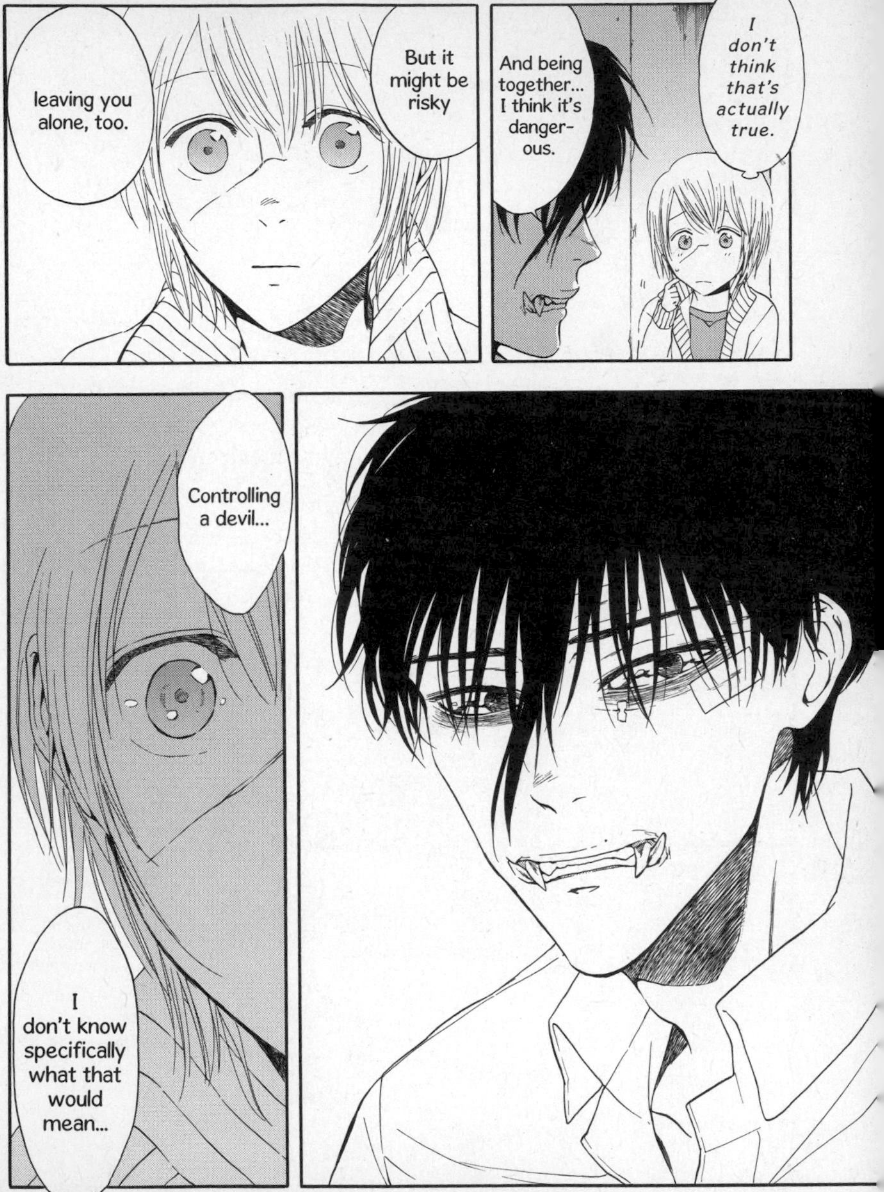
I don't think that's actually true.
And being together... I think it's danger-ous.
But it might be risky
leaving you alone, too.
Controlling a devil...
I don't know specifically what that would mean...

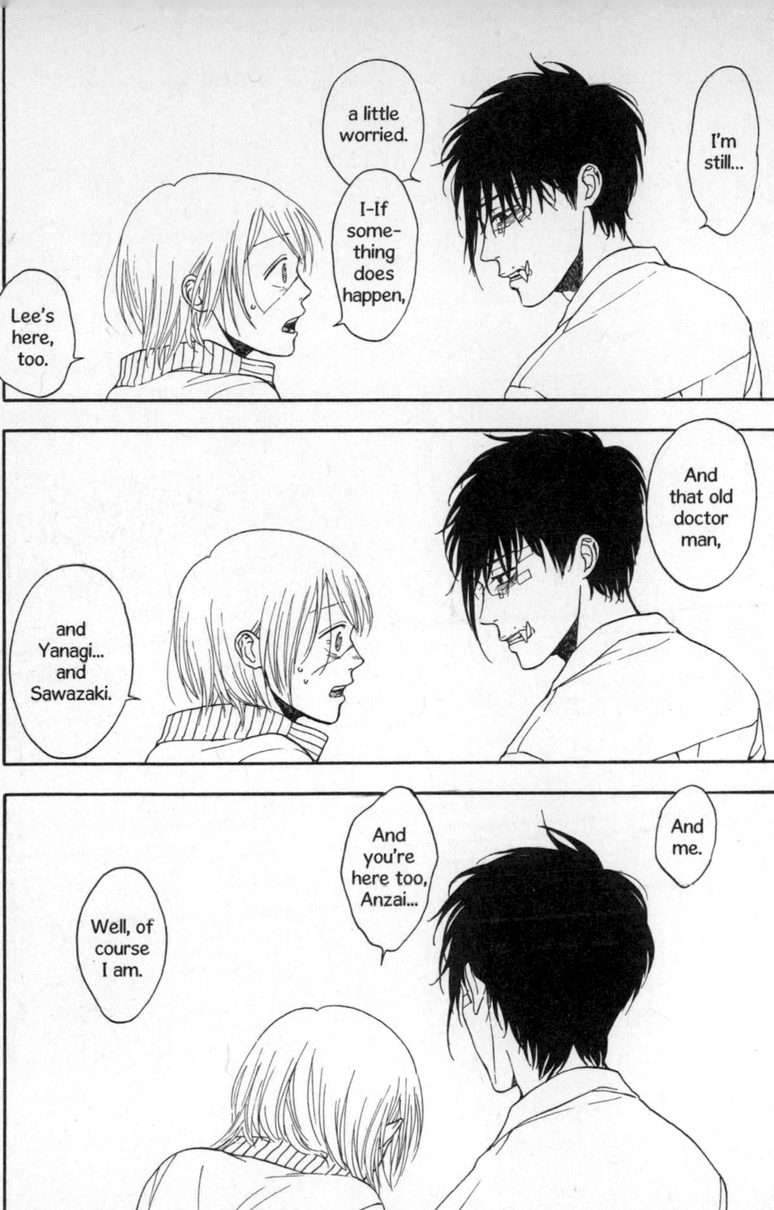
I'm still...
a little worried.
I-If something does happen,
Lee's here, too.
And that old doctor man,
and Yanagi... and Sawazaki.
And me.
And you're here too, Anzai...
Well, of course I am.

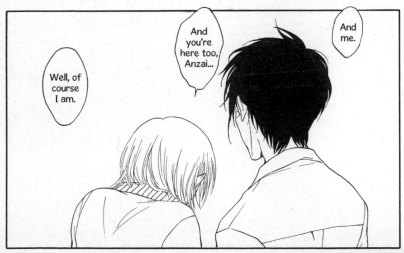

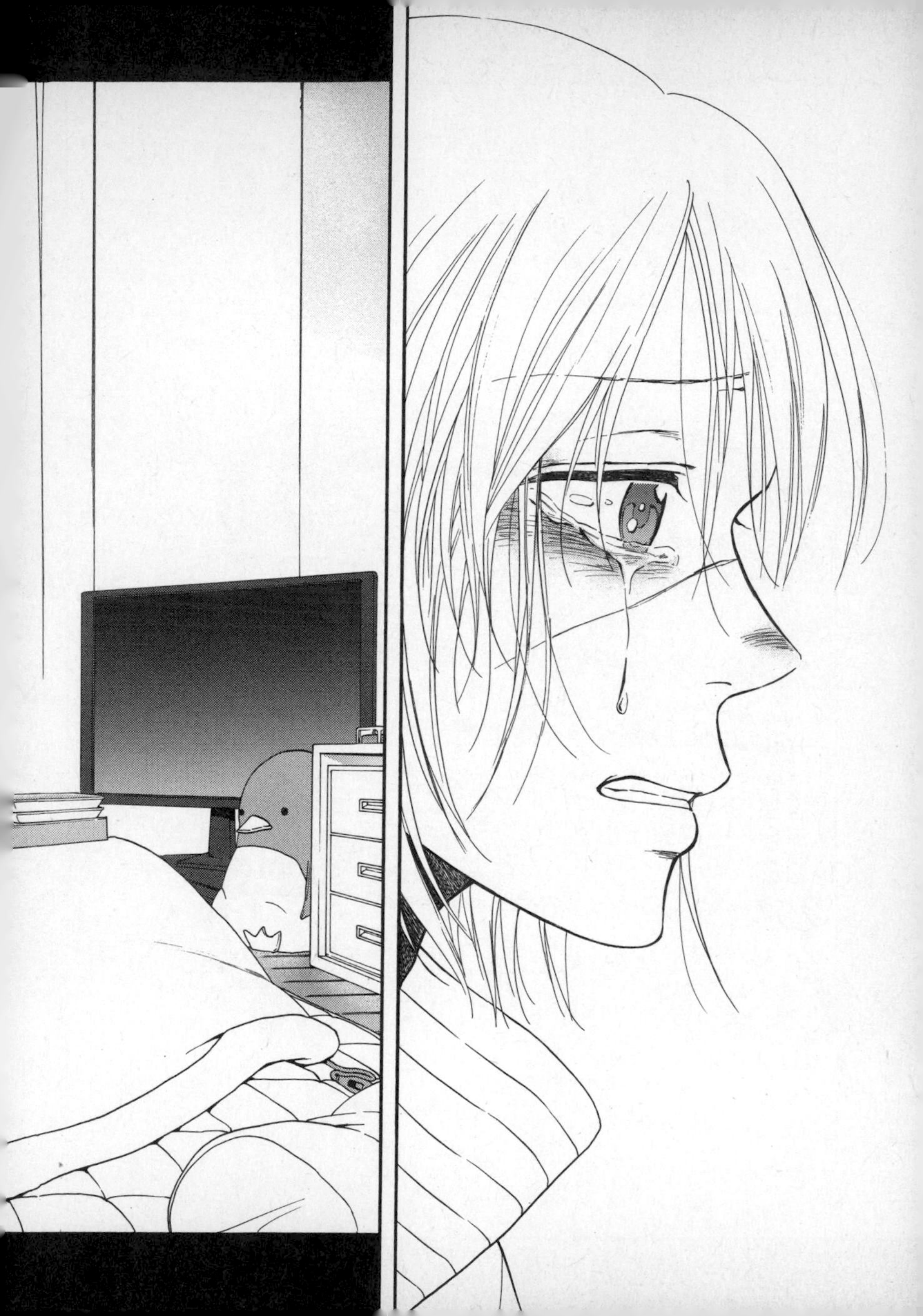

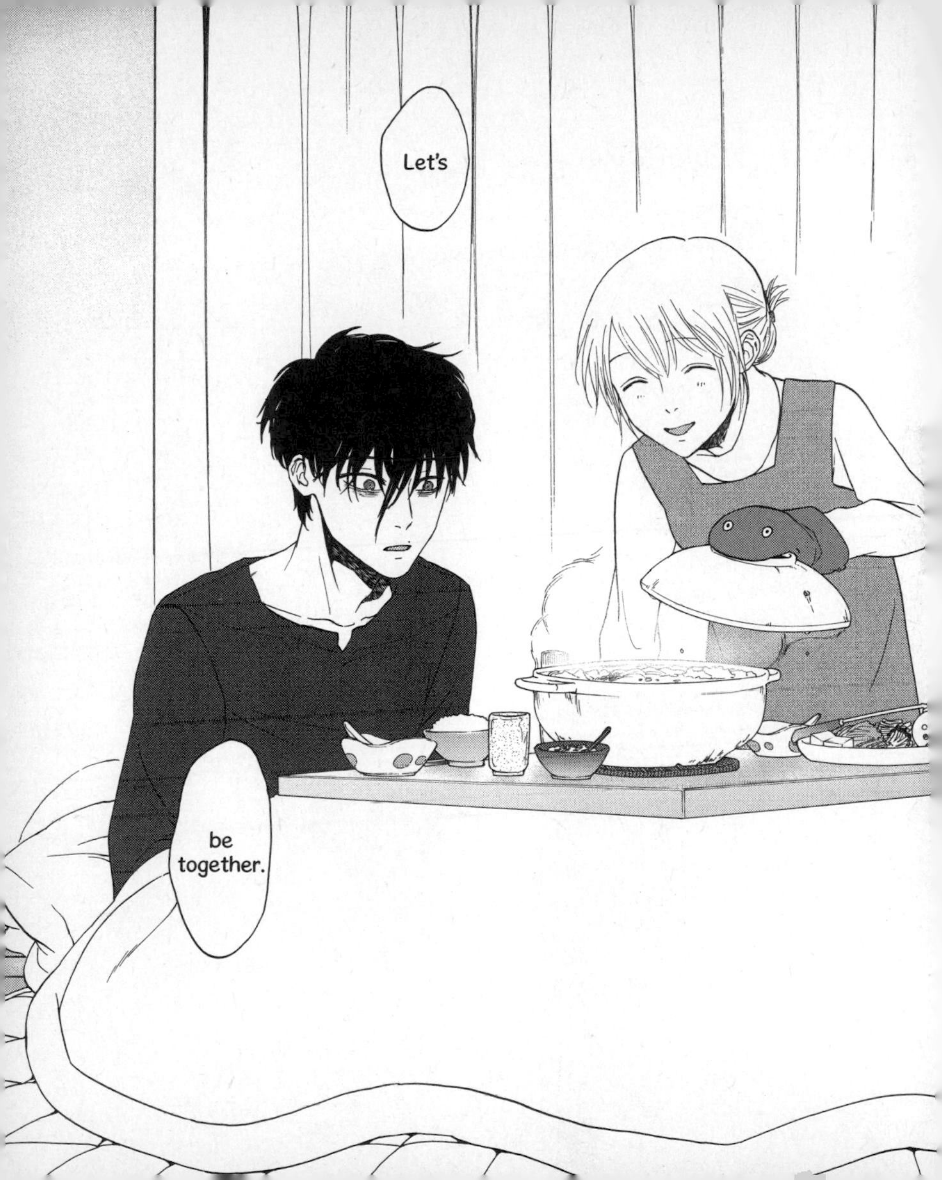
Let's
be together.

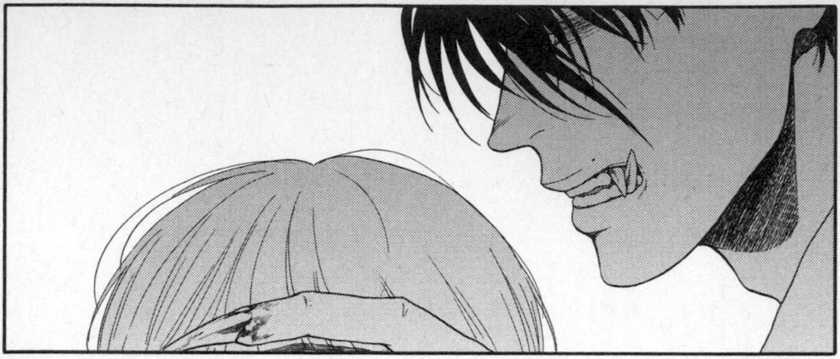

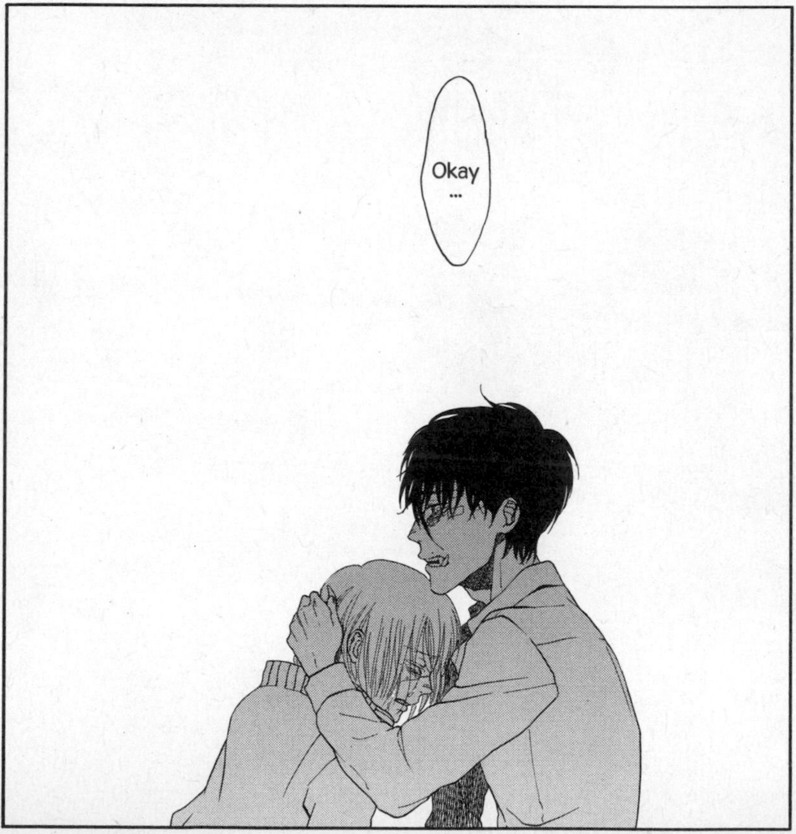
Okay
...

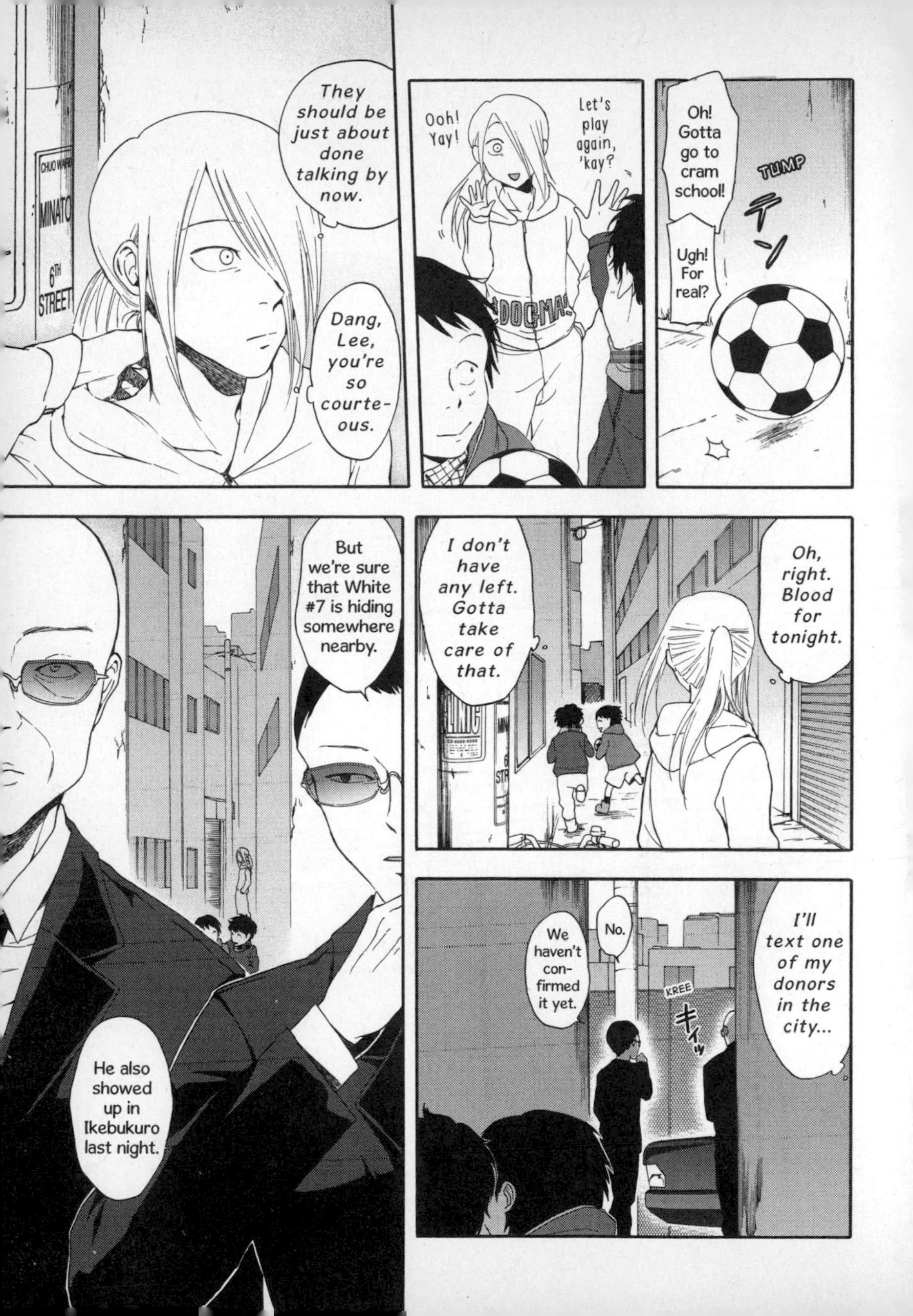
Oh! Gotta go to cram school!
Ugh! For real?
TUMP
テン
Let's play again, 'kay?
Ooh! Yay!
DOGMA
They should be just about done talking by now.
Dang, Lee, you're so courteous.
MINATO
6TH STREET
Oh, right. Blood for tonight.
I don't have any left. Gotta take care of that.
I'll text one of my donors in the city...
No.
We haven't confirmed it yet.
KREE
キイッ
But we're sure that White #7 is hiding somewhere nearby.
He also showed up in Ikebukuro last night.

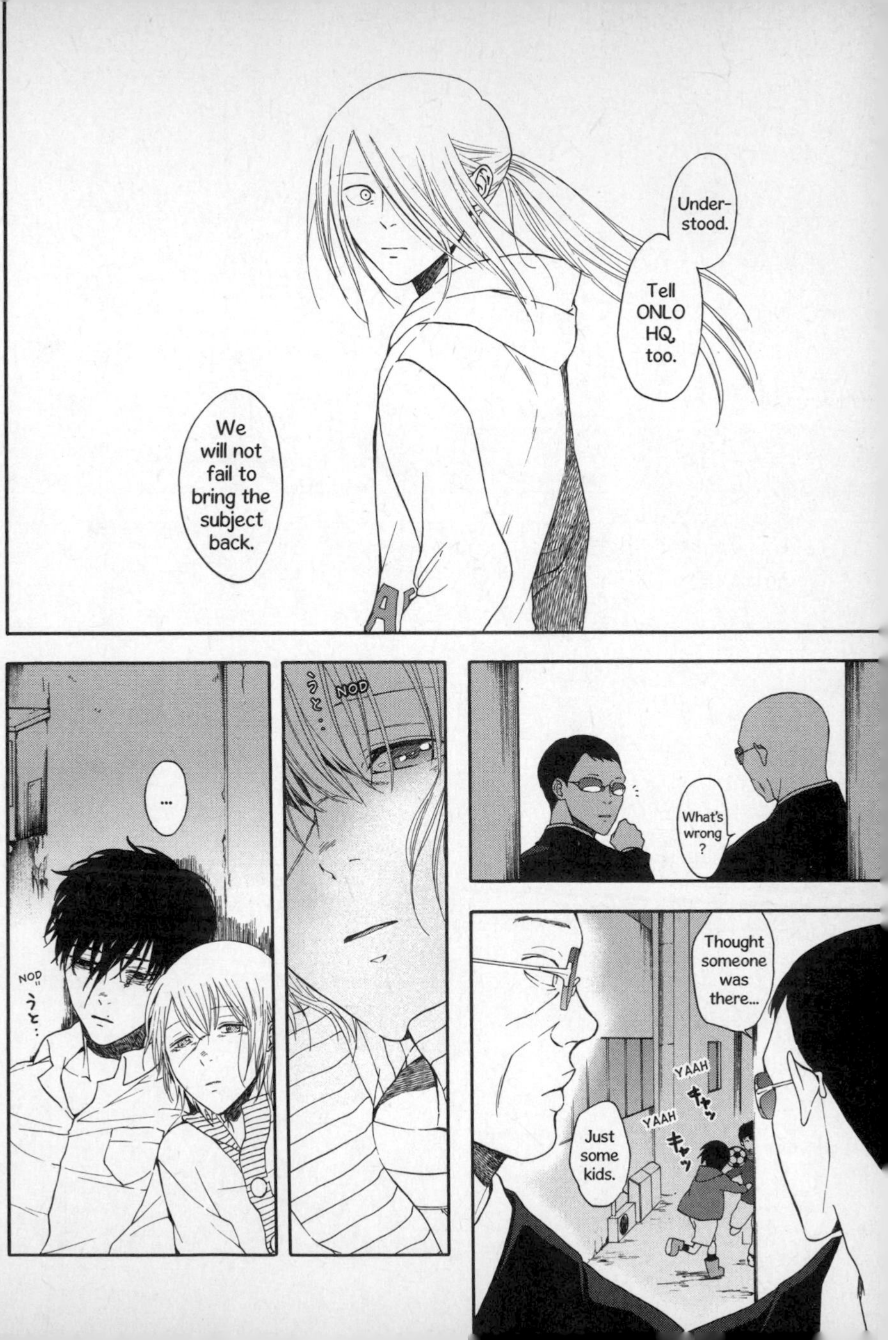

Under-stood.
Tell ONLO HQ, too.
We will not fail to bring the subject back.
What's wrong?
Thought someone was there...
YAAH
キャッ
YAAH
キャッ
Just some kids.
うと‥
NOD
...
NOD
うと‥

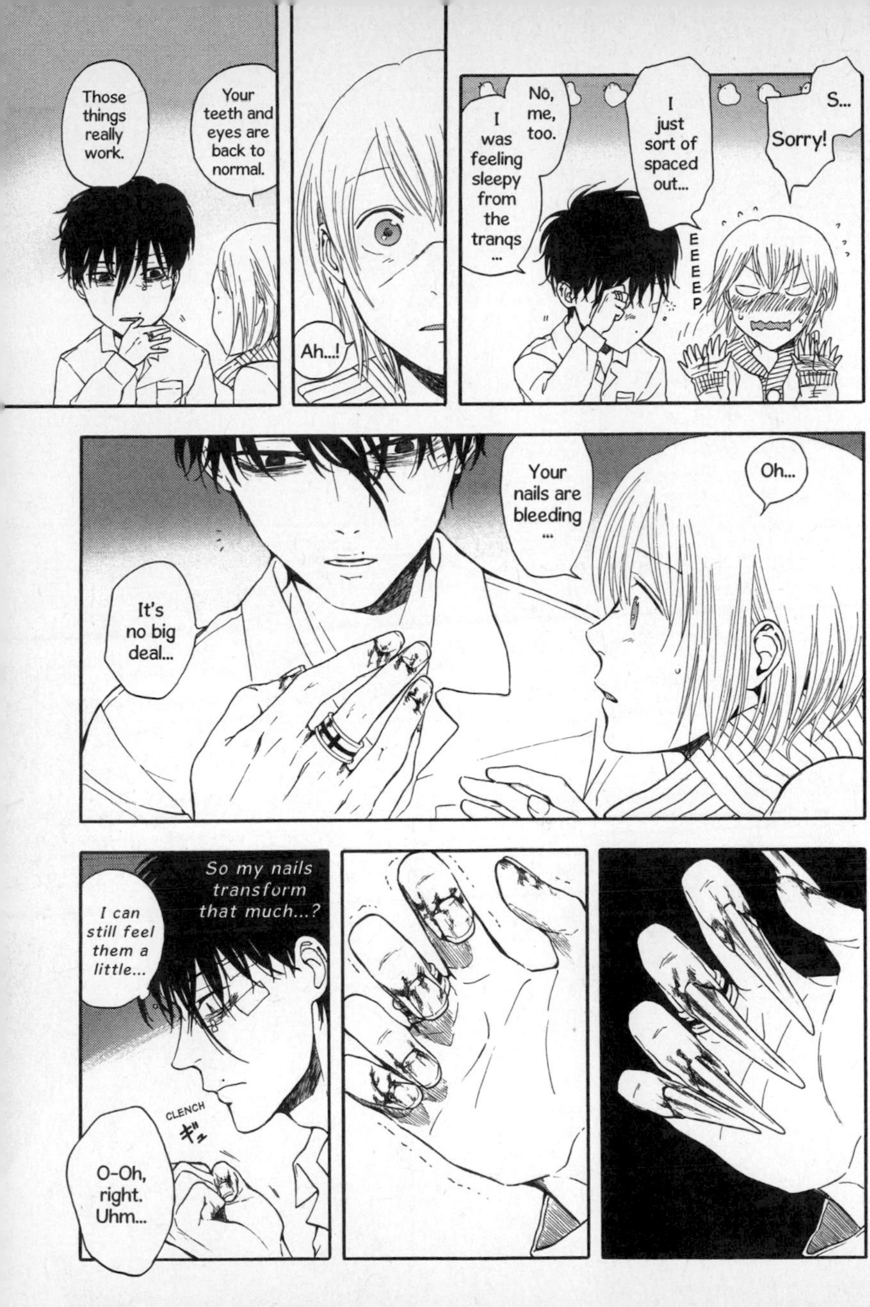
S... Sorry!
I just sort of spaced out...
EEEEP
No, me, too. I was feeling sleepy from the tranqs ...
Ah...!
Your teeth and eyes are back to normal.
Those things really work.
Oh...
Your nails are bleeding ...
It's no big deal...
So my nails transform that much...?
I can still feel them a little...
CLENCH
ギュ
O-Oh, right. Uhm...

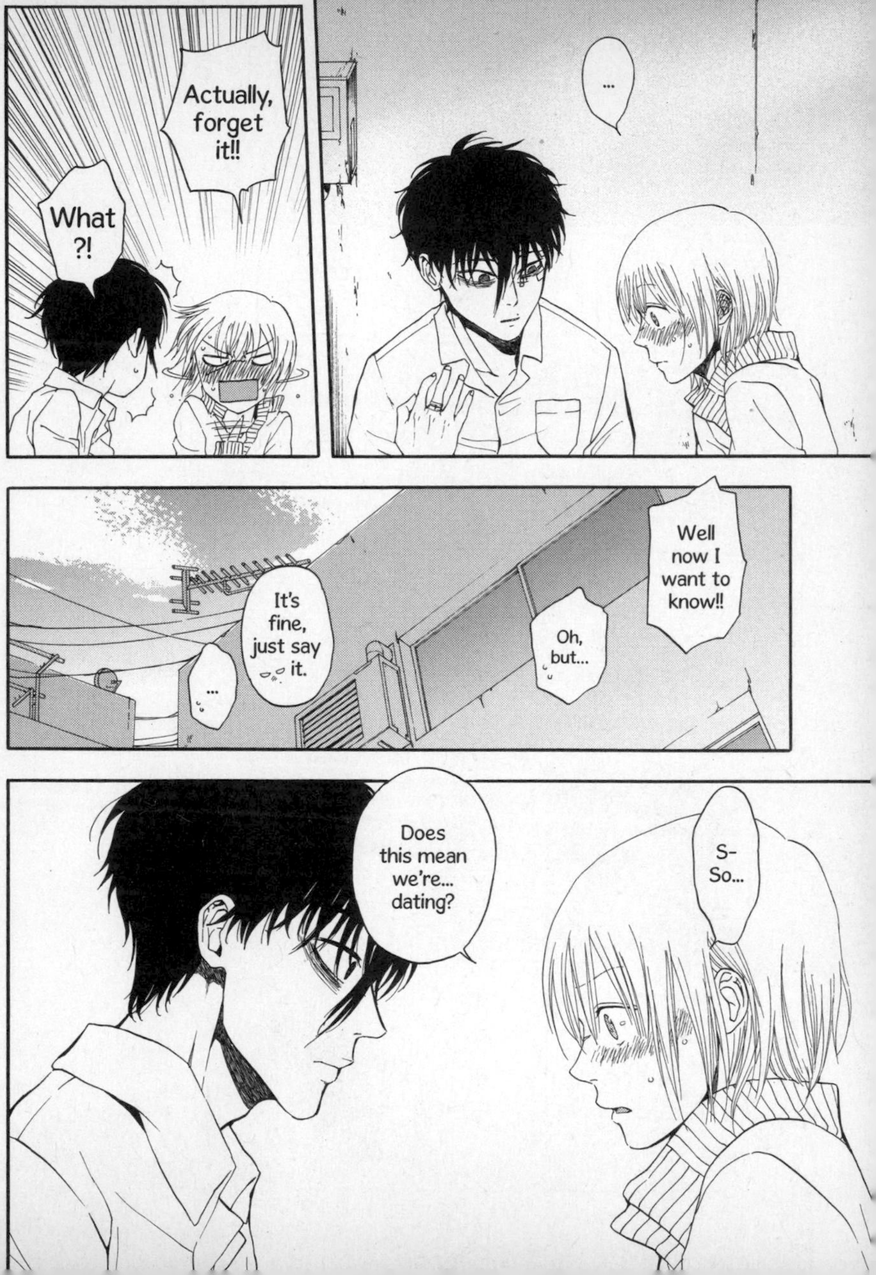
...
Actually, forget it!!
What ?!
Well now I want to know!!
Oh, but...
It's fine, just say it.
...
S- So...
Does this mean we're... dating?

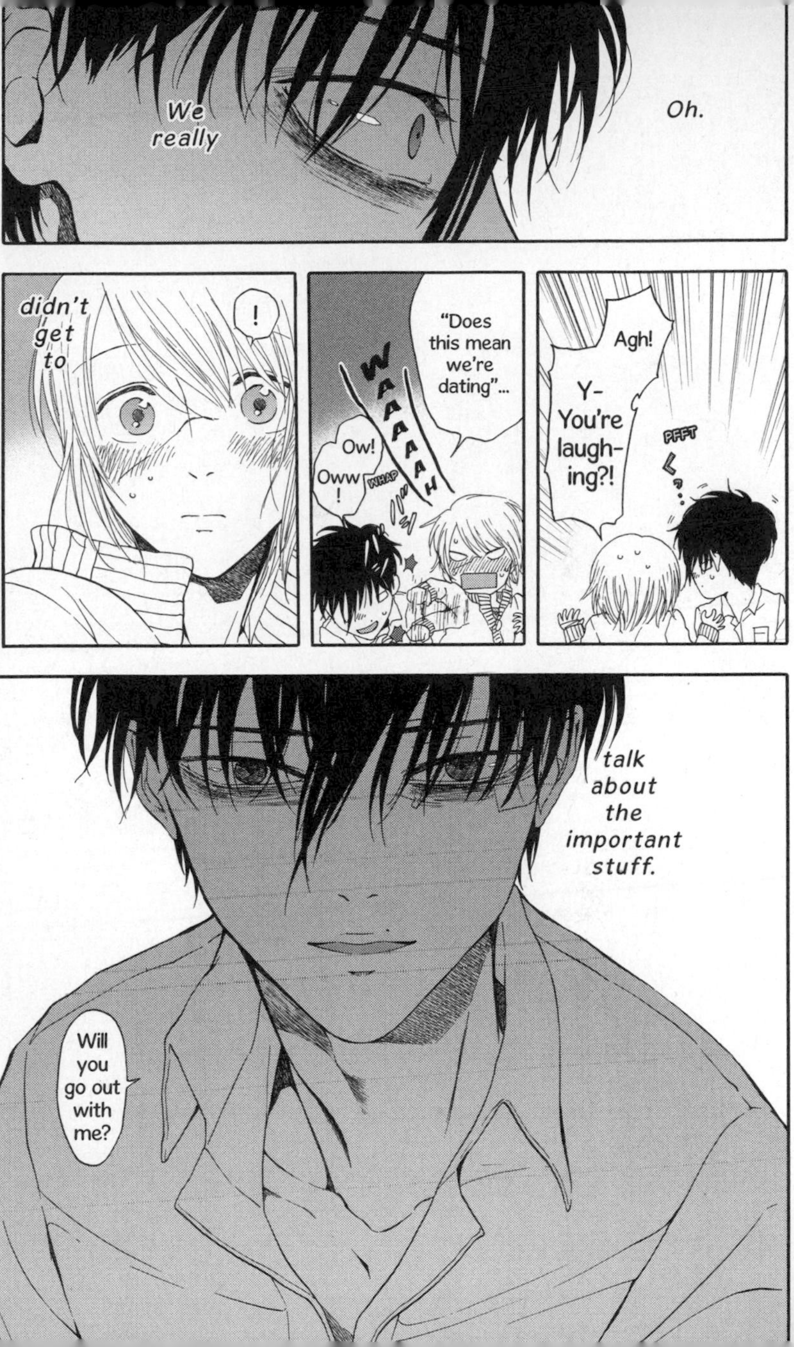
Oh.
We really
Agh!
Y-You're laughing?!
PFFT
"Does this mean we're dating"...
WAAAAAH
Ow!
Oww!
WHAP
!
didn't get to
talk about the important stuff.
Will you go out with me?

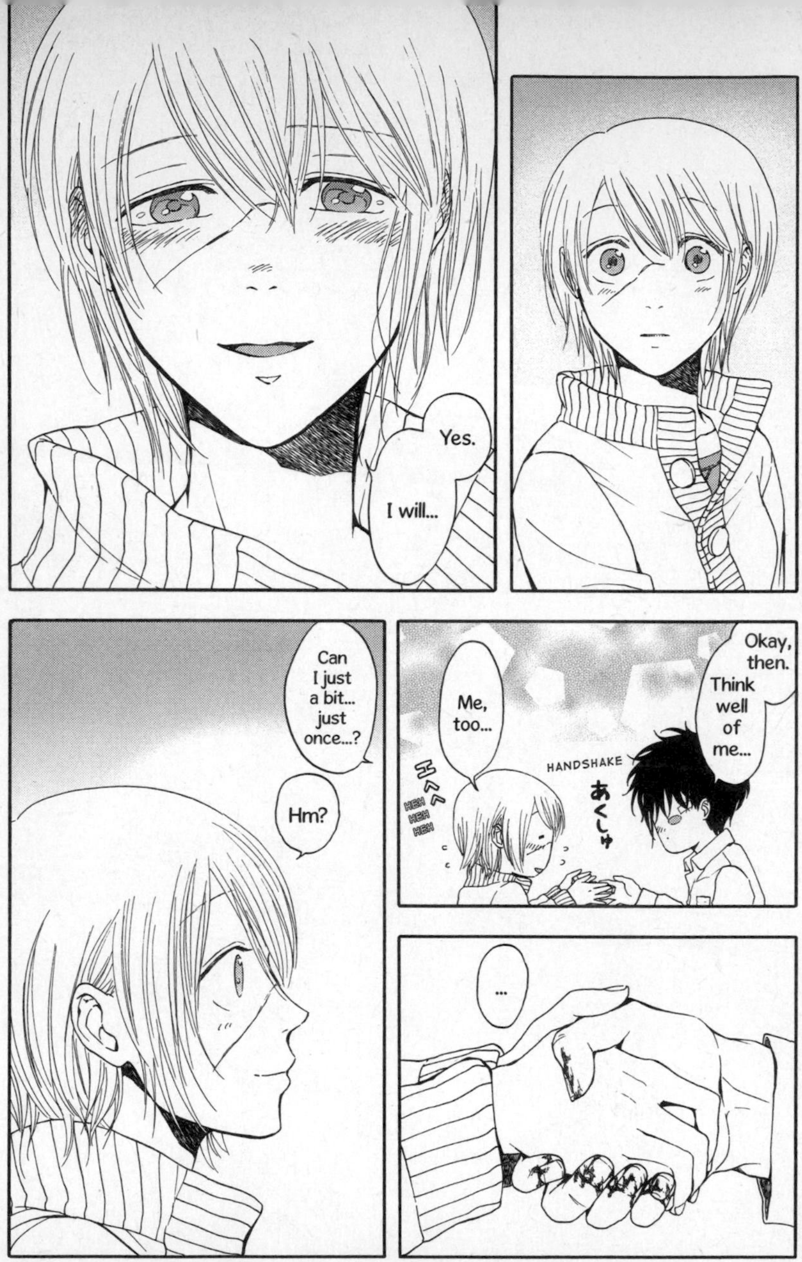
Yes.
I will...
Okay, then. Think well of me...
HANDSHAKE
あくしゅ
Me, too...
えへへ
HEH HEH HEH
...
Can I just a bit... just once...?
Hm?

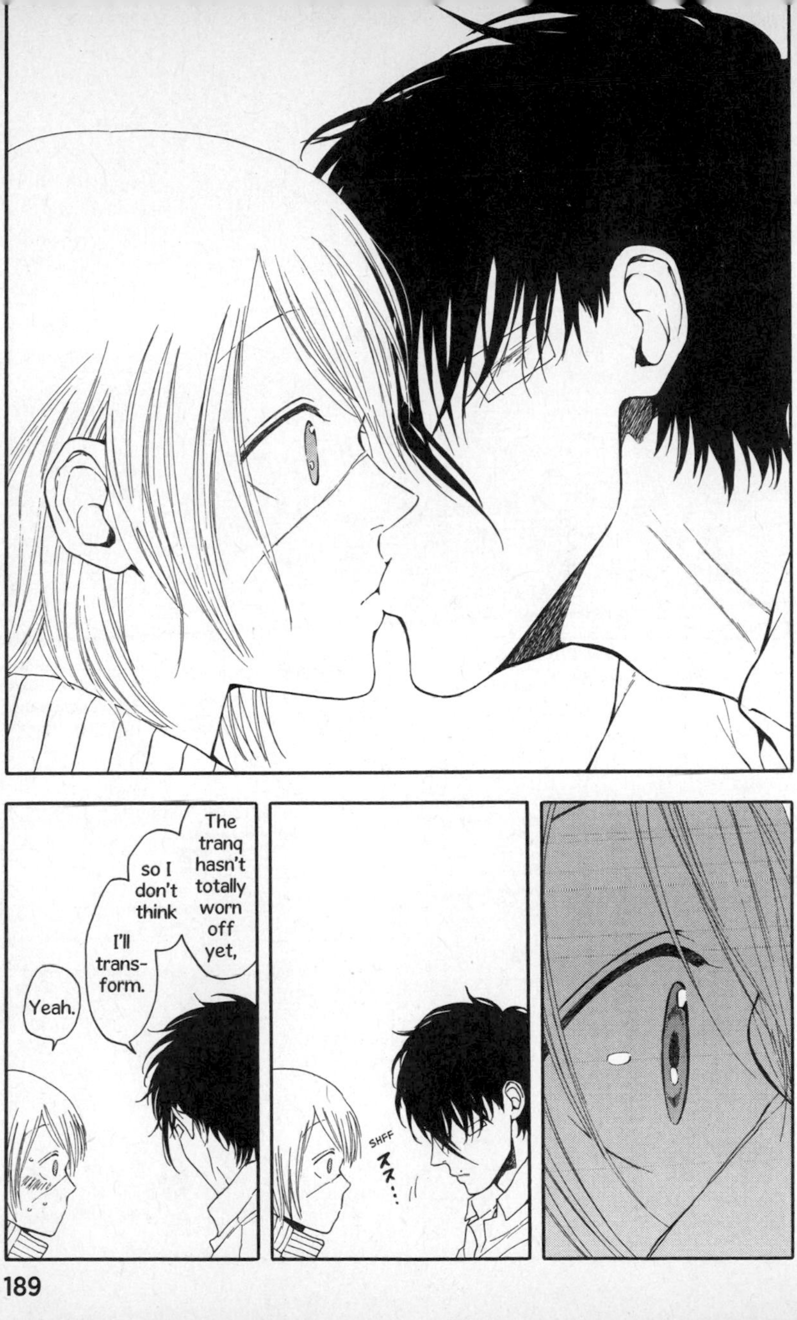
SHFF
スス…
The tranq hasn't totally worn off yet,
so I don't think I'll transform.
Yeah.

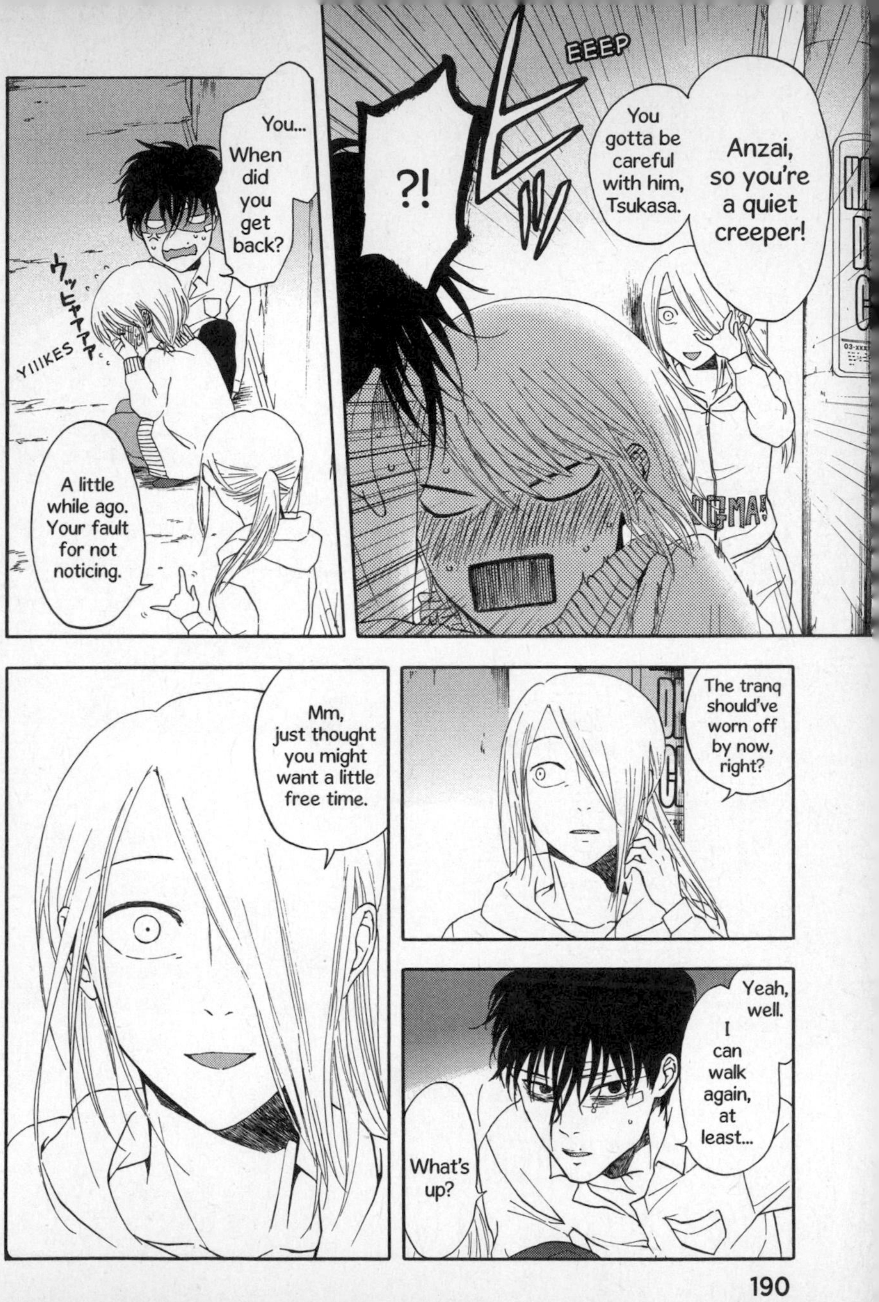
EEEP
Anzai, so you're a quiet creeper!
You gotta be careful with him, Tsukasa.
?!
You... When did you get back?
ウッヒャアアア
YIIIKES
A little while ago. Your fault for not noticing.
The tranq should've worn off by now, right?
Yeah, well. I can walk again, at least...
What's up?
Mm, just thought you might want a little free time.

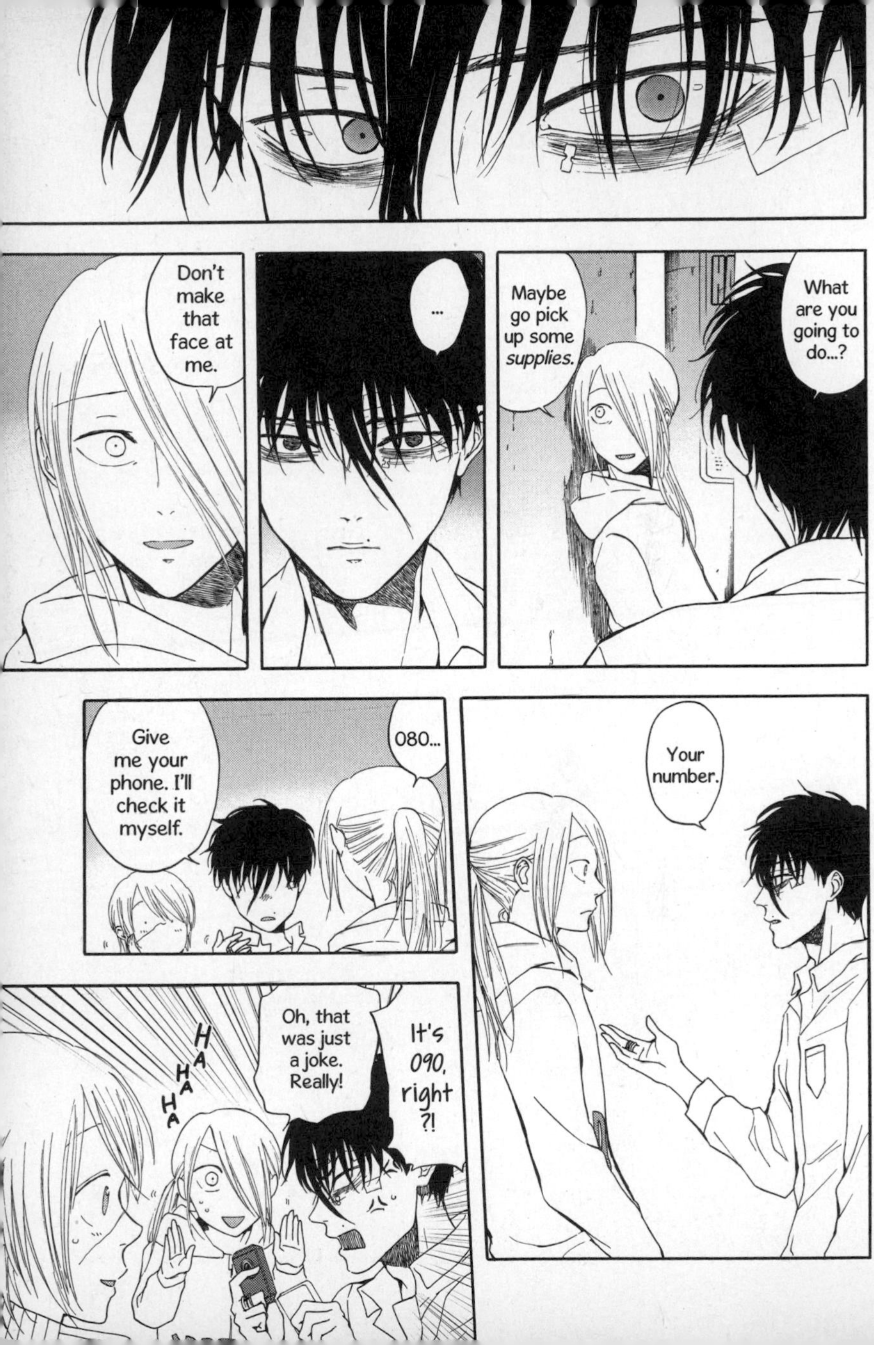
What are you going to do...?
Maybe go pick up some *supplies*.
...
Don't make that face at me.
Your number.
080...
Give me your phone. I'll check it myself.
It's 090, right?!
Oh, that was just a joke. Really!
HA HA HA

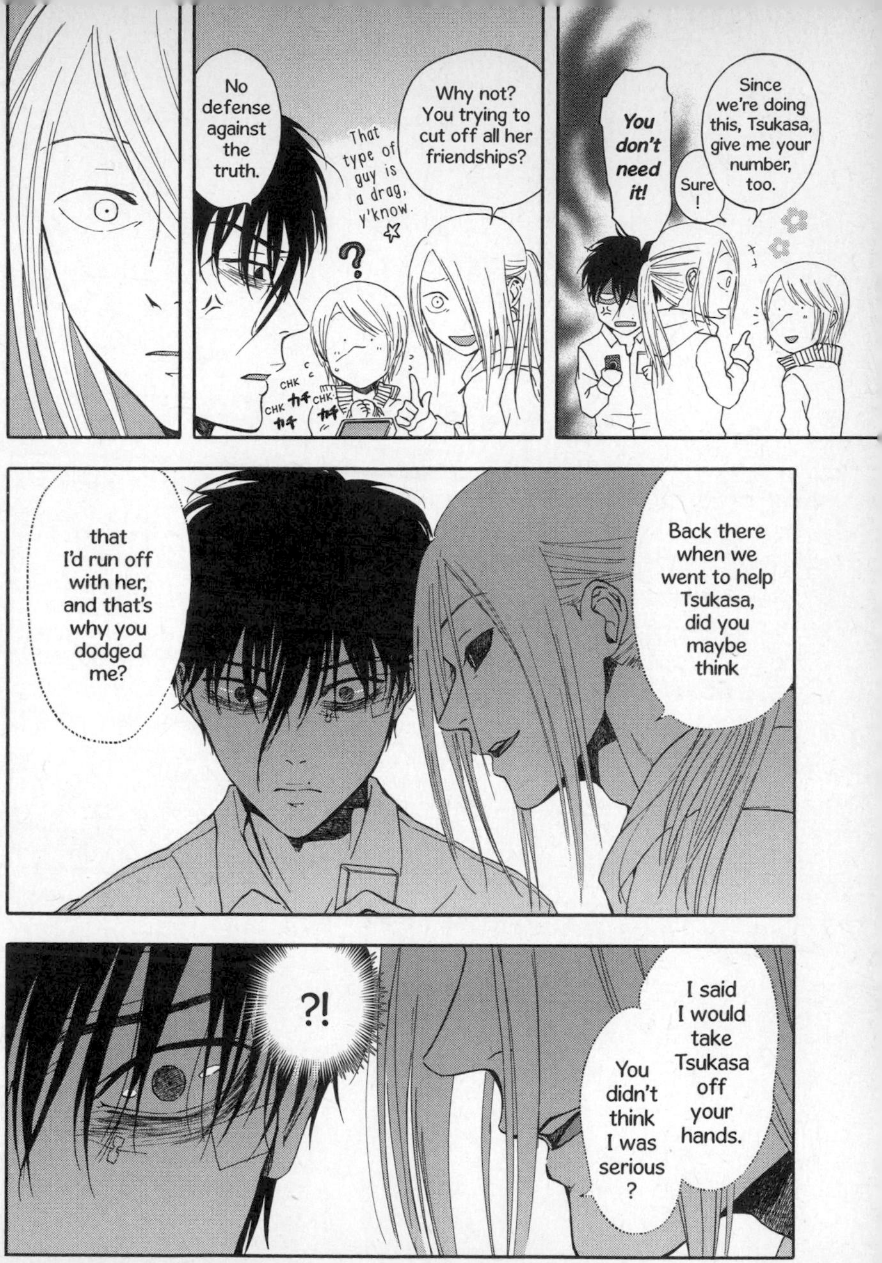
Since we're doing this, Tsukasa, give me your number, too.
Sure!
You don't need it!
Why not? You trying to cut off all her friendships?
That type of guy is a drag, y'know.
No defense against the truth.
CHK CHK CHK
Back there when we went to help Tsukasa, did you maybe think
that I'd run off with her, and that's why you dodged me?
I said I would take Tsukasa off your hands.
You didn't think I was serious?
?!

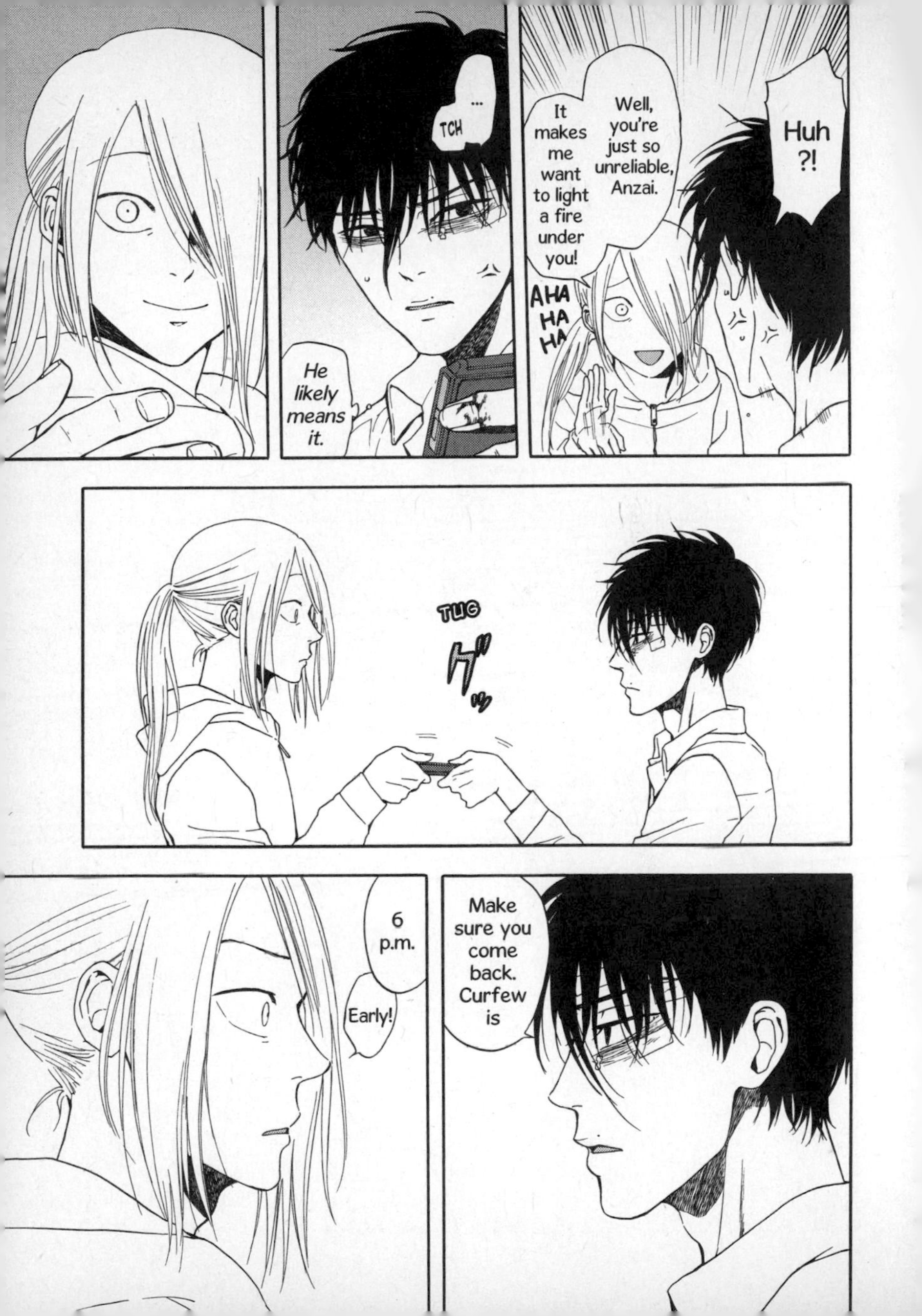
Huh ?!
Well, you're just so unreliable, Anzai.
It makes me want to light a fire under you!
AHA HA HA
...
TCH
He likely means it.
TUG
グッ
Make sure you come back. Curfew is
6 p.m.
Early!

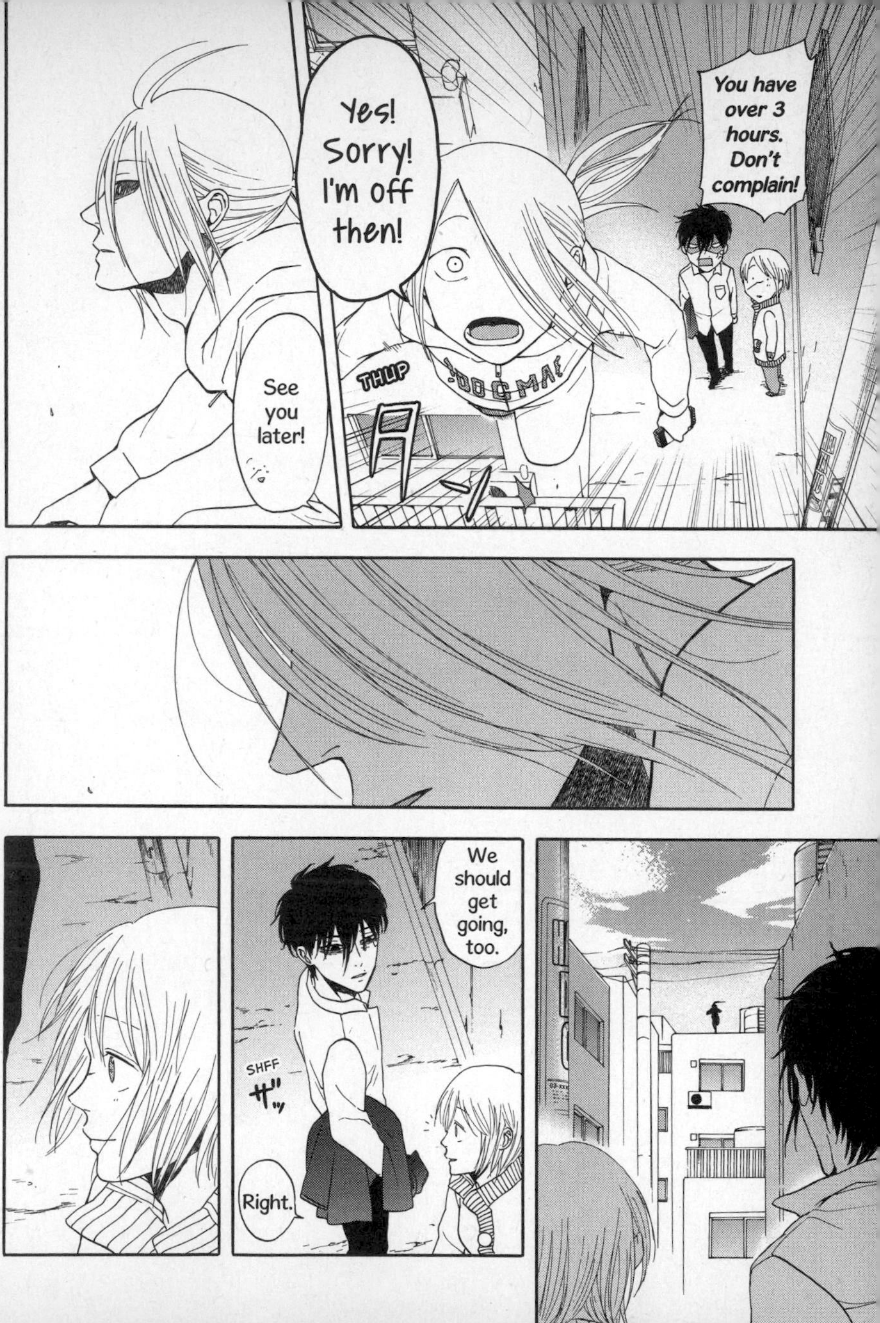

You have over 3 hours. Don't complain!
Yes! Sorry! I'm off then!
THUP
See you later!
We should get going, too.
SHFF
ザッ
Right.

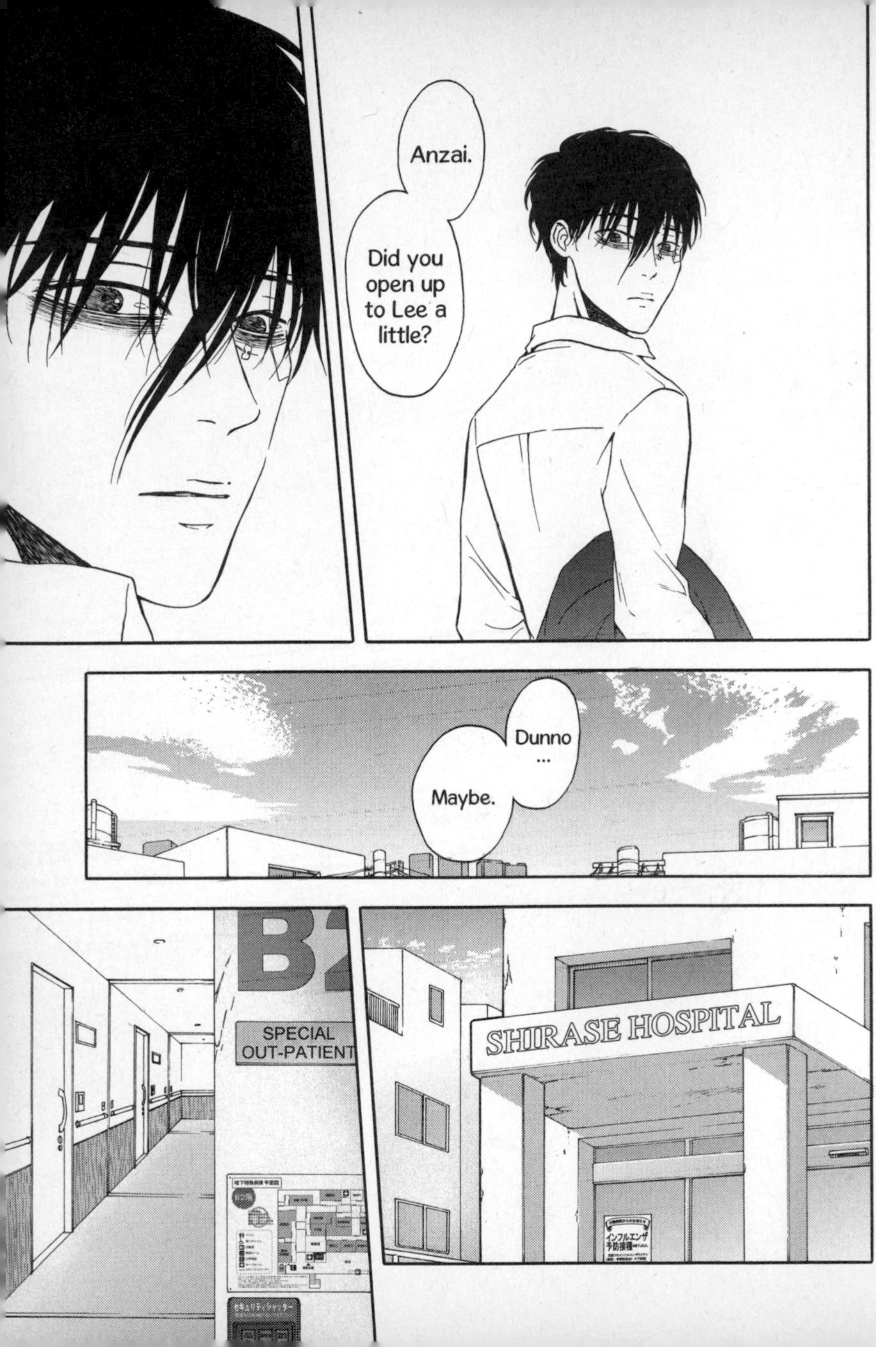
Anzai.
Did you open up to Lee a little?
Dunno...
Maybe.
SHIRASE HOSPITAL
インフルエンザ
予防接種
B2
SPECIAL
OUT-PATIENT

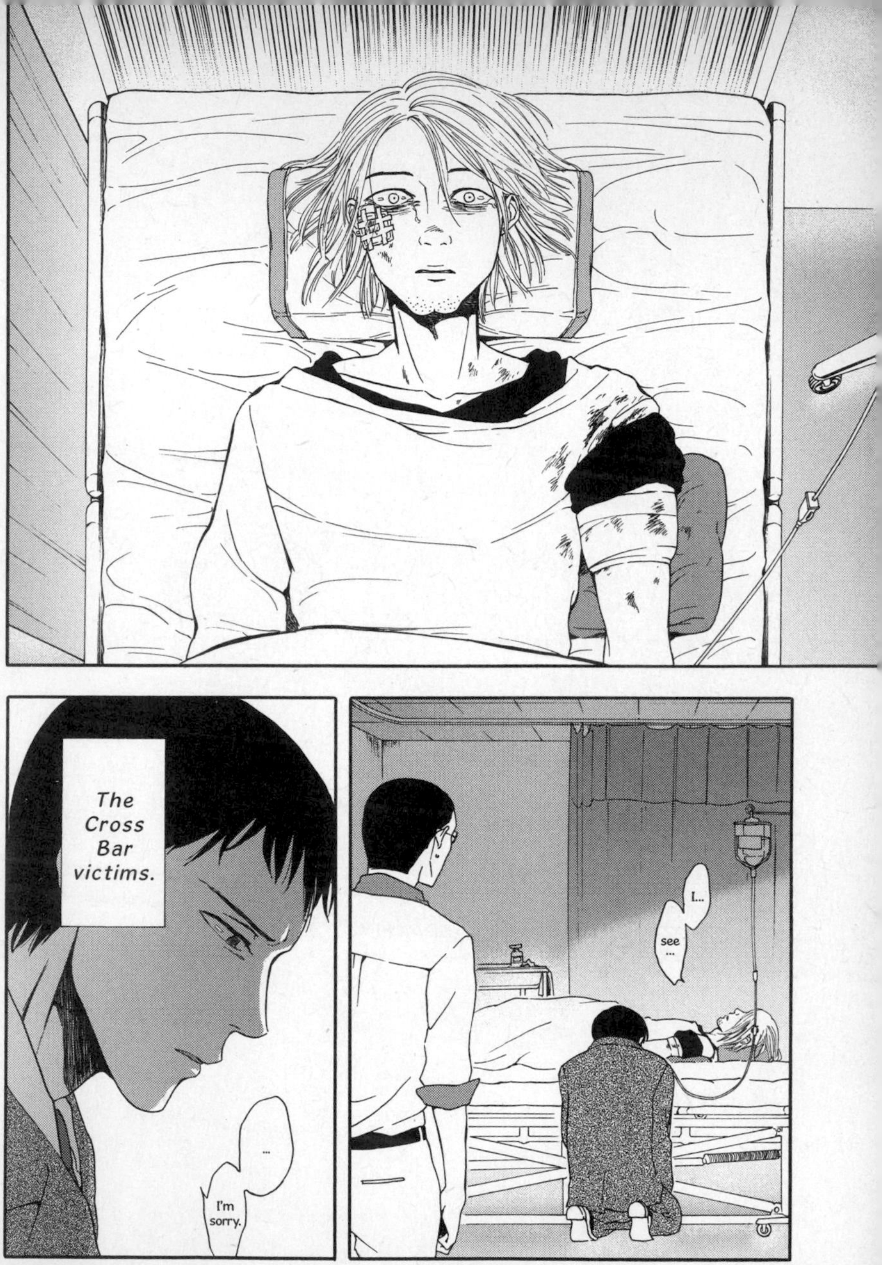
I... see...
The Cross Bar victims.
...
I'm sorry.

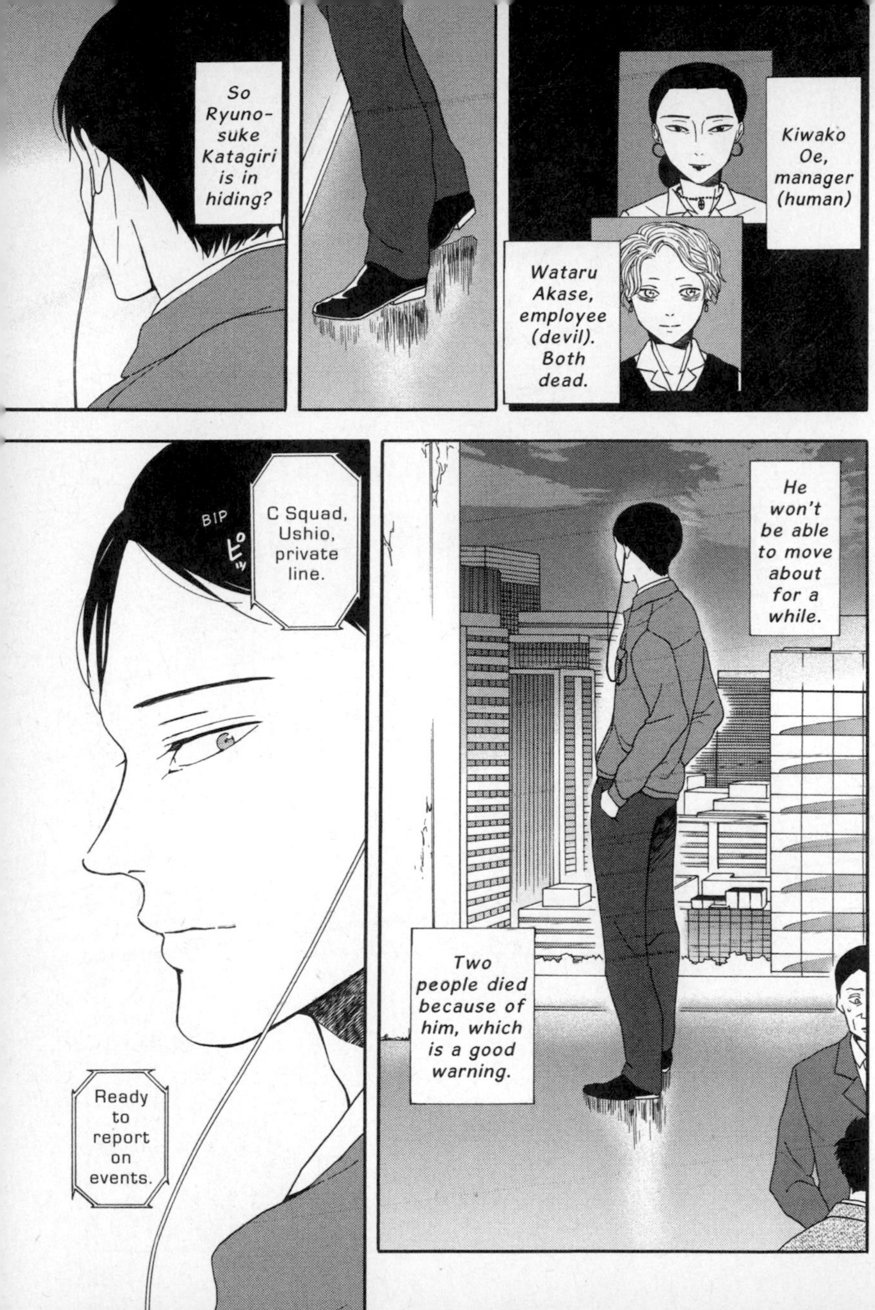
Kiwako Oe, manager (human)
Wataru Akase, employee (devil). Both dead.
So Ryunosuke Katagiri is in hiding?
He won't be able to move about for a while.
Two people died because of him, which is a good warning.
C Squad, Ushio, private line.
BIP
ピッ
Ready to report on events.

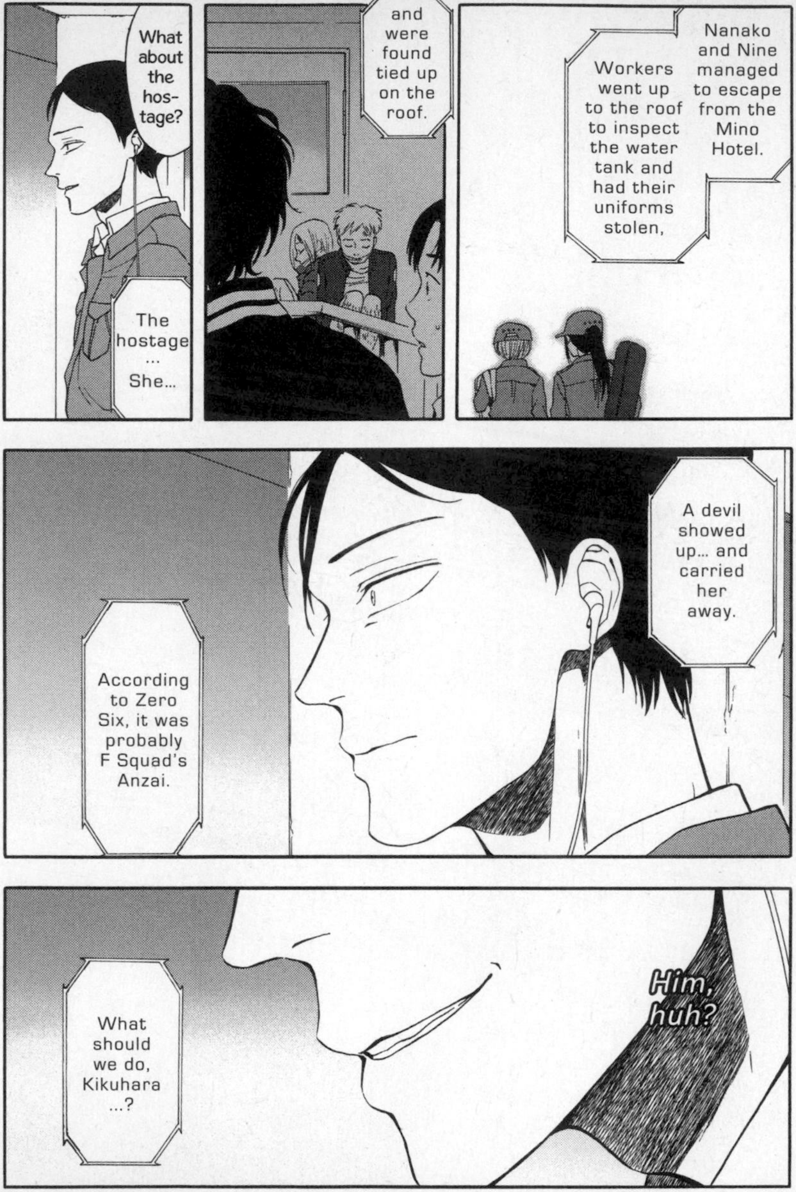
Nanako and Nine managed to escape from the Mino Hotel.
Workers went up to the roof to inspect the water tank and had their uniforms stolen,
and were found tied up on the roof.
What about the hos-tage?
The hostage ... She...
A devil showed up... and carried her away.
According to Zero Six, it was probably F Squad's Anzai.
Him, huh?
What should we do, Kikuhara ...?

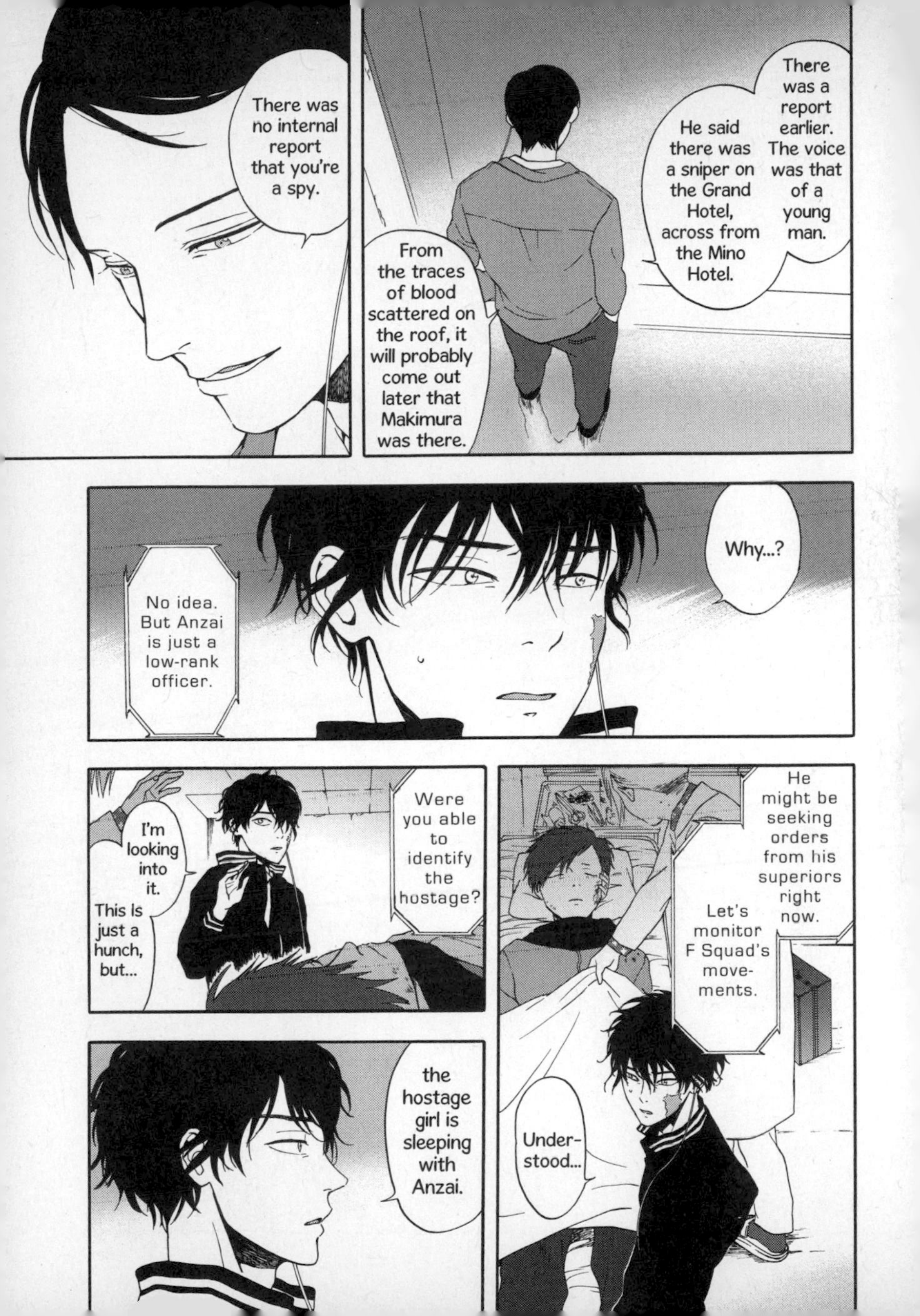
There was a report earlier. The voice was that of a young man.
He said there was a sniper on the Grand Hotel, across from the Mino Hotel.
From the traces of blood scattered on the roof, it will probably come out later that Makimura was there.
There was no internal report that you're a spy.
Why...?
No idea. But Anzai is just a low-rank officer.
He might be seeking orders from his superiors right now.
Let's monitor F Squad's movements.
Understood...
Were you able to identify the hostage?
I'm looking into it.
This Is just a hunch, but...
the hostage girl is sleeping with Anzai.

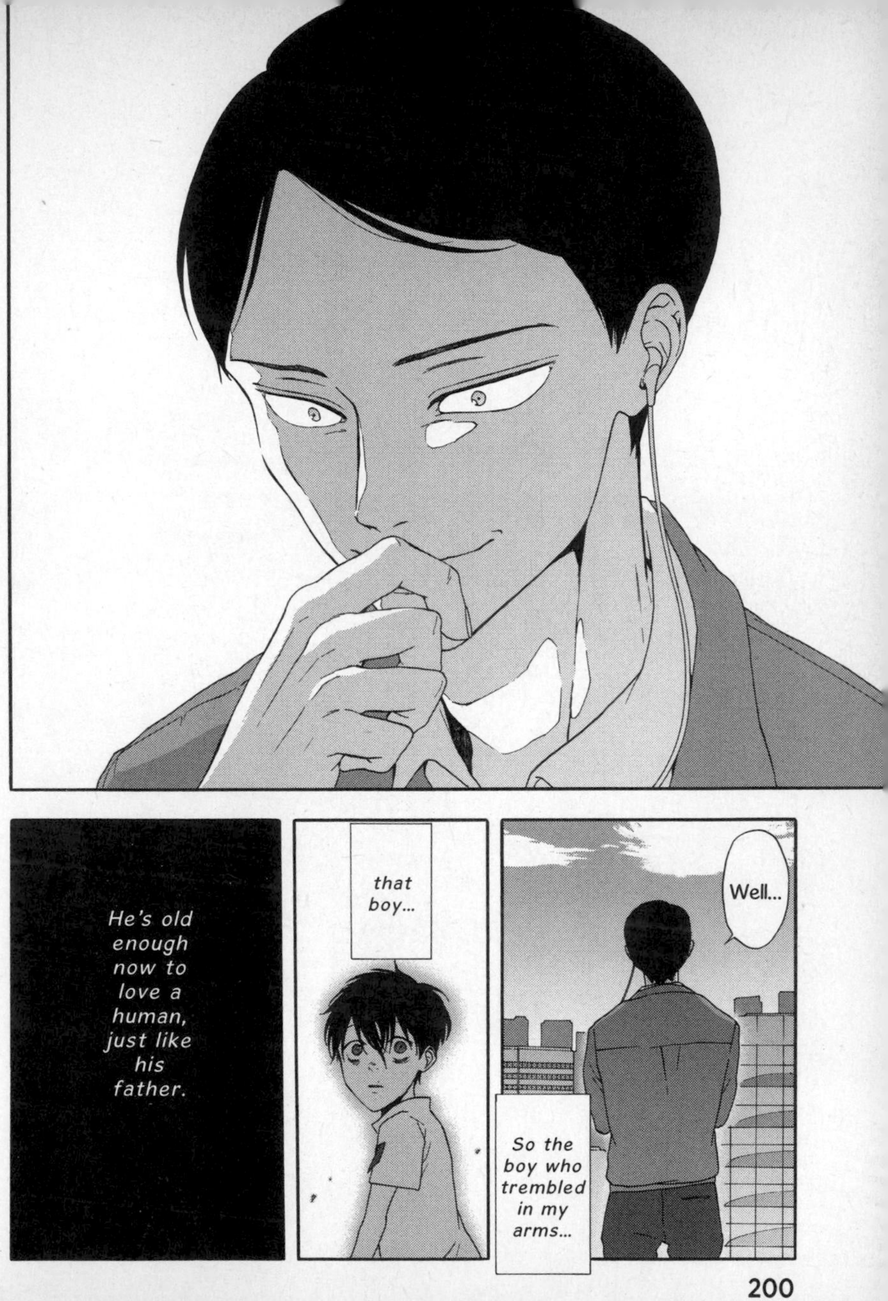
Well...
So the boy who trembled in my arms...
that boy...
He's old enough now to love a human, just like his father.

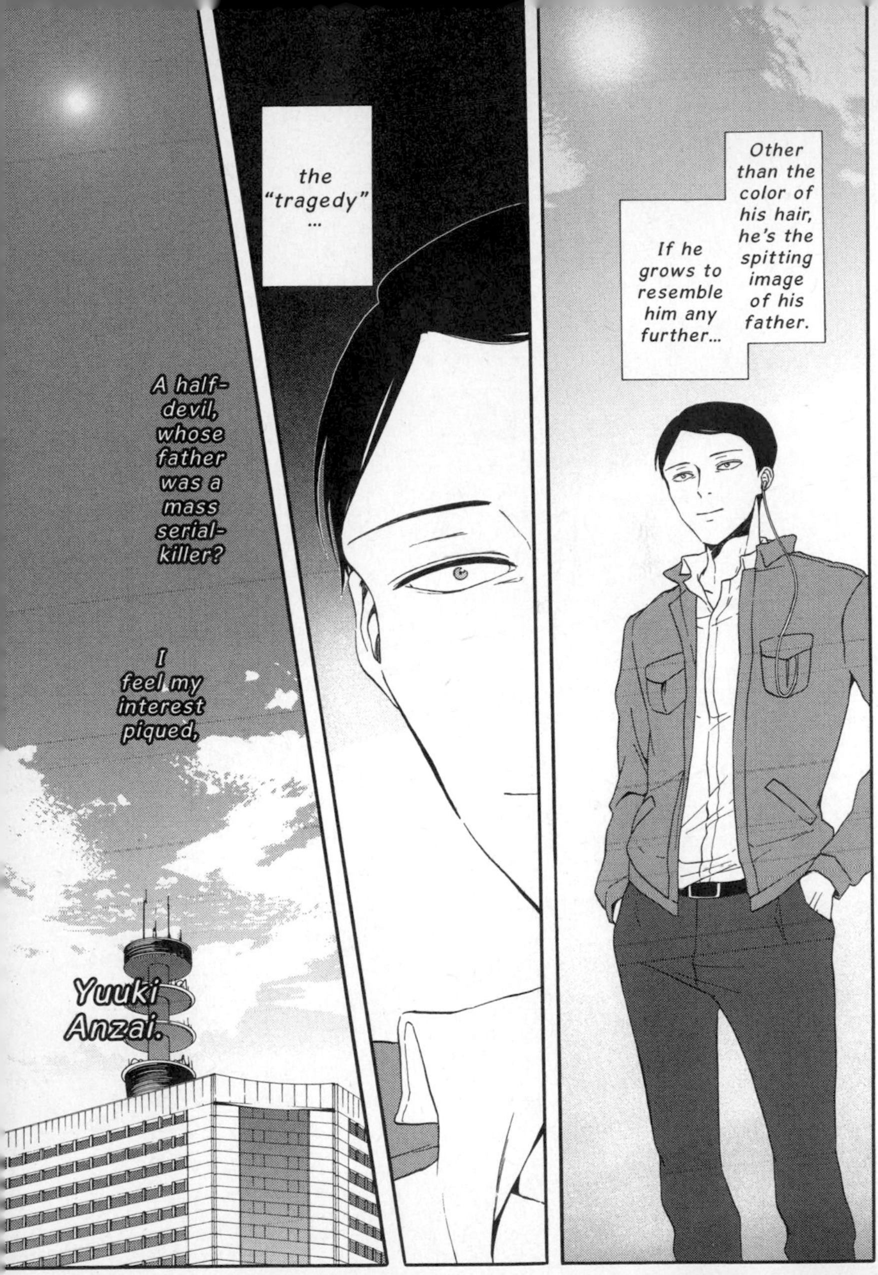
Other than the color of his hair, he's the spitting image of his father.
If he grows to resemble him any further...
the "tragedy" ...
A half-devil, whose father was a mass serial-killer?
I feel my interest piqued,
Yuuki Anzai.

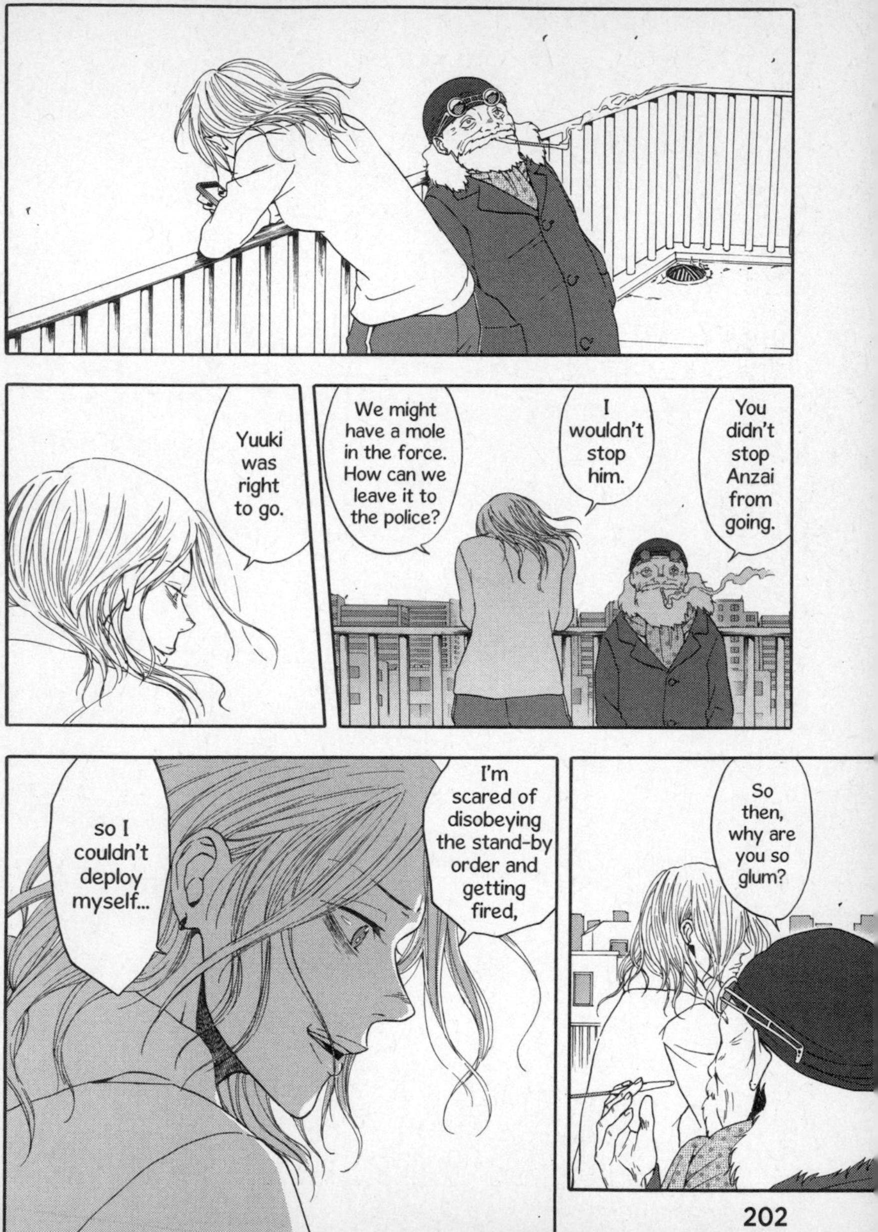
You didn't stop Anzai from going.
I wouldn't stop him.
We might have a mole in the force. How can we leave it to the police?
Yuuki was right to go.
So then, why are you so glum?
I'm scared of disobeying the stand-by order and getting fired,
so I couldn't deploy myself...

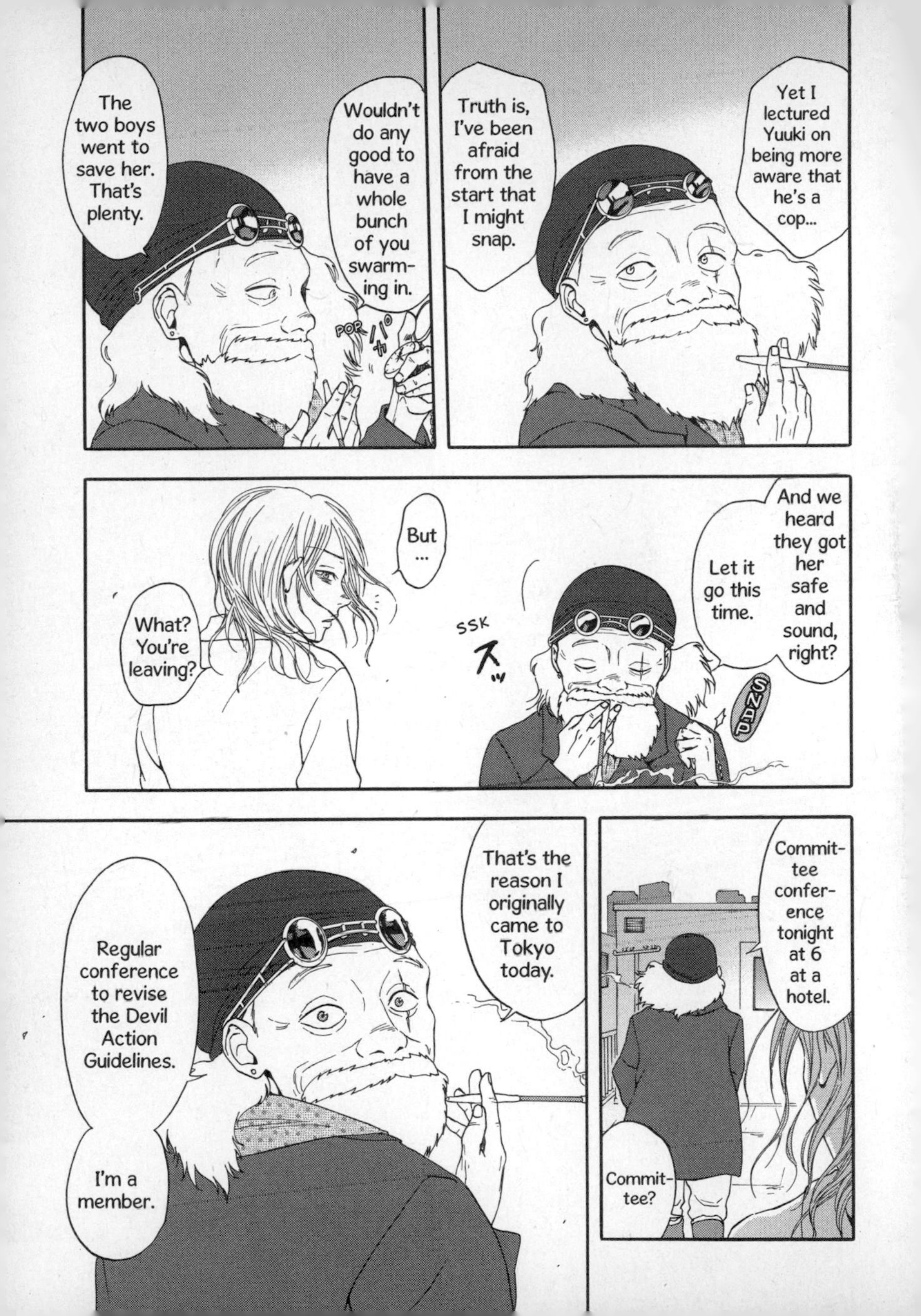
Yet I lectured Yuuki on being more aware that he's a cop...
Truth is, I've been afraid from the start that I might snap.
The two boys went to save her. That's plenty.
Wouldn't do any good to have a whole bunch of you swarming in.
POR
And we heard they got her safe and sound, right?
Let it go this time.
SNAP
SSK
But ...
What? You're leaving?
Committee conference tonight at 6 at a hotel.
Committee?
That's the reason I originally came to Tokyo today.
Regular conference to revise the Devil Action Guidelines.
I'm a member.

到着 Arrivals

航空会社 Airline	便名 Flight No.	出発地 Origin	定刻 Scheduled	変更 Will Arrive	備考 Remarks
HDO	66	Obihiro	15:00	15:07	Baggage Claim Closed
AJA	4766	Obihiro	15:00	15:11	Baggage Claim Closed
AJA	126	Naha	15:05	15:12	Baggage Claim Closed
AJA	3790	Ooita	15:10	15:10	Baggage Claim Closed
AJA		Kumamoto	15:15	15:15	Exit: 5・6
SkyLines	16	Kumamoto	15:15	15:15	Exit: 5・6
AJA	646	Kumamoto	15:20	15:20	Exit: 1・2
	414	Kobe	15:35	15:35	Exit: 1・2

	定刻 Scheduled
航空会社 Airline AJA	15:35
	15:35
	15:45
	15:45
	16:00
	16:00
	16:05
SA 旭川	16:15

The members are coming today from all over the country.

From Hokkaido too...

Redeyes' Rights Protection Committee, also known as R2PC.

It's sunny out.

到着出口
Exit

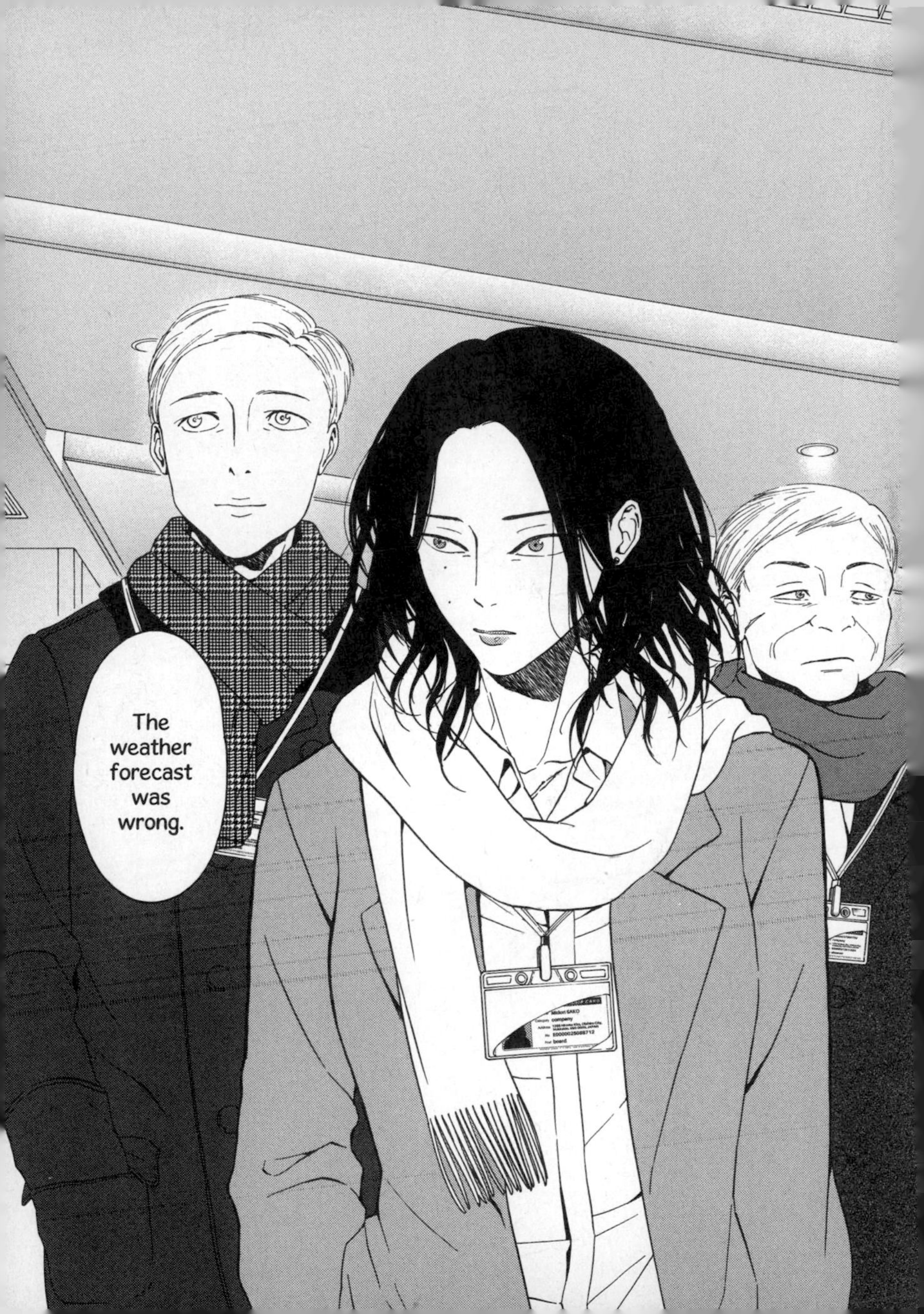
The weather forecast was wrong.

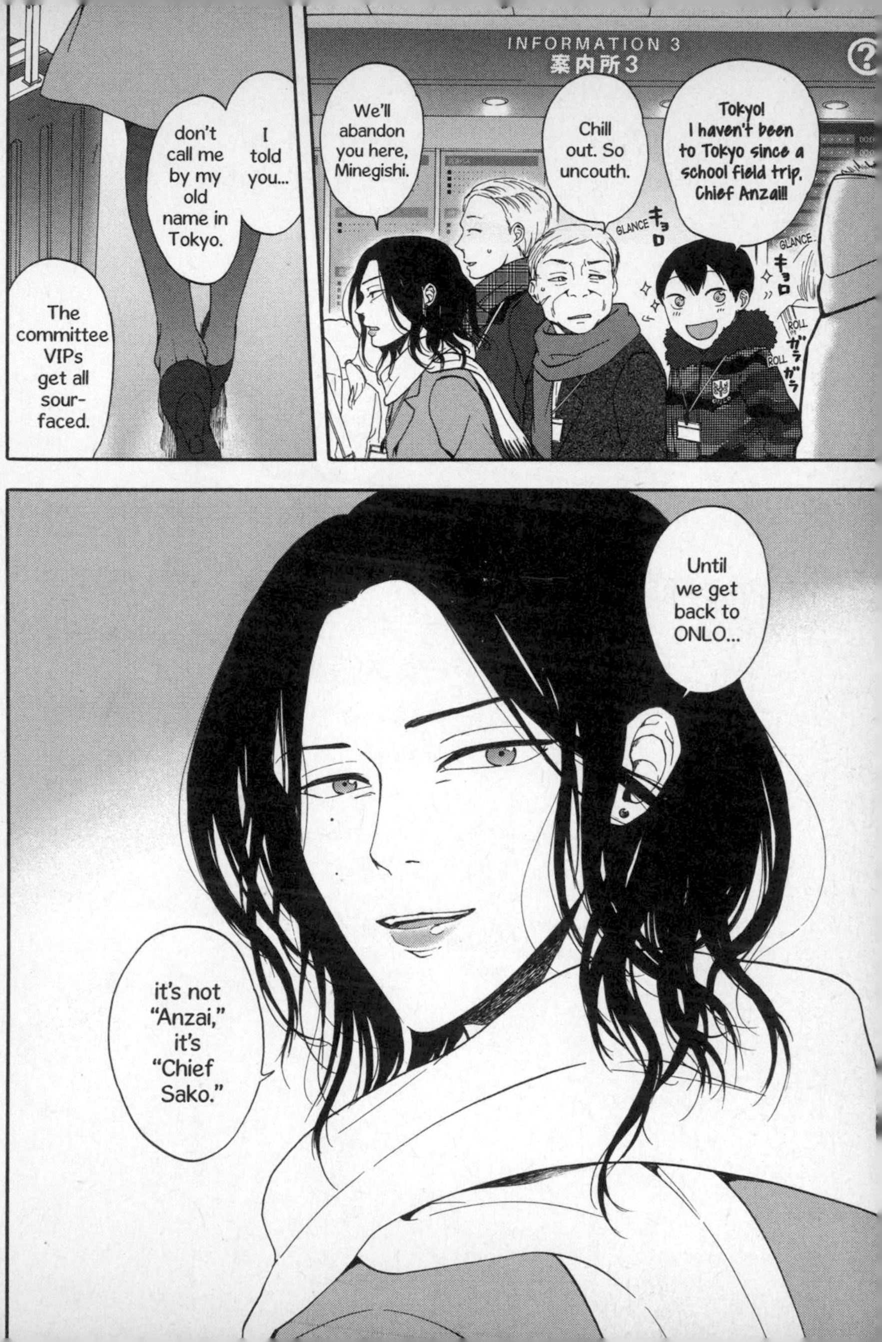
INFORMATION 3
案内所3
Tokyo! I haven't been to Tokyo since a school field trip, Chief Anzai!!
GLANCE キョロ
GLANCE キョロ
ROLL ガラ
ROLL ガラ
Chill out. So uncouth.
We'll abandon you here, Minegishi.
I told you...
don't call me by my old name in Tokyo.
The committee VIPs get all sour-faced.
Until we get back to ONLO...
it's not "Anzai," it's "Chief Sako."

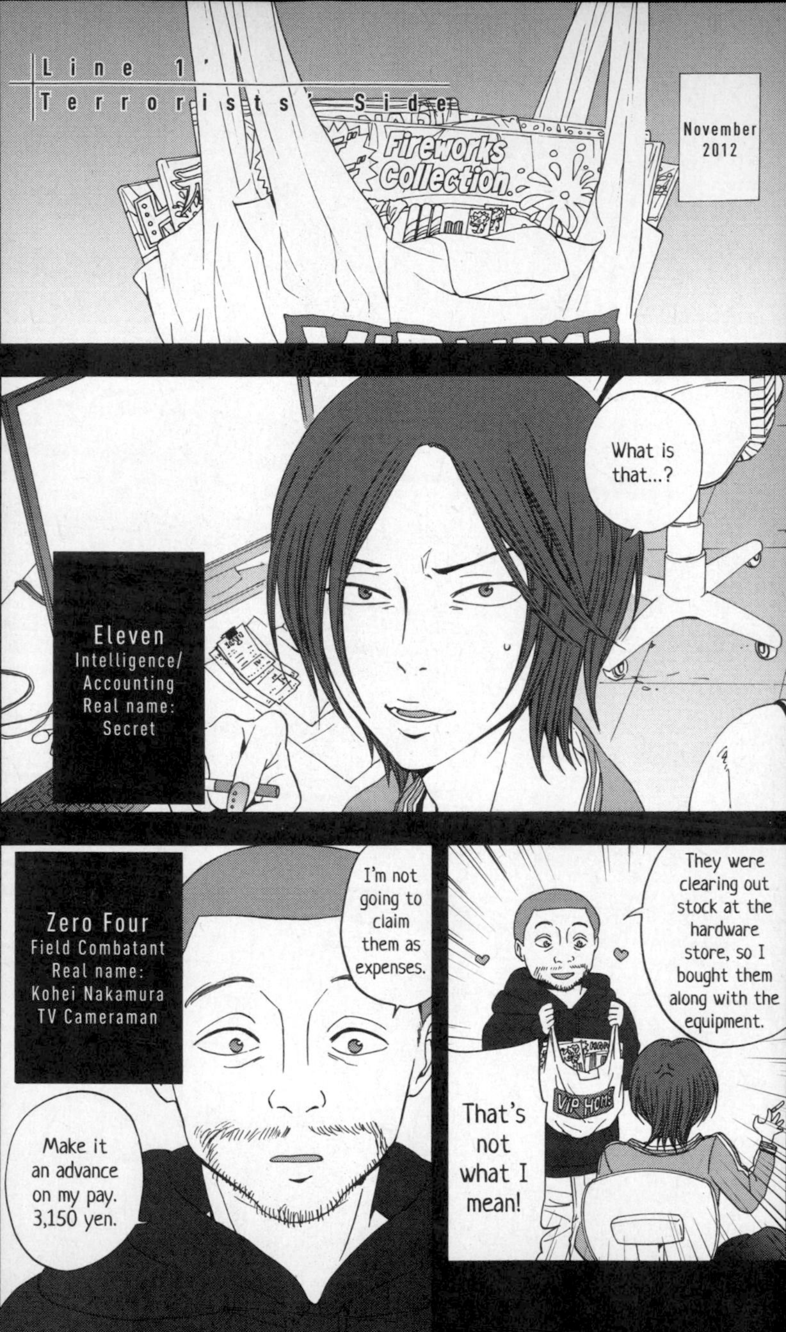
Line 1'
Terrorists' Side
November 2012
Fireworks Collection
What is that...?
Eleven
Intelligence/ Accounting
Real name: Secret
They were clearing out stock at the hardware store, so I bought them along with the equipment.
VIP HOME
That's not what I mean!
I'm not going to claim them as expenses.
Zero Four
Field Combatant
Real name: Kohei Nakamura
TV Cameraman
Make it an advance on my pay. 3,150 yen.

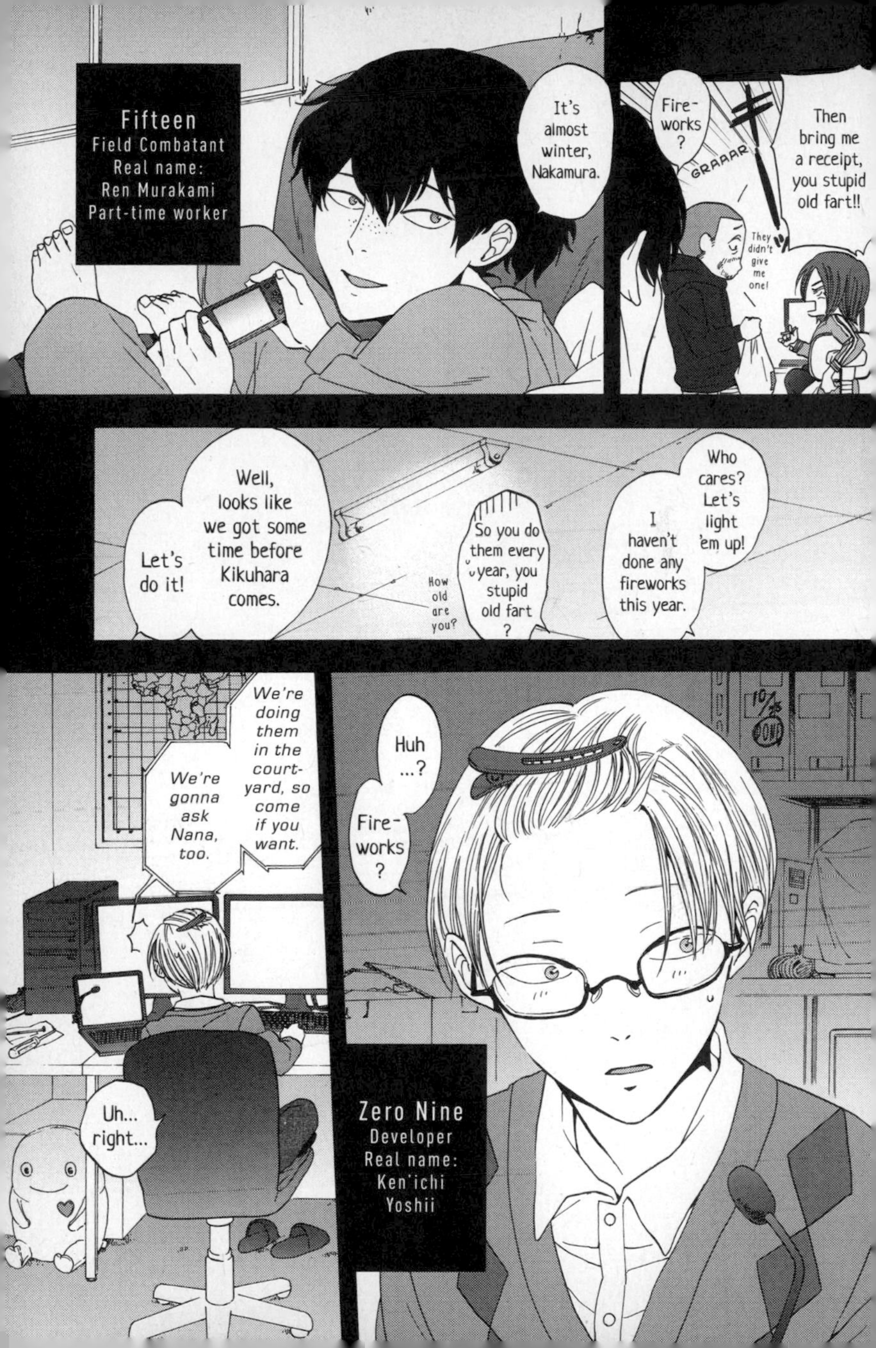
Then bring me a receipt, you stupid old fart!!
They didn't give me one!
Fire-works?
GRAAAR
It's almost winter, Nakamura.
Fifteen
Field Combatant
Real name: Ren Murakami
Part-time worker
Who cares? Let's light 'em up!
I haven't done any fireworks this year.
So you do them every year, you stupid old fart?
How old are you?
Well, looks like we got some time before Kikuhara comes.
Let's do it!
Huh...?
Fire-works?
Zero Nine
Developer
Real name: Ken'ichi Yoshii
We're doing them in the court-yard, so come if you want.
We're gonna ask Nana, too.
Uh... right...

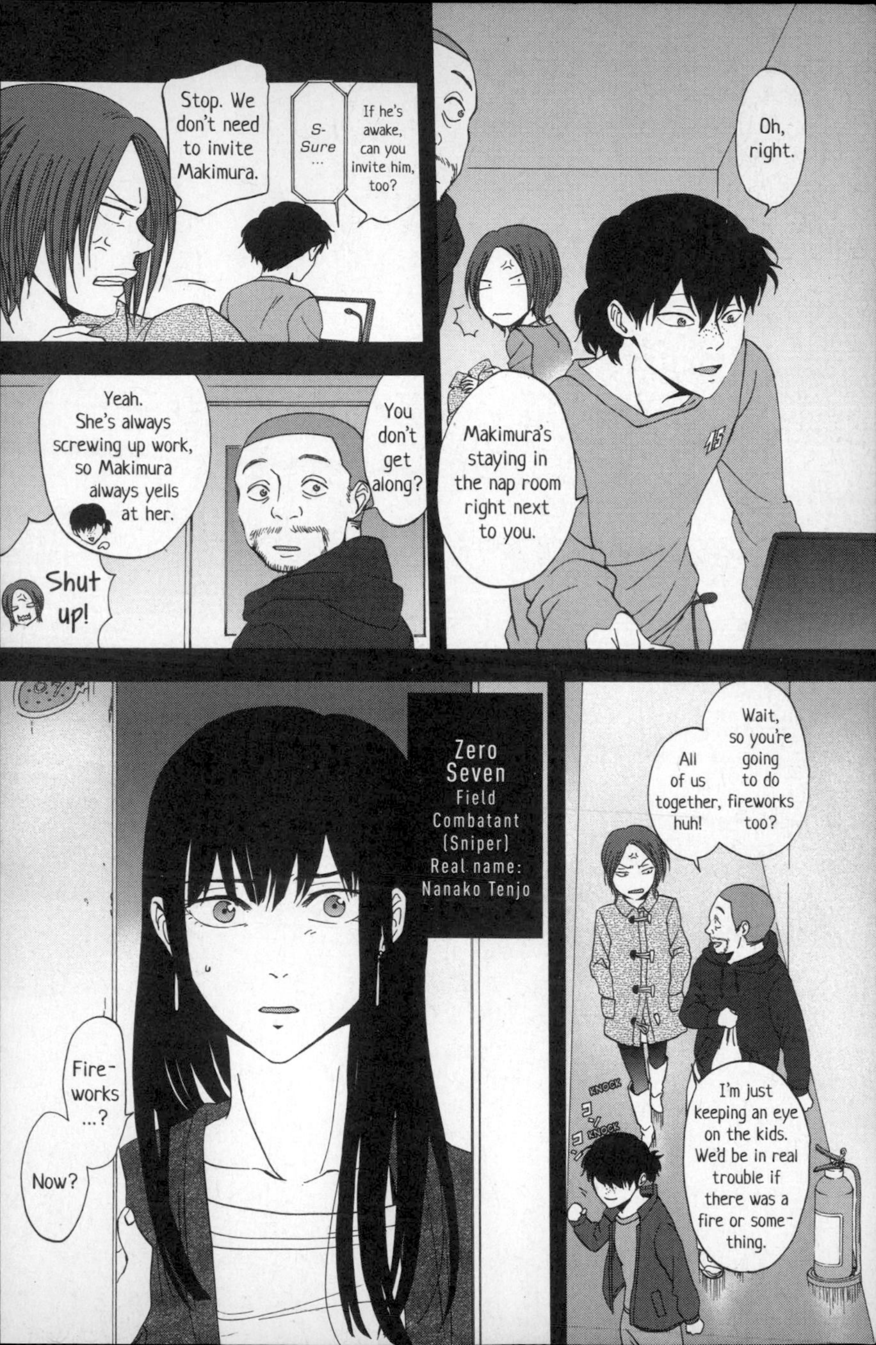

Oh, right.
Makimura's staying in the nap room right next to you.
If he's awake, can you invite him, too?
S-Sure ...
Stop. We don't need to invite Makimura.
You don't get along?
Yeah. She's always screwing up work, so Makimura always yells at her.
Shut up!
Wait, so you're going to do fireworks too?
All of us together, huh!
I'm just keeping an eye on the kids. We'd be in real trouble if there was a fire or some-thing.
KNOCK
KNOCK
Zero Seven
Field Combatant (Sniper)
Real name: Nanako Tenjo
Fire-works ...?
Now?

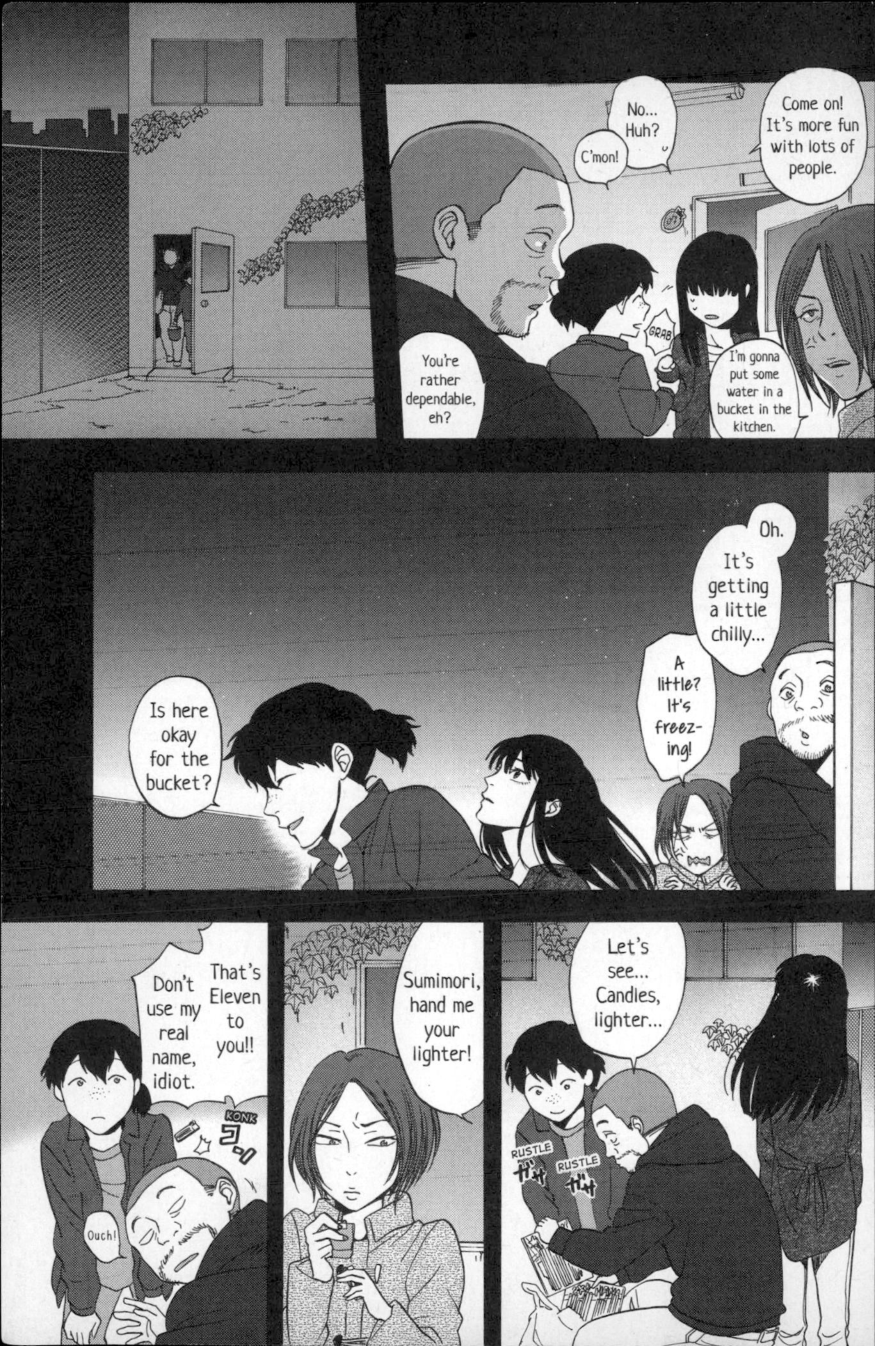
Come on! It's more fun with lots of people.
No... Huh?
C'mon!
I'm gonna put some water in a bucket in the kitchen.
GRAB
You're rather dependable, eh?
Oh. It's getting a little chilly...
A little? It's freez-ing!
Is here okay for the bucket?
Let's see... Candles, lighter...
RUSTLE
RUSTLE
Sumimori, hand me your lighter!
That's Eleven to you!!
Don't use my real name, idiot.
KONK
Ouch!

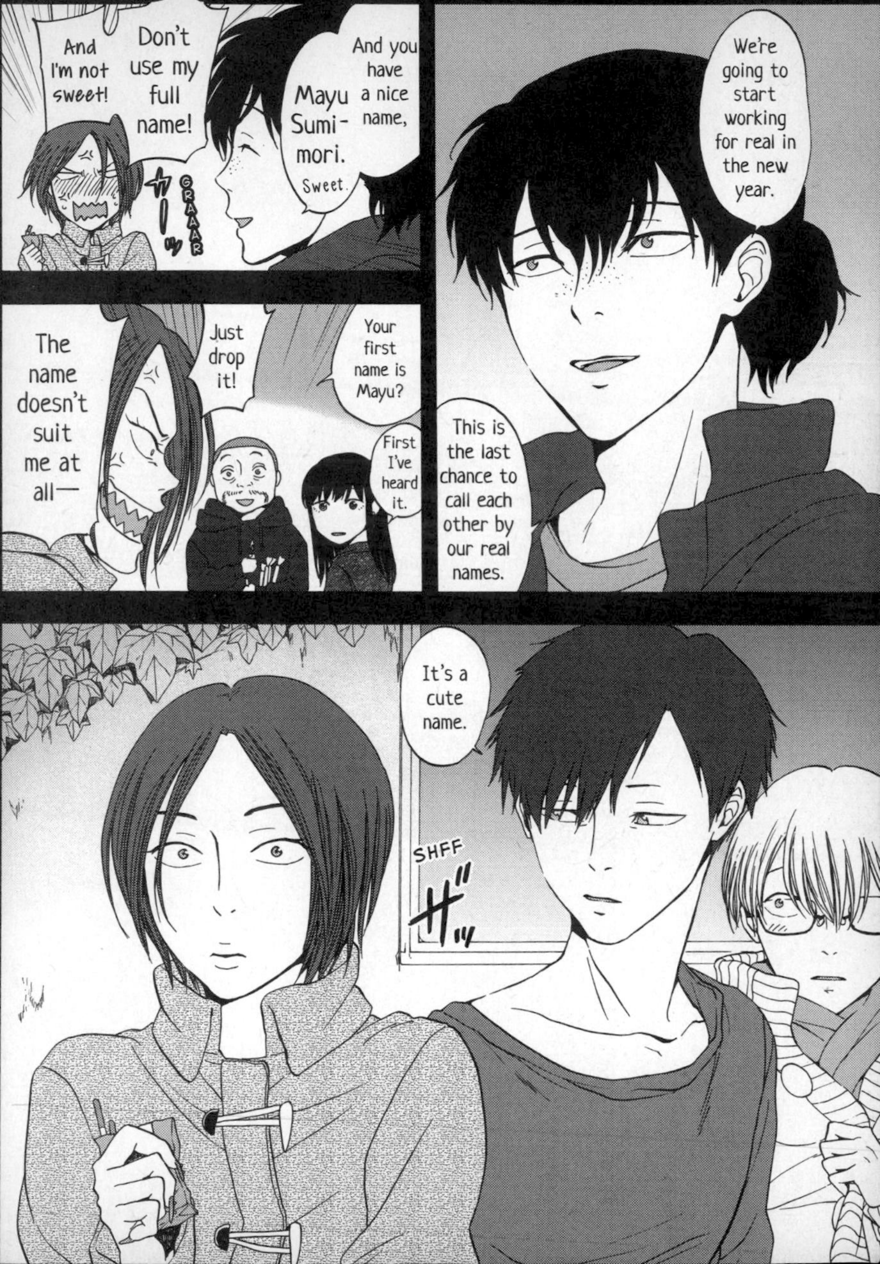

We're going to start working for real in the new year.
This is the last chance to call each other by our real names.
And you have a nice name,
Mayu Sumimori.
Sweet.
Don't use my full name!
And I'm not sweet!
GRAAAR
Your first name is Mayu?
First I've heard it.
Just drop it!
The name doesn't suit me at all—
It's a cute name.
SHFF

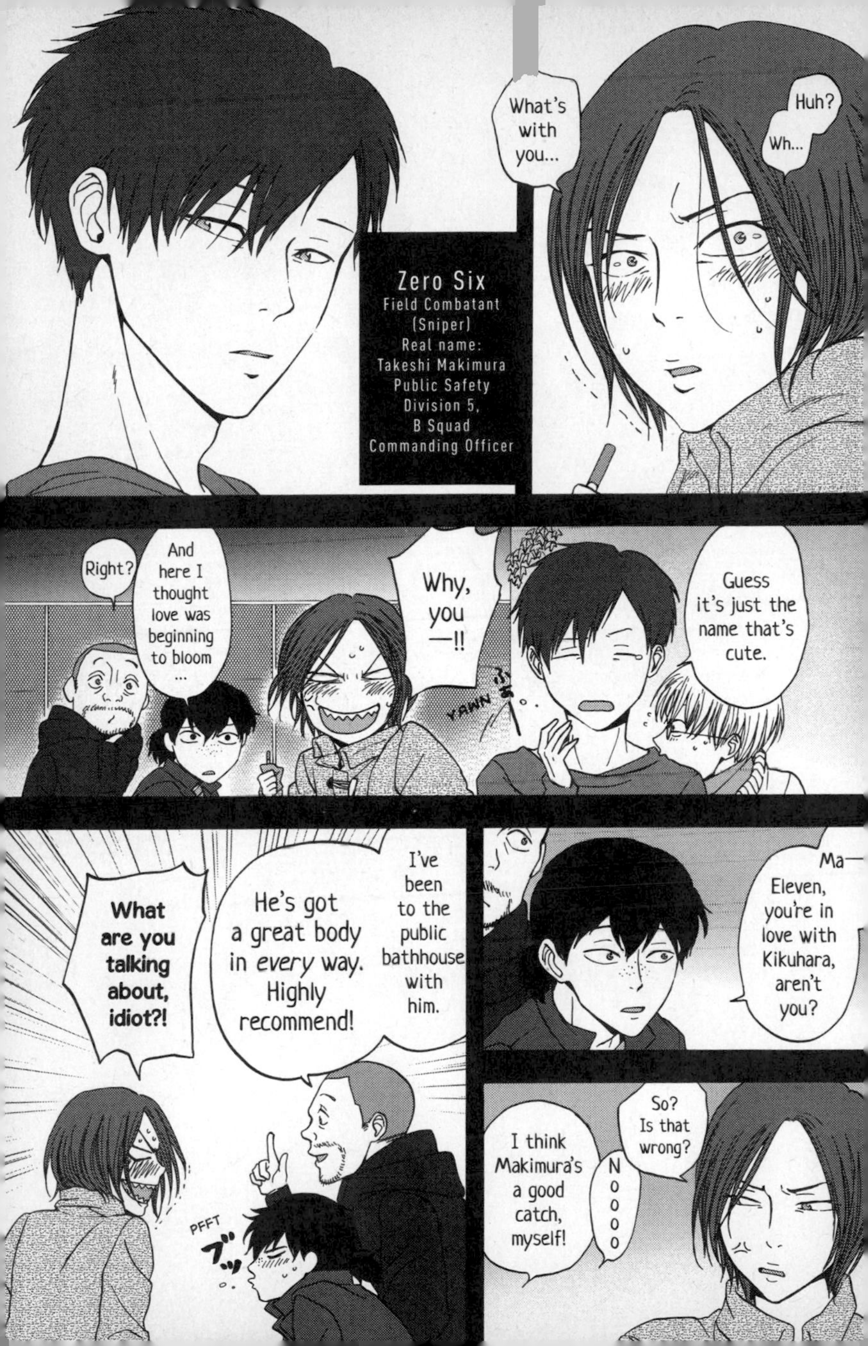
Huh?
Wh...
What's with you...
Zero Six
Field Combatant (Sniper)
Real name: Takeshi Makimura
Public Safety Division 5, B Squad Commanding Officer
Guess it's just the name that's cute.
YAWN
Why, you—!!
And here I thought love was beginning to bloom ...
Right?
Ma— Eleven, you're in love with Kikuhara, aren't you?
So? Is that wrong?
Noooo
I think Makimura's a good catch, myself!
I've been to the public bathhouse with him.
He's got a great body in *every* way. Highly recommend!
What are you talking about, idiot?!
PFFT
ブッ

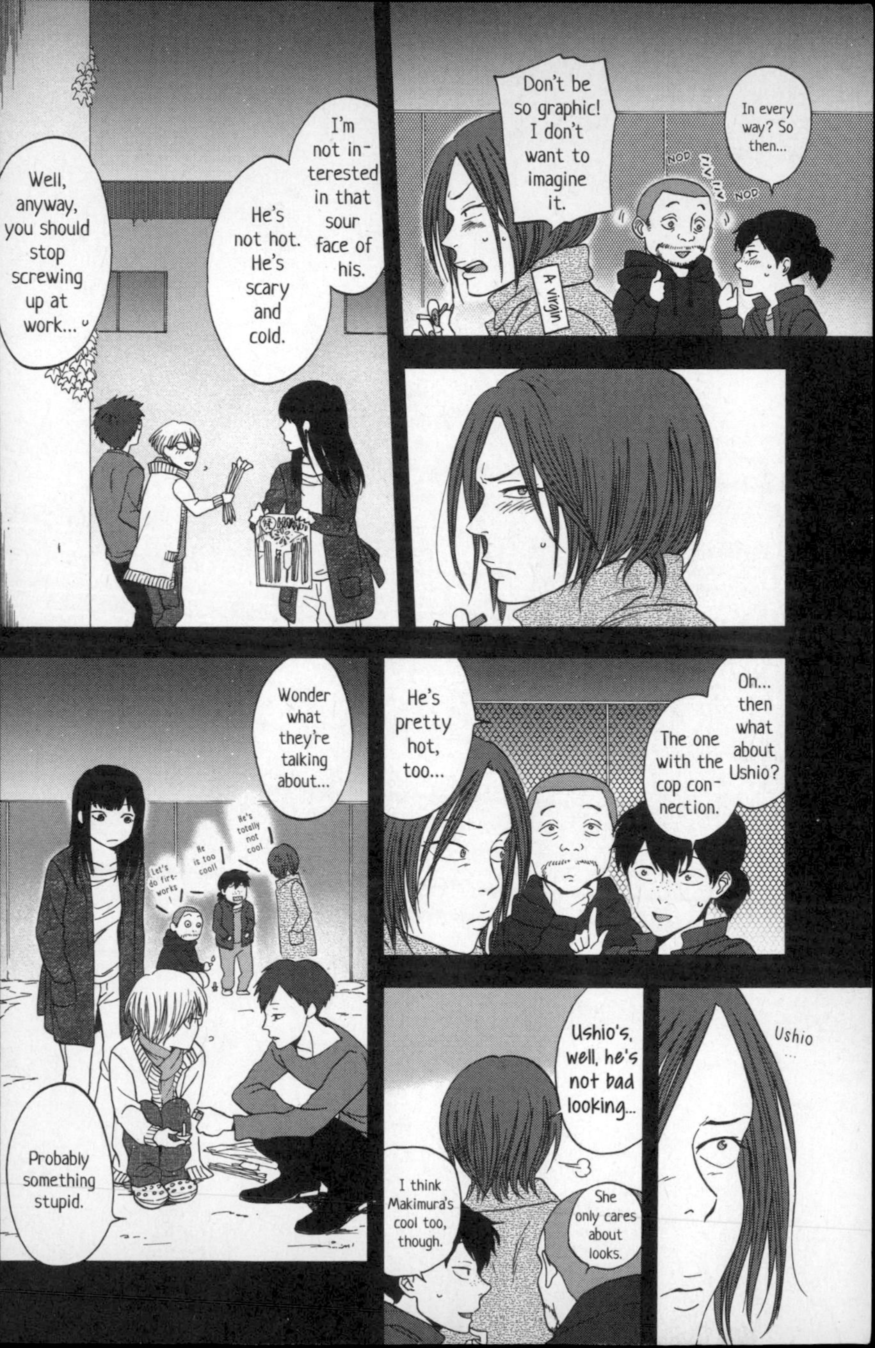
In every way? So then...
NOD NOD
Don't be so graphic! I don't want to imagine it.
A virgin
I'm not interested in that sour face of his.
He's not hot. He's scary and cold.
Well, anyway, you should stop screwing up at work...
Oh... then what about Ushio?
The one with the cop connection.
He's pretty hot, too...
Ushio ...
Ushio's, well, he's not bad looking...
She only cares about looks.
I think Makimura's cool too, though.
Wonder what they're talking about...
He's totally not cool.
He is too cool!
Let's do fireworks!
Probably something stupid.

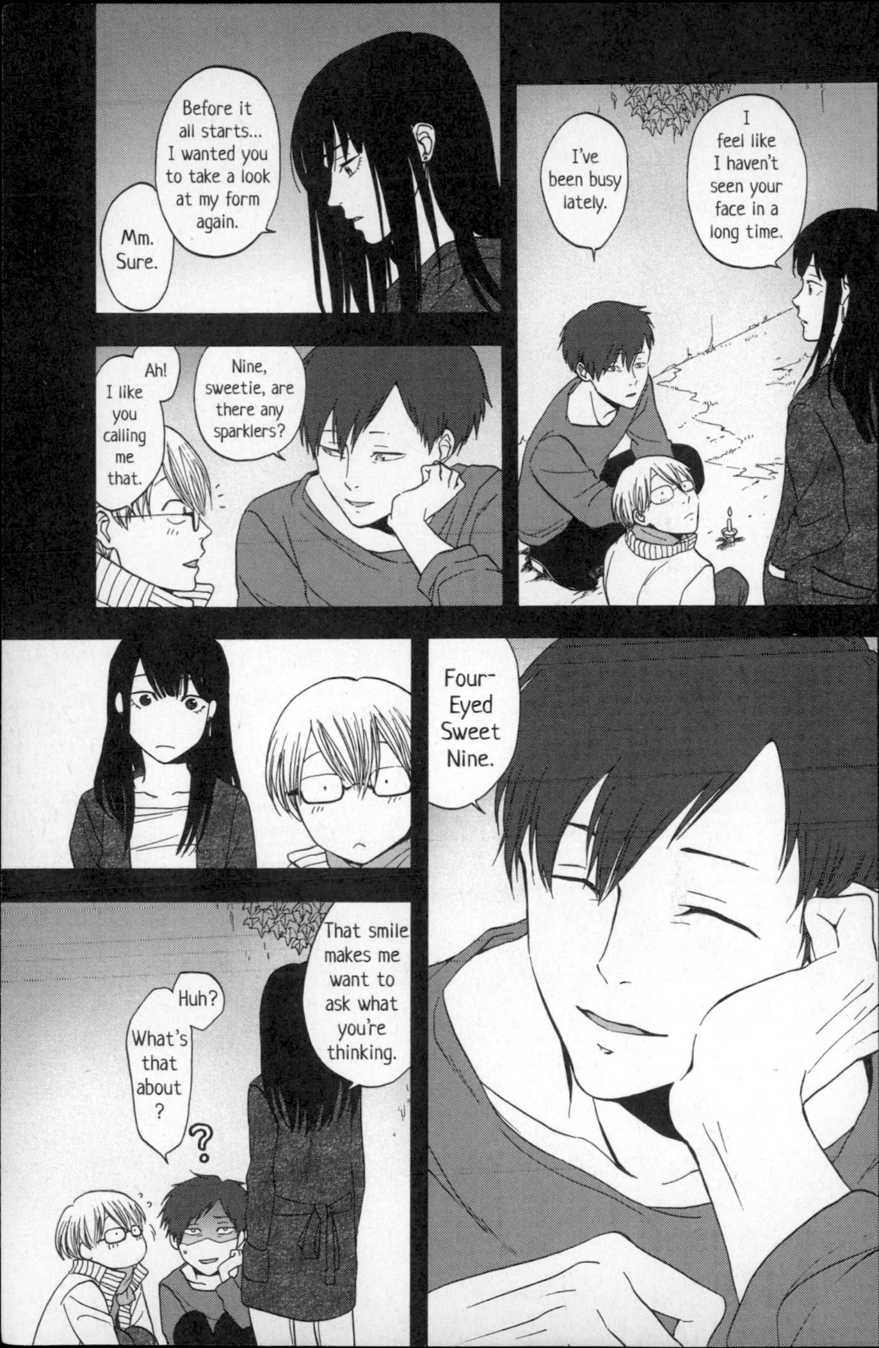
I feel like I haven't seen your face in a long time.
I've been busy lately.
Before it all starts... I wanted you to take a look at my form again.
Mm. Sure.
Nine, sweetie, are there any sparklers?
Ah! I like you calling me that.
Four-Eyed Sweet Nine.
That smile makes me want to ask what you're thinking.
Huh?
What's that about?
?

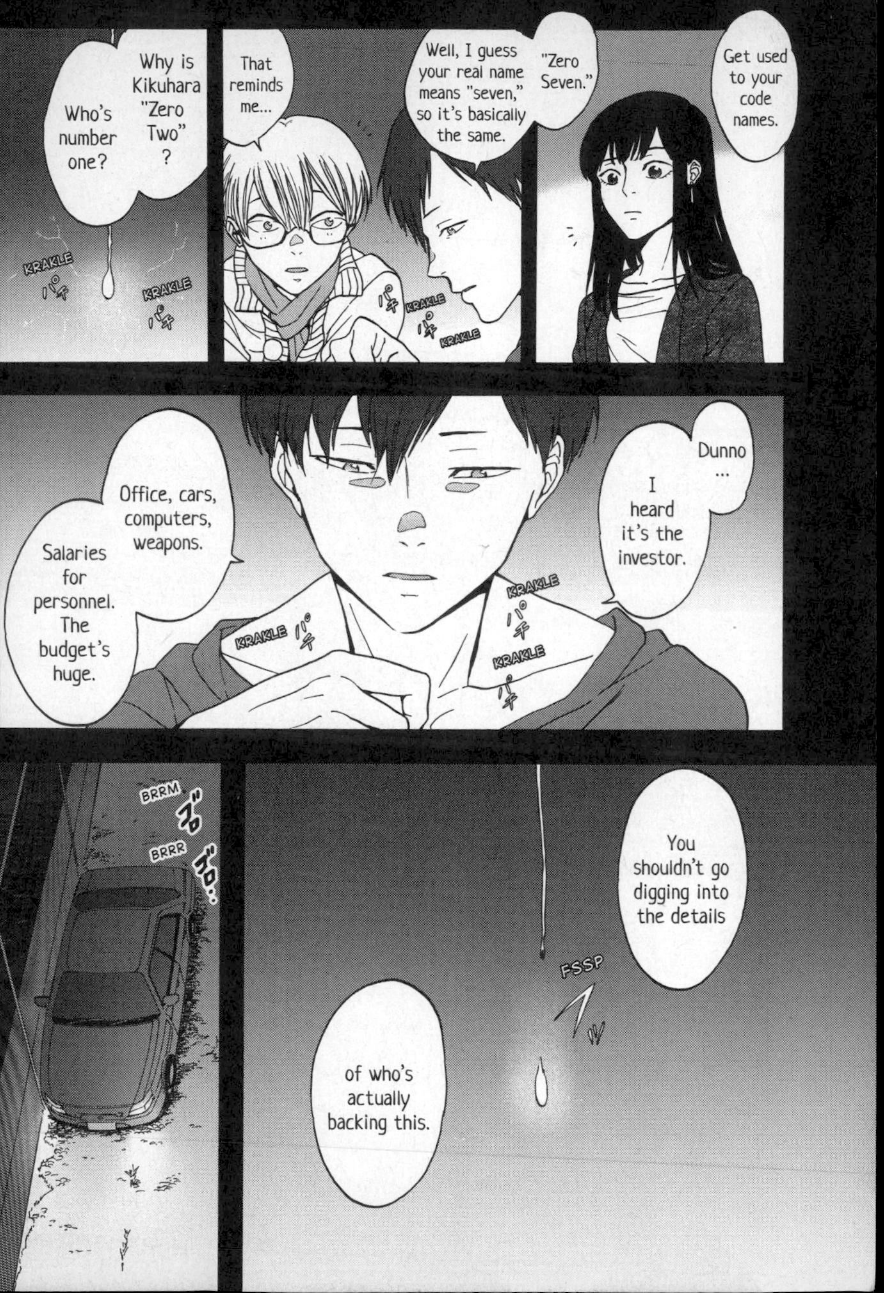
Get used to your code names.
"Zero Seven."
Well, I guess your real name means "seven," so it's basically the same.
KRAKLE パチ
KRAKLE
That reminds me...
Why is Kikuhara "Zero Two"?
Who's number one?
KRAKLE パチ
KRAKLE パチ
Dunno... I heard it's the investor.
KRAKLE パチ
KRAKLE パチ
KRAKLE パチ
Office, cars, computers, weapons.
Salaries for personnel. The budget's huge.
You shouldn't go digging into the details
FSSP
of who's actually backing this.
BRRM ブロ
BRRR ブロロ...

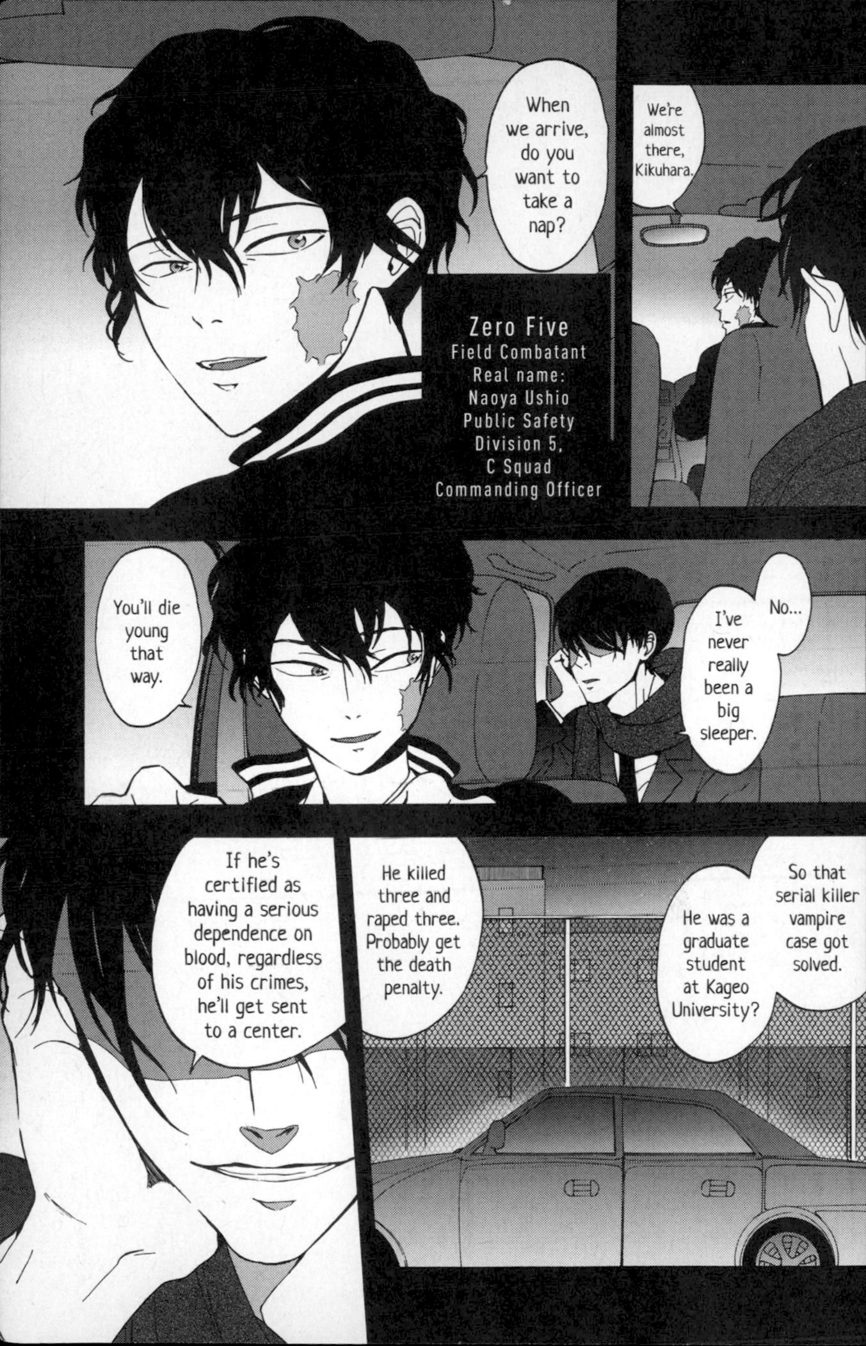
We're almost there, Kikuhara.
When we arrive, do you want to take a nap?
Zero Five
Field Combatant
Real name: Naoya Ushio
Public Safety Division 5, C Squad Commanding Officer
No...
I've never really been a big sleeper.
You'll die young that way.
So that serial killer vampire case got solved.
He was a graduate student at Kageo University?
He killed three and raped three. Probably get the death penalty.
If he's certified as having a serious dependence on blood, regardless of his crimes, he'll get sent to a center.

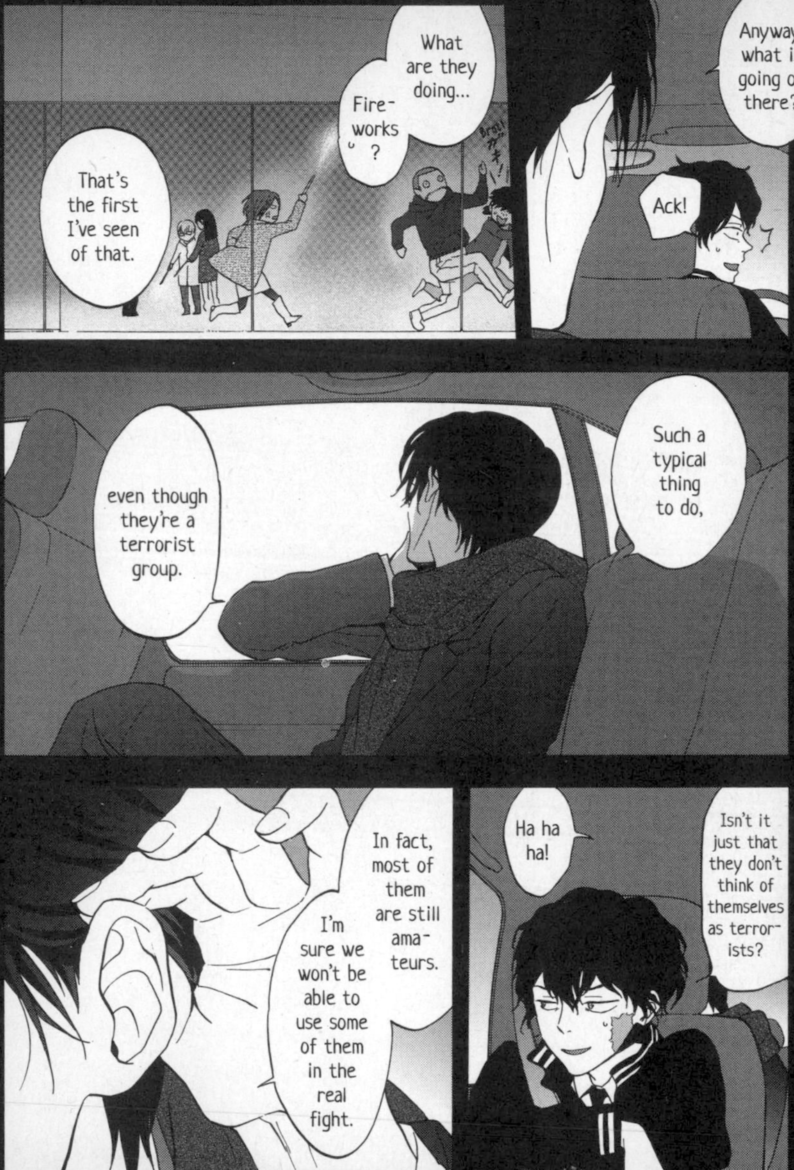
Anyway, what is going on there?
Ack!
What are they doing...
Fire-works?
That's the first I've seen of that.
Such a typical thing to do,
even though they're a terrorist group.
Isn't it just that they don't think of themselves as terror-ists?
Ha ha ha!
In fact, most of them are still ama-teurs.
I'm sure we won't be able to use some of them in the real fight.

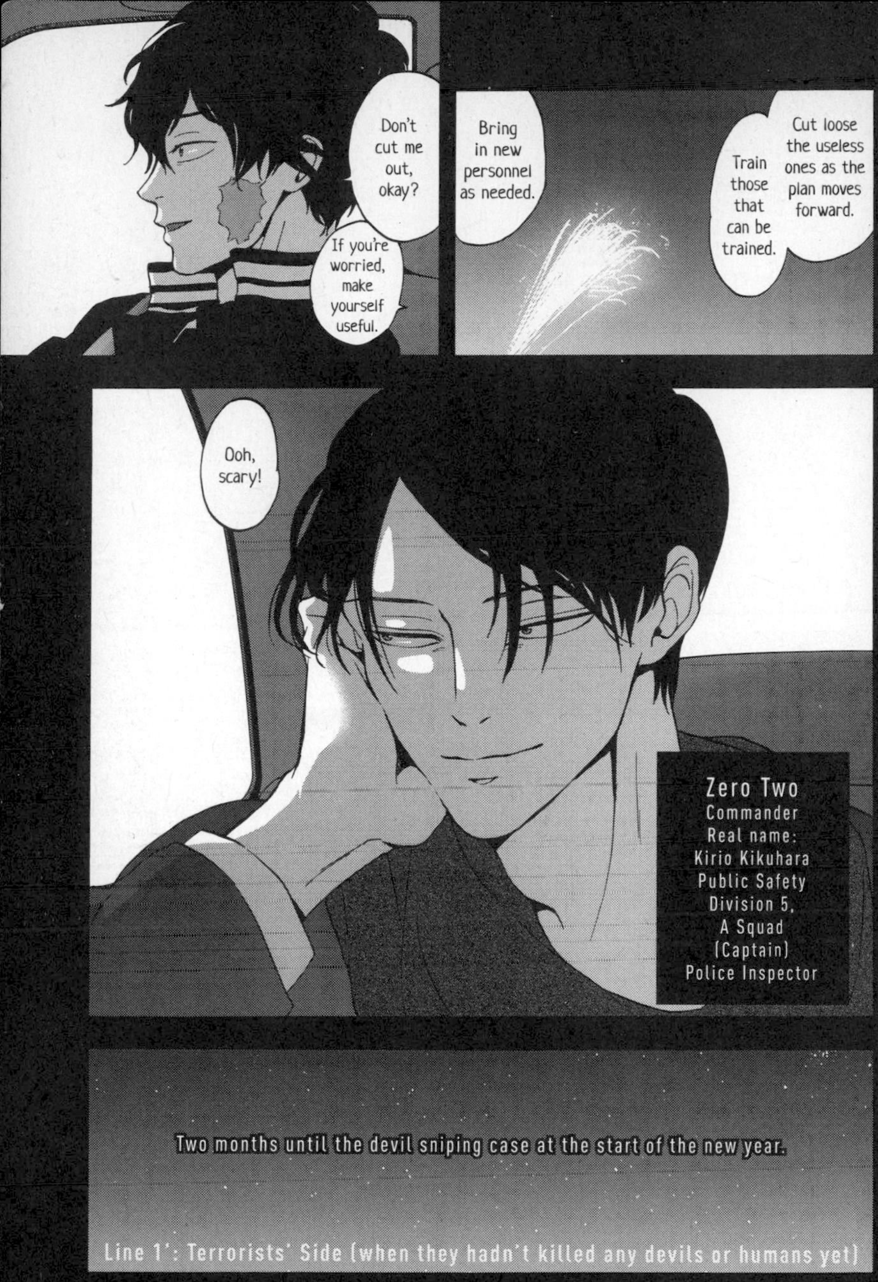
Cut loose the useless ones as the plan moves forward.
Train those that can be trained.
Bring in new personnel as needed.
Don't cut me out, okay?
If you're worried, make yourself useful.
Ooh, scary!
Zero Two
Commander
Real name: Kirio Kikuhara
Public Safety Division 5, A Squad (Captain)
Police Inspector
Two months until the devil sniping case at the start of the new year.
Line 1': Terrorists' Side (when they hadn't killed any devils or humans yet)

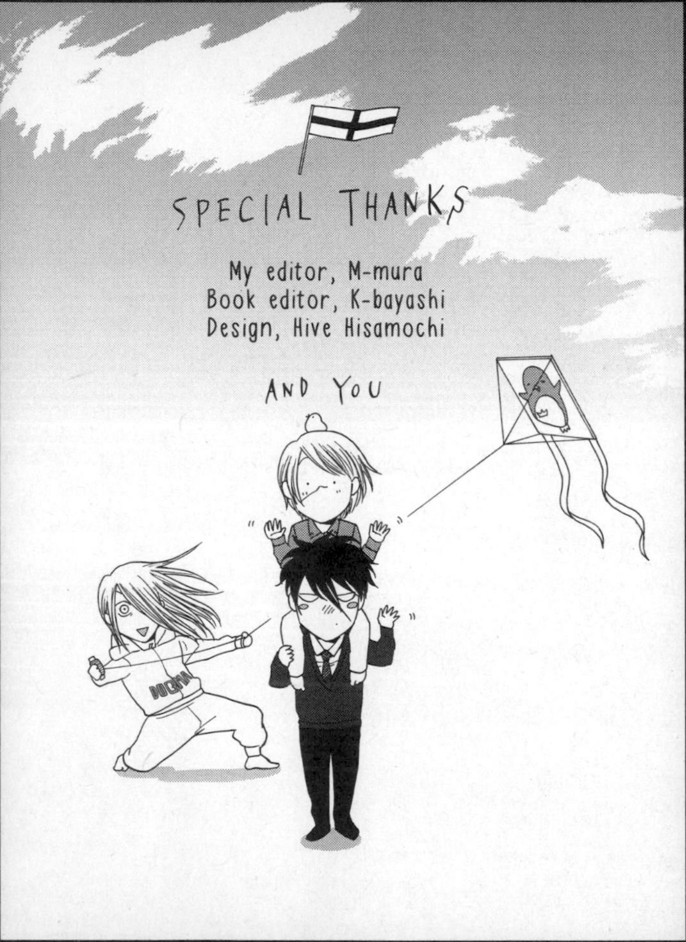
SPECIAL THANKS
My editor, M-mura
Book editor, K-bayashi
Design, Hive Hisamochi
AND YOU

DEVILS' LINE 4

A Vertical Comics Edition

Translation: Jocelyne Allen
Production: Risa Cho
Lorina Mapa

First published in Japan in 2015 by Kodansha, Ltd., Tokyo
Publication rights for this English edition arranged through Kodansha, Ltd., Tokyo
English language version produced by Vertical, Inc., New York

Translation provided by Vertical Comics, 2016
Published by Vertical, Inc., New York

Originally published in Japanese as *Debiruzurain 4* by Kodansha, Ltd., 2015
Debiruzurain first serialized in *Morning two*, Kodansha, Ltd., 2013-

ISBN: 978-1-942993-40-7

Manufactured in the United States of America

First Edition

Vertical, Inc.
451 Park Avenue South
7th Floor
New York, NY 10016
www.vertical-comics.com

Vertical books are distributed through Penguin-Random House Publisher Services.

Motivation

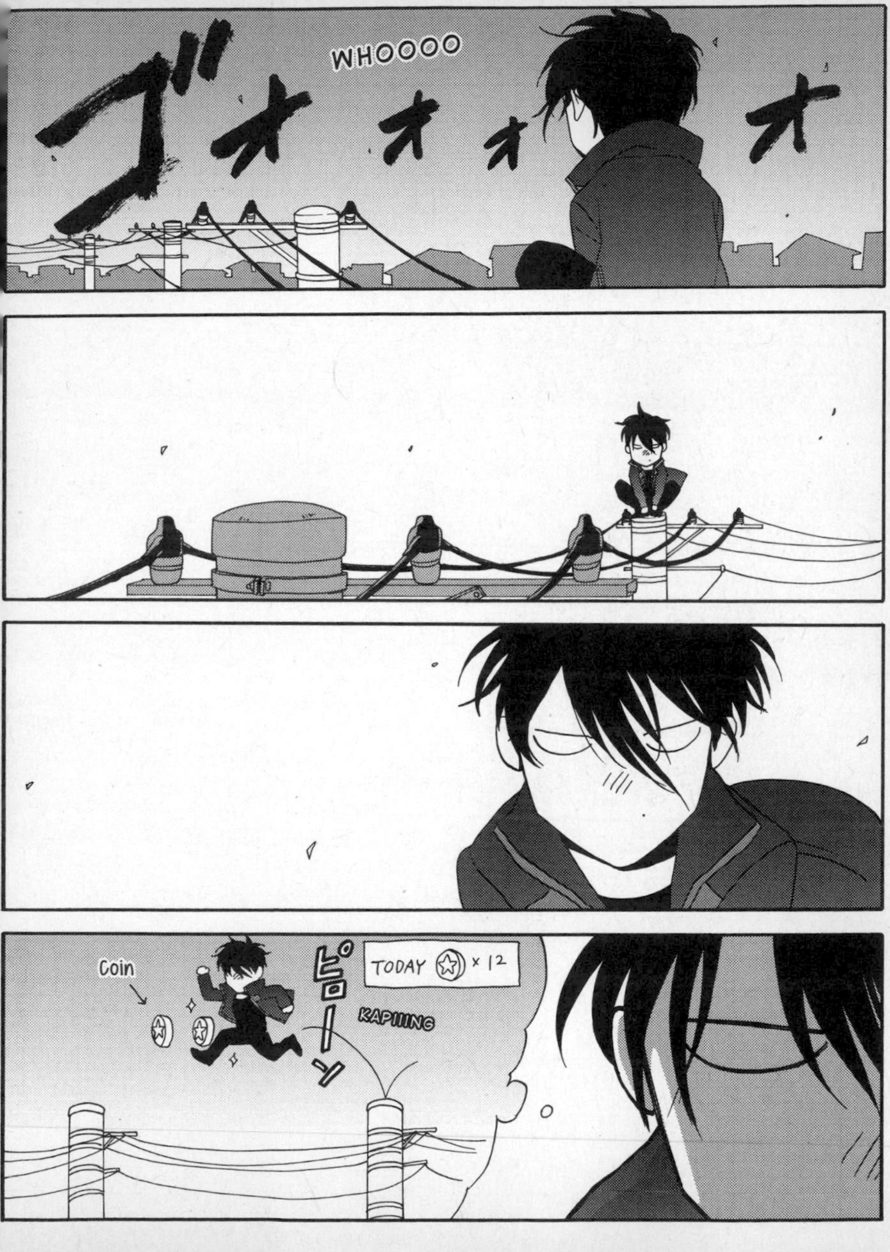
WHOOOO
ゴオォォオ
TODAY x 12
ピローン
KAPIIING
Coin

Happens to All Vampires

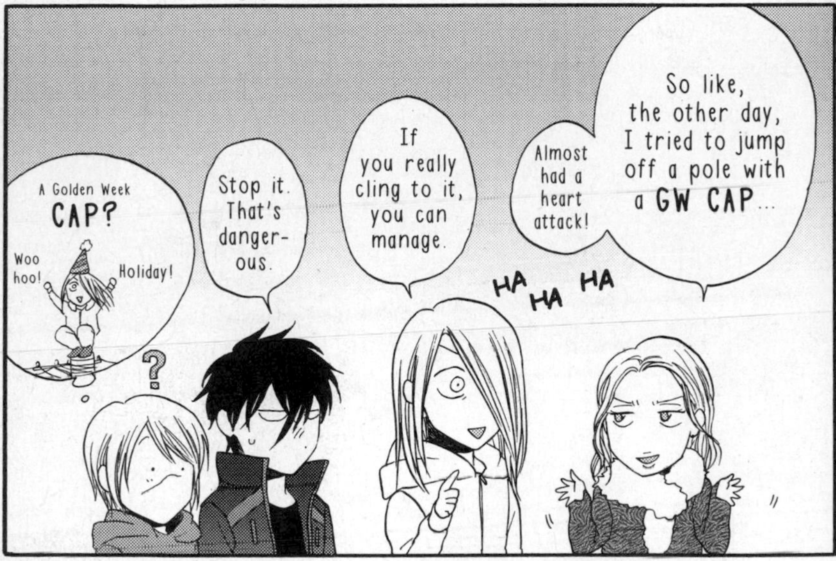
So like, the other day, I tried to jump off a pole with a GW CAP...
Almost had a heart attack!
HA HA HA
If you really cling to it, you can manage.
Stop it. That's danger-ous.
A Golden Week CAP?
Holiday!
Woo hoo!
?

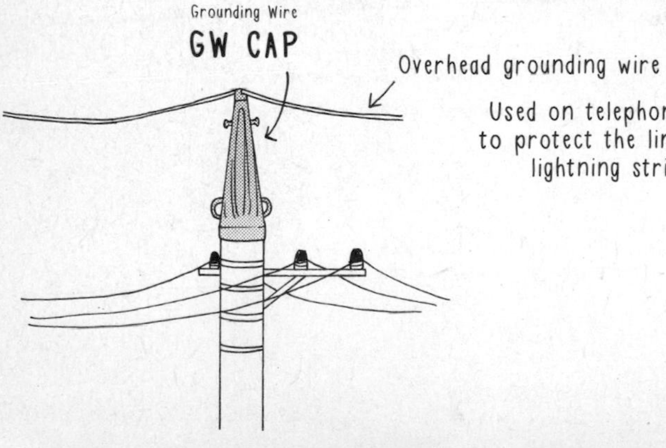
Grounding Wire
GW CAP
Overhead grounding wire

Used on telephone poles to protect the lines from lightning strikes.